Lecture Notes of the Institute for Computer Sciences, Social Informatics and Telecommunications Engineering

178

More information about this series at http://www.springer.com/series/8197

Ronald Poppe · John-Jules Meyer
Remco Veltkamp · Mehdi Dastani (Eds.)

Intelligent Technologies for Interactive Entertainment

8th International Conference, INTETAIN 2016
Utrecht, The Netherlands, June 28–30, 2016
Revised Selected Papers

 Springer

Editors
Ronald Poppe
Department of Information and Computing
  Sciences
Utrecht University
Utrecht
The Netherlands

Remco Veltkamp
Department of Information and Computing
  Sciences
Utrecht University
Utrecht
The Netherlands

John-Jules Meyer
Department of Information and Computing
  Sciences
Utrecht University
Utrecht
The Netherlands

Mehdi Dastani
Department of Information and Computing
  Sciences
Utrecht University
Utrecht
The Netherlands

ISSN 1867-8211   ISSN 1867-822X (electronic)
Lecture Notes of the Institute for Computer Sciences, Social Informatics
and Telecommunications Engineering
ISBN 978-3-319-49615-3   ISBN 978-3-319-49616-0 (eBook)
DOI 10.1007/978-3-319-49616-0

Library of Congress Control Number: 2016957383

Printed on acid-free paper

This Springer imprint is published by Springer Nature
The registered company is Springer International Publishing AG
The registered company address is: Gewerbestrasse 11, 6330 Cham, Switzerland

Preface

The International Conference on Intelligent Technologies for Interactive Entertainment (INTETAIN) is the premier platform for research on advances in interactive technology and the application to entertainment. These are the proceedings of the eighth edition of the series, which was held during June 28–30 2016, in Utrecht, The Netherlands, following previous editions in Madonna di Campiglio (2005), Cancun (2008), Amsterdam (2009), Genoa (2011), Mons (2013), Chicago (2014), and Turin (2015).

The conference was focused on bringing together researchers to present and discuss novel interactive techniques, their application in entertainment, education, culture, and art, and to identify challenges and solutions. The single-track program featured 23 talks from international speakers. These talks were selected from 37 paper submissions, each of which was reviewed by at least three reviewers. Several demos showed the state of the art of interactive technology for entertainment.

The conference featured six thematic sessions: Serious Games, Novel Applications and Tools, Exertion Games, Persuasion and Motivation, Interaction Technologies, and Game Studies. We were delighted to have internationally renowned keynote speakers Elisabeth André (Laboratory for Human-Centered Multimedia, Augsburg University, Germany) and Mark Riedl (School of Interactive Computing, Georgia Institute of Technology, USA), who gave outstanding talks on "Emotion-Sensitive Technologies for Games and Interactive Entertainment" and "Computational Narrative Intelligence: From Games to Robots," respectively. Also, the Oscar-nominated trio Job, Joris, and Marieke (Utrecht, The Netherlands) provided an inspirational overview of their creative work in animation, illustration, character design, and music.

Two workshops were part of the conference: "Virtual Agents for Social Skills Training (VASST)" focused on serious games in which virtual agents play a vital role in training and rehearsing social skills; "Playable Cities: The City as a Digital Playground," brought together researchers exploring ways to make urban areas smarter by engaging citizens in playful ways. Clare Reddington (Creative Director, Watershed, Bristol, UK) provided the keynote talk.

The venue of the eighth edition of INTETAIN was the Instituto Cervantes at the Dom Square in Utrecht. The social program included a reception, boat trip on the Utrecht canals, and a conference dinner in the main historic Utrecht University building the Academiegebouw.

The conference chairs would like to thank all presenters who made this edition so interesting and enjoyable, as well as the invited speakers Elisabeth André, Mark Riedl, and Job Roggeveen of Job, Joris, and Marieke for their outstanding speeches. Many thanks go to the sponsors Utrecht Center for Game Research, EAI, ECCAI, and NWO for their support. The chairs also thank the members of the Technical Program Committee and of the Organizing Committee, who made this conference possible. We would like to thank the EAI representatives Ivana Allen, Sinziana Vieriu, Jana Vlnkova, and Lenka Laukova for their invaluable help in organizing INTETAIN 2016.

Special thanks also to the INTETAIN Steering Committee Board, who assigned Utrecht University the organization of the 2016 INTETAIN edition.

June 2016   Ronald Poppe
                                                          John-Jules Meyer
                                                          Remco Veltkamp
                                                            Mehdi Dastani

Organization

General Chair

John-Jules C. Meyer   Utrecht University, The Netherlands

General Co-chairs

Remco Veltkamp   Utrecht University, The Netherlands
Mehdi Dastani   Utrecht University, The Netherlands

Program Chair

Ronald Poppe   Utrecht University, The Netherlands

Local Arrangements Chair

Arjan Egges   Utrecht University, The Netherlands

Workshop Chair

Dirk Heylen   University of Twente, The Netherlands

Publicity Chair

Zerrin Yumak   Utrecht University, The Netherlands

Sponsor Chair

Marieke Peeters   Delft University of Technology, The Netherlands

Demo Chair

Roland Geraerts   Utrecht University, The Netherlands

Web Chair

Coert van Gemeren   Utrecht University, The Netherlands

EAI Conference Coordinator

Lenka Laukova   EAI — European Alliance for Innovation

Program Committee

Albert Ali Salah	Bogazici University, Turkey
Alejandro Lopez Rincon	Institut des Systemes Complexes, France
Anton Nijholt	Imagineering Institute, Malaysia
Ben Falchuk	Applied Communication Sciences, Vencore Labs, USA
Ben Schouten	Amsterdam University of Applied Sciences, The Netherlands
Benjamin Kenwright	Edinburg Napier University, UK
Bipin Indurkhya	AGH University, Poland
Christian Jacquemin	LIMSI-CNRS, France
Dirk Heylen	University of Twente, The Netherlands
Fabrizio Lamberti	Politecnico di Torino, Italy
Fabrizio Valpreda	Politecnico di Torino, Italy
Giancarlo Iannizzotto	University of Messina, Italy
Helmut Hlavacs	University of Vienna, Austria
Jon George Rokne	University of Calgary, Canada
Maic Masuch	University of Duisburg-Essen, Germany
Marc Cavazza	Kent University, UK
Marco Gori	University of Siena, Italy
Marco Pasin	IrisCube Reply, Italy
Marinka Copier	University of the Arts, Utrecht, The Netherlands
Matt Flagg	PlayVision Labs, USA
Milton Luiz Horn Vieira	Federal University of Santa Catarina, Brazil
Olivier Debeir	Free University of Brussels, Belgium
Radu-Daniel Vatavu	University Stefan cel Mare of Suceava, Romania
Rainer Malaka	TZI, University of Bremen, Germany
Richard Kronland-Martinet	CNRS — LMA, France
Rui Prada	University of Lisbon, Portugal
Sergio Canazza	University of Padova, Italy
Sylvain Marchand	University of La Rochelle, France
Thanos Vasilakos	University of Western Macedonia, Greece
Theresa-Marie Rhyne	Consultant
Tsvi Kuflik	The University of Haifa, Israel

Steering Committee

Imrich Chlamtac	CREATE-NET, Italy
Anton Nijholt	Imagineering Institute, Malaysia
Antonio Camurri	University of Genoa, Italy

Contents

Workshop: Playable Cities

Workshop: Virtual Agents for Social Skills Training

Serious Games

Designing Collaborative Games for Children Education on Sustainable Development

Alysson Diniz Dos Santos[1,2]([✉]), Francesco Strada[1], Andrea Martina[1],
and Andrea Bottino[1]

[1] Dipartimento di Automatica e Informatica, Politecnico di Torino, Turin, Italy
[2] Instituto Universidade Virtual, Universidade Federal do Ceara, Fortaleza, Brazil
`alysson@virtual.ufc.br`

Abstract. Recent research in the digital learning game area strives for defining a solid grounding methodology, capable of driving the game design process towards the maximization of the intended educational results. In this work, we investigate the mix of tangible interaction, immersive environments, collaborative multiplay and validated theoretical background in the design of WaterOn!, an educational game focused on teaching water cycle contents for children. The paper presents the design decisions taken in light of the adopted methodologies, and discusses some open questions related to the use of these tools.

Keywords: Educational game · Tangible · Collaborative · Sustainable development · Water · Children

1 Introduction

Serious games have been used in several fields to convey training or learning [5]. When focused on learning, well designed games must provide an experience in which entertainment and instruction are seamlessly integrated. How to achieve such an ideal scenario is the research objective of an increasing number of publications [13]. In spite of the growing research interest, the digital learning area still lacks an overarching methodology capable of covering the whole development process, from design to evaluation [13]. Although some theoretical tools exist [7], they have not been extensively used yet [20].

The objective of this work is to investigate the use of practical and theoretical design background in the development of WaterOn!, a collaborative multiplayer game focused on teaching water cycle contents for 8–10 years old children. The game exploits tangible and multitouch interaction on mobile devices and a projected virtual environment in order to foster collaboration among co-located users, reinforce the emotional impact of the game [11], and improve the players feeling of immersion into the game story. The WaterOn! design is based on both the RETAIN framework [9] and the practical guidelines for collaborative games described in [1].

© ICST Institute for Computer Sciences, Social Informatics and Telecommunications Engineering 2017
R. Poppe et al. (Eds.): INTETAIN 2016, LNICST 178, pp. 3–12, 2017.
DOI: 10.1007/978-3-319-49616-0_1

As for the related works, sustainability issues has already been approached in collaborative digital environments, like the game Futura [1,19] and the learning activity Youtopia [2]. Both works exploit tangibles as interaction tools, since they were found to be preferred by their audience, in comparison with purely graphic interaction. However, further investigation over the correlation of tangibles, collaboration, and educational games for children audience is needed. For example, [19] relates that collaborative activities are more influenced by group dynamics than by interaction modality and [17] argues that multi-touch interfaces do not always promote effective collaboration, since there is always the risk that players are engaged with their own task with little consideration for their nearby peers.

In this paper, we thoroughly discuss the choices taken in the design of WaterOn! and how the selected design models influenced them. We stress the fact that, to the best of our knowledge, our work is the first that exploits RETAIN as a design model rather than as a mere evaluation tool (like, for instance, in [4,9]). For this reason, although actually the implementation of WaterOn! is still in its preliminary phase and some instructional units are missing, we deemed interesting to share our initial results with the research community. We expect our contribution to rise a discussion on the use of these tools, hopefully providing answers to some of the questions arisen in our work.

The rest of the paper is organized as follows. In Sect. 2 we present the theoretical background related to the design of collaborative educational games. Then, we describe the WaterOn! game in Sect. 3 and we discuss our preliminary results in Sect. 4. Finally, we present the conclusions and outline future works in Sect. 5.

2   Theoretical Background

Recent researches proposed various methodological frameworks that offer structured principles to enhance game-based learning by coupling instructional theories and strategies with traditional game design aspects [12]. Among the possible options, we decided to base the design of WaterOn! on both the RETAIN framework [9] and the key design factors for collaborative games outlined in [1].

The reasons for choosing RETAIN were threefold: (i) it is both a design model and an evaluation tool; (ii) its theoretical bases are closely aligned with modern game design principles; and (iii) it is based on Piaget's theory of cognitive development [16] and, thus, well suited for a children game audience.

According to the RETAIN framework the game design should consider six key factors that can be summarized as follows. The learning materials should be *relevant* to the learners and their needs, the instructional units should be related to each another and the game should underline the relevance of the educational contents in the real life of the players. Then, the educational content should be seamlessly *embedded* into the game fantasy[1]. The game should also foster

---

[1] In this paper the term fantasy is used, as in [9], to encompass the game storyline, its narrative structure and the player experience.

the players' capabilities to use the acquired knowledge in other forms (*transfer*) or to *adapt* it to different contexts. Since an educational game is still a game, *immersion*, or the subjective sensation of "being there", is a key point for enhancing learner motivation. Gunter suggests a step ahead, that is reaching a "full immersion", where players are willing to intellectually invest in the learning situation. Finally, a game with high level of re-playability stimulates *naturalization* of the content, i.e., how well players develop automated or spontaneous use of the learned information.

A drawback of RETAIN is that, being based on the Piaget's theory of cognitive development [16], it offers little or no emphasis to the collaborative part of the learning process. To overcome this issue, we made explicit references in our design to the guidelines for collaborative game designs outlined in [1], which can be summarized in the following points:

– the use of spatially separate but shareable individual territories and resources to facilitate negotiation and learning from others;
– the prevention of a single player to take over the game; and
– the use of discrete world events to pause fast-paced interaction in order to facilitate reflection and self-regulation.

3   WaterOn!

The motivating factors for the choice of water as the educational focus of the WaterOn! game were two. First, education towards water in its different aspects, such as consumption, quality, supply and management, is the basis for understanding other knowledge needed by elementary school children (e.g., the life-cycle of plants and animals, natural disorders, energy production and so on [10]). Second, although being a fundamental topic, some studies show that there are still misconceptions in water education of school-age children [18].

The game design and the instructional units have been centered around the target audience, i.e. 8–10 years old children. This range corresponds to the center of concrete operational stage of children (7–11 years old according to Piaget [16]). The game mechanics have been defined taking into account that children at this age demonstrate logical and concrete reasoning and are more capable of taking part in cooperative activities, with respect to their younger peers [16].

With reference to both the national curriculum standards alignment developed by the water.org foundation [15] and the educational materials available from Project Wet [14], the following three instructional units were defined:

1. identifying the three states of the water and the transitions between them;
2. describing the movement of water within the water cycle;
3. recognizing solar energy as main driver of water movements on earth.

As for the development process, we actually completed the implementation of the first unit, which will be the focus of the rest of the paper. While the remaining units are still in their prototypical phase, we will provide in Sect. 5 hints on their mutual relationships.

3.1 The Game Design

WaterOn! is meant to foster collaboration among children since, in each level, it requires both communication and coordination between players to fulfil the objectives. In order to strengthen such cooperation, the game features a projected virtual environment (Fig. 1(a)). This screen shows the overall game scenario, where players are acting as individuals, and the game status, which is aimed at offering a shared understanding of what has been achieved and what has to be completed yet. Players interact with the game through a tablet (thus being free to move inside the physical game environment), exploiting both multitouch and tangible interaction. Each tablet displays a portion of the whole environment (Fig. 1(b)) and the system provides a direct feedback of players position on the projected scenario (Fig. 1(c)).

Unit 1: Level Design. The first three levels of the game are aimed at teaching children the states of water and the fact that the transition between them occur when heat energy is added or lost. The story of these three levels is played around a bunch of villains trying to plunder water resources while players are

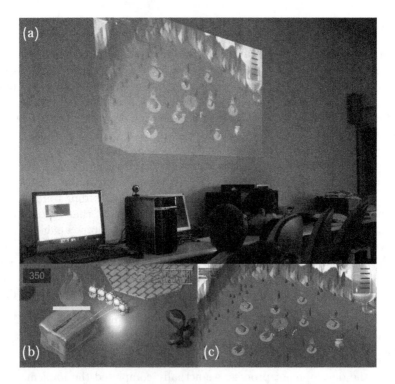

Fig. 1. (a) An image of the projected scenario; (b) View on the tablet screen; (c) Feedback of player positions (the coloured boxes) on the main screen. (Color figure online)

the village dwellers fighting the enemies. In the first level, *melting*, the villains have frozen all the available water to incorporate the village houses into giant ice cubes. Players have to melt the ice and fight against the enemies, which are trying to freeze again the water (Fig. 1). In the second level, *vaporization*, players have to blow up an air balloon, which is necessary to chase the (escaped) villain in chief, by transforming the collected water into steam. Players have to pour water into huge pots and to fuel the fire below them while enemies try to steal water from the pots (Fig. 2(a)). The last level, *deposition*, is preceded by an introductory scene showing that the air balloon has been attacked by enemies, which punched holes in it. The steam flowed out and condensed into clouds, while the air balloon crashed on a mountain top. The goal of the players is to move the clouds towards the mountain, cool them down to start snowing and create a snow ramp allowing to rescue the balloon passengers. Here the enemies use fans to hamper the cloud movements (Fig. 2(b)).

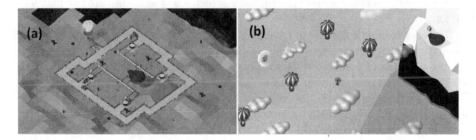

Fig. 2. Screenshots of vaporization (a) and deposition (b) levels.

In all three levels, the lose condition is associated with the extinction of the shared resources (i.e. the water in the desired state). The aim of aggregating win-lose conditions to the communal resources is to stimulate negotiation and players learning from others [1]. Another feature aimed at fostering cooperation is the absence of individual failure or success in-game, since it is only possible to win or lose in group.

3.2   Interaction Design

Players can move around the environment using either controls on the tablet screen or a map-based travel metaphor. As for the game interaction, players can use tangibles as tools to generate in-game actions. Examples are the *heat token* (the heat source used to melt the ice in the first level and evaporate the water in the second; both have effect only when placed in the proper position), the *cold token* (required to cool down the clouds and generate the deposition effect) and the *blower token* (used to move clouds in the third level; the position where the marker is placed around the cloud in the tablet screen determines the wind direction and force).

To enrich the game mechanics, direct touch interaction is also available. Besides enabling navigation, player touches can activate specific actions in the game. For instance, in all levels, each player can tap on an enemy to imprison it for some seconds. Each player has a limited number of cages, which can be unlocked according to the points acquired by the player. The choice for a limited amount of weapons is aimed at forcing a more "strategical" approach (i.e. requiring, again, collaboration). These touch interactions are not directly associated with the educational content of the game, but are meant to keep the player immersed by creating a more active gameplay and complexity progression among the levels.

Implementation Details. WaterOn! has been implemented into Unity 3D, a cross-platform game engine, which offers advanced lighting and rendering options, built-in support for spatialized audio, physics management, complex animations, multitasking, pipeline optimization and networking. Multiplayer collaborative interaction has been managed implementing a client-server architecture, where the server controls the primary screen and the clients are the players' tablets.

In order to enable the use of tangibles with devices equipped with commercial capacitive touch screens, we developed custom passive markers characterized by unique patterns of conductive touch points that encode both their position and ID [3]. Our markers use four contact points per marker, where three of them define an orthogonal Cartesian reference system capable of providing position and orientation information, and the fourth one, the data point, defines the marker ID. We experimentally found that the minimal size allowing a robust marker identification is 30 mm. With this size, the number of unique IDs that can be represented is 8, and a larger set of distinct markers can be obtained increasing the marker size. Since four touch points are required for a tangible, a maximum of two markers and two finger touches can be recognized at the same time on a standard tablet. Markers are 3D-printed, using conductive graphene filaments to create the contact points, which are attached to a common base and then enclosed in a plastic PLA shield (Fig. 3).

(a)   (b)   (c)

Fig. 3. The capacitive tangible (c) consists in a set of contact points (a) enclosed in a PLA shield (b).

4   Results and Discussion

The main goal of this study was to investigate the mix of tangible interaction, immersive environments, collaborative multiplay and pedagogical background in the design of an educational game for children. Based on this consideration, how can we assess the preliminary results of our research?

Beside defining the key elements to be considered in game-based learning design, the work of Gunter proposes as well an evaluation model that classifies each of these six aspects into four levels. However, we believe that the application of such evaluation scheme is too preliminary in our case, due to the fact that WaterOn! is still in its development stage and some instructional units are missing. Nevertheless, we think it is interesting to summarize how the RETAIN model and the principles expressed in [1] influenced our design and where we are planning to focus our future evaluation.

We underline that we actually tested our application with some volunteers (aged between 8 and 10). Although their number does not allow a systematic evaluation, we obtained positive feedbacks from our testers. Children expressed enjoyment and found challenging to progress in the game, which they commented was a factor increasing their fun. We observed that children rapidly find out they have to cooperate to successfully complete a level, although not instructed to do that. To this end, the shared scenario was effective in coordinating their efforts. Another positive finding was that all our testers enjoyed the use of tangibles as interaction tools.

WaterOn! and RETAIN. In the following we will discuss the influence to our design of each of the RETAIN aspects.

Relevance. The game mechanics (i.e., the use of simple interactions relying on previous knowledge on touchscreen devices and tangibles) were designed to match the developmental level of our target players. The learning objective is clearly defined (the three states of water and the transitions among them) and the game fantasy is intrinsically related to the educational goals, thus preventing the focus to shift away from the targeted contents.

Embedding. The educational content is endogenous to the fantasy context, i.e. the story and gameplay are tightly coupled with the information we want to transfer. We think that the level of engagement shown by our testers is a possible indicator of this fact. However, this point requires further investigation.

Transfer. The keys to progress in the game are mastering the instructional elements, which are introduced in a hierarchical manner, and using active problem solving approaches. The emulation of realistic scenarios intends to foster the transfer between the learned contents and real life. Gunter suggests reinforcing this transfer by introducing post acquisition events (e.g. by exploiting accessory educational material or reviews). We will investigate this aspect in our future work.

Adaptation. The first three game levels put forth the basis for adaptation, which will be necessary to progress in the following instruction units. Indeed, players will have to extend the learned state transition concepts in order to gain a clear understanding of the water cycle and, thus, advance in the game.

Immersion. The use of tangibles and the progressive presentation of mechanics (i.e., the introduction of new mechanics in each level) intend to maintain the cognitive immersion of the players. The game plot, the shared environment and animations aim to harness belief creation. Nevertheless, the achievement of a "fully involvement to invest in the belief", as referred by Gunter, needs to be further investigated.

Naturalization. In the preliminary tests, our users always asked us to replay the game. Beside being a positive indication of their attitude towards the game, replaying helps content retention and improves the speed of cognitive response. This, in turns, leads to positive effects in terms of naturalization, i.e. making it easier to use the acquired knowledge in novel scenarios. Clearly, further analyses are required to confirm this conjecture.

WaterOn! and the Guidelines for Collaborative Game Design. The guidelines described in Sect. 2 were adopted in WaterOn! as follows.

The use of spatially separate but shareable individual territories and resources is at the base of the game design. The tablets offer single manipulation over a common territory and allow to increase the number of simultaneous players, since they do not need to share the physical space over the same screen.

The prevention of a single player to take over the game is guaranteed mainly through game balancing. The quantity of enemies is adapted to the number of players and their power, when they act in group, overcome the capabilities of a single player. Therefore the artificial intelligence acts to group enemies and prevent a player to win alone.

The first three levels did not require the introduction of **discrete world events to pause fast-paced multi-touch interaction**. Indeed, the game design does not permit fast-paced interaction. The tools controlled by the tangible tokens have a limited speed of action, and the number of items to be used with direct touches is also limited. On the contrary, we plan to introduce such events in the extension of WaterOn! game. For instance, in the second instruction unit, the players will have to use the tokens presented in the first unit to re-stablish the balance of the water cycle, which was scrambled by the enemies. During the levels, periodic discrete events like precipitation, glaciation and transpiration will affect water states in the whole game scenario. This will change the natural balance, requiring players to collaboratively plan new actions, e.g. to decide which tool to use, where to use it in the scenario and how to face the enemies.

Open Questions. As we stated in the introduction, the RETAIN framework has been previously used to evaluate serious games [4,9], and our work is the first attempt to use it explicitly during the design process. As a result, some questions arose:

How to make the player interested in keep learning about the topic after the game experience? This point was not discussed in the work of Gunter. However, we think it would be necessary to develop in-game strategies capable of stimulating the children interest after the game finishes, although we have no clear suggestions yet on how to achieve this objective.

How to assess the fully involvement to invest in the belief (i.e. the full immersion)? Although Gunter links this requirement to the achievement of the highest level possible of content embedding, we found hard to detect which strategies can lead to this full immersion. We suggest that this feature can be re-modeled taking it account as well the flow concept [6].

Concerning the collaborative dimension, we found that the guidelines in [1] were clearly defined and useful. However, we think they do not completely enclose the collaborative design of the game. For example, we witnessed that during the first level played by all our groups of testers, although the majority of the players understood the need to collaborate, some of them initially attempted to simply complete their personal goals. Although this problem was readily solved, one possible solution to avoid it from the very beginning could be the introduction of challenges requiring multiple actions from different players. While this approach was successfully tested with young adults [8], further investigation on its adequacy to a children audience is needed.

5   Conclusions

In this work we described the preliminary implementation of an educational game for children. The game design has been based on solid and validated models and on sound guidelines that, according to our initial results, seem to provide: (i) a valuable contribution towards the achievement of the planned educational goals and (ii) a satisfactory level of engagement of our players.

As for future works, we will complete the implementation of WaterOn! with the introduction of the missing instruction units outlined in Sect. 3. Then, we will thoroughly evaluate our work exploiting both user surveys, panels of experts and the evaluation schema defined by the RETAIN model.

References

1. Antle, A.N., et al.: Futura: design for collaborative learning and game play on a multi-touch digital tabletop. In: Proceedings of the Fifth International Conference on Tangible, Embedded, and Embodied Interaction, pp. 93–100. ACM (2011)
2. Antle, A.N., et al.: Youtopia: a collaborative, tangible, multi-touch, sustainability learning activity. In: Proceedings of the 12th International Conference on Interaction Design and Children, pp. 565–568. ACM (2013)
3. Bottino, A., Martina, A., Toosi, A., Strada, F.: Gaine - a portable framework for the development of edutainment applications based on multitouch and tangible interaction. Entertainment Computing, pp. 207–216 (2016, to appear)
4. Campbell, L.O., Gunter, G., Braga, J.: Utilizing the retain model to evaluate mobile learning applications. In: Society for Information Technology & Teacher Education International Conference, vol. 2015, pp. 732–736 (2015)

5. Crookall, D.: Serious games, debriefing, and simulation/gaming as a discipline. Simul. Gaming **41**(6), 898–920 (2010)
6. Csikszentmihalyi, M.: Beyond Boredom and Anxiety. Jossey-Bass, New York (2000)
7. dos Santos, A.D., Fraternali, P.: A comparison of methodological frameworks for digital learning game design. In: De Gloria, A., Veltkamp, R. (eds.) GALA 2015. LNCS, vol. 9599, pp. 111–120. Springer, Heidelberg (2016). doi:10.1007/978-3-319-40216-1_12
8. Fan, M., et al.: Exploring how a co-dependent tangible tool design supports collaboration in a tabletop activity. In: Proceedings of the 18th International Conference on Supporting Group Work, pp. 81–90. ACM (2014)
9. Gunter, G.A., Kenny, R.F., Vick, E.H.: Taking educational games seriously: using the retain model to design endogenous fantasy into standalone educational games. Educ. Technol. Res. Dev. **56**(5–6), 511–537 (2008)
10. Hrennikoff, M.: Implementing an imaginative unit: wonders of the water cycle. Educ. Perspect. **39**(2), 27–33 (2006)
11. Iwata, T., et al.: Traditional games meet ICT: a case study on go game augmentation. In Proceedings of the Fourth International Conference on Tangible, Embedded, and Embodied Interaction, pp. 237–240. ACM (2010)
12. Kebritchi, M., et al.: Examining the pedagogical foundations of modern educational computer games. Comput. Educ. **51**(4), 1729–1743 (2008)
13. Mayer, I., et al.: The research and evaluation of serious games: toward a comprehensive methodology. Br. J. Educ. Technol. **45**(3), 502–527 (2014)
14. Online. Project wet's discover water, 02 2016
15. Online. Water.org foundation, 02 2016
16. Piaget, J., Cook, M., Norton, W.: The Origins of Intelligence in Children, vol. 8. International Universities Press, New York (1952)
17. Rick, J., et al.: Beyond one-size-fits-all: how interactive tabletops support collaborative learning. In: Proceedings of the 10th International Conference on Interaction Design and Children, pp. 109–117. ACM (2011)
18. Shepardson, D.P., Wee, B., Priddy, M., Schellenberger, L., Harbor, J.: Water transformation and storage in the mountains and at the coast: midwest students' disconnected conceptions of the hydrologic cycle. Int. J. Sci. Educ. **31**(11), 1447–1471 (2009)
19. Speelpenning, T., Antle, A.N., Doering, T., van den Hoven, E.: Exploring how tangible tools enable collaboration in a multi-touch tabletop game. In: Campos, P., Graham, N., Jorge, J., Nunes, N., Palanque, P., Winckler, M. (eds.) INTERACT 2011. LNCS, vol. 6947, pp. 605–621. Springer, Heidelberg (2011). doi:10.1007/978-3-642-23771-3_45
20. Whitton, N.: Digital Games, Learning: Research and Theory. Routledge, Abingdon (2014)

Towards Serious Gaming for Communication Training - A Pilot Study with Police Academy Students

Tibor Bosse[1(✉)] and Charlotte Gerritsen[2]

[1] Department of Computer Science, Vrije Universiteit Amsterdam,
De Boelelaan 1081, 1081 HV Amsterdam, The Netherlands
t.bosse@vu.nl
[2] Netherlands Institute for the Study of Crime and Law Enforcement,
De Boelelaan 1077, 1081 HV Amsterdam, The Netherlands
cgerritsen@nscr.nl

Abstract. Serious games are increasingly being used for training of communicative skills. The main idea is to create a virtual environment in which a trainee can interact with graphically embodied virtual characters. By designing scenarios in such way that the character's behaviour provides direct feedback on the correctness of the trainee's choices, an interactive learning experience is created. This paper explores the potential of this approach in the domain of law enforcement. A prototype has been developed of a serious game that enables police academy students to train their communicative skills. A pilot study with 41 students has been conducted. The results show that this is a promising instrument for education in this domain, but also point out several suggestions for improvement.

Keywords: Serious gaming · Virtual characters · Communication training

1 Introduction

"On Friday, August 16th, around 14.30, a report was received of a man and a woman being heavily under the influence of alcohol in a park in Zutphen. A number of police officers went to the park, and found the man and woman there. The man approached the officers with clenched fists while speaking aggressive language. He refused to show his ID. The woman that accompanied him did not want to show her ID either. As a result, both of them were arrested and transferred to the police station. The man showed much resistance to his arrest. Both on the way to the station and at the station, both arrested persons still showed verbally and physically aggressive behaviour towards the police. Both were remanded in custody for insulting and threatening behaviour towards police officers."

Although it is just one example[1], this incident illustrates that aggressive behaviour against police officers is an ongoing concern in The Netherlands. The aggression can range from verbal threats and intimidations to physical violence. In 2006, the Dutch

---

[1] Source: http://www.politie.nl/nieuws/2013/augustus/17/02-zuthen-agressie-tegen-politieagenten.html.

© ICST Institute for Computer Sciences, Social Informatics and Telecommunications Engineering 2017
R. Poppe et al. (Eds.): INTETAIN 2016, LNICST 178, pp. 13–22, 2017.
DOI: 10.1007/978-3-319-49616-0_2

Ministry of the Interior (BZK) initiated a preventive program 'Veilige Publieke Taak' [1]. Part of this initiative was monitoring the incidence of violence in the public sector. According to this study, around 60 % of the employees in the public sector has been confronted with undesired behaviour in the last 12 months. Despite interventions initiated by the Minister of Justice, only a tiny improvement for some services was found in the period 2006–2011 [1]. For the police domain, no significant improvement has been achieved at all, so the situation is still very actual.

There is an ongoing discussion about what can be done to better prepare police officers for such incidents. One of the solutions that are currently considered is to put substantial effort in *training of communicative skills*. The underlying idea is that the way in which employees communicate with citizens might have an effect on whether or not the citizens misbehave. Indeed, communication training and resilience training have become important elements in the education program at the Dutch Police Academy [2]. Such training is typically performed in a group setting, for instance based on role-play, where student learn to communicate with (aggressive) citizens in such a way that the situation does not escalate. Although this form of training has shown to be successful, it is quite expensive with respect to both money and time. Furthermore, the training is not always easy to control or repeat systematically.

As a complementary approach, in our research we propose the use of simulation-based training to learn communicative skills. This is in line with a number of recent initiatives that show promising results regarding the possibility to train social skills based on simulated environments involving virtual humans [3–7]. These projects have addressed a variety of tasks in different domains, including police interviews [3], leadership training for naval officers [4], medical consultations [5], negotiation in different cultures [6], and manager-employee conversations [7].

The main idea of the current system is that Police Academy students can practice their communication skills by engaging in conversations with virtual citizens. By designing the scenarios in such a way that the virtual characters behave well if they are being approached correctly, but misbehave if they are being treated inappropriately, trainees will receive immediate feedback on their performance. With such a system, students have the ability to practice their communication skills in a cost-effective, personalized and systematic manner.

In this paper, a prototype of such a serious game for simulation-based training is presented, which has been developed in collaboration with the Dutch Police Academy. In addition, a pilot study is described that has been performed to evaluate different aspects of the system. The emphasis of the proposed system is on decision making aspects in a graphically realistic environment. By using a combination of motion capture technology and state-of-the-art software from the gaming industry, a realistic environment with human-like virtual characters is created. To achieve this, the choice has been made to use a relatively simple interaction paradigm, based on multiple choice menus and dialogue trees. Hence, the focus of this paper is on developing a learning tool for decision making in familiar environments, and not so much on affective multi-modal interaction (which obviously is an important aspect of simulation-based training too, and which we will integrate with our current system in the future).

2 Theoretical Basis

To design an effective training tool, a first question to be asked is what should be the learning goals of the system. For the current context, these learning goals are similar to the ones used in the existing education program of Police Academy students.

In [2], an overview is presented of the theories that are used in this education program for teaching social skills. The document covers a wide variety of skills, including 'core qualities', cooperation, feedback, communication, general conversation skills, task-specific conversation skills, conflict resolution, and emotion/stress regulation. For the proposed project, which has an emphasis on (verbal) communication and aggression de-escalation, especially the last four skills are of relevance. The idea is to capture the knowledge available in the relevant theories within the training system, to enable it to provide appropriate feedback to the actions performed by the trainee (cf. [8, 9]). Regarding *general conversation skills*, there are a number of techniques that students should include in their repertoire by repeated practice; these include techniques at a verbal (e.g., paraphrasing, asking questions) and a non-verbal level (e.g., nodding and using eye contact). Regarding *task-specific communication skills*, there are several more sophisticated methods that students should learn to apply in the right context. For instance, in ticket issuing conversations, students can make use of the 'Van der Steen method'. This method divides the conversation in three phases (opening, dealing with reactions, and administrative closure), and prescribes recommended behaviours for different types of reactions of the conversation partner [10]. Similarly, several theories are used that enable people to take away resistance during difficult conversations, such as the Leary Circumplex [11] (which classifies behaviour along the axes of dominance and cooperation, and provides guidance for selecting a type of behaviour that facilitates successful interaction), and the Transactional Analysis [12] (a psychological theory that helps understanding how people express their personality in terms of behaviour). Regarding *conflict resolution*, an important theory is the one by Giebels and Euwema [13], which distinguishes five styles for solving conflicts (namely forcing, avoiding, problem solving, yielding, and compromising), and enables people to make strategic choices between these styles in a particular situation. In addition, the CIPA model is often used, which identifies four phases within difficult conversations (making contact, gathering information, problem solving, and closure), and provides behavioural guidelines for each phase [2]. Finally, regarding *emotion/stress regulation*, students should learn to recognise the aggression level of their conversation partner as well as their own stress level, and be able to find a suitable match between the two by switching between stress levels and corresponding interaction techniques [14]. Although this overview of communication skills was established specifically for the Police Academy, it shows much overlap with the techniques that are prescribed for other domains in which aggression de-escalation plays a role, such as public transport and health care [15].

2.1 Focus of This Pilot Study: The 'Door Scene'

As it would be impossible to address all of the above skills within one pilot study, the focus of the current paper is on one specific learning goal. This learning goal is taken from the module 'Noodhulp' (Emergency Assistance), which is one of the modules in the education program at the Police Academy. As part of this module, students have to learn to correctly handle the so-called 'Door Scene'. This is a situation in which a police officer has just been informed about an incoming emergency call. For the current prototype, we focus on the domain of domestic violence (e.g., a call from a crying woman who claims that her boyfriend is abusing her). The scenario starts at the moment that the police officer (together with his or her partner) arrives at the address from which the call was made, and rings at the door. Typically, the door is then opened by one of the key characters in the scenario (e.g., the woman how made the call, or her boyfriend). The main goal for the trainee is to find out what is going on (e.g., is this indeed a case of domestic violence?) and to decide whether or not there is sufficient evidence to enter the house, while at the same time preventing the situation from escalating by applying the appropriate communication skills.

3   Training Environment

To develop the training environment, the same approach as in [16] has been followed: the environment has been implemented in InterACT[2], a training platform developed by the company IC3D Media.[3] The InterACT platform is especially suitable for designing simulation-based training of interpersonal skills, since it focuses on smaller situations, with high realism and detailed interactions with virtual characters. An example screenshot of a training scenario for students of the Police Academy is shown in Fig. 1.

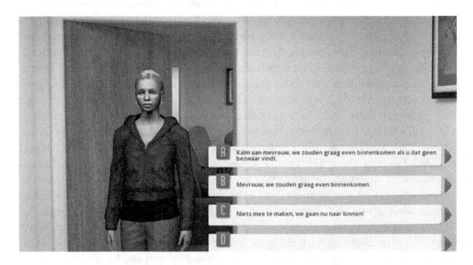

Fig. 1. Example screenshot of a training scenario.

[2] http://www.interact-training.nl/.

[3] http://ic3dmedia.com/.

In the example displayed in Fig. 1, the trainee plays the role of a police officer, responding to a potential domestic violence situation. The goal in this situation is to engage in a conversation with the lady to persuade her to let you help her.

A dialogue system based on conversation trees has been used to enable trainees to engage in a conversation with the embodied conversational agent (ECA). The system is based on the assumption that a dialogue consists of a sequence of spoken sentences that follow a turn-taking protocol. In these scenarios, the trainees starts the conversation by saying something (e.g. "Good morning, we have been informed that your neighbour heard someone cry this morning"). After that, the ECA can respond, followed by a response from the trainee, and so on. These dialogues are represented by conversation trees, where vertices are either decision nodes or atomic ECA behaviours, and the edges are transitions between nodes.

The atomic ECA behaviours consist of gestures, combined with pre-generated fragments of speech, synchronised with facial expressions. Scenario developers can generate their own fragments using a motion sensing input device such as the Microsoft Kinect camera and a commercial software package called FaceShift.[4] The recorded fragments are independent from a particular avatar and they can be projected on arbitrary characters.

Each decision node is implemented as a multiple choice menu. By using this menu, the trainee has the possibility to choose between multiple sentences. Hence, the emphasis of the current system is on the verbal aspects of aggression de-escalation. In the system used for the current study, two to four options are available for every decision node.

For the current evaluation study, four representative scenarios for the 'Door Scene' have been developed, in collaboration with (and approved by) domain experts of the police academy. In two scenarios the ECA is male, and in two scenarios the ECA is female. The scenarios have been designed in such a way that the ending can be either positive (e.g., the ECA lets the police officer enter the house) or negative (e.g., the ECA closes the door and refuses to open again), depending on the appropriateness of the trainee's choices. However, in the current study, no explicit 'score' was assigned to the player's performance.

The contents of the scenarios (i.e., the conversation fragments) have been recorded with the help of professional actors (one male and one female). On average, a scenario lasts about 5 interactions (i.e., both the user and the virtual character speak about 5 sentences before the scenario ends), which means that it takes about 2–3 min to play a scenario.

4 Pilot Study

To obtain feedback from potential end users on the prototype, a pilot study has been performed with students of the Police Academy. In the following sections, the participants, experimental design, and procedure of the study are described, respectively.

---

[4] http://www.faceshift.com/.

4.1 Participants

In total, 41 people were selected to participate in the experiment. All participants were students of the Police Academy, who were following the module 'Emergency Assistance'. The participants came from three different classes, who participated at different days: the first class consisted of 16 students, the second class of 11 students, and the third class of 14 students. No participants dropped out. Out of the 41 participants, 31 were male and 10 were female. The average age of the participants was 27.1 ($\sigma = 6.5$).

4.2 Procedure

The pilot experiment was executed in a computer room at the Police Academy (see Fig. 2).

Fig. 2. Impression of the pilot experiment.

At the start, all participants filled out an informed consent form and provided their personal data. This, as well as all other data gathered in this experiment, was collected anonymously. After that, participants received a document with instructions about how to work with the training software. Participants had to play all four scenarios consecutively. They were instructed to first solve each scenario to the best of their ability by carefully observing the situation and by selecting the appropriate responses in the multiple choice menu. After that, they could play each scenario again, in order to explore what would happen in they selected different responses. After having read the instructions, they could start the training software.

Upon launching the software, the start menu shown in Fig. 3 was displayed. In the upper part of the menu, participants had to input their personal ID and gender. Below that, they could select the scenario they wanted to run. As mentioned, there were 4 training scenarios, which were chosen in such a way that they were representative for the types of situations encountered on the job.

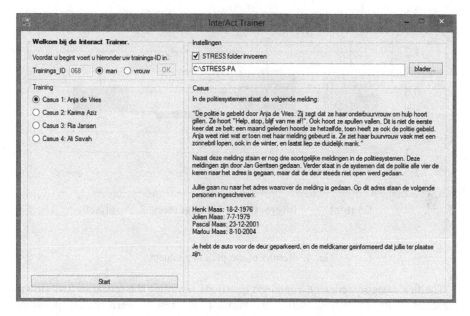

Fig. 3. Start menu of the training software (in Dutch).

4.3 Questionnaire

After the training, the participants were asked to fill out a usability questionnaire. This questionnaire consisted of 20 statements about which the participants had to express their opinion on a 7-point Likert scale. The questionnaire was inspired by Witmer and Singer [17], and included statements about issues such as user experience, presence, and perceived effectiveness. In the end, the statements were grouped into 4 categories, namely *content*, *interaction*, *engagement*, and *effect*, to obtain an average score on these aspects. The *content* category contained statements about the perceived realism of the scenarios and the characters (e.g., 'the scenarios were representative for real world situations'). The *interaction* category contained statements about how natural it was to interact with the characters (e.g., 'I felt that my answers had an influence in the behaviour of the virtual characters'). The *engagement* category addressed the perceived sense of presence of the participants (e.g., 'during training I felt engaged in the scenarios'). Finally, the *effect* category contained statements asking the participants for their opinion about the effectiveness of the training (e.g., 'I think this type of training is a useful addition to real world training').

5 Results

As explained above, the statements included in the questionnaire were grouped into four categories: interaction, content, engagement and effect. The aggregated answers for these categories are (on a scale from −3 up to 3) are shown in Fig. 4.

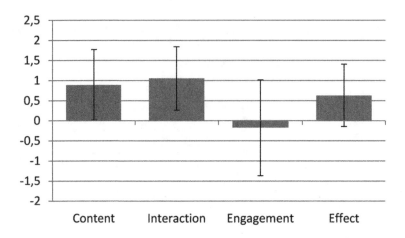

Fig. 4. Results of the pilot experiment.

The first category, *content*, contained questions regarding the scenarios and virtual characters. With an average score of almost 1, the results were mainly positive, however there were critical remarks as can be seen by the rather larger standard deviation. Similar results are found for the second category, *interaction,* and are, with an average score of just above 1, again mainly positive. The worst results are found on the category asking about the *engagement* aspects of the training. This entailed questions about the participants' personal involvement in the scenario, asking for instance about whether they got frightened by the aggression of the virtual characters. With an average score of −0.1 the results do not look promising, however again the standard deviation is very large, indicating a large variation in the answer. The last category contained questions about the participants' personal belief whether such a training has an *effect.* For example, they had to answer if they thought that this type of training was a useful addition to the current role-play scenarios, and if it would improve their communication skills. Overall, responses to these questions were positive (average 0.6), although there is room for improvement.

In all, these results are encouraging, in the sense that participants from a possible group of end users sees the potential of simulation as an instrument for communication training. Also, it is promising that the content of the scenarios and the way of interacting is considered fairly positive. Nevertheless, there is room for improvement, as witnessed, among other, by the responses given on the topic of 'engagement'. In this respect, it was also interesting to consider the feedback given by individual participants. Some examples of remarks made by the participants were:

- The scenarios were relatively short; I wanted to continue playing after I was allowed to enter the house.
- The emotional impact needs to be increased. I found the behaviour of the virtual characters insufficiently intimidating.
- I did not completely 'buy' the conversation with the virtual character. Compare to training based on role play, I was too much aware that I was only playing a game.
- It might be interesting to include a juridical component in the learning goals of the scenarios.
- It might be interesting to enable interaction with your partner as part of the game.

Based on these suggestions, we are currently working on improving the game.

6 Discussion

The current paper introduced a prototype of a simulation-based training environment that enables Dutch Police Academy students to practice their communication skills during face-to-face conversations. The emphasis of the prototype is on learning how to handle the 'Door Scene' in the context of domestic violence situations.

The prototype was evaluated by means of a pilot study in which 41 students of the Police Academy participated. The results indicate that with respect to user satisfaction, participants were positive about the content of the virtual scenarios and the mechanisms to interact with the characters. Also, they were moderately positive about the potential of the system as an effective learning tool. This was confirmed by some of the teachers, who were also allowed to play the game. Nevertheless, also a number of points for improvement were identified, which mainly have to do with the emotional aspect of the game. In other words, for many participants their sense of presence was limited because they did not 'feel' the emotion in the virtual conversation partner. One interesting way to improve this situation, which we are currently considering, is to combine the scenarios with haptic feedback (e.g., by using a vibrating vest designed for video games). Based on such technology, a situation can be created in which an (aggressive) virtual character can actually 'touch' the user. Another obvious possible extension would be to use a head-mounted display instead a flat video screen. Our hope is that such extensions will in the future lead to a more engaging, and therefore more effective training tool.

Acknowledgments. This research was supported by funding from the National Initiative Brain and Cognition, coordinated by the Netherlands Organization for Scientific Research (NWO), under grant agreement No. 056-25-013. The authors wish to thank Annet Beunk, Bianca Korporaal, Jeroen de Man, Frank Mosterd, Hans van Velzen, and all participants in the study for their contribution to the project.

References

1. Abraham, M., Flight, S., Roorda, W.: Agressie en geweld tegen werknemers met een publieke taak. Onderzoek voor Veilige Publieke Taak. DSP, Amsterdam (2011)
2. de Vries, R.: Reader SOVA. School voor Politiekunde, (Allround) Politiemedewerker, Kwartiel 1. Drachten, Januari 2011 (2011)
3. Bruijnes, M., Linssen, J.M.: op den Akker, H.J.A., Theune, M., Wapperom, S., Broekema, C., Heylen, D.K.J.: Social behaviour in police interviews: relating data to theories. In: D'Errico, F., Poggi, I., Vinciarelli, A., Vincze, L. (eds.) Conflict and Multimodal Communication. Computational Social Sciences, pp. 317–347. Springer, Heidelberg (2015)
4. Hays, M., Campbell, J., Trimmer, M., Poore, J., Webb, A., Stark, C., King, T.: Can role-play with virtual humans teach interpersonal skills? In: Interservice/Industry Training, Simulation and Education Conference (I/ITSEC) (2012)
5. Jeuring, J., et al.: Communicate! — A serious game for communication skills —. In: Conole, G., Klobučar, T., Rensing, C., Konert, J., Lavoué, É. (eds.) EC-TEL 2015. LNCS, vol. 9307, pp. 513–517. Springer, Heidelberg (2015). doi:10.1007/978-3-319-24258-3_49
6. Kim, J., Hill, R.W., Durlach, P., Lane, H.C., Forbell, E., Core, C., Marsella, S., Pynadath, D., Hart, J.: BiLAT: a game-based environment for practicing negotiation in a cultural context. Int. J. AI Educ. 19(3), 289–308 (2009)
7. Vaassen, F., Wauters, J.: deLearyous: training interpersonal communication skills using unconstrained text input. In: Proceedings of ECGBL, pp. 505–513 (2012)
8. Christoph, N.: The role of metacognitive skills in learning to solve problems. Ph.D. thesis, University of Amsterdam (2006)
9. Heuvelink, A., Mioch, T.: FeGA: a cognitive feedback generating agent. In: Proceedings of the Seventh IEEE/WIC/ACM International Conference on Intelligent Agent Technology (IAT 2008), pp. 567–572. IEEE Computer Society Press (2008)
10. Mandemaker, L., de Pater, H.: Bejegening bij verkeershandhaving. In: Berkhout, R. (ed.) Bejegenen bij handhaving, pp. 86–96. Politieacademie, Apeldoorn (2009)
11. Leary, T.: Interpersonal Diagnosis of Personality. Ronald Press, New York (1957)
12. Stewart, I., Joines, V.: TA Today: A New Introduction to Transactional Analysis. Lifespace Publishing (1987)
13. Giebels, E., Euwema, M.: Conflictmanagement: analyse, diagnostiek en interventie. Wolters-Noordhoff, Groningen/Houten (2006)
14. Breakwell, G.M.: Coping with Aggressive Behaviour. Wiley, Hoboken (1997)
15. Anderson, L.N., Clarke, J.T.: De-escalating verbal aggression in primary care settings. Nurse Pract. 21(10), 95, 98, 101–102 (1996)
16. Bosse, T., Gerritsen, C., de Man, J.: Evaluation of a virtual training environment for aggression de-escalation. In: Proceedings of GAME-ON 2015. Eurosis (2015)
17. Witmer, B.G., Singer, M.J.: Measuring presence in virtual environments: a presence questionnaire. Presence Teleoperators Virtual Environ. 7, 225–240 (1998)

A Serious Game for Learning Social Networking Literacy by Flaming Experiences

Kaoru Sumi[(✉)] and Kodai Kasai

Future Universiyu Hakodate, Hakodate, Japan
kaoru.sumi@acm.org

Abstract. In this study, we developed a serious game in which fifth and sixth grade elementary school students who have yet to use Twitter experience flaming in a fictitious setting, with the goal of teaching information literacy and online manners. In our system, elementary school children were able to see their Twitter timeline alongside concurrent real-world conditions. This virtual experience gave them an understanding of Twitter without actually using the service, as well as the opportunity to actively learn what types of posts lead to flaming and to cultivate crisis management skills. Upon evaluation of fifth and sixth grade test subjects, it was found that our system is an effective for information literacy and online manners learning.

Keywords: Social networking literacy · Flaming · Experience · Serious games

1 Introduction

With the diffusion of household internet connectivity, it has become possible for anyone to make casual statements over the internet. What's more, the proliferation of smartphones has enabled easy access to the internet even among those unable to use a computer, contributing to an internet user base of ever lowering age. In recent years, inappropriate speech and flaming on social networking services (SNS) have become a problem. On SNS, flaming describes a situation in which a user who has engaged in inappropriate speech is criticized by a large number of other users. Flaming has resulted in many cases in which the offending user is identified, or—based on the content of the speech—has evidence of his or her actions submitted for prosecution. Posters of such inappropriate speech are frequently junior and senior high schoolers, leading some to call for restrictions on their smartphone ownership and SNS usage, while others call for pertinent education. In this study, we followed the latter way of thinking and developed an effective SNS education system. Knowing that smartphone ownership increases sharply in fourth grade, and that smartphone-related trouble often occurs shortly after purchase, we decided that fifth and sixth grade students could be educated most effectively. We then developed a serious game that allows children of this age range to experience flaming in a fictitious setting, with the purpose of teaching information literacy [1–4] and online manners.

Our goals in developing this serious game [5–7] were to give children a simulated experience of actual events, and bring resolution to the societal problem of flaming. Education was the main objective, not simply entertainment. Serious games are in use at

© ICST Institute for Computer Sciences, Social Informatics and Telecommunications Engineering 2017
R. Poppe et al. (Eds.): INTETAIN 2016, LNICST 178, pp. 23–33, 2017.
DOI: 10.1007/978-3-319-49616-0_3

schools and other educational settings in England, where—despite their status as games —they have been demonstrated to be educationally useful. Related studies include one which used a roleplaying game for experiential learning of information ethics [8], and another which evaluated the use of both a serious game and worksheet [9].

One advantage of employing a serious game is that it allows children to actively use a mock version of Twitter to experience realistic flaming. Also, it visualizes the complicated mechanisms of SNS, making them easier to understand. Furthermore, we by allowing children to make mistakes and experience flaming—something that had not yet been possible in education—we believed they would be better able to recall what they had learned due to the Zeigarnik effect [10, 11]. The Zeigarnik effect is a phenomenon in which people remember uncompleted tasks better than completed ones. We believed that active learning via a serious game would be a highly effective device for learning about information ethics, and our goal was to get children to understand SNS and flaming by experiencing them within such a game. As it is impossible to educate children on SNS when they have not used them before, we thought that a serious game in which they use a mock SNS and get instant feedback on their actions would be the most suitable form of education.

2 A Serious Game for Learning SNS Manners by Flaming Experiences

We developed the main system using GameMaker: Studio, as it readily lends itself to event-driven programming. GameMaker: Studio is a piece of game development software that was developed by YoYo Games.

As seen in Fig. 1, the Twitter screen is displayed on the left side of the game screen, and the virtual world is displayed on the right. The protagonist's tweets are those with the cat thumbnail. On the top right is the Navigator, a character that teachers

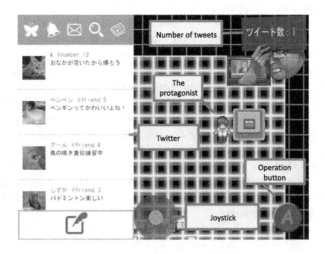

Fig. 1. The game screen.

the user about Twitter and the system, and shows the user the number of tweets he or she has posted so far.

In this exploration RPG, the protagonist and three of his or her friends are lost in the world of Twitter, and to return to the real world, they must master tweeting. The Twitter world contains a number of sparkling spots, which the user must search for to progress through the game. When the user finds such a spot and examines it, an event is triggered which the user can then tweet about. A total of 15 tweets have been prepared, 4 of which are inappropriate. Tweeting triggers another event, which has been carefully designed to convey—in a way that is easy for children to understand—the fact that the user's tweets are being viewed by both friends and a large number of strangers. If the user posts an inappropriate tweet it will trigger flaming and a game over, an event that makes the user aware of his or her wrongdoing. In addition to the four characters lost in the Twitter world, there are two other friends in the real world, and these characters can communicate with the protagonist via Twitter. The Twitter used in this study's system is not the real thing, but a mere imitation that can only be used within the system itself. If the user tweets, that tweet will not be posted online.

2.1   Inputting

We anticipated the game being played on an iPad, so we made input entirely touch and slide-based. At the start of the main system the user selects a sex and inputs his or her last name, Twitter user name, and password. This allows the user to control a protagonist of the same sex and name, who tweets under the username he or she selected. If flamed, the user will be identified and his or her last name spread across the internet. Password selection was enabled for an event in which the user, having revealed his or her password to a stranger, has his or her account hijacked. The purpose of this personalization was to increase the sense of immersion and realism, and cause the user to feel remorse after being flamed.

2.2   Tweeting

The user does not write the in-game tweets; he or she tweets messages that have been prepared in advance. The user examines sparkling spots scattered across the Twitter world, triggering events which he or she can tweet about. For instance, if the user examines an ambulance, he or she will be able to tweet about that ambulance. When a tweeting event is triggered, the user will be asked if he or she would like to tweet. If the user selects "no," the event will be suspended. If the user selects "yes," he or she will be able to tweet, the event will progress, and the sparkling spot will disappear. Reactions to the user's tweet will appear on his or her timeline, and the user's surroundings will change. For example, if the user tweets about an ambulance, reactions to the post will appear on his or her timeline, and other users who saw the post will gather in the area. There are three possible types of tweet: text-only tweets, reply tweets, and tweets with a picture attached. The following tweets have been created for the system.

2.3 Flaming

Of the game's events, the following four involve the user posting a tweet that leads to flaming:

- The user tweets a picture of him or herself inside a patrol car
- The user tweets a picture of him or herself inside of an ice cream freezer case
- To find the owner of a lost smartphone, the user tweets a photo of the phone's home screen picture (the owner's face)
- The user tweets a picture of him or herself standing on railroad tracks

If the user posts any of these tweets, he or she will be praised by friends, but shortly thereafter will be bombarded with third-party criticism, resulting in flaming. The user's timeline will be inundated with criticism, and the Twitter world screen will turn red and then to an image of white-noise-like static. Afterward, the police will come arrest the user, and the scene ends in a game over. All of these events are actual incidents from the past.

- The protagonist and friends have a picture taken of themselves inside a patrol car, believing they will be praised by their other friends. To share the picture with said friends, the protagonist casually posts it on Twitter.
- Caught up in the moment, someone climbs inside of an ice cream freezer case, and a friend, thinking it is funny, snaps a picture. The friend, wanting to share the picture with other friends, decides to tweet it.
- The protagonist and friends come across a lost smartphone. Wondering how they can return it to the owner, they check the home screen and find that it has a picture of what appears to be the owner. Following the suggestion of a friend, the protagonist tweets a picture of the home screen, believing that it will allow them to locate the owner quickly.
- The protagonist and friends, at a loss for what to tweet about, come to a train station. They take a picture on the railroad tracks and talk about how their friends would praise them if they were to tweet it. The protagonist decides to act on this idea, and tweets a picture of him or herself standing on the tracks (Fig. 2).
- Following a game over, the screen transitions to a description of the inappropriate tweet posted by the user (Fig. 3). This screen shows the actual real-life tweet and explains what happened to the person who tweeted it and what about the tweet was inappropriate (Fig. 4). After reading this information, the user will be returned to a point just before the flaming incident and will have another chance to play the game.

The main system includes another event involving not an inappropriate tweet, but a hijacking of the user's account. In this event, a suspicious fortune teller promises to tell the user's fortune after hearing his or her username and password. If the user divulges this information, his or her account will be hijacked and used to post tweets. Changing the password will stop these tweets from being posted. This event was inspired by an incident with a suspicious site onto which people would enter their Twitter user name and password. Subsequently hijacked user accounts were used to tweet advertisements for suspicious websites (which included the sites' URLs), replies to users' friends

Fig. 2. Wanting to share the picture with other friends.

Fig. 3. The police coming arrest the user.

asking them to buy prepaid credit cards, unintelligible messages posted when a company's account was hijacked, and more.

2.4   Strategy for Getting Children to Tweet

There exist gates scattered about the Twitter world, each of which is opened by posting a certain number of tweets. Therefore, users must tweet in order to play the game. Advancing deeper brings the user to a teleportation machine, which can be used to return to the real world and beat the game.

Fig. 4. Game over Screen. Actual incidents from the past are shown.

Elementary school level SNS education (including Twitter) is challenging because of children's difficulty in grasping abstract concepts like SNS, as well as the difficulty in making children aware of the people on the other side of the screen. So it is beneficial to portray SNS in a concrete, visual manner. To accomplish this, we had the protagonist and his or her friends get lost in the Twitter world, where tweeting would cause changes to their surroundings. In other words, we expressed the various effects of tweeting visually. This simulated experience gave children an understanding that their tweets are constantly being viewed by both acquaintances and complete strangers. This is extremely important, as a misunderstanding of the breadth of the internet, such as the belief that one's tweets will only be seen by one's acquaintances, is one of the reasons given for inappropriate tweets.

2.5 Experimental Control System

To demonstrate the learning effectiveness of the main system, as imparted by the Zeigarnik effect, we developed a control system with which to compare it to. It is different from the main system in that when the user attempts to make an inappropriate tweet, he or she is stopped by friends that are also lost in the Twitter world. Afterward, the friends and the Navigator warn the user about the danger of the tweet: while the tweet may gain the user praise from friends, there will be a flood of third-party criticism, and in the worst-case scenario, evidence of his or her actions will be submitted for prosecution. The following is an excerpt of such a warning used by the system: "If you use tweets to brag about reckless horseplay or other behavior that causes trouble, you'll be attacked by many people and may even be arrested." After the warning, there is no game over, and the user is able to continue playing the game. Everything else is identical to the main system.

3   The Experiments

In this study, we performed a preliminary experiment followed by two full-scale experiments. Before conducting the experiments, we performed a preliminary survey testing the depth of children's knowledge on smartphones and SNS. 19 fifth graders (9 boys and 10 girls) from Akagawa Municipal Elementary School and 81 sixth graders (41 boys and 40 girls) from Showa Municipal Elementary School participated in the survey, for a total of 100 participants. Both schools are located in the City, which cooperated in the subsequent main experiments. We then analyzed the children's knowledge base, and used the information to improve the main system's design.

In the preliminary experiment, 47 students from a High School, aged 14–17, used the main system or watched it in action, and evaluated whether it was an accurate portrayal of flaming, and whether the system could be used for learning. When asked if the main system had accurately portrayed flaming on Twitter, 96 % of students replied that it was an accurate portrayal, while 4 % replied that while it was an accurate portrayal, there needed to be more innovative elements. We used this feedback to improve the main system's design, including its innovative elements and UI.

The first full-scale experiment had 19 fifth grade subjects (9 boys and 10 girls) from Akagawa Elementary School, and used 2 kinds of educational tools—the main system and control system. The purpose of this experiment was to verify whether making mistakes and experiencing flaming would increase learning effectiveness.

The second full-scale experiment had 81 sixth grade students (41 boys and 40 girls) from Showa Elementary School, and used 3 kinds of educational tools—the main system, control system, and video materials on flaming created by the IPA (Information-Technology Promotion Agency, an Incorporated Administrative Agency). The goals of this experiment were to verify whether learning effectiveness was increased by making mistakes and experiencing flaming, to verify whether learning effectiveness was increased by engaging in active learning, and to verify the difference in learning effectiveness between the main system and the video-based teaching materials. A simple test was used for this verification. In creating this test, we referred to and cited test questions found in information ethics teaching materials [12] created by GREE for junior and senior high school students. Questions are as follows. Q1: Posting your wrongdoing on the Internet stays on the right side of the law. (Y/N), Q2: Posting your comments on the Internet cannot be seen anyone except your friends. (Y/N), Q3: It will be flaming on the Internet only if someone perpetrates a crime and runs afoul of the law. (Y/N), Q4: We can post photos on the Internet without prior consent by a person in a picture. (Y/N), Q5: We can post photos of a close friend on the Internet without prior consent by a person in a picture. (Y/N), Q6: In the case of flaming on the Internet, if you erase your posts the problem will be solved. (Y/N), Q7: Even posting under anonymity, your real name sometimes come out. (Y/N), Q8: We have to observe the rule and know manners on the Internet as actual life. (Y/N) Q9: What is the twitter? (written questionnaire) Q10: What kinds of tweets will be flaming? (written questionnaire).

Subjects were divided into two groups (groups one and two) during the first full-scale experiment and three groups (groups three, four, and five) during the second full-scale experiment. These groups and the teaching methods employed on them are described in the table below (Table 1).

Table 1. Groups and conditions

	Teaching method
Group 1: akagawa elementary school	Flaming/main system
Group 2: akagawa elementary school	No flaming/control system
Group 3: showa elementary school	Flaming/main system
Group 4: showa elementary school	No flaming/control system
Group 5: showa elementary school	Video materials

We first held a simple class on SNS for each group, and then taught them in greater detail using the prescribed educational tools (main system/control system/video materials). Afterward we gave each group an identical post-test to measure the learning effectiveness of the educational tool used.

4   Results

The average scores for the post-test administered to each group at the two elementary schools are listed in Table 2. In terms of average score for multiple choice questions, there was not much of a difference observed between groups. In fact, when comparing each of the groups to one another, no significant difference was observed in most cases. However, large differences were observed between groups when comparing average scores for written response questions.

Table 2. Average scores for post-test

	Average for multiple choice questions (100 point maximum)	Average for written response questions (100 point maximum)
Group 1: akagawa elementary school	77.50 points	65.00 points
Group 2: akagawa elementary school	61.11 points	36.11 points
Group 3: showa elementary school	91.96 points	80.55 points
Group 4: showa elementary school	90.48 points	38.88 points
Group 5: showa elementary school	80.41 points	34.26 points

To determine whether there was a statistically significant difference between the average scores of the groups that used the main system and the groups that used the control system, two-sided t-tests with a significance level of five percent were performed on groups one and two and groups three and four (Table 3). The average scores were found to be significantly different, with the groups that used the main system scoring significantly better.

Table 3. Two-sample test of groups that used the main system and groups that used the control system

	Multiple Choice Questions	Written Response Questions		Multiple Choice Questions	Written Response Questions
Group 1-Group 2	t(17) = 2.45, p = 0.0252	t(17) = 2.18, p = 0.0435	Group3-Group 5	t(52)=1.57,p=.1221	t(52)=5.14,p=.000004
Group 3-Group 4	t(52) = 2.99, p = 0.0043	t(52) = 4.84, p = 0.00001	Group 4-Group 5	t(52)=0.98,p=.3316	t(52)=0.43,p=.6647

Next, to determine whether there was a statistically significant difference between the average scores of the groups that used the main or control system and the group that used the video-based teaching materials, two-sided t-tests with a significance level of five percent were performed on groups three and five and groups four and five (Table 3). The only significant difference was found in the written response question scores for groups three and five, in which group three (a group that used the main system) scored significantly better than group five.

5   Discussion

In this study we developed a serious game for experiential learning of SNS manners, and performed experiments comparing the main system with the control system and video-based teaching materials.

In terms of average scores for multiple choice questions, there was not much of a difference between groups, with no significant difference observed in most cases. However, large differences were observed between groups when comparing average scores for written response questions. We believe this is because the multiple choice questions were easier and could be solved with less knowledge, while the written response questions were difficult to solve without acquiring the proper knowledge. The average scores for written response questions, when arranged in order of highest to lowest, were as follows: all groups taught using the main system came in at the top, followed by groups taught using the control system, and the group that was taught using the video-based teaching materials came in at the bottom. From these findings it can be said that the main system, by having children experience flaming as part of their education, was the most effective learning device. Furthermore, judging from the fact that the control system reaped higher average scores than the video-based teaching materials, it can be said that active learning and the visualization of Twitter's mechanisms are more effective learning devices than passive learning.

When comparing the groups that used the main system with those that used the control system, it was found that the main system had significantly higher learning effectiveness. We believe this is because subjects, stimulated through their experience with flaming, endeavored to gain a precise understanding of Twitter—an inference which is supported by evidence. The majority of children who (under the control system) did not experience flaming exhibited a lack of understanding of not only flaming and inappropriate speech, but of Twitter itself. The only difference between the main system and the control system was the presence or lack of flaming; all other aspects of the systems, including their explanations of Twitter, were identical. What's more, it was observed that groups using the main system frequently performed slide-based operations on the left-hand Twitter portion of the screen, while groups using the control system rarely used these slide-based operations and instead just watched the right-hand virtual portion of the screen. It is possible that the children's flaming experience stimulated an interest in Twitter, causing them to carefully watch that portion of the screen.

We were worried that in performing a preliminary test (administered before the main and control systems were used) the children would inadvertently learn about inappropriate speech, rendering accurate measurement of each system's learning effectiveness impossible. Thus, we only administered the test to groups three and four. However, there was no significant difference observed between these groups and the group in which the preliminary test was not administered, suggesting that the preliminary test did not have an influence on the experiment. In comparing the results of the preliminary test and the post-test, no significant difference was observed in the multiple choice questions, while the average score of the written response questions was found to be significantly higher in the post-test, demonstrating the learning effectiveness of the systems.

Regarding Table 3, no significant difference was observed in the average scores of written response questions, while a significant difference was observed in the average scores of multiple choice questions. This indicates higher learning effectiveness for the sixth grade group. This could be related to a difference in the knowledge base of fifth and sixth graders.

The test results for the written response questions differed greatly between the group that used the video-based teaching materials and the group that used the main system. The former lacked an understanding of Twitter itself, and exhibited less variation in its answers to written response questions. A possible reason for this is the fact that, compared to the video-based learning materials, the main system provided subjects with an opportunity to see a greater variety of tweets, including inappropriate tweets. These results show a large difference in the learning effectiveness of active learning and passive learning, suggesting that active learning may be more effective. It can also be said that by visualizing Twitter, the main system succeeded in making the SNS easier for children to understand, enabling them to learn more about it in a short amount of time.

6 Summary

In this study we developed a serious game for experiential learning of SNS manners. Under this system, subjects used a mock version of Twitter to actively learn about information ethics. To confirm the learning effectiveness of this main system, we performed experiments comparing it with a control system and video-based learning materials, with fifth and sixth grade elementary school students used as subjects. The main system was found to have higher learning effectiveness than both the control system (in which children were not allowed to make mistakes or experience flaming) and the video-based learning materials (a passive method of learning).

References

1. What is the NFIL?. National Forum on Information Literacy. Accessed 25 Oct 2012
2. Presidential Committee on Information Literacy: Final Report, 10 January 1989. Accessed 25 Oct 2012
3. Gillmor, D.: Mediactive. Accessed 2 Feb 2013
4. Toth, M.: Definitions of Information Literacy. http://www.plattsburgh.edu/library/instruction/informationliteracydefinition.php
5. Abt, C.: Serious Games. The Viking Press, New York (1970)
6. Aldrich, C.: The Complete Guide to Simulations and Serious Games, p. 576. Pfeiffer (2009). ISBN: 0-470-46273-6
7. Reeves, B., Reed, J.L.: Total Engagement: Using Games and Virtual Worlds to Change the Way People Work and Businesses Compete. Harvard Business School Publishing, Boston (2009)
8. Matsukura, T.: The teaching materials development for learning an information ethic, Kanazawa University, Departmental Bulletin Paper (2006). http://hdl.handle.net/2297/7227
9. Yukari, S., Yukino, A., Shinsuke, M., Taketoshi, I.: Evaluation of learning effectiveness of worksheets in a educational serious game. Research report of JET Conferences, vol. 2012, no 1, pp. 381–386, 03 March 2012
10. Kurt, K.: Principles of Gestalt Psychology, p. 334 (1935)
11. Zeigarnik, B.G.: Das Behalten erledigter und unerledigter Handlungen. Psychol. Forsch. 9, 1–85 (1927)
12. GREE teaching materials. http://corp.gree.net/jp/ja/csr/statement/internet-society/educational-activity/teaching-materials

Game@School. Teaching Through Gaming and Mobile-Based Tutoring Systems

Annalisa Terracina[1]([✉]), Massimo Mecella[1], Riccardo Berta[2],
Francesco Fabiani[1], and Dario Litardi[1]

[1] Sapienza Università di Roma, Rome, Italy
terracina@dis.uniroma1.it
[2] Università di Genova, Genova, Italy

Abstract. In this work, we describe an approach and a conceptual architecture of a supporting teaching tool that takes into account two main objectives in new teaching trends: Virtual Learning Environments (VLEs) and Intelligent Pedagogical Agents (IPAs). We additionally present an Android application that uses the IPA as a standalone application as an initial step towards the realization of such an architecture.

Keywords: Virtual Learning Environment · Intelligent Pedagogical Agent · Serious game

1 Introduction

In the past years, the rapid growth of the game industry has aroused wide interest, particularly among educational technology researchers. It is known that the possibilities to use digital games in education have been considered since the 70s, even if actually the quality of produced games has not met the expectations of educators and the use of games has not become as general as expected [5]; on the other hand we find commercial games used for learning purposes, famous examples are PORTAL2[1] or MINECRAFT[2].

In this context, we followed the idea to integrate the most up-to-date technologies in new teaching trends, namely Virtual Learning Environments (VLEs, [2]) and Intelligent Pedagogical Agent (IPAs), as deeply investigated in [10]. The VLE is developed as an immersive 3D environment and the game is a role playing game in which each student becomes a player with her abilities and her tasks. In order to succeed, all the players should work to achieve a common objective/goal. The storyboard is designed in a way that there is an evolution in the role playing game and a progress in the level of learning as well. The use of IPAs is proposed as support during the game evolution and each student has her own IPA: IPAs act as learning facilitators and guide the learners in the virtual environment. In fact, as suggested in [13], one of the Artificial Intelligence (AI) grand challenges in education is "mentors for every learner".

---

[1] http://www.teachwithportals.com/.
[2] https://minecraftedu.com/.

© ICST Institute for Computer Sciences, Social Informatics and Telecommunications Engineering 2017
R. Poppe et al. (Eds.): INTETAIN 2016, LNICST 178, pp. 34–44, 2017.
DOI: 10.1007/978-3-319-49616-0_4

In this paper, after introducing in Sect. 2 some background concepts about learning that motivates our approach, we present the pillars of our game and its architecture in Sect. 3. Then, in Sect. 4 we focus on the initial Android app which provides the mobile IPA (as described in the architecture) to be used by students during learning, and a preliminary validation in real teaching contexts in Sect. 5. We conclude by comparing with relevant work in Sect. 6 and provide some final remarks in Sect. 7.

2 Background

The idea of helping students during their learning through a different way wrt. the classical approach finds support in many psychological studies and previous work. In particular, Howard Gardner already in 1983 theorized [3]: "My own belief is that any reach, nourishing topic - any concept worth teaching - can be approached in at last five different ways that roughly speaking map onto the multiple intelligence. We might think of the topic as a room with at least five doors or entry points into it. Students vary as to which entry point is most appropriate for them and which routes are most comfortable to follow once they have gained initial access to the room. Awareness of these entry points can help the teacher introduce new materials in ways in which they can be easily grasped by a range of students; then, as students explore other entry points, they have the chance to develop those multiple perspectives that are the best antidote to stereotypical thinking". For each of the five entry points theorized by Gardner, as reported in Table 1, we provide a motivation for the adoption of a role playing game and a concrete example of a possible game-play situation, based on teaching physics (we argue the approach is applicable to STEM in general). Notably, in 1999 Gardner added a sixth entry point [4]: *Social - Use group settings, role-play and collaborative arrangements*, which perfectly complies with our proposed approach.

The learning objectives of the game are: the physics aspects of a space mission (gravity, propellent, orbits, trajectories, etc.); which are the conditions in which humans can live (gravity, oxygen, pressure, temperature, etc.) and many other interdisciplinary aspect of the proposed topic. The learning aspects are well integrated in the game mechanics. There are simulation rooms where players, depending on their roles, can solve problems, simulate certain conditions, etc.

As shown in Fig. 1, the teacher introduces the scenario to the students and explains the problems that they have to solve during the game. After that, the teacher designates a

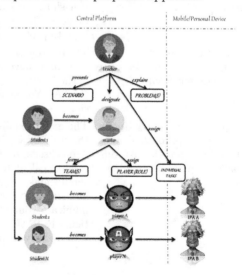

Fig. 1. Use case scenario

Table 1. Gardner' s theory of five entry points and role-playing game

Howard Gardner five entry points	Plot and roles' examples in the game
Narration entry point (read or tell a story)	The game has a plot (tell a story) that evolves during the game. The story has been designed to address several physics problem linked to a space mission. In addition several physics tasks are proposed in an interdisciplinary way. *Story*: The Near Earth Object, classified as 2017 Titan, will impact the Earth 25 May 2017. A huge team of scientists is studying 2017 Titan, but unfortunately there is no way to destroy the asteroid before it will impact the Earth. The best way to avoid the disaster is to prepare a space mission and colonize a new planet. The team challenge is to choose an exoplanet to colonize among three possible ones
Logical-quantitative entry point (provide data, use deductive reasoning, examine numbers, narrative plot structure, cause and effect relationship)	During the game, students should solve problems and specific assigned tasks. *Mathematicians*. To perform a flight to one of the exo-planets, a vehicle must first escape from the Earth. Achieving the right speed, however, is only part of the problem; other factors must be considered, e.g., the Sun's gravitational field and the motion of the Earth about the Sun. You should trace the trajectory to the three exo-planets and share your results with the engineers
Philosophical entry point (big questions about reasoning and the way of reasoning)	Students should consider pros and cons of every possible solution. They should discuss all together and understand the implications of their choices. *Astrobiologists*: you should evaluate the consequences of colonizing a planet. What to do if the planet is already inhabited? How to protect the local environment?
Aesthetic entry point (emphasize sensory, activate aesthetic sensitivities)	The information/social space is explicitly represented as a 3D immersive world. *Space artists*: you are a member of the International Association of Astronomical Artists (IAAA). You should draw the vexillum of the space mission
Experimental entry point (hands-on-approach, dealing directly with materials, simulation, personal explanations)	The game requires that students take actively part to the story by solving problems and finding solutions. The team discussion is also a must. *Physics scientists*: you need to calculate the gravity on the three planets. You should make some comparison with terrestrial gravity and suggest which is the best planet to colonize. Communicate your results to other team members, in particularly to the astrobiologists and discuss with them. Can we survive in those gravity condition?

master (among the students) that behaves at the same level as the teacher, by following the approach in which a student can "learn how to learn by teaching". Then, the master with the help of the teacher, can form teams and assign a specific role to each student. Each student, from now on, becomes a player with her specific role and her own task as well. In this phase, an IPA is assigned to each student/player that will drive her all along the game. The relation between the student and her IPA should progress all along two paths: the learning aspect (giving tips and advices related to the topics and to the tasks assigned) and the emotional/pedagogy one (the interaction depends on the feelings of the student). IPA behaviour has been implemented and tested in the Android app, as explained in Sect. 4.

3   Overall Architecture

The envisioned role playing game partly runs on a central server (e.g., an interactive whiteboard) and partly on mobile devices directly provided by the school or owned by the students themselves. In our current implementation, the VLE functionalities, related to class management and handled by the teacher, are built on top of Opedia[3], and are available on the interactive whiteboard. The VLE indeed allows teachers to manage games, players, teams, etc. A player is a student that has already registered and that has a previously assigned role, (see Fig. 1), each player is part of a team, formed by 5/6 players.

The main component that runs on the whiteboard is the Game Manager engine that control the Unity Server, the Chat Server and the Knowledge Forum Server. Information and logs about game sessions and related activities are stored on the whiteboard as well. The game has been conceived to be used in classes but can be used at home as well, therefore some services should be always up and running (like login/register, sentiment analysis, etc.). Information about students/players is stored in a database. The game is developed using Unity 3D as a multi-players game, that is the reason why there are both Unity server and client components. The components that run on the mobile device, in addition to the Game Manager client, concern all the additional functionalities of the game that can be used by the student, as further explained below. Figure 2 shows the overall architecture and its main components.

For each team there is a shared space, displayed on the interactive whiteboard, in which are shown: the list of players, the live chat among members of the same team and the Knowledge Forum, as depicted in Fig. 3. If the teacher touches a player, all the related info (as role, assigned tasks, individual score, level, power, etc.) are shown. The Knowledge Forum (KF) gives the possibility to the student to add notes about the game, the assigned tasks, or any learning aspect of the game. The added notes appear on the shared VLE and are visible to other students and teacher. The Big Brain (BB) is a peculiar type of help in the game: if the player uses this kind of help, she could gain points instead of losing them. In order to gain points, the player should ask the right questions to BB. For each session just few (2 or 3) questions are foreseen.

---

[3] http://www.opedia.it/.

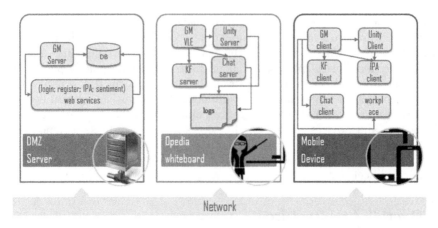

Fig. 2. Game architecture

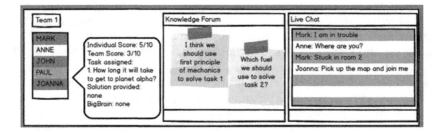

Fig. 3. Shared VLE view

Players are able to chat during a game session. The chat is among team members and it is visible on players' mobile devices and on the shared VLE. The IPA live chat gives the possibility to the student to chat with her virtual tutor that should guide her trough the emotional and learning aspect of the game. In the workplace, players can analyse their tasks, simulate solutions, read notes about task topics and provide solutions to the assigned tasks.

Fig. 4. Mobile device game view

Players play on their mobile devices, as shown in Fig. 4. In the right corner, there is the *assigned task* panel; the central bar lists all the available functionalities; in the left corner, there is the *IPA live chat* panel. In the top left corner, there is the individual score. The IPA live chat is a core part of our research: players can chat with their virtual tutors; the system allows the player to freely express her thoughts in textual form. A more detailed description of how the developed IPA works is reported in Sect. 4.

4 The Android App

In order to verify our approach, during the development of the whole game, we have realized a stand alone application in Android that uses the IPA as interlocutor while studying specific contents. The student registers to the application and once she is logged, she can choose among a list of topics and available IPAs (with different aspects). Once the topic has been chosen, students can chat with the IPA simulating a natural dialogue about the topic covering pedagogical and learning aspects. The app follows a game approach, in fact the session starts with an initial quest to which the student should answer at the end of her learning path. The score of the game depends on how many questions the student asked in order to devise the solution. Some Android application screenshots are reported in Fig. 5).

Students interact with the IPA via chat, expressing in natural language. Natural language analysis is then performed on students phrases to detect their emotions, by exploiting a back-end Web service that analyses the sentence and returns an emotional state: it returns a label representing the identified sentiment (positive, negative, neutral), along with a numeric score ranging from strongly positive (1.0) to extremely negative (−1.0). Depending on the label and on the numeric score the user gets back an adequate answer: each possible

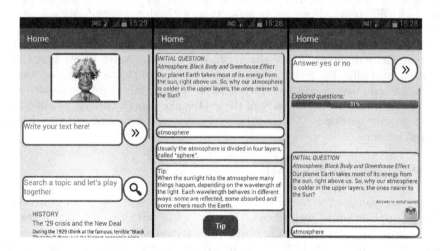

Fig. 5. Android app screenshots

answer corresponds to a pre-registered mp4 file in which an animated avatar has been modelled (mimic expressions and motivational phrases). For example, when player logs in, avatar says "Hello, welcome to our app. How are you today?". The system analyses the player sentence and reply something like "I am happy to ear that you are fine" in case of extremely positive label or "I am sorry that you are not fine" in case of extremely negative label. This approach aims to establish an empathic feeling between the student and her virtual tutor.

In order to collect emotions, expected IPA behaviors and motivational phrases, we worked with a group of 20 students from an Italian high school aged 16–17 years old (target age of our serious game). The work done with students lasted three months (from September 2014 to December 2014) and has been conducted in collaboration with teachers from literature and computer science classes. We divided the work into two main parts: a study of the emotions in school context and the prototyping of animated agents, as described in [12]. The results of the study have been used to model the avatar and his reaction.

In addition to the emotional relation between the student and the IPA, the student is able to chat with the IPA about the subject of study via textual messages: the best answer to learning questions is provided by using a specific AI algorithm, starting from [8]. As a matter of fact, while in state-of-the-art games, the user usually interacts by choosing a sentence among a set of predefined possibilities, our system allows the user to freely express his thoughts in textual form and provides the user with an adequate answer (selected from a database of answers provided by an expert). The core of the AI algorithm is an implementation of Naïve Bayes Text Classification [7], which is a probabilistic classification method based on Language Modelling under the hypothesis of words conditional independence (unigram or bag of word model). The first task consists in a sentence lemmatization, which transforms all the terms of the sentence in a form suitable for word analysis and computation. We then evaluate the Interrogative/Adjective Pronoun (IAP) of the question, in order to assign a higher classification score to the sentences from the database with a matching IAP. Instead of excluding all the sentences in the database with a different IAP, we just penalize them with a lower classification score; in fact it might happen that an answer might be the best one to respond to the user's question even if each of the expected questions that were associated to it in the database had a different IAP. We then proceed with the Naive Bayes Text Classification, and filter the result by applying the threshold criterion. If the answer passes the test, then it will be returned to the player, otherwise the answer will be replaced with a verbal message of the avatar like "Sorry, there is no adequate answer to your question". Threshold criterion have been verified and tuned with real test sessions.

5   Preliminary Evaluation

In order to evaluate the use of the Intelligent Pedagogical Agent, we tested the Android application in real schools. The app came with two different learning paths: one in STEM, in particular physics (the terrestrial atmosphere) and one in humanities, in particular history (the new deal). Those two learning paths have been developed by field experts. Each student was free to choose the preferred topic.

Appreciation, usability and learnability of the Android app have been specifically assessed in three experimental sessions. The first run of test validation occurred the 19 November 2015 (11 students, all males, aged 17–18), the second run occurred the 20 of January 2016 (16 students, two female, aged 17–18). After a preliminary evaluation of the first two test runs, we calibrated the AI algorithm lowering the threshold for the response to the asked question. The third run occurred the 8 February 2016 (13 students, 8 males and 5 females, aged 17–18). In all three runs, students were able to play with the application roughly 40 min (a bit less of a standard lesson time); we just asked them to play with the application asking question to the IPA about the subject of study. After that they compiled a questionnaire that has been structured in three main sections: liking, usability and learnability.

Appreciation. The first set of questions aimed at understanding if students like the idea of a personalized learning path and the possibility to ask free questions guided by a virtual agent: 75 % of students like this possibility. The aspect of the empathetic guide was felt as well: 68 % of students liked the idea to have an empathic guide and would like to chat also about personal matters. 68 % of students enjoyed the app and would recommend it to others, even if just 56 % of them perceived it as a game. 50 % declared the app is more effective for STEM subject while the other 50 % per cent said both STEM and humanistic.

Usability. It emerged that 68 % finds the interface and the touch screen function clear. Just 50 % of the students used the side menu and the majority of them declare they wish to add other functionalities. Most of the interviewed disliked the scientist avatar (70 %) while liked the young girl (72 %).

Learnability. Tests revealed that 78 % of students thought avatar explanations are clear and declared that provided answers are in line with asked questions. 64 % declared tips were useful. We asked how many questions they asked to the avatar before quitting the game: 46 % gave up after few questions, 34 % ended the game after roughly 10 questions, 15 % around 20 and just 1 student declared to ask more then 20 questions. Those results were obtained in the first two runs. That is mainly because very often pertinent questions received no answers due to the very high threshold settings of the AI algorithm. However, after AI algorithm threshold calibration, in the third test run we obtained that 38 % ended the game after roughly 20 questions while 30 % gave up after few questions. So we had an increment of roughly 20 % in content exploration.

6   Related Work

An example of VLE is the one described in [9]. The research is based on multiple pre-existing projects which embody virtual technologies. All of them have their respective benefits, and the goal of the project was to fuse them into a new collaborative learning environment. Within such a collaborative environment, those tools provided the opportunity for teachers and students to work together as avatars as they control equipment, visualize physical phenomenon generated by the experiment, and discuss the results.

Concerning emotional learning, [1] presents an approach to a possible modelling of user affect designed to assess a variety of emotional states during interactions: knowing the details of a user's emotional reaction can enhance a system capability to interact with the user effectively. Instead of reducing the uncertainty in emotion recognition by constraining the task and the granularity of the model, the proposed approach explicitly encodes and processes this uncertainty by relying on probabilistic reasoning. The authors discuss their model in the context of the interaction with pedagogical agents designed to improve the effectiveness of computer-based educational games. They also introduce Dynamic Decision Networks and illustrate how they can be used to enable pedagogical agents for educational games to generate interactions tailored to both the user's learning and emotional state. [14] presented a pedagogical agent capable of active affective support, guided by the logic which integrates the learner's cognitive and affective states. They developed an algorithm for feature tracking which utilizes a combination of common image processing techniques, such as thresholding, integral projections, contour-tracing and Haar object classification. The experiment results indicate a range of preferences associated with pedagogical agents and affective communication. According to the authors, affective interaction is individually driven, and they suggest that in task-oriented environments affective communication carries less importance for certain learners. This paper inspired us in the modelling of the avatar in a process of reverse engineering. In fact, the animated avatar is a preregistered mp4 file in which the avatars face expresses emotions. [11] presents a system that embodies the idea of virtual humans that act and interact like humans, bringing social elements in the interaction: a couple of twins that are virtual teachers in the Museum of Science in Boston designed to engage visitors and raise their awareness and knowledge of science. The twins have some aspects that were built in advance, and some that operate in real time as the user interacts with them. The aspects built in advance include the character bodies, animations, textual content, and spoken output. The speech recognition, natural language understanding, and dialogue management decisions of what to say are computed in real time, as is the scheduling and rendering of spoken and gestural outputs. Speech recognition, natural language understanding, and dialogue policies also make use of knowledge sources constructed in advance, using supervised machine learning.

In [8], the system allows the player to express himself in natural language. The system processes users' input sentences and returns the best answer among a set of possible stored answers. The communication is implemented through an NLP algorithm based on an ad hoc text retrieval problem solver and on a Naive Bayes text classifier with an inner product-based threshold criterion. The algorithm implemented in the system is a variation of a text retrieval algorithm. We extended the work done in this paper has reported in paragraph 4.

7   Concluding Remarks

The proposed use of IPAs in the game, and the related Android app, follows an inquiry based approach. It starts by posing questions, problems or scenarios rather than simply presenting established facts or portraying a smooth path to knowledge. In the app, the initial quest posed to the student is a sort of incipit that serves to encourage her to start reasoning about a specific topic of study. Then, students ask free questions to the virtual tutor, designing their specific learning path and not following a predetermined one. As previously reported, 75 % of students like the idea of a personalized learning path and the possibility to ask free questions.

We also found that 68 % of students liked the idea to have an empathic guide. It is important for teachers to create a positive, emotionally safe environment to provide for the optimal learning of students. Learning how to manage feelings and relationships constitutes a kind of "emotional intelligence" that enables people to be successful. Emotional intelligence expands on Howard Gardner's theory of multiple intelligences. Although the interplay of affective and cognitive processes always underpins learning outcomes, affective interaction sometimes may need to remain in the background, as found in other study [14]; whatever the case, an Intelligent Tutoring System should let the user decide on the level of affective feedback. That is the case of our game in which the player can choose if and when chat with her IPA.

In summary, we believe our Android application, although only preliminarily validated, gave us a proof that the developed IPA could be an important plus for the envisioned role playing game. In the future we are planning to asses the learning outcome of the app comparing control and experimental group.

References

1. Conati, C.: Probabilistic assessment of users emotions in educational games. J. Appl. Artif. Intell. **16**, 555–575 (2002)
2. Dillenbourg, P., Schneider, D., Synteta, P.: Virtual learning environments. In: 3rd Hellenic Conference Information and Communication Technologies in Education (2002)
3. Gardner, H.: Frames of Mind: The Theory of Multiple Intelligences. Basic Books, New York (1983)
4. Gardner, H.: Intelligence Reframed: Multiple Intelligences for the 21st Century. Basic Books, New York (1999)
5. Ketamo, H., Kiili, K., Arnab, S., Dunwell, I.: Integrating games into the classroom: towards new teachership
6. Lease, M.: Natural language processing for information retrieval: the time is ripe (again). In: Proceedings of ACM Ph.D. Workshop in CIKM (2007)
7. Manning, C.D., Raghavan, P., Schtze, H.: Introduction to Information Retrieval. Cambridge University Press, Cambridge (2008)
8. Mori, D., Berta, R., De Gloria, A., Fiore, V., Magnani, L.: An easy to author dialogue management system for serious games. J. Comput. Cult. Herit. **6**(2), 10 (2013)
9. Scheucher, B., Bailey, P.H., Gütl, C., Harward, J.V.: Collaborative virtual 3D environment for internet-accessible physics experiments. iJOE **5**(S1), 65–71 (2009)
10. Soliman, M., Guetl, C.: Intelligent pedagogical agents in immersive virtual learning environments: a review. In: Proceedings of MIPRO 2010. IEEE (2010)
11. Swartout, W., Artstein, R., Forbell, E., Foutz, S., Lane, H.C., Lange, B., Morie, J.F., Rizzo, A.S., Traum, D.: Virtual humans for learning. AI Mag. **34**, 13–30 (2013)

12. Terracina, A., Mecella, M.: Building an emotional IPA through empirical design with high-school students. In: 9th European Conference on Game Based Learning
13. Woolf, B.P., Lane, H.C., Chaudhri, V.K., Kolodner, J.L.: AI grand challenges for education. AI Mag. **34**, 9 (2013)
14. Zakharov, K., Mitrovic, A., Johnston, L.: Towards emotionally-intelligent pedagogical agents. In: Woolf, B.P., Aïmeur, E., Nkambou, R., Lajoie, S. (eds.) ITS 2008. LNCS, vol. 5091, pp. 19–28. Springer, Heidelberg (2008). doi:10.1007/978-3-540-69132-7_7

Interaction Technologies

Exploring User-Defined Gestures and Voice Commands to Control an Unmanned Aerial Vehicle

Ekaterina Peshkova[✉], Martin Hitz, and David Ahlström

Alpen-Adria-Universität Klagenfurt, Klagenfurt, Austria
{ekaterina.peshkova,martin.hitz,
david.ahlstroem}@aau.at

Abstract. In this paper we follow a participatory design approach to explore what novice users find to be intuitive ways to control an Unmanned Aerial Vehicle (UAV). We gather users' suggestions for suitable voice and gesture commands through an online survey and a video interview and we also record the voice commands and gestures used by participants' in a Wizard of Oz experiment where participants thought they were manoeuvring a UAV. We identify commonalities in the data collected from the three elicitation methods and assemble a collection of voice and gesture command sets for navigating a UAV. Furthermore, to obtain a deeper understanding of why our participants chose the gestures and voice commands they did, we analyse and discuss the collected data in terms of mental models and identify three prevailing classes of mental models that likely guided many of our participants in their choice of voice and gesture commands.

1 Introduction

Over the past decade, researchers have shown increased interest in developing interfaces to interact with a UAV (Unmanned Aerial Vehicle) that is partially explained by recent availability of low-cost UAVs (e.g., Parrot AR.Drone), which became affordable to a larger range of researchers. Much of the current works investigated novel input modalities in order to provide more natural ways of interaction such as speech [1], gestures (including head [2–4], hand [5–8], and upper body movements [9, 10]), face detection [11], gaze direction [12, 13], and even brain activity [14].

When designing a human-machine interface, the way users imagine interaction with the system has to be carefully investigated as it is of crucial importance for the intuitiveness of the resultant interaction vocabulary. Accordingly, a good understanding of users' mental models is believed to be a key aspect to consider in a user-centered design. A number of authors have explored users' mental models with the aim to improve interface usability [15] and to design intuitive interfaces, both for human-computer interaction [16, 17] and human-robot interaction [18, 19]. Regarding interaction with a UAV, to our best knowledge, our work is the first attempt to investigate users' truly 'natural' behavior (i.e., unguided and without instructions and a set of predefined and imposed commands) with their associated mental models when navigating a single UAV.

© ICST Institute for Computer Sciences, Social Informatics and Telecommunications Engineering 2017
R. Poppe et al. (Eds.): INTETAIN 2016, LNICST 178, pp. 47–62, 2017.
DOI: 10.1007/978-3-319-49616-0_5

The goal of our study is to create a collection of user-defined gestures and voice commands to control a UAV and to gain insights regarding any possible underlying mental models. Accordingly, we let users define their own input (voice and gesture) vocabulary for ten main commands to operate a drone: *takeoff*, *land*, *up*, *down*, *left*, *right*, *rotate left*, *rotate right*, *forward*, and *backward*. We target our study towards an interface for users with no previous experiences in navigating UAVs and explore the behavior of novice users in order to understand what gestures and voice commands are intuitive for users whose mental models are not influenced by previous knowledge and experiences with UAVs.

Our exploration of user-defined commands to navigate a UAV is based on three data sources: (1) an online survey where we collected suggestions for voice commands, (2) a video interview where we recorded suggested gestures, and (3) a Wizard of Oz experiment where we observed and recorded participants' behavior and spontaneous voice and gesture command choices while piloting a drone (a skilled drone pilot, the 'wizard', secretly interpreted participants' commands and operated the drone accordingly using the standard touchscreen-based interface). With our study, we aim to address the following questions:

- What are intuitive gestures and voice commands to navigate a UAV?
- Are there commonalities in users' behavior and command choices?
- What mental models do novice users have regarding the navigation of a UAV?
- Do novice users rely on one coherent mental model when they navigate a UAV or do they rely on concepts and notions drawn from different mental models?

The main contribution of our work is a collection of user-defined gestures and voice commands that can serve as a source of inspiration and guidance for future research and projects on interaction with unmanned agents (Unmanned Ground Vehicles or Unmanned Underwater Vehicles). We also provide insights regarding the mental models novice users rely on when navigating a drone. Although our exploration is focused on commands for a UAV, we anticipate that the obtained results could easily be extended to the more general case of human-robot interaction and related navigation tasks. Finally, we also see a minor contribution in our methodological approach by demonstrating the strengths of combining three techniques to elicit user-defined voice commands and gestures to allow interaction designers to come up with close to optimal natural user interfaces.

Next, we provide a brief overview of related work and then describe the used materials and procedures of the online survey, the video interview, and the Wizard of Oz experiment. After that we report our findings, discuss mental models in the context of UAV control, and then analyse our findings in terms of mental models. We conclude with a summary and an outline of promising directions for future work.

2 Related Work

Over at least two past decades, most research has investigated unconventional input modalities such as speech, gestures, gaze direction, and facial expressions to interact with a robot [20]. It is a widely held view that the use of natural cues peculiar to human-human interaction could contribute to the development of a more natural human-robot interaction. In some sense, much human-robot interaction research and work on interfaces for UAV control, including ours, are guided by the motto of designing robots or vehicles capable of perceiving and interpreting human behavior, not the reverse. Previous work has also demonstrated strong advantages of interfaces that allow the user to interact through multiple "natural" input modalities, such as body movements and speech. We review inspiring related work on multimodal control interfaces and work on speech and gesture interaction.

In early work, Hauptmann and McAvinney [21] investigated the use of gestures and speech to rotate, translate, and scale a 3D cube on a screen. They reported that the study participants preferred to use a combination of gestures and speech rather than a single modality. Similarly, Sharma et al. [22] pointed out that multimodal interaction promotes natural conversation and presented several arguments for multimodality. Among them was an argument that a fusion of multiple senses is inherent in human nature. In particular, the combination of speech and gestures has received close attention [23, 24]. In the context of navigation, Jones et al. [25] explored the use of speech and gestures to control the flight of a group of UAVs and found that many study participants found it intuitive to interact with the system using both speech and gestures.

Quigley et al. [26] compared several user interfaces that employ different modalities to interact with a UAV. These were: *physical interfaces* (an altitude joystick, a physical icon controller or "phicon" – a real object used to interact with a system, and an altitude TrackPoint^{TM}), *direct manipulation* (PDA- and laptop-based interfaces), *voice-based interface*, and an interface with *numerical parameter entry*. The study found that users prefer simple intuitive interfaces with a lower precision level rather than numerical parameter-based interfaces that require entering exact flight data. The main reasons were that high-precision interfaces result in unreasonably high workload and that the provided precision would not be needed in most situations. The study also showed that a future user interface should require reasonable levels of mental and physical demands and leave out unnecessary complications that impede the operators' work. Quigley et al. stressed the effectiveness of voice-based control when a UAV is within an operator's field of view, as the operator could fully focus visual attention on the operated UAV instead of continuously switching visual focus between the UAV and the input controls.

In more recent years, numerous projects on gesture-based interaction, both with a single UAV and a group of UAVs, have been presented. These projects have compared gesture control to standard touchscreen-based interfaces [9] and joystick input [2]. Pfeil et al. [9] explored five different gesture sets to pilot a UAV (e.g., a user spreads the arms to the sides and navigates the UAV by bending and rotating the upper body; a user holds an imagined UAV and its movements are mapped to movements of the actual UAV) along a predefined path. Pfeil et al. reported that ten of their fourteen participants preferred gestures over the touchscreen-based interface and that six participants rated the touchscreen-based interface as the least fun technique to use. Higuchi and Rekimoto [2] evaluated and compared their gesture-based interface to the use of joystick input. The suggested head-gesture interface synchronized the position and orientation of the operator's head with those of a UAV. In the study, participants had to control a UAV and take pictures of both stationary and moving objects with the on-board camera. A better performance, in terms of time required to complete the tasks and in terms of the accuracy of taken pictures (i.e., how close photographed objects were to the center of a picture), was achieved with the gesture-based interface. In addition, post-questionnaires revealed that participants found it simpler to control the UAV with the head-gestures than with the joystick.

Most of the suggested gesture-based interaction techniques were defined by designers [3, 5, 6, 8, 10–12, 27] and only in some of them the vocabulary was further evaluated by users [2, 4, 7, 9]. Jones et al. [25] investigated users' natural behavior using speech and gestures to control the flight of a group of UAVs in their Wizard of Oz study conducted in a simulated environment. In a single UAV case, there are two works where users were let to define the vocabulary. Burke and Lasenby [28] provided five persons with verbal descriptions of UAV's responses and recorded the suggested gestures, and Cauchard et al. [29] used a Wizard of Oz study to explore users' spontaneous command suggestions. None of the two works provided a list of collected user-defined commands. However, Cauchard et al. reported that most of the nineteen participants used a "human to human-like" interaction style. This finding makes sense considering that the participants did knew about the human operator who was interpreting and translating their commands. However, this knowledge might also have influenced participants' behavior and command choices. Nevertheless, the study by Cauchard et al. clearly demonstrates the feasibility of exploring users' natural behavior and intuitive gesture and voice commands for UAV interaction.

While the review above shows a great deal of work on natural interaction with UAVs, the main novelty brought by our work consists in the identification of mental models [30] for UAV navigation and their association with natural interaction gestures and voice commands, especially for novice users.

3 Data Collection

For our exploration we picked the eight basic motion commands that are necessary to manoeuvre a UAV: *up, down, left, right, rotate left, rotate right, forward,* and *backward*. We also included the *takeoff* command and the *land* command. Each of these two commands is a combination of a functional command, *turn on* respectively *turn off* the rotors, and a motion command, *up* respectively *down* (until a certain height is reached or until the ground is touched). We collected gesture and voice command suggestions for the ten commands from 110 persons: 50 persons (aged between 25 and 68 years (mean 37, s.d. 12), 19 female) participated in an online survey, 27 persons (aged between 21 to 52 years (mean 31, s.d. 8), 12 female) participated in a video interview, and 33 persons (aged between 21 and 62 years (mean 30, s.d. 9), 11 female) participated in a Wizard of Oz session. Only five experiment participants and twelve interview participants indicated having previous (childhood or more recent) experiences in operating remote-controlled toys such as cars, boats, or drones. Among the participants there were no experienced UAV pilots. Survey respondents were not questioned regarding their previous experiences. Five persons participated in both the experiment and in the interview.

The online survey was open during five weeks and consisted of ten questions (excluding instructions and demographic questions), one for each of the ten commands. Each question showed one image to illustrate the outcome of one of the ten commands and the participant was asked to provide one word, or a short phrase, that he/she thought would be a suitable voice command for the depicted outcome. The used images are shown in Fig. 1(a to j).

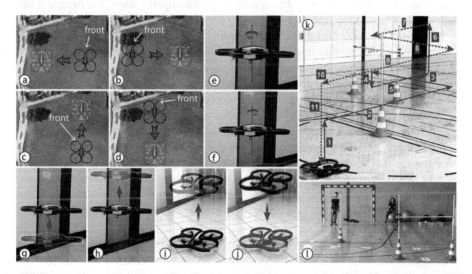

Fig. 1. Materials used in the survey (a–j) and experiment (k and l). Survey images to illustrate commands: (a) *left*, (b) *right*, (c) *forward*, (d) *backward*, (e) *rotate left*, (f) *rotate right*, (g) *down*, (h) *up*, (i) *takeoff*, and (j) *land*. (k) Obstacle path. (l) Experiment setup with participant (left) and wizard (right).

In the video interview participants watched ten short video clips (2–6 s long, one for each command) of a drone performing each of the ten commands (e.g., a drone *taking-off* from the ground, a drone turning *left* in the air). After having watched a clip the participant was asked to suggest a gesture that would be suitable to command the drone to perform the shown action. Participants' gestures were captured on video for later analysis and demographic data were collected through a short questionnaire.

The experiment was conducted in a gymnasium. The participant's task was to use voice and gesture commands to navigate a UAV (Parrot AR.Drone 2.0) along a pre-defined path that was indicated by arrows on the floor, as shown in Fig. 1k and l. To complete the path all of the ten commands under study had to be used. First, the participant had to command the drone to *takeoff* (Fig. 1k, segment 1) from a fixed start position. After takeoff, the drone had to fly *forward* (Fig. 1k, segment 2) to the right of the first vertical pole and then fly *left* (Fig. 1k, segment 3) without changing its orientation. When the drone was approximately in the middle between the two most distant vertical poles, the participant had to command the drone to fly *down* (Fig. 1k, segment 4) until it could pass below the horizontal pole that connected the vertical poles.

After having flown below the horizontal pole (Fig. 1k, segment 5) the drone had to fly *up* (Fig. 1k, segment 6) higher than the horizontal pole and then fly *backward* (Fig. 1k, segment 7) above the pole. Once the horizontal pole was passed, it had to fly sideways to the *right* (Fig. 1k, segment 8). Next, the drone had to continue *backwards* (Fig. 1k, segment 9) until it was approximately above its initial position. On reaching the initial position (Fig. 1k, position 10), the participant had to *rotate* the drone by 180° (either *rotate left* or *rotate right*) so that its front faced the participant. After that, the drone had to be rotated back in the opposite direction by 180°. Finally, the drone had to *land* at the start position (Fig. 1k, segment 11).

The participant was told that the drone could be manoeuvred through both voice commands and gestures and that the purpose of the task was to verify the accuracy of the voice and gesture recognizers. Two video cameras on tripods facing the participant (Fig. 1l was taken by one of the cameras) served both as visual props to make voice and gesture detection seem realistic and to record the participant's voice and gesture commands for later analyses. The 'wizard' who secretly interpreted and translated the participant's commands and manoeuvred the drone using a tablet was sitting behind the participants (Fig. 1l). The participant was told that the 'wizard's' role was to take notes about the recognizers' performance during the task. The navigation task required a constant attention of the participants on the operated drone due to its dynamic nature. One experimenter was standing next to the participants to clarify potential doubts of the participants. In that way, the participants did not have time and need to look at the "wizard".

In order to avoid giving away hints about possible voice and gesture commands while explaining the task and the required path, the experimenter showed the path by carrying the drone along the path. After that, the participant did the same to confirm that he/she had understood the required path. The participant was asked to stand during the task and to remain within a 2×2 m large square that was marked on the floor.

4 Results

We divide our presentation of the results in three parts: we first report on results regarding voice commands (obtained from the survey and from the experiment). Next, we present our findings regarding gestures (obtained from the experiment and from the interview), and finally we discuss how our participants combined voice and gesture commands during the experiment. The results are summarised in Table 1[1]. The table lists the most frequently suggested and used voice commands and gestures. The numbers in the table represent the rounded relative frequency (%) with which the listed words and gestures occurred among all word suggestions, respectively used gestures, for the specified command (columns). Numbers in italics (row 4–6) show the number of experiment participants who used a voice command (*Voice*), a gesture (*Gesture*), or a combination (*V + G*) for the specified command.

---

[1] Please contact the authors for the full collection of voice and gesture commands.

Table 1. The most frequently used/suggested voice and gesture commands.

		Up & Down	Left & Right	Rotate Left & Rotate Right	Forward & Backward	Takeoff & Land
Survey	Voice	up (81) upward (8) down (83) downward (4)	left (82) west (6) right (84) east (6)	turn left (30) rotate left (26) rotate counter clockwise (17) turn right (31) rotate right (25) rotate clockwise (17)	forward (58) go (13) straight (8) north (6) back/backward (42) reverse/south (6)	up (28) takeoff (21) lift/start (17) land (56) down (23)
Experiment	Voice	up (88) higher (12) down (100)	left (80) turn left (12) right (92) turn right (8)	turn (48) turn left (12) turn (50) turn right (12)	forward (56) straight (32) back (76) backward (16)	up (42) start (32) land (40) stop (33) down (13)
Experiment	Gestures	31 58	24 (left) and 26 (right)	35	23 35	–
Voice		7 9	8 10	10 9	7 7	9 15
Gesture		9 10	9 9	8 9	9 9	2 3
V+G		17 14	16 14	15 15	17 17	22 15
Interview	Gestures	33 37	30 30	22	22 37	–

4.1 Voice Commands

The first row in Table 1 lists the most frequently suggested voice commands in the survey. The second row lists the most common voice commands that were used among the experiment participants who either used a voice command or a combination of speech and a gesture for the corresponding command.

In the study we observed many commonalities between the voice commands suggested in the survey and those being used in the experiment. The majority of all suggestions for the *up* and *down* commands in the survey were 'up' (81 %) and 'down' (83 %). The second most frequent words were 'upward' (8 %) respectively 'downward' (4 %). Also in the experiment, 'up' was the most frequent (88 %) voice command used to manoeuvre the drone *up* among the seven participants who used a voice command. In the experiment, 'higher' was the second most frequent (12 %) voice command for *up*. All nine participants who used a voice command for *down* used the word 'down'.

In the survey, the most frequent suggestions to command a UAV to fly *left* or *right* were the words 'left' (82 %), respectively 'right' (84 %). When a voice command was used for flying *left* or *right* in the experiment (8 resp. 10 participants), the mostly used words were 'left' (80 %) respectively 'right' (92 %).

The short phrases 'turn left' (30 %), 'rotate left' (26 %), and 'rotate counter clockwise' (17 %) were the most frequent suggestions in the survey for the *rotate left* command. For the *rotate right* command, an almost identical distribution was observed between the phrases 'turn right' (31 %), 'rotate right' (25 %), and 'rotate clockwise' (17 %). In the experiment, nine participants used a voice command for *rotate left* and for *rotate right*. Nearly half of the participants (48 %) used either 'turn' or 'turn around' in a combination with a gesture to specify the direction to rotate. 'Turn left' and 'turn right' were used by 12 % of the participants.

Both in the survey and in the experiment, more than half (58 %) of the participants used 'forward' to command the UAV to fly *forward*. 'Go' and 'straight' were other frequently used commands provided in the survey and in the experiment.

In the survey, the same number of the respondents suggested 'back' (42 %) and 'backward' (42 %) to command a UAV to fly backward. In the experiment, a majority of the participants who used a voice command preferred the shorter version 'back' (76 %) instead of 'backward' (16 %). This difference indicates the practical use of the experiment that allowed us to observe natural behavior of novice users when navigation a real vehicle in a concrete scenario.

In the survey, the suggestions for the *takeoff* command were divided between 'up' (28 %), 'takeoff' (21 %), 'lift' (17 %), and 'start' (17 %). In the experiment, the most frequently used voice commands for *takeoff* were 'up' (42 %) and 'start' (32 %). The survey respondents and the experiment participants frequently suggested, and used, 'land' (56 % resp. 40 %) and 'down' (23 % resp. 13 %) to command the UAV to *land*. In the experiment, 'stop' was also the second most frequently (33 %) used voice command to *land* the drone.

Interestingly, the respondents and the participants used 'up' both for the *up* and *takeoff* commands and 'down' for the *down* and *land* commands. This observation suggests that there was a tendency to neglect the functional difference of the *takeoff* and *land* commands.

Overall, the strongest agreement on voice commands was for the *up*, *down*, *left*, and *right* commands. For the *forward* and *backward* commands, the suggestions were mainly divided between two options. There were other interesting ideas such as 'let's go' for the *takeoff* command; 'park' and 'that's it' to command *land*; a phrase 'ready, steady, go' was used for the first forward command.

In the experiment, over half of the participants (58 %) used 'stop' to command the UAV to stop. In addition, the participants kept interacting with the UAV using 'go on', 'again', '(a bit) more', '(it's) ok', 'yes', and 'no' to continue or discourage the current movement of the UAV. Two survey participants and four participants in the experiment specified attributes for commands such as '1 m up' or '180° counter clockwise'.

4.2   Gestures

Row 3 and 7 in Table 1 show the most frequently observed gesture for each of the eight motion commands (*up*, *down*, *left*, *right*, *rotate left*, *rotate right*, *forward*, and *backward*) during the experiment and in the video interview, respectively. Overall, we observed a variety of gestures, including small finger gestures, such as pointing with a finger, and full-body gestures, such as taking a step towards in a desired direction. However, hand gestures were the most common. The majority (52 %) of interview participants and the majority (62 %) of the experiment participants who used hand gestures tended to consistently use either one or both hands for all the commands; the others mixed one-handed and two-handed gestures. In case of two-handed gestures, it is interesting to note that most of the time the involvement of the second hand was redundant as it simply duplicated the movements of the other. Furthermore, we did not observe any overlaps between the gestures used for the eight motion commands.

In order to command a UAV to fly up, 33 % of the interviewees and 31 % of the participants showed the following gesture: arms bent at the elbows in front of the person point upwards with palms facing the ceiling. The same number of the interviewees moved either one (37 %) or two hands (37 %) down with palms facing the floor. In the experiment, 68 % of those who showed gestures used both hands for the down command and the remaining 32 % used one hand.

The most frequently observed gestures for *left* and *right* in the experiment were to put out both hands in front of the torso and then move the hands to the left, respectively to the right. Most interview participants (30 %) suggested the same gestures, but used only one hand, the left for the *left* command and the right hand for the *right* command.

The most popular gestures, both in the experiment and in the video interview, for the *rotate left* and *rotate right* commands were to put out the dominant hand, bend the elbow, and then circle the hand/forearm counter clockwise or counter clockwise (experiment 35 %, interview 22 %).

In the experiment, the most frequently used gesture (23 %) for the *forward* command among participants who used a gesture or combined a gesture with speech was to extended both arms in front of the upper chest and "pushed" the hands away. The same gesture, but with only one hand, was also the most popular (22 %) gesture for *forward* in the video interview. For the opposite direction, the *backward* command, experiment participants most frequently (35 %) used both hands and "waved" towards themselves. Interview participants used only one hand (37 %).

4.3   Combination of Voice Commands and Gestures

Our analysis of the video recordings during the experiment revealed that 11 participants (33 %) mostly (at least for 8 out of 10 commands) used a combination of voice and gesture commands, six participants (18 %) mostly used a gesture only (at least for 8 out of 10 ten commands), and seven participants (21 %) mostly used voice commands only. For each command, the usage of voice commands only, gestures only, and a combination of both modalities was approximately the same: 25 %, 25 %, and 50 %, respectively. The exceptions were the *takeoff* (27 %, 6 %, and 67 %) and *land* (45 %, 9 %, and 45 %) commands, for which only few participants used gestures only. The reason might be the functional difference: while the other eight commands suggest only a certain movement of the UAV, the *takeoff* and *land* commands involve an additional function: turning on and off the rotors, which is possibly more easily communicated through a voice command.

In a combination with voice commands, gestures often served to explicitly indicate the direction, e.g., 'go up' accompanied with a hand pointing upwards. The exceptions were the *rotate left* and *rotate right* commands for which 45 % of the participants used gestures to specify the direction e.g., 'rotate' accompanied with a gesture indicating the direction of rotation.

4.4   The Takeoff and Land Commands

Gestures used for the *takeoff* and *land* commands are left out from Table 1. The reason is their sameness with the gestures shown for the *up* and *down* commands, respectively.

In the experiment, the wizards were asked to hesitate with taking off and landing the UAV to give the participants time to figure out gestures different from those used for the *up* and *down* commands. For most participants, in the end, after the ineffective insisting on using the *up/down* gesture to command the UAV to takeoff/land, most of the participants used a voice command such as 'start' and 'stop'. The fact that the participants used voice commands instead of inventing a separate gesture for the *takeoff* and *land* commands suggests that speech fits more naturally for the given commands.

Those who participated in the video interview were asked to suggest only gestures and, as a result, several variations of *land* gestures different from *down* gestures were observed. Almost one fifth of the participants (22 %) separated the *land* and *down* commands either by using a totally different gesture, as visualized in Fig. 2a, or by augmenting the down gesture (Fig. 2b and c). The gestures shown in Figs. 2b and c were used both individually and in a combination with the most frequently used down gesture (Table 1). However, these gestures give an impression of being more "forced" rather than being natural and intuitive since their mental models are less obvious.

Fig. 2.   Gestures used to distinguish the land from the down command: (a) vertical clap, (b) a horizontal clap, (c) crossed hands move to the sides.

5   Discussion

We set out this study to provide insight into intuitive interaction using voice and gestures to operate a UAV. The most frequently used voice commands and gestures listed in Table 1 are apparently the most intuitive ones for novice users and the answer to our question "What are intuitive gestures and voice commands to navigate a UAV?" We now present and discuss our main findings that answer the remaining three questions:

5.1 Commonalities in Users' Behavior and Command Choice

The analysis of the observed gestures and voice commands within each part of the study individually showed that less diversity of voice commands and gestures was observed in the experiment compared to the survey and the interview, respectively. With regard to the survey, this finding may partly be explained by the number of the respondents that is higher than the number of those participated in the experiment (50 vs. 33). As for the interview, though the number of the participants was slightly lower than in the experiment (27 vs. 33), the same tendency was detected. There is, however, another possible reason to which we are inclined. The observed diversity is likely to be related to a number of "degrees of freedom". Survey and interview participants had full discretion to suggest any relevant idea. Whereas participants in the experiment were also encouraged to use any voice command and/or gesture, we cannot exclude that experiment participants tried to give commands that they thought could be more easily recognized by the pretended voice and gesture recognizer or that they tried to guess and use the commands chosen by the developer. This finding suggests that the survey and interviews are mutually complementary with the experiment as the limitation of one is compensated by the strong side of the other. Accordingly, we emphasize the importance of considering all three sources of data to make the picture complete.

In terms of gestures, the data obtained from the interview and the experiment revealed that the absolute majority of the participants indicated the direction to fly with their hands and specified the direction to rotate by rotating the forearm. Likewise, there were many commonalities among the collected voice commands. These findings suggest that, in the considered context, there is indeed a potential in the development of gestures and voice commands that are intuitive for novice users.

Overall, the obtained gesture set (Table 1) included from 9 to 17 options for each of the eight commands. However, if we neglect the orientation of the palms and the cases where the second hand was used explicitly, meaning that a command would have been

Table 2. Final gesture set, suitable for all participants.

clear even if only one hand was involved, then an interface able to correctly interpret the set of gestures presented in Table 2 would allow all our experiment participants to navigate a UAV without any initial instructions.

5.2   Mental Models

To answer our third and fourth questions "What mental models do novice users have regarding the navigation of a UAV?" and "Do novice users rely on one coherent mental model when they navigate a UAV or do they rely on concepts and notions drawn from different mental models?" we first briefly explain what we mean with 'mental models'. The concept of mental models originates from cognitive science and its introduction is most often attributed to Craik [30], more than seventy years ago. Since then it has been widely used within the field of Human-Computer Interaction [31] to reason about, and to understand, human behavior. However, less HRI-related work can be found on mental models. A mental model about the functionality and behavior of a system is formed mainly by previously acquired knowledge (e.g., from documentation or instructions) and experiences with similar systems. Moreover, a system is often considered to be intuitive to use if the way the system works matches the user's expectations, which in turn are dictated by his/her mental model of how the system works. Accordingly, and since we are interested in designing intuitive interactions using gestures to manoeuvring a UAV, we tried to identify any patterns regarding mental models in participants' behavior.

Of course, one could argue that it is unlikely that an interface designer can design an interface that meets the expectations of all the potential users. While it is true that it is hardly possible to predict the users' behavior, mental models might help to guide a user to the desired behavior. In many cases, a hint can be enough to guide a user to a certain mental model. The following example illustrates the key idea behind the concept. For example, a user is asked to guide a UAV by imitating the desired actions using hand movements, as illustrated in Fig. 3. Following this scenario, the user could intuitively control the flight of the UAV without further instructions simply by adhering to the mental model "my hand represents the UAV" (imitative class of mental models in our classification; cf. below). Therefore, the use of mental models that define a behavior that is intuitive for an individual or a group of users under a certain scenario could help in stimulating the desired behavior. Accordingly, we aimed to identify user-defined mental models, which seemed to guide each participant's behavior, in order to come up with intuitive interaction techniques.

Fig. 3. Gestures associated with the imitative class of mental models with the hand imitating the required commands: (a) *up/down*; (b) *left/right*; (c) *rotate left/rotate right*; (d) *forward/backward*.

Our analysis of mental models in terms of their commonalities and differences led to clustering of related mental models into three classes: *imitative, intelligent,* and *instrumented.* In the *imitative* class, a part of the operator's body e.g., a hand, as in Fig. 3, serves as a surrogate of the UAV and thus movements of this body part are directly mapped to movements of the UAV. Gestures include those where the UAV follows the motions of the head, one hand, two hands, the upper-body, or the whole body.

In the *intelligent* class, an operator expects a certain level of intelligence of a UAV that enables the UAV to interpret a given command correctly. Gestures include those where an indication of the direction is given with the index finger, thumb, hand, forearm, arm, and "come to me" or "go away" gestures.

In the *instrumented* class, an operator gives the flight instructions using an imaginary tool. This class is represented through four mental models. We call these the 'virtual UAV', the 'puppet ruler', the 'joystick', and the 'super power'. With the 'virtual UAV' the operator holds in the hands a virtual UAV whose movements are mapped directly to the movements of the real UAV. With the 'puppet ruler' the operator holds an imaginary UAV right in front of the body that is 'connected' with the UAV through two invisible 'strings', the real UAV copies the movements of the 'puppet' UAV. With the 'joystick' the operator associates the forearm with a joystick and tilts the forearm as if it was a joystick: forward, backward, left or right to command a UAV to go forward, backward, left, and right, respectively. Finally, with the 'super power' the operator keeps the arms in front of the body at chest-height with the palms facing forward and 'pushes' or 'pulls' the UAV in the desired direction, as if having a magic super power.

Most of our participants seem to have preferred an *intelligent* type of mental model and seem to have expected that the UAV could correctly interpret all the given commands, including high-level commands such as the "come to me". A reason behind this preference might be the strong resemblance to human-to-human interaction.

Another important finding is the tendency participants had to stick to one and the same mental model while navigating the UAV. Particularly, almost a quarter (24 %) of all participants who used gestures in the experiment used at least six gestures (out of 8) that were associated with one mental model and more than one third (38 %) of the participants used at least four gestures that were associated with one mental model. In the survey, almost one fifth (19 %) of the interview participants suggested gestures associated with one mental model and the majority (63 %) suggested at least five gestures belonging to the one and same mental model. These observations underline the importance of considering mental models to define a coherent gesture set.

A possible reason for using more mental models could be the inability of the 'main' model to cover all commands. For example, tilting the forearm as if it was a joystick could be intuitively associated with the *forward, backward, left,* and *right* commands, however, the rest of the studied commands are not that intuitively mapped to any such forearm movement. Another reason could involve aspects related to physical ergonomics. For example, imitation of UAV movements with one hand with the palm facing downwards can naturally cover all the studied commands except for the *rotate left* and *rotate right* as rotation of the hand at the wrist about vertical axis is not physically comfortable (Fig. 3c).

The gesture vocabulary composed of the most frequently used gestures (Table 1) does not necessarily warrant the coherence of its components. For instance, each gesture considered individually seems to make sense. However, the gesture set on the whole seems to be inconsistent. In particular, the *up* gesture looks like if the operator holds a virtual UAV in the hands. The *down* gesture can be seen as the imitation of the required UAV's motion with both hands. An operator simply indicates the direction to fly with a fully extended arm when commanding a UAV to fly left and right as well as the direction to rotate by rotating the forearm. The *forward* gesture looks like if the operator has the 'super force' to push the UAV forward. The *backward* gesture resembles the "come to me" gesture. Although the gestures might be interpreted differently, it is worth mentioning that it is not possible to give an operator only one single hint that uniquely defines the set of gestures presented in Table 1 and that allows the operator to navigate the UAV without further instructions. In addition, it seems illogical to use both hands to command a UAV to fly up and down while only one hand is used for the remaining commands. In such a case, an operator would have to learn by heart when to use one hand and when to use both hands. This inconsistency makes the gesture set shown in Table 1 harder to remember and might lead to a confusion of gestures. For the set of commands studied, this issue does not seem to cause serious problems as the vocabulary is small and could be easily learned. However, in cases where a larger gesture vocabulary is necessary, such inconsistencies might cause confusion and notably increase the user's mental workload. In order to avoid such problems, we recommend avoiding a mixture of mental models, as far as possible. It is our strong believe that an interaction technique composed of gestures belonging to one mental model would lead to a lower mental workload.

6　Conclusion

The present exploration used three sources (an online survey, a Wizard of Oz experiment, and a video interview) to elicit *intuitive* gestures and voice commands for controlling a UAV from novice users. With our approach we could identify: (1) the most intuitive gestures and voice commands; (2) important commonalities in users' behavior and command choices; and (3) various mental models that guided our novice users in their voice and gesture choices. With our exploration, we also provided evidence that indicates that novice users tend to rely on concepts and notions drawn from one mental model rather than drawn from different mental models.

The main outcome of our exploration is a collection of user-defined voice commands and gestures to manoeuvre a UAV. Although the focus of the exploration was on UAVs, the proposed collection of gestures and voice commands, as well as, the underlying methodology (using several methods to elicit what users' find intuitive) might serve as a source of inspiration for other researchers and interface designers in their development of natural and intuitive interactions for a broader range of unmanned agents, including Unmanned Ground Vehicles and Unmanned Underwater Vehicles.

For future work we plan to compare the use of the user-defined gestures and voice commands to other interaction modalities. Further studies are also needed to investigate the influence of mental models on various usability-related interface aspects, such as learnability, memorability, ergonomics, satisfaction, and intuitiveness. In addition, it would be interesting to compare experiences of individuals within the same task but with gesture sets associated with different mental models.

References

1. Supimros, S., Wongthanavasu, S.: Speech recognition - based control system for drone. In: Proceedings of the 3rd ICT International Student Project Conference (ICT-ISPC 2014), pp. 107–110 (2014)
2. Higuchi, K., Rekimoto, J.: Flying head: a head motion synchronization mechanism for unmanned aerial vehicle control. In: CHI 2013 Extended Abstracts on Human Factors in Computing Systems, pp. 2029–2038 (2013)
3. Teixeira, J.M., Ferreira, R., Santos, M., Teichrieb, V.: Teleoperation using google glass and AR.Drone for structural inspection. In: Proceedings of the XVI Symposium on Virtual and Augmented Reality (SVR 2014), pp. 28–36 (2014)
4. Pittman, C., LaViola, J.J.: Exploring head tracked head mounted displays for first person robot teleoperation. In: Proceedings of the 2014 ACM International Conference on Intelligent User Interfaces (IUI 2014), pp. 323–328 (2014)
5. Mashood, A., Noura, H., Jawhar, I., Mohamed, N.: A gesture based kinect for quadrotor control. In: Proceedings of the 2015 International Conference on Information and Communication Technology Research (ICTRC 2015), pp. 298–301 (2015)
6. Naseer, T., Sturm, J., Cremers, D.: FollowMe: person following and gesture recognition with a quadrocopter. In: Proceedings of the 2013 IEEE/RSJ International Conference on Intelligent Robots and Systems (IROS 2013), pp. 624–630 (2013)
7. Ng, W.S., Sharlin, E.: Collocated interaction with flying robots. In: Proceedings of the 20th IEEE International Symposium on Robot and Human Interactive Communication (RO-MAN 2011), pp. 143–149 (2011)
8. Soto-Guerrero, D., Ramírez Torres, J.G.: A human-machine interface with unmanned aerial vehicles. In: Proceedings of the 10th International Conference on Electrical Engineering, Computing Science and Automatic Control (CCE 2013), pp. 307–312 (2013)
9. Pfeil, K., Koh, S.L., LaViola, J.: Exploring 3d gesture metaphors for interaction with unmanned aerial vehicles. In: Proceedings of the International Conference on Intelligent User Interfaces (IUI 2013), pp. 257–266 (2013)
10. Ikeuchi, K., Otsuka, T., Yoshii, A., Sakamoto, M., Nakajima, T.: KinecDrone: enhancing somatic sensation to fly in the sky with kinect and AR.Drone. In: Proceedings of the 5th Augmented Human International Conference (AH 2014), no. 53 (2014)
11. Nagi, J., Giusti, A., Gambardella, L.M., Di Caro, G.A.: Human-swarm interaction using spatial gestures. In: Proceedings of the IEEE/RSJ International Conference on Intelligent Robots and Systems (IROS 2014), pp. 3834–3841 (2014)
12. Monajjemi, V., Wawerla, J., Vaughan, R., Mori, G.: HRI in the sky: creating and commanding teams of UAVs with a vision-mediated gestural interface. In: Proceedings of the IEEE/RSJ International Conference on Intelligent Robots and Systems (IROS 2013), pp. 617–623 (2013)
13. Hansen, J.P., Alapetite, A., MacKenzie, I.S., Møllenbach, E.: The use of gaze to control drones. In: Proceedings of the ACM Symposium on Eye Tracking Research and Applications (ETRA 2014), pp. 27–34 (2014)

14. Kos'myna, N., Tarpin-Bernard, F., Rivet, B.: Bidirectional feedback in motor imagery BCIs: learn to control a drone within 5 minutes. In: CHI 2014 Extended Abstracts on Human Factors in Computing Systems, pp. 479–482 (2014)
15. Davidson, M.J., Dove, L., Weltz, J.: Mental Models and Usability (1999)
16. Rust, K., Malu, M., Anthony, L., Findlater, L.K.: Understanding child-defined gestures and children's mental models for touchscreen tabletop interaction. In: Proceedings of the 2014 Conference on Interaction Design and Children (IDC 2014), pp. 201–204 (2014)
17. Valdes, C., Eastman, D., Grote, C., Thatte, S., Shaer, O., Mazalek, A., Ullmer, B., Konkel, M.K.: Exploring the design space of gestural interaction with active tokens through user-defined gestures. In: Proceedings of the SIGCHI Conference on Human Factors in Computing Systems (CHI 2014), pp. 4107–4116 (2014)
18. Kiesler, S., Goetz, J.: Mental models of robotic assistants. In: CHI 2002 Extended Abstracts on Human Factors in Computing Systems, pp. 576–577 (2002)
19. Powers, A., Kiesler, S.: The advisor robot: tracing people's mental model from a robot's physical attributes. In: Proceedings of the 1st ACM SIGCHI/SIGART Conference on Human-Robot Interaction (HRI 2006), pp. 218–225 (2006)
20. Fong, T., Nourbakhsh, I., Dautenhahn, K.: A survey of socially interactive robots. Robot. Auton. Syst. **42**(3–4), 143–166 (2003)
21. Hauptmann, A., McAvinney, P.: Gestures with speech for graphic manipulation. Int. J. Man-Mach. Stud. **38**(2), 231–249 (1993)
22. Sharma, R., Pavlović, V.I., Huang, T.: Toward multimodal human-computer interface. Proc. IEEE **86**(5), 853–869 (1998)
23. Rogalla, O., Ehrenmann, M., Zöllner, R., Becher, R., Dillmann, R.: Using gesture and speech control for commanding a robot assistant. In: Proceedings of the 11th International Workshop on Robot and Human Interactive Communication (RO-MAN 2002), pp. 454–459 (2002)
24. Urban, M., Bajcsy, P.: Fusion of voice, gesture, and human-computer controls for remotely operated robot. In: Proceedings of the 7th International Conference on Information Fusion (FUSION 2005), pp. 1644–1651 (2005)
25. Jones, G., Berthouze, N., Bielski, R., Julier, S.: Towards a situated, multimodal interface for multiple UAV control. In: Proceedings of the IEEE International Conference on Robotics and Automation (ICRA 2010), pp. 1739–1744 (2010)
26. Quigley, M., Goodrich, M.A., Beard, R.W.: Semi-autonomous human-UAV interfaces for fixed-wing mini-UAVs. In: Proceedings of the IEEE/RSJ International Conference on Intelligent Robots and Systems (IROS 2004), pp. 2457–2462 (2004)
27. Lichtenstern, M., Frassl, M., Perun, B., Angermann, M.: A prototyping environment for interaction between a human and a robotic multi-agent system. In: Proceedings of the 7th Annual ACM/IEEE International Conference on Human-Robot Interaction (HRI 2012), pp. 185–186 (2012)
28. Burke, M., Lasenby, J.: Pantomimic gestures for human–robot interaction. IEEE Trans. Robot. **31**(5), 1225–1237 (2015)
29. Cauchard, J.R., E, J.L., Zhai, K.Y., Landay, J.A.: Drone & me: an exploration into natural human-drone interaction. In: Proceedings of the 2015 ACM International Joint Conference on Pervasive and Ubiquitous Computing (UbiComp 2015), pp. 361–365 (2015)
30. Craik, K.: The Nature of Explanation. Cambridge University Press, Cambridge (1943)
31. Norman, D.A.: The Design of Everyday Things. Basic Books, Inc., New York (2002)

Monitoring Interactions

Felix Meißner$^{(\boxtimes)}$ and Remco C. Veltkamp

Department of Information and Computing Sciences,
Universiteit Utrecht, 3508 TB Utrecht, The Netherlands
fnmeissner@gmail.com

Abstract. This work proposes a human interaction recognition based approach to video indexing that represents a video by showing when and with whom was interacted throughout the video. In order to visualize the length of an interaction, it is required to recognize individuals that have been detected in earlier parts of the video. To solve this problem, an approach to photo-clustering is extended to video material by tracking detected faces and using the information from tracking to improve the recognition of human beings. The results of the tracking based approach show a considerable decrease of false cluster assignments compared to the original method. Further, it is demonstrated that the proposed method is able to correctly recognize the appearance of five out of the six individuals correctly.

Keywords: Computer vision · Video indexing · Bag of words · Human recognition

1 Introduction

The current advance of head mountable video recording devices calls for supportive technology regarding the collection of recorded material. The ever increasing size of personal video collections can be approached by an automated video indexing system that supports users by giving concise summaries of lengthy videos. This work proposes a human interaction recognition based approach to video indexing that represents a video by showing when and with whom was interacted throughout the video. By interaction we mean any interaction between the filmmaker and a person that is visible in the video, which includes social interactions like meeting friends as well as non-social interactions like paying the groceries at the store. In Fig. 1, several frames are presented that show the cashier of a store interacting with the filmmaker who is paying groceries.

The index we propose is visualized as a horizontal axis representing the time in the video. Each detected interaction partner is represented as a bar above the axis together with a picture extracted from the video. The length and position of the bar represents the moment in time in the video. For an example of an index please see Fig. 3, which shows the index representing the ground truth of the dataset we have recorded for the evaluation of this work. We approach the problem of creating a human interaction based index by detecting all individuals

© ICST Institute for Computer Sciences, Social Informatics and Telecommunications Engineering 2017
R. Poppe et al. (Eds.): INTETAIN 2016, LNICST 178, pp. 63–73, 2017.
DOI: 10.1007/978-3-319-49616-0_6

Fig. 1. An example of an interaction is the interaction of the movie maker with a cashier when paying groceries at a shop.

using face detection. All detections are clustered based on visual appearance. Optimally, each cluster contains all detections from one individual so that the first and the last frame within one cluster represents the start and the end time of an interaction.

The aim of our work is to improve the quality of the clustering as well as the visual index by extending the work by Song and Leung (2006) [1] to include video specific information. We identify groups of the same individual by tracking faces through several frames.

2   Related Work

In the work by Song and Leung (2006) [1], consumer photo albums are clustered based on the individuals they show. For the detection of individuals face detection is used. The recognition is based on a combined distance measure that considers the appearance of detected faces as well as the appearance of clothes. Clothes are detected by selecting a predefined area below any detected face. To prevent the clothes detections of two individuals that are near to each other from overlapping with the other individual's clothes, the clothes detections are segmented by maximizing the difference between the color histograms of both detections. We propose an extension to the work by Song and Leung (2006) [1] to adapt to egocentric video material.

Everingham et al. [2] propose a similar approach of integrating information from tracking into a distance measure between two detection groups. Opposed to our approach, they use the maximum distance between all possible pairs of detections within the detection groups as the distance between two detection groups. In our work, we build a single descriptor per detection group, modeling appearances and its changes as a statistical model. By including information from multiple detections into the descriptor, we improve the quality of the measure of distance between two detection groups that are known to contain detections of the same individual.

3   Approach

We assume that any interaction between the filmmaker and another person involves looking at each other, meaning an interaction can be detected by repeatedly recognizing a frontal human face. Thus, to detect interactions, we apply face detection as proposed by Viola and Jones (2001) [3], which detects human beings looking at the camera. We track faces using optical flow as described by Everingham et al. (2009) [2], resulting in detection groups that are known to contain detections of the same individual. To prevent bypassing people from being shown as interaction partners, the detection groups can be required to contain a minimum number of detections.

Optical flow cannot always track a face during the complete interaction, for example because the interaction partner is temporarily out of sight or occluded. That means that an interaction can consist of one or more detection groups. In order to recognize when an interaction starts and where it ends, all detection groups belonging to the same interaction need to be found. We approach this problem by clustering all detections based on their visual appearance into a set of clusters. From the clusters we learn the first and the last frame of the interaction.

For the process of clustering we use and extend the approach of Song and Leung [1], which combines face recognition with clothes recognition to cluster consumer photo sets. In this section, we first give a summary of how the original approach works and then present the extensions that we propose in order to improve the clustering results when applied to egocentric video material.

In the approach of Song and Leung [1], for each detection of clothes, overlapping patches are extracted to form a global bag of patches. In order to prevent parts of skin that might overlap clothes, a skin detector is trained based on extracted skin patches from below the eyes. Patches that are classified as skin are ignored in the further. To all patches from all detections principal component analysis is applied. The first 15 principal components are clustered by k-means to form a dictionary of visual words. The patches of each detection are quantized with respect to the visual word dictionary and each bin is multiplied with $\log(\frac{1}{w_i})$, with w_i being the fraction of all patches that has been assigned to the ith bin of all descriptors. This adjustment emphasizes rare patches as they contain more information compared to patches that are frequent in all detections. The dot product of both vectors gives the distance between two clothes detections. Regarding the distance between two faces, we use descriptors based on facial features as described by Everingham et al. [2]. The distance between two face descriptors is given by the Euclidean distance between the two vectors.

To combine the two distance measures between faces and between clothes into a single distance value between two detections, Song and Leung [1] uses linear regression. The probability that two detections are the same person is given by

$$P(Y = 1|x_f, x_c) = \frac{1}{1 + exp(-w_f x_f - w_c x_c - w_0)}, \qquad (1)$$

where x_f is the similarity between the faces and x_c is the similarity between clothes. The weights w_f and w_c control how much influence each of the similarities has on the combined outcome, and w_0 provides an offset. Given a labeled training set, the values for w_0, w_c and w_f can be learned by applying iterative reweighted least squares. In this work the values has been chosen experimentally due to the lack of an appropriate data set.

Based on the combined distance measure, the affinity matrix is calculated, holding all pairwise similarities between all detections. The similarity matrix is used to apply spectral clustering, with the clusters being the desired grouping of the detected individuals. We currently set the number of clusters manually, but existing heuristics to estimate the correct number of clusters can easily be implemented. The work of Luxburg [4] presents several approaches to this problem.

Until here, the approach of Song and Leung [1] is explained and will be referred to as the original approach in our experimental evaluation. In the following, we propose two extensions, multiple dictionaries of visual words and descriptors for multiple detections.

3.1   Multiple Dictionaries of Visual Words

Using multiple dictionaries has the advantage that the dictionaries can be calculated before the data is completed, which is important for possible real time applications. In our application, detection groups are a good candidate for having an individual bag of words dictionary. When using separate dictionaries per detection group, it is not possible to compare descriptors to each other directly as they refer to different dictionaries. In the following, two different approaches are presented that can solve this issue by integrating the dictionaries into the distance measure between two descriptors.

Multiple Separate Dictionaries. Aly et al. [5] propose to approach multiple dictionaries by building a descriptor per detection per dictionary. We evaluate this approach in our experiments.

Multiple Dictionaries with the Earth Movers Distance. Another possibility is to change the distance measure used to compare the descriptors. Instead of using the dot product between two descriptors, the Earth Mover's Distance (EMD) can be used, which allows to take into account the distance between the dictionaries as well. The EMD can be though of the minimum amount of work that is required to fill holes in the ground with earth from piles in some distance to the holes.

In [6], the EMD between two signatures $P = \{(p_1, w_{p1}), \ldots, (p_n, w_{pn})\}$ and $Q = \{(q_1, w_{q1}), \ldots, (q_n, w_{qn})\}$ is defined as

$$\mathbf{EMD}(P, Q) = \frac{\sum_{i=1}^{m} \sum_{j=1}^{n} f_{ij} d_{ij}}{\sum_{i=1}^{m} \sum_{j=1}^{n} f_{ij}}, \tag{2}$$

where $\mathbf{D} = [d_{ij}]$ is the ground distance matrix, with d_{ij} holding the distance between p_i and q_j, and $\mathbf{F} = [f_{ij}]$ being the flow matrix, holding the flows between weights w_{pi} and w_{qj} that minimize the overall cost

$$WORK(P, Q, \mathbf{F}) = \sum_{i=1}^{m} \sum_{j=1}^{n} f_{ij} d_{ij}, \tag{3}$$

subject to

$$
\begin{aligned}
f_{ij} &\geq 0 && 1 \leq i \leq m, 1 \leq j \leq n \\
\sum_{j=1}^{n} f_{ij} &\leq w_{pi} && 1 \leq i \leq m \\
\sum_{i=1}^{m} f_{ij} &\leq w_{qj} && 1 \leq j \leq n \\
\sum_{i=1}^{m} \sum_{j=1}^{n} f_{ij} &= \min(\sum_{i=1}^{m} w_{pi}, \sum_{j=1}^{n} w_{qj}).
\end{aligned}
\tag{4}
$$

Intuitively, applying the EMD to compare descriptors of visual words can be explained as follows: When comparing two descriptors, the visual words of the dictionaries they refer to represent the location of the piles and holes that are to be filled. The visual words of the first descriptor represent the location of the piles and the visual words of the second descriptor represent the location of the holes that are to be filled. The distance between two visual words is the difference in their appearance. As the descriptors are histograms of visual words, their entries represent the size of the holes and the weight of the piles. Consequently, high values in the histograms can only be *moved* to the other descriptor at low cost when the visual words they represent have a similar appearance and similar size.

Formally speaking, the first part of the signature, $p_1, \ldots, p_n$, are the back-projected visual words. The visual words are back-projected because each *detection group* uses an individual PCA transformation vector. As a result, the principal components cannot be compared with each other in PCA space, because the principal components of each group have a completely different meaning in original space. The second part of the signature, the weights $w_1, \ldots, w_n$, are the histograms of visual words. The ground distance matrix $\mathbf{F}$ is calculated by taking the L1-distance between every two visual word vectors p_i and q_j. By normalizing the histograms to sum up to 1, all descriptors have the same amount of weight and the EMD between them becomes a metric.

3.2 Descriptors from Multiple Detections

In the original approach by Song and Leung [1], the appearance of each detection is modeled as a histogram of visual word frequencies. To build a descriptor that contains information of more than one of such descriptors, this work evaluates a way of modeling multiple histograms as a single descriptor.

The most simple approach is to build a vector containing the average values of each bin. The advantage of this approach is that the effect of outlining values is reduced significantly. On the other hand, bins with a high variance within one detection group will not be represented appropriately, as the information about the variance is lost.

A better approach is to use two vectors containing not only the average, but also including the standard deviation for each histogram bin. In histograms or a vector of average bin values, the values of each bin cannot be compared by simply subtracting the values. Instead, each bin is interpreted as a Gaussian distribution and the distance between two bins is the probability of them describing each other. For this, the normalized L2 distance between two Gaussian distributions is used, which is described in the work of Jensen et al. [7] as

$$d_{nL2}(p_1, p_2) = \int (p'_1(x) - p'_2(x))^2 \mathrm{d}x, \tag{5}$$

where

$$p'_i = p_i(x) / \sqrt{\int p_i(x)^2 \mathrm{d}x}. \tag{6}$$

In the implementation, $\int p_i(x)^2 \mathrm{d}x$ is approximated by sampling 1000 linear data points between 0 and 1.

4   Experiments

For the experimental evaluation of the proposed extensions we recorded a custom dataset. The dataset consists of recordings of paying groceries from an egocentric perspective and shows 6 different individuals. The resulting number of detections and detection groups resulting from applying face detection and tracking the detected faces with optical flow is shown in Table 1. The face detector is the only component that requires training, but since we use the trained classifier from OpenCV we have no training phase at all and consequently use the complete dataset for testing.

Table 1. Number of detections and detection groups in the evaluation dataset from face detection and tracking.

Individual	#1	#2	#3	#4	#5	#6
Detections	59	201	52	44	81	66
Detection groups	3	3	3	2	3	5

4.1   Clustering Performance

In order to evaluate the proposed extensions we first measure the resulting receiver operating characteristics (ROC) of the clustering step. As proposed by Song and Leung [1], the Rand index as proposed by Rand [8] is used to calculate the true positive rate (TPR) and false positive rate (FPR): Given a set of N detections,

"[...] any clustering result can be seen as a collection of $N(N-1)/2$ pair-wise decision. A false alarm happens when a pair actually from different individuals, but the algorithm claims they are the same individual. A true positive (detection) is when a pair actually from the same individual and the algorithm also claims so" ([1]).

The results of clustering the dataset using the multiple dictionaries bag of words approach with Earth Mover's Distance (MDBOW EMD) as well as the multiple dictionaries bag of words approach with separate dictionaries (MDBOW SD) are compared to the results of the original approach in Table 2. The number of clusters C is initially set to $C = 2$ and increased with increasing step size to calculate the receiver operating characteristic. The correct number of clusters is $C = 6$. For this experiment, only descriptors from clothes are used because the approaches do not influence the distance measure between detected faces.

For the correct number of clusters $C = 6$, the MDBOW EMD approach has a 21 % lower FPR than the original approach, while the TPR only decreases about 4 %. When the detections are clustered into $C = 12$ clusters, the FPR of the same approach is 62 % higher, which show the importance of having the correct number of clusters. When using the MDBOW SD, compared to the original approach the TPR is decreased and the FPR is increased independent of the number of clusters that has been set.

Table 2. Measuring clustering performance: The resulting true positive rate (T) and false positive rate (F) for the original approach and the two multiple dictionary bag of word approaches using the Earth Mover's Distance (MDBOW EMD) and separate dictionaries (MDBOW SD) as described in Sect. 3.1. The number of ground truth clusters is $C = 6$.

Approach	C=2		C=4		C=6		C=12		C=18	
	T	F	T	F	T	F	T	F	T	F
Original	1.00	0.73	0.99	0.28	0.98	0.28	0.98	0.29	0.97	0.29
MDBOW EMD	0.99	0.48	0.95	0.23	0.94	0.22	0.98	0.47	0.92	0.22
MDBOW SD	0.97	0.46	0.97	0.45	0.96	0.45	0.96	0.44	0.95	0.44

In Table 3, the results of clustering the dataset with detection group based descriptors are compared to those of the original approach. Again, the number of clusters C is initially set to $C = 2$ and increased with increasing step size to calculate the receiver operating characteristic. The correct number of clusters is $C = 6$. For this experiment, both face and clothes descriptors are used as the proposed method applies to both. To relate the measurement to the preceding experiment, the true and false positive rate are calculated based on the detections and not the detection-groups.

For the correct number of clusters $C = 6$, clustering detection groups results in a TPR decreased by 1 % and a FPR decreased by 89 %. When increasing the number of cluster to 10, which is 1.6 times the correct number of clusters, the FPR becomes 0.001 and the TPR is 0.95.

Table 3. Measuring clustering performance: The resulting true positive rate (T) and false positive rate (F) for the original approach and the detection group based descriptors (DG) as described in Sect. 3.2. The number of ground truth clusters is $C = 6$.

Approach	C=2		C=4		C=6		C=8		C=10	
	T	F	T	F	T	F	T	F	T	F
Original	1.00	0.73	0.99	0.28	0.98	0.28	0.98	0.29	0.97	0.28
DG	1.00	0.37	1.00	0.09	0.97	0.03	0.96	0.02	0.95	0.001

4.2   Retrieval Performance

To analyze the quality of the different bag of words based visual descriptors, the average precision of the first K neighbors is looked at. Since all detections from the same detection group are already known to belong to the same cluster, only those detections are considered which are in different detection groups than the original detection, when retrieving the nearest neighbors. Given a set of detections D and the K nearest neighbors of each detection K_D, the average precision p is the number of correct neighbors divided by the total numbers of neighbors, given by

$$p = \frac{\sum_{d \in D} \sum_{k \in K_D} knn(d, k)}{\sum_D \sum_{K_D} 1}, \quad \text{where} \quad knn(d, k) = \begin{cases} 1 & \text{if same person} \\ 0 & \text{otherwise} \end{cases} \quad (7)$$

The average precision of retrieving the first 10 nearest neighbors for each detection from our complete dataset is shown in Fig. 2. The precision of the original approach for $K = 1$ is 0.82 and decreases approximately linearly to 0.68 for $K = 10$. The MDBOW EMD approach and the MDBOW SD approach have an overall better precision, which is about the same for both approaches. For $K = 1$ the precision for the two new approaches is about 0.95 and decreases to 0.8, which is about 18 % better compared to the original approach.

4.3   Resulting Index

The ground truth index for our dataset is depicted in Fig. 3, whereas ground truth refers to the ground truth of the clustering results. Each horizontal rectangle represents the presence of the depicted individual within the video.

In Fig. 4, the index is shown that is constructed by the framework. Individuals 1,2 and 5 are detected at the correct position and with approximately the correct number of frames. Individual 6 is detected at the correct position, although clearly several occurrences are not recognized, letting the index entry begin later and end earlier than the entry in the index representing ground truth.

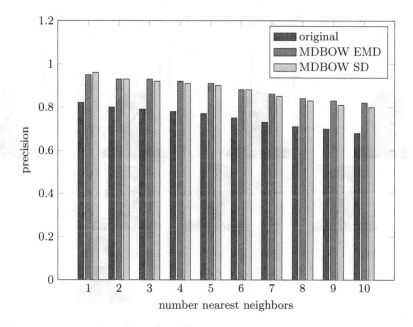

Fig. 2. Measuring retrieval performance: The average precision of different clothes descriptors when retrieving the K nearest neighbors for each detection in dataset 2.

For individuals 3 and 4, two separate index entries are shown. While individual 4 is represented correctly, the 3rd individual's last frame is wrongly recognized at the end of the video. Since our algorithm uses the first and the last frame of a cluster to calculate the beginning and the end of an interaction, the bar for individual 3 spans the second half of the index.

Fig. 3. The index produced for ground truth clustering results.

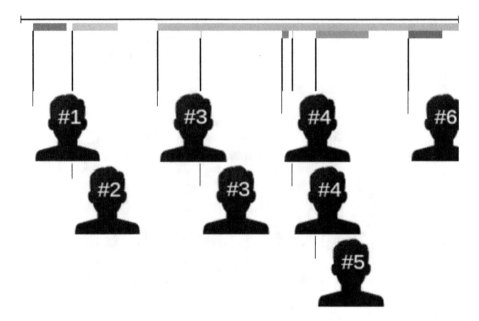

Fig. 4. The index produced for clustering results when using detection group based descriptors.

5   Conclusion

We have presented two different approaches to extend the work by Song and Leung [1] to cluster egocentric video material: Using multiple dictionaries of bag of words and aggregating separate detections into group-descriptors by using tracking.

Regarding the first approach, the experiments show that using multiple dictionaries with the Earth Mover's Distance results in a 21 % lower false positive rate than the original approach, while the true positive rate only decreases 4 %. Furthermore, the k-NN experiment suggests that both methods perform better than the original approach when used to query for similar detections. In other words, the methods might render very useful in other applications.

The second approach, including multiple detections in a single model, shows good results in our experiments. The false positive rate is reduced by 89 %, given the correct number of clusters. Furthermore, we show that the clustering approach can be used to create a time based index representing human interactions for short length video.

References

1. Song, Y., Leung, T.: Context-aided human recognition - clustering. In: Leonardis, A., Bischof, H., Pinz, A. (eds.) Computer Vision - ECCV 2006. LNCS, vol. 3953, pp. 382–395. Springer, Berlin Heidelberg (2006)
2. Everingham, M., Sivic, J., Zisserman, A.: Taking the bite out of automatic naming of characters in TV video. Image Vis. Comput. **27**(5), 545–559 (2009)
3. Viola, P., Jones, M.: Rapid object detection using a boosted cascade of simple features (2001)
4. Luxburg, U.: A tutorial on spectral clustering. Stat. Comput. **17**(4), 395–416 (2007)
5. Aly, M., Munich, M., Perona, P.: Multiple dictionaries for bag of words large scale image search. In: International Conference on Image Processing (ICIP), Brussels, Belgium, September 2011
6. Rubner, Y., Tomasi, C., Guibas, L.J.: The earth mover's distance as a metric for image retrieval. Int. J. Comput. Vis. **40**(2), 99–121 (2000)
7. Jensen, J.H., Ellis, D.P., Christensen, M.G., Jensen, S.H.: Evaluation distance measures between Gaussian mixture models of mfccs. In: ISMIR, (2011) Observation of Strains: Proceedings of the 8th International Conference on Music Information Retrieval, 23–27 September 2007, Vienna, Austria, pp. 107–108. Austrian Computer Society (2007)
8. Rand, W.M.: Objective criteria for the evaluation of clustering methods. J. Am. Stat. Assoc. **66**(336), 846–850 (1971)

Hold Me Tight: A Tangible Interface for Mediating Closeness to Overcome Physical Separation

Carina Gansohr, Katharina Emmerich$^{(\boxtimes)}$, and Maic Masuch

Entertainment Computing Group, University of Duisburg-Essen,
Forsthausweg 2, 47057 Duisburg, Germany
{carina.gansohr,katharina.emmerich,
maic.masuch}@uni-due.de

Abstract. This paper presents a sense appealing tangible user interface as an innovative technological solution to increase a feeling of closeness for two physically separated persons: an interactive pillow pair allowing intimate voice message exchange over a distance. The pillow shape incorporates the comfortable characteristics of the intimate going-to-bed ritual and is meant to provoke a relaxed and reflective ambience in which dedication for one another can be revealed. A working proof of concept prototype is evaluated in a qualitative study based on a combination of cultural probes and interviews to investigate its applicability for couples living in long-distance relationships. Initial findings indicate that the pillow concept is successful in the matter of providing an appealing solution to make lovers feel closer over a geographical distance. Users slow down, feel warm and safe and compose messages meant to express support, consolation, love and appreciation.

Keywords: Tangible interface · User experience · Closeness · Physical separation · Long distance relationship · Cultural probes

1 Introduction

Flexibility and mobility are major aspects of today's society. Education and career paths are no longer limited to local areas. Additionally, online dating platforms facilitate finding the right partner outside the local scope. As a result, many couples live in Long Distance Relationships (LDR) today. Digital technology keeps them connected over vast geographical distances and theoretically enables them to interact with each other at anytime and anywhere. However, it is questionable whether these common tools are sufficient enough to create meaningful and pleasant interactions that ease coping with separation. The aim of this paper is to explore the target group of physically separated loved ones and to present a reasonable and effective technical solution to overcome the distance between them.

Social interactions, love and the feeling of belonging are major human needs [1]. Interactions taking place in enduring and stable frameworks with the same person are particularly important to satisfy this human need to belong, while a lack of belongingness is considered as harmful, causing ill effects such as loneliness and isolation [2].

© ICST Institute for Computer Sciences, Social Informatics and Telecommunications Engineering 2017
R. Poppe et al. (Eds.): INTETAIN 2016, LNICST 178, pp. 74–85, 2017.
DOI: 10.1007/978-3-319-49616-0_7

A reasonable model to define close relationships is provided by Sternberg's Triangular Theory of Love, which includes three basic components of love: intimacy (closeness felt to another person and emotional investment), passion (state of physical or psychological arousal) and commitment (decision to build a significant bond with someone) [3]. In order to strengthen love, it is important to translate these components into perceivable actions, which is challenging over a distance.

2   Overcoming Separation in Long Distance Relationships

Couples living in LDRs have to overcome several difficulties. Firstly, they need to establish and hold up a certain level of intimacy. This can only be accomplished in a private setting, since reciprocal self-disclosing acts like revealing secrets and desires are essential to build intimacy [4]. Secondly, physical contact is severely missed while being separated [5]. Hence, using physical objects acting as a proxy for the distant partner is a common strategy of LDR couples to feel the partner's presence [6, 7]. These are often received as gifts, which signal great intimate knowledge about the receiver and can thus be seen as responses to self-disclosing acts by displaying understanding, care and appreciation. Thirdly, joint actions and rituals are important for taking part in each other's life, but are hard to schedule and are often mediated by technology. Due to that, LDR couples tend to establish digitally mediated rituals to counteract weakening emotional ties [8]. Recent research investigated how well commonly available tools and novel design approaches are able to counteract these issues and will be discussed in the following.

Video mediated communication (VMC) is a wide-spread technique to communicate over long distances and is used in diverse fields of application [5, 9, 10]. Video connection enables to perceive rich subliminal information by body language, facial expression or the partner's surrounding, which can be used to gain a deeper understanding about the partner's mood and constitution. Hence, VMC is often described as particular natural and offers the opportunity to join in specific actions and rituals [10]. The time synchronously spent with each other demonstrates presence in absence and illustrates effort and engagement since the couple grants a dedicated moment in time in which both are totally focused on the conversation [10]. However, VMC requires great timing, which is hard to schedule for LDR couples. Besides, being captured by a camera diminishes the privacy aspect, which is important to reveal self-disclosing acts [5, 10]. Furthermore, it was observed that the unfulfilled desire to touch the partner causes a sense of an even greater distance between both of them [5].

Smartphones provide a more flexible usage of VMC or at least voice transmission, because they can be used on the go. However, being theoretically available 24/7 does not mean that people are permanently approachable and in the mood for intimate conversations. This might lead to false expectations: Although it is technically possible to respond asynchronously at a later time, people expect each other to respond fast and equally extensive [11]. Delayed responses might result in frustration and negatively influence the enjoyment of intimate messages on both sides, either by waiting for a message or by feeling forced to rush. In contrast, handwritten letters follow a slowed down process that provides time for reflection and demonstrates how much time and effort were spent to create a message, which was found to increase the perceived meaningfulness [7, 11]. As a consequence, future designs should focus on efficient timing that allows taking a dedicated moment in time for reflection as well as a personal and contextual fitting to create meaningful intimate messages.

Most of the commonly available technology sets its focus on explicit information exchange and neglects typical emotional and subtle communication patterns in close relationships [12]. Following a more recent user experience design approach that focuses on the user's emotions, affects and desires, there are various ways of mediating closeness and intimacy over a distance by addressing awareness or expressivity [12]. Those range from simple yet valuable "one-bit communication" like an on/off signal effectively used based on great intimate knowledge [13] to complex synchronous joint actions like having dinner over a distance [14].

Since taking time for synchronous communication can be hard to schedule, innovative asynchronous approaches were more recently developed and tested [15–17]. Here again, results indicate that abstract cues such as texts or visible cues are able to reflect emotions and are sufficient for creating a sense of awareness when being deployed in an interpretable context [16]. Furthermore, recent designs and studies focus on physicalness by providing various approaches: A feeling of relatedness can be enhanced by reconstructing specific movements [17], displaying physical parameters such as heart beat rates [18] or using inflatable vests meant to mimic hugs over a distance [19]. However, finding appropriate ways to physically interact with each other over a distance is a great challenge, since tools might be perceived as too artificial leading to uncomfortableness [15]. Hassenzahl et al. [12] suggest that instead of focusing on directly simulating touch, the experience connected with touch should be addressed by future designs. Following a metaphorical approach, tangible user interfaces can provide pleasant interaction possibilities. Tangible objects inherently have a certain affordance character, which invites users to perform a certain action [20]. Furthermore, a tangible device could serve as a proxy for the distant partner, which helps people to feel closer to each other by interacting with it [7, 9]. Chien et al. [21] introduce a well translated interaction concept in which a pillow is used to leave messages for the partner, but since one pillow has to be shared by the couple, it cannot be used over a great distance. Using a pillow as an interaction device is also followed by two recent commercial projects: Pillow Talk[1], which allows listening to the partner's heartbeat, and Pillo[2], which uses a pillow as an interface for playing games.

3 Development of an Interactive Good Night Pillow Pair

In summary, transmitting intimacy over a distance is important to achieve a feeling of closeness. In this context, privacy and trustworthiness are basic conditions for reciprocal self-disclosure and hence intimacy. The ambiance created should allow users to relax and take time in order to demonstrate appreciation and care by composing

---

[1] http://www.littleriot.com/.

[2] http://pillogames.com/.

reflective messages and to enjoy receiving them. This should be further supported by the device's physicality and interaction pattern. All of these criteria are bundled up to a novel design approach that uses an asynchronous communication pattern, in which interaction depends more on the experience of being connected in a similar mood and environment, rather than on being time-dependent.

3.1 Good Night Pillow Concept

Two interactive pillows connected to each other were designed allowing intimate voice message exchange. Both partners have their own pillow each in order to record a message by talking to it. This message can then be send to the partner's pillow where it waits for the partner to come home and to listen to it in an equally relaxed manner by placing the head on it. The pillow pair is implemented in the context of a couple's goodnight ritual, which is located in the private bedroom offering a trustworthy surrounding for intimate communication. The timing is advantageous for reflective messages, because daily duties are already fulfilled. The pillow shape is associated with coziness and comfort and has the affordance character to calm down and relax. It can be cuddled and hold tight when used as a proxy for the distant partner (see Fig. 1).

Consistent with this conceptual idea the interaction concept is based on quite sound to support the relaxed setting and to shield the conversation in an intimate way. Voice messages can be equally created, send and listened to on both pillows. To preserve the soft and comfortable nature of a pillow, common user input solutions such as buttons cannot be implemented. Instead, the three core functionalities are triggered by gestures performed on the pillow. In order to start the recording, the user needs to hold the pillow tight as long as he/she wants the recording to take place. Through this hugging gesture, the user is forced to concentrate on the message by spending a dedicated moment in time without any distractions. Likewise, the listening function is activated by gently pressing ones head in the cushion. In regard of usability and safety, feedback

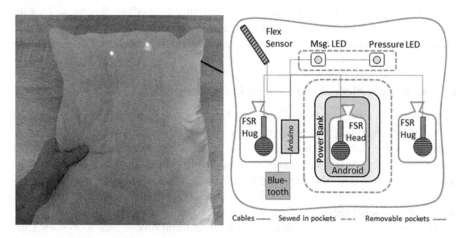

Fig. 1. Final pillow interface on the left and schematic overview on the right.

mechanisms are implemented. A message is not automatically uploaded. Instead, the user is able to listen to the recorded message and potentially revise it before consciously sending it by bending one designated corner of the pillow. In addition, visual feedback is provided by two color changing lights to inform the user about applied pressure, as well as the message's state (see Fig. 1).

3.2 Technical Implementation

Technically, three main components are used: An Arduino board with attached sensors and modules, an Android smartphone for recording as well as playing back sounds and the Dropbox Sync API working as a server to store messages. The Arduino Nano board is equipped with three force sensitive resistors (FSR) (see Fig. 1). Two are placed in small pockets and stowed at both sides of the pillow to detect a hug, the remaining one is placed in the middle of the pillow to detect if the user's head is placed on the pillow. A flex sensor is embedded in the upper left corner of the pillow to control message upload. Two LEDs provide visual feedback: The hug LED changes its color according to applied pressure, whereas the message LED changes its color to indicate an ongoing recording, a waiting message to be send as well as a successful or unsuccessful upload. A Bluetooth module is attached to the board in order to establish a connection to the Android smartphone, which is stuffed inside the pillow's cushion and reacts to incoming Bluetooth commands. The smartphone starts and handles the recording of messages as well as their playback and provides additional user feedback through vibration. Furthermore, its Wi-Fi access is used to connect remote pillow pairs with each other by using the Dropbox Sync API, which allows storing and exchanging messages between remote pillows.

4 Prototype Evaluation

The evaluation followed a user-centered approach focused on user experience to point out initial findings about the prototype's applicability to mediate closeness. To gain in-depth insights about the users and their interaction context, the evaluation was based on qualitative research extended by descriptive quantitative data.

4.1 Evaluation Method and General Procedure

The exploratory survey strategy consisted of two phases. In the first phase the current use of technology was requested to compare the prototype with already existing strategies and to identify most promising fields of application. Participants were encouraged to report personal rituals, such as saying goodnight. The pillow was then presented and tested in the second phase. Here, emotional aspects and the overall interaction context were focused including ambiance, timing, content of messages, physicality, personal meaning of the prototype and attitude towards it.

Two closely interwoven methods were used: cultural probes and interviews. Cultural probes are packages including assortments of artifacts, such as diaries or craft materials. Along with evocative tasks they are meant to record inspirational responses to specific events, feelings or interactions [22]. They subjectively focus on the everyday life and can be used flexibly within private settings without disturbing or unsettling participants [23]. Since results gained by this method are often ambiguous and less appropriate to be formally analyzed [24], additional follow-up interviews in which participants explained the completed materials were conducted. This strategy allowed participants to concisely reflect on their behavior before being interviewed.

The center piece of the first cultural probe package was a handbook in which participants were proposed to answer questions with several techniques: text based methods (e.g. writing story fragments or expressing thoughts by brainstorming) and graphical presentations (e.g. sketching or completing comic scenarios) (see Fig. 2). The cultural probe package of the second phase included the pillow prototype and a diary for recording experiences with it. The two semi-structured interviews followed a pre-defined guideline and took approximately 30 min with each participant being interviewed separately. The interviews were audio recorded, transcribed word-by-word and pseudonymized. In a second step they were analyzed by using the bottom-up technique affinity diagramming in order to identify thematic clusters [24].

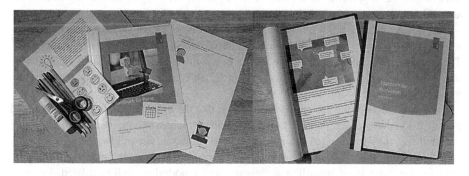

Fig. 2. Cultural probes material including diaries and craft materials.

Only couples living in a LDR were included and were chosen based on divergent patterns (e.g. distance between them, length of love relationship and prior experiences with sharing a flat) in order to gain a wide spectrum of answers while keeping the number of participants small. Three heterosexual couples were recruited ranging in age from 23 to 27, with an average distance of 165 km between them (70–325 km) and approximately 8.6 days spend together per month. The first couple (C1) was together since 1.5 years, never lived in the same city and only met each other at weekends. Couple two (C2) experienced both residing together and being separated across country boarders within their 5.5 years as a couple. The third couple (C3) (together since 0.5 years) was in a transition phase at the study's point in time because he just moved to another city.

The study was conducted in two phases and required three appointments with participants. In the beginning, participants were introduced to the study and equipped with the first package. After 7 days to fill out the material participants were met again for the first interview. Afterwards, the second phase started with handing out the second cultural probe package. The couples had 10 days to test the pillow and were then met for the final 30-min interviews.

4.2 Results

Results from the first study phase confirmed the assumptions made about LDR couples: While being separated, physical aspects were missed most and difficulties of planning shared activities occurred. The partner was mostly missed in the evenings (56 %) and mainly due to situations that would usually be experienced together. Two of the three couples follow a ritual pattern to communicate while being apart: C2 uses Skype every evening and keeps the video connection open the whole night while sleeping. C1 uses text messages in the evenings and reported that sometimes an almost synchronous chatting unfolds, whereas other messages were not read until the next morning. This ritual behavior was important for both couples. Yet, C1 thinks that the text messages themselves could be replaced by any other medium, whereas C2 reported that the video connection was too important to be replaced and that e.g. a phone call would not create the same sense of presence in absence. C3 was newly challenged with living in a LDR and did not show established routines yet.

In the second phase the pillow prototype was deployed. In summary 60 messages were exchanged over the pillows, hence approximately 10 messages per participant. The average length of messages was 00:29 min with the shortest message being only one second and the longest message lasting 02:38 min. A tendency was found that messages got longer over time.

The interviews of the second phase revealed that the basic interaction concept of the pillow worked for participants. They particularly emphasized the cozy interface and reported that they felt invited to calm down and to cuddle the pillow. The interaction concept of lying down on the pillow in order to trigger message playback and to hold it tight for the purpose of recording a message was reported as well-translated. Participants enjoyed the interaction with the pillow and particularly stressed the importance of the LEDs' visible feedback responding to the user's applied pressure as well as the tactile vibratory feedback. Furthermore, the low sound volume and the fact that the pillow was exclusively used among the couple were mentioned to support intimate communication. The going-to-bed setting was another important factor, because this limited context attached further meaning to the messages: Participants reported that they were able to immerse into the situation captured by their partners.

All these factors build the basement for three types of unique experiences participants made with the pillow (identified by affinity diagramming): slow movement, moment capturing and reflection. Participants reported that due to the soft interface, the low sound volume and the timing, they felt slowed down and focused on the partner. They consciously tried to prevent potentially disturbing factors, e.g. an enabled TV, in order to not compromise the ambiance. Additionally, besides taking time for oneself to record a message, it was also meant to spend a dedicated moment in time while listening to the partner's saying. Not being able to intervene the partner was reported as beneficial. On the one hand it is a matter of respect and devotion, on the other hand it facilitates the opportunity to capture a moment in which one can immerse. One participant explained: *"I can't exercise influence on what she is saying. Therefore, it is something, it shall not sound too enthusiastic, but it is something monumental that you can't influence this moment. [...] [The message] was like a small glass of compote, which you filled and then you can simply open it and then due to these scents, to carry this metaphor further, through these scents or this taste, you were able to immerse into this situation"* (C2, male, 27).

Furthermore, having time to phrase a message was believed to support reflective behavior. The participants' messages were thought through and they took a significant amount of time to compose a valuable and meaningful message before sending it to their partners. They tried to put themselves in the partner's place to figure out what content would be enjoyed most. The playback mechanism of a recorded message before being able to send it fostered this behavior. One participant explained that this mechanism would be advantageous in disputes. Instead of reacting too emotional, it would help to calm down before responding hastily and improperly.

Regarding the content of messages, different topics and purposes could be identified. There were messages meant to keep the other one on track about daily activities and to verbally express love and care. Other messages were more creative (e.g. containing songs or bedtime stories) and considered as more special. Furthermore, the meaning of a message was believed to be increased by well-considered timing, like an up-cheering message in the night before an important exam. Besides effort being demonstrated by time and emotional investment, one participant indicated the physical investment of applying pressure to the pillow while recording a long message. In his opinion it further underlined the effort and thus the dedication for one another, again increasing meaningfulness. Generally, messages were interpreted as small gifts, rather than as a source of information. Joyful curiosity was reported before lying on the pillow to hear a new message. Accordingly, participants claimed that no negative messages should be transmitted through the pillow, since it would ruin the caring experience. In this context one participant explained: *"The pillow [suppresses unfriendly utterances] because it is so soft. It gives you closeness and as a child you also had this cuddle-pillow. That is something familiar, where you seek for solace"* (C2, female, 26).

In response to questions about the perceived level of connectedness, a range of responses was elicited. C1, who was used to exchange text-based messages, reported an increased sense of connectedness using the pillow due to voice transmission as well as the cozy overall situation and exclusivity of messages. This view was echoed and expanded by C3, who particularly referred to the physical aspects of the pillow when giving reason to higher perceived connectedness. Although C2 appreciated the tactile interaction experience as well, they both agreed that the pillow could not replace their daily Skype ritual in the matter of perceived connectedness. The main reason was the lack of direct synchronous communication that they were used to. However, most participants indicated that the pillow had or would have helped them to overcome moments in which they missed their partners. Advantageous was the fact that the pillow could be used as a proxy when the partner was not directly available. Participants reported that in contrast to smartphones and computers, the soft texture was more human-like and that a feeling similar to cuddling with the partner evoked by interacting with it.

During the testing period, most participants required time to make themselves comfortable with using the pillow. Speaking to a pillow, listening to one's own voice and thinking about pleasant content was unfamiliar and constituted an inhibition threshold that needed to be overcome. Furthermore, some participants were initially concerned about the pillow's trustworthiness and felt insecure if their message would please their partner, since they did not get a direct reaction to it in response. However, all of these initial concerns diminished over time. Receiving a message in response eased the feeling of uncomfortableness and the couples fell into a routinized pattern.

Finally, participants were asked if they could imagine themselves using the pillow again over a longer time span. Half of them agreed to this question, whereas two answered with yes, but felt unsure about possible wear-out effects and only one participant explained that he would not need to use the pillow again, because of his already successfully established Skype ritual that was more beneficial in his opinion.

4.3 Discussion

Although results do not allow for universally valid statements due to the small group of participants, the combination of cultural probes and semi-structured interviews led to profound insights about the target group, their opinions and attitudes towards the pillow concept. The pillows are supposed to provide an intimate setting in which meaningful messages are exchanged aiming at a greater sense of connectedness. In the following it is discussed how well the concept was able to meet these requirements.

Since the pillow was exclusively used among designated partners and locally limited to the bedroom, a sufficient sense of privacy evolved to transmit intimate messages. This was further supported by the low sound volume that did not expose the partner. However, in the beginning an inhibition threshold was identified. On the one hand, participants felt unsure about the trustworthiness of the device, which might be due to its novelty and the lack of prior experiences with comparable products. On the other hand, using the pillow is an act of self-disclosure. As it is explained by the intimacy model [4], this kind of interaction requires an equivalent response to provide reciprocity. This leads to the assumption that initial inhibition thresholds result from intermittently delayed feedback (and might be higher compared to a synchronous communication). Furthermore, this can also explain why participants felt much more comfortable about sending messages after they received a similar message or positive feedback of their partner. Accordingly, we observed an increasing length of messages over time.

In respect of meaningfulness the chosen going-to-bed setting and the matching pillow shape can be identified as important facilitators. Participants stated that they inherently associated the pillow with relaxation, which explicitly invited them to take time for their messages. Thus, results indicate strong tendencies of reflective behavior: It was considered what kind of content would be delightful and in what kind of mood the other might be when receiving the message. Furthermore, participants appreciated the implemented play-back function and revised their messages before sending them off. Similar to findings about handwritten letters [11], we assume that taking time to choose the right words intensified the meaning of messages. Another important aspect was the familiar environment in which messages were recorded, since it allowed participants to immerse in the situation and to experience a sense of taking part in this moment. This not only fits to results stated by King et al., who assume that a shared experience is often related to a specific location [7], but also fosters the approach to experience joint actions based on a specific individual moment rather than on time. Accordingly, this promotes the assumed potential of asynchronous techniques to mediate intimacy and closeness over a distance.

Generally, the pillow was less seen as a tool to communicate with each other, but rather as a device to demonstrate love, awareness, care and appreciation due to its gift-giving character, which moreover allowed immersion into a specific moment. Furthermore, the pillow acted as a proxy for the distant partner to some extent, which led to a feeling of being warm and safe and therefore completed the overall ambiance. Based on the discussion above, we conclude that the pillow concept works. However, that does not give evidence to its general suitability for every type of couple. Regarding everyday applicability, the three divergent couple manifestations indicate that prior experience of using technology to mediate intimacy and connectedness influences the likeliness of establishing a ritual framework. When being used to communicating synchronously, the pillow might not be sufficient to create a greater sense of connectedness due to its asynchronicity. However, all participants identified the tactile experience as well as the embedding into a specific context as added values. This seems to be a supplement and the major advantage towards common tools.

5 Conclusion and Future Work

The qualitative evaluation of the pillow concept with couples in LDRs led to reasonable initial findings proofing the general concept and supporting its applicability in the tested field. The pillow's distinctive characteristics like the soft and cozy tangible interface, it's embedding into the specific, intimate application context of the going-to-bed ritual and the hug-alike interaction mechanisms result in reciprocal acts of self-disclosure and great perceived connectedness. Hence, those features distinguish the device from commonly existing communication tools and provide additional value regarding meaningfulness and intimacy. Though the pillow device is not sufficient to replace synchronous communication between partners, it is supposed to be a valuable complement to enrich interaction, to retain love despite physical separation and thus to support the quality of human relationships. While results from the initial evaluation display predominantly positive resonance, future long-term comparative studies should be conducted that also include quantitative methodology in order to further elaborate on the pillows' effects and the potential advantages and disadvantages compared to other communication tools, particularly in situations such as disputes or moments of great yearning for the partner. Furthermore, an experimental comparison with other objects, which are for example less soft or which are deployed in other home-settings, can be conducted to prove benefits of the pillow shape and the bedroom setting.

Besides, the pillow concept is supposed to be applicable to other target groups of separated loved ones as well. While LDRs were focused in the study at hand, parent-child relationships might also benefit from the device in case of physical separation.

Social support and care are particularly needed in serious situations such as illness and significantly help in regard to well-being and health [25, 26]. Accordingly, we initially tested the pillow with a family who was physically separated due to cancer therapy of one child, as well. Within this serious context, the pillow appeared to have a positive effect in providing support and care, and its consolation character was emphasized. The mother claimed that she would like to use the pillow when her children feel sad and seek for solace while she is unable to be physically present. Yet, the trial revealed that the simple pillow shape seemed to be less appropriate for children. Hence, we suggest a teddy bear shape and an additional focus on more playful interaction methods to further engage children as well. Future research in this field will follow to investigate the pillows' applicability in other context than LDRs and to particularly prove its benefits regarding coping strategies for loneliness in hospitalized settings.

References

1. Maslow, A.H.: Motivation und Persönlichkeit. Rowohlt Taschenbuchverlag, Reinbeck bei Hamburg (2005)
2. Baumeister, R.F., Leary, M.R.: The need to belong: desire for interpersonal attachments as a fundamental human motivation. Psychol. Bull. 117(3), 497–529 (1995)
3. Hendrick, S.S., Hendrick, C.: Liking, Loving and Relating. Brooks/Cole Publishing Company, Pacific Grove (1992)
4. Jiang, C.L., Hancock, J.T.: Absence makes the communication grow fonder: geographic separation, interpersonal media, and intimacy in dating relationships. J. Commun. 63(3), 556–577 (2013)
5. Neustaedter, C., Greenberg, S.: Intimacy in long-distance relationships over video chat. In: CHI 2012 Proceedings of the SIGCHI Conference on Human Factors in Computing Systems, pp. 753–762. ACM, Austin (2012)
6. Vetere, F., Gibbs, M.R., Kjeldskov, J., Howard, S., Mueller, F., Pedell, S., Mecoles, K., Bunyan, M.: Mediating intimacy: designing technologies to support strong-tie relationships. In: CHI 2005 Proceedings of the SIGCHI Conference on Human Factors in Computing Systems, pp. 471–480. ACM, Portland (2005)
7. King, S., Forlizzi, J.: Slow messaging: intimate communication for couples living at a distance. In: DPPI Designing Pleasurable Products and Interfaces, Newcastle upon Tyne, pp. 452–454 (2007)
8. Lim, H., Suh, B.: Now here or nowhere: conflict resolution strategies for intimate relationship in diverse geographical contexts. In: CSCW Companion 2014 Proceedings of the Companion Publication of the 17th ACM Conference on Computer Supported Cooperative Work & Social Computing, pp. 197–200. ACM, Baltimore (2014)
9. Yarosh, S., Abowd, G.D.: Mediated parent-child contact in work-separated families. In: CHI 2011: Proceedings of the SIGCHI Conference on Human Factors in Computing Systems, pp. 1185–1194. ACM, Vancouver (2011)
10. Kirk, D., Sellen, A., Cao, X.: Home video communication: mediating "closeness". In: Proceedings of the 2010 ACM Conference on Computer Supported Cooperative Work (CSCW), pp. 135–144. ACM, Savannah (2010)

11. Lindley, S.E., Harper, R., Sellen, A.: Desiring to be in touch in a changing communications landscape: attitudes of older adults. In: CHI 2009 Proceedings of the SIGCHI Conference on Human Factors in Computing Systems, pp. 1693–1702. ACM, Boston (2009)

12. Hassenzahl, M., Heidecker, S., Eckoldt, K., Diefenbach, S., Hillmann, U.: All you need is love: current strategies of mediating intimate relationships through technology. ACM Trans. Comput. Hum. Interact. **19**(4), 1–19 (2012). Article 30

13. Kaye, J., Levitt, M.K., Nevins, J., Golden, J., Schmidt, V.: Communicating intimacy one bit at a time. In: CHI 2005 Extended Abstracts on Human Factors in Computing Systems, pp. 1529–1532. ACM, Portland (2005)

14. Wei, J., Cheok, A.D., Nakatsu, R.: Let's have dinner together: evaluate the mediated co-dining experience. In: ICMI 2012: Proceedings of the 14th ACM International Conference on Multimodal Interaction, pp. 225–228. ACM, Santa Monica (2012)

15. Nawahdah, M., Inoue, T.: Virtually dining together in time-shifted environment: KIZUNA design. In: CSCW 2013 Proceedings of the 2013 Conference on Computer Supported Cooperative Work, pp. 779–788. ACM, San Antonio (2013)

16. Kwok, T.C., Huang, M.X., Tam, W.C., Ngai, G.: Emotar: communicating feelings through video sharing. In: IUI 2015 Proceedings of the 20th International Conference on Intelligent User Interfaces, pp. 374–378. ACM, Atlanta (2015)

17. Schmeer, J., Baffi, T.: Touch trace mirror: asynchronous, collaborative messaging as a concept for creating a relatedness experience. In: TEI 2011 Proceedings of the Fifth International Conference on Tangible, Embedded, and Embodied Interaction, pp. 303–304. ACM, Funchal (2011)

18. Lotan, G., Croft, C.: ImPulse. In: CHI 2007 Extended Abstracts on Human Factors in Computing, pp. 1983–1988. ACM, San Jose (2007)

19. Teh, J.K.S., Cheok, A.D., Peiris, R.L., Choi, Y., Thuong, V., Lai, S.: Huggy pajama: a mobile parent and child hugging communication system. In: IDC 2008: Proceedings of the 7th International Conference on Interaction Design and Children, pp. 250–257. ACM, Chicago (2008)

20. Norman, D.A.: The Design of Everyday Things. Basic Books, New York (2002)

21. Chien, W.C., Diefenbach, S., Hassenzahl, M.: The whisper pillow: a study of technology-mediated emotional expression in close relationships. In: Design: Cultural Probes, pp. 51–59. ACM, Newcastle upon Tyne (2013)

22. Gaver, B., Dunne, T., Pacenti, E.: Cultural probes. Interactions **6**, 21–29 (1999)

23. Crabtree, A., Hemmings, T., Rodden, T., Cheverst, K., Clarke, K., Dewsbury, G., Hughes, J., Rouncefield, M.: Designing with care: adapting cultural probes to inform design in sensitive settings. In: Proceedings of OzCHI 2003, New Directions in Interaction Information environments, Media and Technology, pp. 4–13. ACM, Brisbane (2003)

24. Martin, B., Hannington, B.: Universal Methods of Design: 100 Ways to Research Complex Problems, Develop Innovative Ideas, and Design Effective Solutions. Rockport Publishers, Beverly (2012)

25. Spiegel, D., Kraemer, H.C., Bloom, J.R., Gottheil, E.: Effect of psychological treatment on survival of patients with metastatic breast cancer. Lancet **2**(8668), 888–891 (1989)

26. Matire, L.M., Lustig, A.P., Schulz, R., Miller, G.E., Helgeson, V.S.: Is it beneficial to involve a family member? A meta-analysis of psychosocial interventions for chronic illness. Health Psychol. **23**(6), 599–611 (2004)

Analyzing Fear Using a Single-Sensor EEG Device

Jeroen de Man$^{(\boxtimes)}$ and Nicolette Stassen

Department of Computer Science,
VU University Amsterdam, Amsterdam, The Netherlands
j.de.man@vu.nl, n.g.m.j.stassen@student.vu.nl

Abstract. Single-sensor EEG hardware provides possibilities for researchers to measure fear in human beings. Previous research show that consumer-grade EEG devices can be used to measure different states of mind. However, as is often the case with similar research, post-hoc questionnaires are used to measure the emotional state. This paper will focus on the physiological and psychological state of an individual in fear, comparing continuous subjective feedback with EEG measurements. Data has been collected using a Myndplay Brainband and a rotary meter, while 30 subjects viewed soothing and scary films. The rotary meter proved useful for obtaining continuous feedback and, although more research is needed, differences in brainwaves for fearful and calm states are found for multiple frequency bands.

Keywords: Fear analysis · EEG · Psychological response · Physiological response

1 Introduction

Emotions like fear are difficult to measure. On the psychological level, subjective ratings can be biased and difficult to compare. On the physiological level, multiple techniques can be used to measure the level of fear, like fMRI's, skin conductance or heart rate monitors. If you measure the physiological effects, it is still very hard to know if these effects are caused by fear, or by another factor. For example, sweating can be caused by experiencing fear, but on a hot summer day it is difficult to say if the sweating is caused by fear or by the heat. More often electroencephalography (EEG) is used to measure physiological changes of a human being. An EEG device measures the brainwaves of an individual.

In several studies, the physiological level of fear is measured using skin conductance and heart rate [1–3]. These studies show that skin conductance is a good method to measure the physiological effects of fear. Though, skin conductance is also a multifaceted phenomenon. It shows elevation in sweating in fear, but also in other emotions [4]. This makes it hard to recognize if the sweating is caused by fear or another emotion. Using an EEG headset, the researcher has a better indication of the emotion of an individual. However, professional EEG devices with over a hundred sensors are difficult to use and very expensive. These days, single-sensor EEG devices are

© ICST Institute for Computer Sciences, Social Informatics and Telecommunications Engineering 2017
R. Poppe et al. (Eds.): INTETAIN 2016, LNICST 178, pp. 86–96, 2017.
DOI: 10.1007/978-3-319-49616-0_8

becoming more readily available. These consumer-grade headsets only have a few sensors and are mostly used for gaming purposes [5].

Because these headsets have fewer sensors, it could be that data retrieved from these headsets are not as reliable or accurate as professional EEG devices. To use these single-sensor headsets in research, it is necessary to know if it is possible to measure emotions like fear with these headsets. If this would be possible, applications would be able to use these single-sensor headsets as an input device, resulting in a more user-friendly setup and possibly even more accurate results. This in turn could be beneficial for any such application, ranging from entertainment to serious gaming and training.

This research project will focus on the question if such psychological and physiological levels of fear are related to each other. In other words, do measurements from single-sensor EEG devices correspond with physiological measurements and subjective ratings with regard to fear. This will be done by first researching if single-sensor EEG devices, in this case the MyndPlay Brainband, can be used to measure fear responses of an individual. Second, using continuous subjective ratings of fear, the EEG measurements are explored to find indicators for different aspects of fear.

2   Background

The limbic system is a set of brain structures that lies directly under the cerebrum. The limbic system is considered to play a major role in emotion processing. Using functional magnetic resonance imaging (fMRI) researchers demonstrate that the amygdala (a part of the limbic system) shows a higher activity in response of fear stimuli [6]. Because the limbic system is a structure deep in the brain, the use of fMRI was the most common non-invasive technique to measure these fear responses.

It was long thought that emotions like fear were only processed in the limbic system. However, more recent research suggests that not only the limbic system is responsible for emotion processing and that there is some kind of emotion circuit in the brain that processes emotions [7]. This would mean that brainwaves are produced while processing emotions. Brainwaves are synchronized electrical pulses from neurons communicating with each other. Brainwaves can be detected by the use of an electroencephalography (EEG) recorder. EEG is a non-invasive measurement of electronic activity on the scalp. Studies used an EEG recorder to find more brain areas involved in emotion processing and one of these studies show that the right frontal region of the brain is activated for negative emotions such as fear [8]. In other research not only different brain regions activated during emotions like fear was looked at, they also investigated a certain ratio called the slow wave/fast wave ratio [9]. Putman et al. found that the slow wave/fast wave ratio (SW/FW) is increased in hyperactivity disorder and that this SW/FW correlates negatively with fearful modulation.

Nowadays, EEG devices are not only available for professionals and more and more consumer-grade devices using dry electrodes become available. This makes the EEG device cheap as well as easy to use for non-professionals. There is however the question to what extent these devices can be used for research and other purposes, including questions such as are the measurements accurate enough or can they be used reliably.

Studies show promising results about the use of these single-sensor EEG headsets for research to detect different mental states [10, 11]. In this paper a further analysis is made of measuring emotions with a single-sensor EEG device.

3 Method

The research conducted for this paper is explained in detail below. First, more information on the participants and measurements taken are given. Thereafter, the procedure for the experiment is explained as is the analysis that will be performed on the data gathered.

Participants. The sample consisted of 30 students and employees from the VU University Amsterdam. From these participants, 70% were male (N = 21) and 30% were female (N = 9). The youngest participant was 18 years old and the oldest participant was 38 years old (M = 22.20, SD = 3.69).

Measures. To measure the psychological level of fear of the subjects, the subject will make use of a rotary potentiometer. The rotary potentiometer will be connected to a Phidget board and gives continuous values from zero to 1000. Every second an average of all the values will be recorded, which will be scaled to a value between 0 and 10, rounded down and averaged over all participants to end up with a single rotary meter value for each second. Besides the rotary meter values, there is a seven-item questionnaire about the feelings of the subject. Individuals answer the items on a five point Likert scale. EEG signals are used to measure the physiological effects. It measures the brain waves of a human, expressed in Hertz. The MyndPlay Brainband, used in this study, is a single sensor EEG headset providing data at a sampling rate of 512 Hz. It can recognize eight different types of EEG frequency bands (brainwaves): delta (0.5–2.75 Hz), theta (3.5–6.75 Hz), low-alpha (7.5–9.25 Hz), high-alpha (10–11.75 Hz), low-beta (13–16.75 Hz), high-beta (18–29.75 Hz), low-gamma (31–39.75 Hz), and mid-gamma (41–49.75 Hz).

Procedure. All the participants from the sample are asked to watch a set of videos used in previous research [11, 12]. Before the subjects watch the video, they will practice using the rotary meter. In this research, four videos will be presented to the subjects. The first video is a relaxing video of a beach, the second video is a documentary, the third video is a stressful video with scary clips, and the last video is again the video of a beach. The EEG is measured during this whole trial. During the trial, the subject is asked to turn the rotary meter if he or she feels more scared in order to measure the subjective thoughts of the individual. After this, the participant is asked to fill in a few questions about how they felt during the trial. All the questionnaires and measurements are anonymous.

Data Analysis. The data analysis of this research consists of three parts. The MyndPlay BrainBand provides EEG measurement per second with brainwaves ranging from delta to mid-gamma, as well as eSense^{TM} values for attention and meditation. The eSense^{TM} values will not be used in this study. The brainwaves are categorized in delta, theta, low-alpha, high-alpha, low-beta, high-beta, low-gamma or mid-gamma waves.

Firstly, the average values of the rotary meter will be used as an approximation of an overall subjective rating of fear for that video. This will be done to see if the rotary values are more or less comparable to subjective ratings given in post-hoc question-naires and results found in previous research.

To determine if there is a difference between the brainwaves in calm and fearful state, a paired t-test will be used. This will be done by comparing peaks of the calm state and fearful state. In this research, the fearful state is measured during the stressful video. The calm state is measured during the documentary and is used as a baseline. Peaks will be determined individually by finding values more than four standard deviations away from the mean value of the individual during the calm state. This will be referred to as the peak-value. Consequently, all the peaks are summed up per person per brainwave.

Next, the brainwaves of the calm and fearful state will be compared. To compare these states, the brainwaves will be processed to get a peak-value ratio. This will be done by dividing the amplitude of the brainwave by the peak-value of the individual. This peak-value ratio will signify a possible discrepancy between a brainwave value and the peak-value. If this ratio is higher than one, it will mean that there is a peak at that moment. This peak-value ratio is calculated in order to dismiss noise of the different individuals. The peak-value ratio will be compared to the video content. This will be a subjective analysis.

Visualizations will be made in order to show the relation between the psychological and physiological levels of the individuals. This is done by making graphs displaying the relation between the rotary meter values and the peak-value ratio of the EEG in fearful state. These graphs will be analyzed manually to find which frequencies of brainwaves correspond with subjective ratings of fear.

4   Results

Below various results of the experiment are presented. At first, the subjective ratings alone are considered, after which these ratings are compared with the measurements taken with the single-sensor EEG device. Here, first the calm and fearful state are compared using various frequencies, after which those frequencies are compared with the continuous subjective ratings of fear gathered with the rotary meter.

4.1   Subjective Feelings

The first aim of this research was to see if the rotary meter is a reliable way to measure the subjective feelings of an individual. Figure 1 shows the average rotary meter values during the different videos. As can be seen, during the scary video the test group was most frightened. However, in the beach videos some people felt a little frightened as well. This pattern corresponds with subjective ratings found in similar experiments using the same videos [11, 12] and is supported by the answers of this questionnaire as well. Here, participants indicated that they did not feel completely calm during the first video of the beach and were even less calm during the second video of the beach.

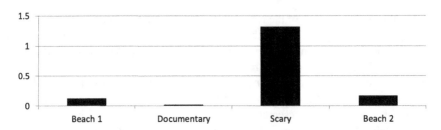

Fig. 1. Average rotary meter values for the different videos.

Moreover, participants did feel frightened during the third video and experienced various startle moments, but did continue to watch the video without closing their eyes.

4.2   Brainwaves in Calm and Fearful State

The first aim of this research was to test if there is a difference between the amount of brainwave peaks in a calm state and a fearful state. To test this, a paired t-test was conducted, comparing the amount of peaks in calm state and fearful state. This was done per brainwave. The paired t-test results show that there is a significant difference between the peak levels in calm state and fearful state for the delta ($p = 0.003$), theta ($p = 0.005$), low-alpha ($p = 0.048$), high-beta ($p = 0.030$), low-gamma ($p = 0.049$) and mid-gamma brainwaves ($p = 0.011$).

Figures 2, 3 and 4 show the peak-value ratio of the brainwaves during the documentary and the scary film of the delta, low-beta and low-gamma bands. The x-axis represents the time and the y-axis represents the average value of all the trials of the peak-value ratio. In these graphs, the grey line corresponds with the brainwave in the fearful state. The black line represents the brainwave in the documentary. The documentary was 180 s long and the scary film was 310 s long.

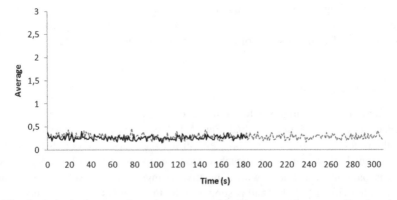

Fig. 2. Delta brainwaves from documentary (black) compared to scary film (grey).

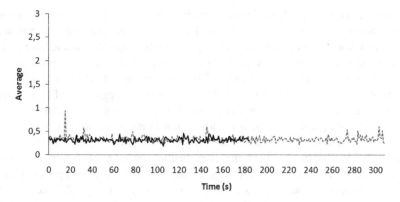

Fig. 3. High-beta brainwaves from documentary (black) compared to scary film (grey).

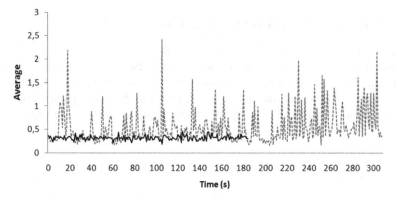

Fig. 4. Low-gamma brainwaves from documentary (black) compared to scary film (grey).

In this study there will be focused on two kinds of fearful states. First, there are the startle moments. In the video used, two of such moments occur at 14 and 30 s into the video. Secondly, there are the moments where the tension is rising for the viewer. These are the moments where the viewer thinks something is going to happen, but nothing did so far. In the video used, two of those scenes were shown from 15 to 30 and 177 to 227 s into the film.

As can be seen in Fig. 2, the delta brainwave does not specifically react to one of these fearful moments. The two lines overlap with each other. This means that the peak-value ratio in the documentary and the scary film are very alike. The delta band does not react on the fearful moments.

As can be seen in Fig. 3, the high-beta brainwaves react on the startle moments, but not to the moments of tension. The dashed grey line from the scary film is higher than the black line of the documentary during the startle moments, but not during the moments of tension. This means that the peak-value ratio of the low-beta band is higher in the scary film during these startle moments than the peak-value ratio during the documentary. The high-beta band reacts only on the startle moments.

As can be seen in Fig. 4, the low-gamma brainwaves react on the startle moments as well as some of the moments of tension. The grey line from the scary film is higher than the black line of the documentary during the startle moments. During the moments of tension, the low-gamma brainwave has more activity during most of this moment. It is seen that from seconds 15 to 20 and 182 to 190 into the film, the low-gamma has a higher peak-value ratio in fearful state. This is during the beginning of these tension moments. The low-gamma band reacts on the startle and tension moments.

Overall, the high-alpha, low-beta and low-gamma brainwaves differ most from each other in the calm and fearful state. These frequency bands react the most in fearful situations. The low-alpha, low-beta, high-beta and low-gamma brainwaves react on the startle moments. The high-alpha, low-beta and low-gamma react on some of the moments of tension. However, this is only a preliminary finding and more (targeted) experiments are required to identify exact causes for each activity in the various frequencies.

4.3   Rotary Meter Values and EEG Peak Levels

The second part of this research was to test if there is a relation between the psychological level, the rotary meter data, and the physiological level, the EEG levels, in fearful state. Figures 5 and 6 show the rotary meter values and the peak-value ratio of the brainwaves of the scary film over time. The dashed grey line represents the rotary meter values, while the black line represents the brainwave values over time.

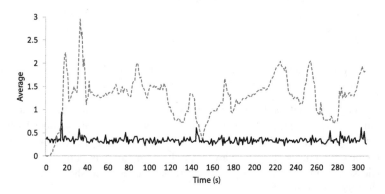

Fig. 5. High-beta brainwaves (solid black) compared to rotary meter values (dashed grey).

Figure 5 represents the high-beta band compared to the rotary meter values. In the previous subsection, it is shown that the high-beta band reacts on startle moments on seconds 14 and 30. It is expected that the rotary meter values will be higher on these moments as well. Looking at the rotary meter values, there are two peaks right after the peaks of the high-beta band, on seconds 20 and 35 into the video. These peaks of the rotary meter show that the subjects were more scared on the startle moments. The rotary meter values do show a delay.

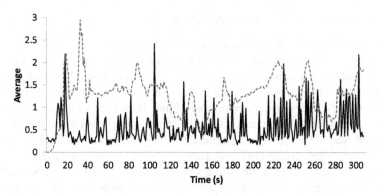

Fig. 6. Low-gamma brainwaves (solid black) compared to rotary meter values (dashed grey).

Figure 6 represents the low-gamma band compared to the rotary meter values. In the previous subsection, it is shown that the low-gamma band reacts on the beginning of tension moments. It is expected that the rotary meter values will get higher over the time on these tension moments. Looking at the rotary meter values, these get progressively higher from seconds 22 and 180 into the film. These progressively higher values of the rotary meter show that the subjects gradually got more frightened. The rotary meter values again show a delay with the tension moments of the videos.

5   Discussion

Different results are reported in the previous section. In this section, the results of the major findings will be discussed. First, the significance found in the peaks of the documentary compared to the scary film will be discussed. Secondly, the results of the peak-value ratios in the different films are of interest. Thirdly, the rotary meter values compared with the questionnaire will be discussed. Lastly, the rotary meter values compared with the brainwaves are of interest.c

5.1   Peaks in Calm and Fearful State

There is a significant difference found in most of the brainwaves of the subjects in calm and fearful state. These findings do not correspond to previous research [11]. This can be explained by the different method used to define peaks in the brainwaves. The method used in this research is based on the method used in the research of De Man, with the main difference being that they used the standard deviation of an individual while watching the first beach video. In this research, the standard deviation of an individual watching the documentary is used. The standard deviation of the documentary is used, because many subjects indicated they were stressed during the first beach video. They expected something scary to happen. In the documentary they were calmer. The documentary therefore is a better baseline. This could be an explanation for the different findings. The fact that significant differences were found, suggests that a low level EEG device like the MyndPlay Brainband can indeed be used to measure an emotion such as fear.

5.2   Brainwaves in Calm and Fearful State

The results of the peak-value ratios in the different films are very promising. Though research about EEG brainwaves in different settings is still very recent, these results show that different brainwaves react on different aspects of fear. The higher frequency bands, like the beta and gamma, seem to have more activity during the fearful film. This corresponds with the hypothesis that higher frequency bands are more active during moments of concentration [13]. If the low-alpha, low-beta, high-beta and low-gamma waves have a higher amplitude, it might suggest that the person has a startle moment. There are however numerous reactions visible in the peak-value ratios which are more difficult to relate to the video content in this manner. As such, it is important to continue this line of research and devise more focused experiments to figure out the exact nature of these reactions.

5.3   Subjective Feelings

Looking at the values of the questionnaire and the rotary meter, it can be seen that the rotary meter gives a good representation of the subjective feelings of the individuals. The rotary meter values reflect the answers in the questionnaire and are in line with results found in previous research. The subjects indicated that they did not feel calmer during the second beach video than during the first beach video. The rotary meter values show a slightly higher average in the second beach video. This can suggest that the rotary meter is a good indicator of the subjective feelings of an individual over time and could result in more fine grained results than Likert scales tend to provide. Using a rotary meter to show the subjective feelings instead of a questionnaire afterwards, can thus be very useful in research. This way, subjects are not distracted by other factors of the test that can change their feelings afterwards. The rotary meter is not difficult to use for either the researcher or the participant. It is necessary to show the participant how the rotary meter works beforehand, otherwise the subject seems to forget to use the rotary meter.

5.4   Rotary Meter Values and EEG Peak Levels

The results show that the rotary meter values have some correlation with the brainwaves. Though it is hard to test this correlation, as different brainwaves seem to react to different aspects of fear. To test the correlation between the brainwaves and the subjective feelings, there has to be a research testing for only one aspect of fear. For example, there could be a study where subjects watch a video with only startle moments. Then it can be statistically tested which brainwave reacts to these startle moments and a correlation test can be conducted. It can be seen in the graphs that there seems to be a delay between the brainwaves and the rotary meter data. This is likely caused by the reaction time of the participant. When testing for correlation between the physiological and psychological effects of fear, the reaction time of the individual has to be taken into account.

6 Conclusion

Using a single-sensor EEG device and a rotary meter, psychological and physiological reactions towards fearful stimuli were analyzed. On various levels, promising results were found. For one, a difference was found in the amount of peaks and in the peak-value ratio between the brainwaves in calm and fearful state. Moreover, it appears that different brainwave frequency bands react to different aspects of fear, like startle moments. On the other hand, using a rotary meter to retrieve continuous subjective ratings of fear worked very well. Although subjects needed to practice using the rotary meter beforehand, using the device did not interfere with the experiment and viewing.

Nevertheless, more research has to be done to determine exactly which brainwaves react to which aspect of fear as well as the response to other types of emotion or activity. Especially experiments focusing on very specific triggers should be considered to underpin the exact causes of the various reactions found in the EEG measurements. It is however clear that even with these low-cost consumer-grade EEG headsets, various emotional responses can be detected.

Acknowledgements. Special thanks go out to Tibor Bosse and Marco Otte, for providing the necessary support for this research.

References

1. Ax, A.F.: The physiological differentiation between fear and anger in humans. Psychosom. Med. **15**, 433–442 (1953)
2. Hodges, W., Spielberger, C.: The effects of threat of shock on heart rate for subjects who differ in manifest anxiety and fear of shock. Psychophysiology (2007)
3. Williams, L.M., Phillips, M.L., Brammer, M.J., Skerrett, D., Lagopoulos, J., Rennie, C., Bahramali, H., Olivieri, G., David, A.S., Peduto, A., Gordon, E.: Arousal dissociates amygdala and hippocampal fear responses: evidence from simultaneous fMRI and skin conductance recording. NeuroImage **14**, 1070–1079 (2001)
4. Figner, B., R.O., M.: Using skin conductance in judgement and decision making research. In: A Handbook of Process Tracing Methods for Decision Research: A Critical Review and User's Guide, pp. 163–184 (2010)
5. NeuroSky: Brain Wave Signal (EEG) of NeuroSky, Inc. (2009)
6. Breiter, H.C., Etcoff, N.L., Whalen, P.J., Kennedy, W.A., Rauch, S.L., Buckner, R.L., Strauss, M.M., Hyman, S.E., Rosen, B.R.: Response and habituation of the human amygdala during visual processing of facial expression. Neuron **17**, 875–887 (1996)
7. LeDoux, J.E.: Emotion circuits in the brain. Ann. Rev. Neurosci. **23**, 155–184 (2000)
8. Ahern, G.L., Schwarts, G.E.: Differential lateralization for positive and negative emotion in the human brain: EEG spectral analysis. Neuropsychologia **23**, 745–755 (1985)
9. Putman, P., van Peer, J., Maimari, I., van der Werff, S.: EEG theta/beta ratio in relation to fear-modulated response-inhibition, attentional control, and affective traits. Biol. Psychol. **83**, 73–78 (2010)
10. Choi, H.S., Jones, A., Schwartz, G.: Using brain-computer interfaces to analyze EEG data for safety improvement

11. de Man, J.: Analysing emotional video using consumer EEG hardware. In: Kurosu, M. (ed.) HCI 2014. LNCS, vol. 8511, pp. 729–738. Springer, Heidelberg (2014). doi:10.1007/978-3-319-07230-2_69

12. Bosse, T., Gerritsen, C., Man, J., Stam, M.: Inducing anxiety through video material. In: Stephanidis, C. (ed.) HCI 2014. CCIS, vol. 434, pp. 301–306. Springer, Heidelberg (2014). doi:10.1007/978-3-319-07857-1_53

13. Dustman, R.E., Boswell, R.S., Porter, P.B.: Beta brain waves as an index of alertness. Science **137**, 533–534 (1962)

Persuasion and Motivation

Design of an Adaptive Persuasive Mobile Application for Stimulating the Medication Adherence

Franci Suni Lopez[1(✉)] and Nelly Condori-Fernandez[2(✉)]

[1] Universidad Nacional de San Agustín, Arequipa, Peru
fsunilo@unsa.edu.pe
[2] VU University Amsterdam, Amsterdam, The Netherlands
n.condori-fernandez@vu.nl

Abstract. There is a variety of persuasive applications that have been proposed in different application domains like well-being, health-care and e-commerce. However many have been designed largely for a general audience. Designers of these technologies may achieve more success if applications consider contextual information of the user for making them more adaptable. This paper is an proposal for improving medication adherence by sending personalized persuasive message and reinforcing feedback. To do this, we propose an adaptive services oriented architecture, and a persuasion strategy defined for selecting the appropriate persuasiveness level according to contextual information such as time and stress. Stress measure is derived from physiological data (e.g. Electro Dermal Activity, heart rate, temperature), which is collected through a wearable wireless multi-sensor device.

Keywords: Medication adherence · Persuasive message · Stress · Fuzzy logic · Inference system

1 Introduction

The World Health Organization[1] (WHO) ensures that the failure of the medical treatment is the main cause that has not obtained all the benefits that medicines can provide patients [1]. In consequence the poor medical adherence carries medical complications, psycho-social and economic in the person and society. It reduces the quality of life due to the complication of the disease and the use of more potent drugs, depression and in the worst cases, death. This is why the importance of generating new strategies that fit the patient's needs for stimulating medication adherence. For instance, a health-care game using a robotic assistant was proposed by Gonzales and Riek [2]. Kamal *et al.* uses text persuasive messages for reminding when to take the medicine [3]. The specific content of the persuasive message is derived based on the Social Cognitive theory and Health Belief

---

[1] http://www.who.int/en/.

© ICST Institute for Computer Sciences, Social Informatics and Telecommunications Engineering 2017
R. Poppe et al. (Eds.): INTETAIN 2016, LNICST 178, pp. 99–105, 2017.
DOI: 10.1007/978-3-319-49616-0_9

model. In contrast to our approach, authors do not consider different persuasiveness levels and reinforcing feedback. Moreover, both approaches do not take in to account internal context information of the user (i.e. physiological data), which can be used not only for providing personalized and adaptive messages but also for monitoring heart rate or skin temperature. We also find other related strategies such as counting of pills, electronic control, telecommunications systems for monitoring and counseling and care equipment [4,5].

With the increasing power of mobile phones and the recent technological advances in non-obtrusive and ubiquitous monitoring technology, in this article, we propose an architecture of a context-aware mobile application that exploits real-time physiological data for delivering self-adaptive persuasive messages that stimulate the medication adherence. We will use the E4-Wristband[2]; a wearable wireless multi-sensor device for real-time computerized biofeedback and data acquisition. The paper is organized as follows, in Sect. 2 we present our adopted persuasion strategy. Section 3 describes the main components of our architecture. Finally, conclusions and future work are discussed in Sect. 4.

2   Persuasion Strategy

Cialdini [6] developed six principles of persuasion (i.e. Reciprocity, Commitment and Consistency, Social Proof, Authority, Liking and Scarcity), which have been successfully applied in different domains, such as e-commerce [7] or well-being [8]. Based on these six principles [6], we identify four levels of persuasiveness as the most appropriate for stimulating the medication adherence:

1. **Scarcity (Level 1):** When something is scarce, people will value it more (e.g. I believe rare products (scarce) are more valuable than mass products).
2. **Consensus (Level 2):** People do as other people do. When a persuasive request is made people are more inclined to comply when they are aware that others have complied as well (e.g. when I am in a new situation I look at others to see what I should do).
3. **Commitment (Level 3):** People do as they said they would. People try to be consistent with previous or reported behavior, resolving cognitive dissonance by changing their attitudes or behaviors to achieve consistency. If a persuasive request aligns with previous behavior people are more inclined to comply (e.g. I try to do everything I have promised to do).
4. **Authority (Level 4):** When a request or statement is made by a legitimate authority, people are more inclined to comply or find the information credible (e.g. I always follow advice from my general practitioner).

The hierarchical ordering of persuasiveness levels is defined based on the findings reported by Kaptein *et al.* [9], who found the authority and commitment principles as the most influential, and scarcity as the least. We adopt also the liking principle ("People prefer to say *'yes'* to those they know and like" [6])

---

[2] https://www.empatica.com/e4-wristband.

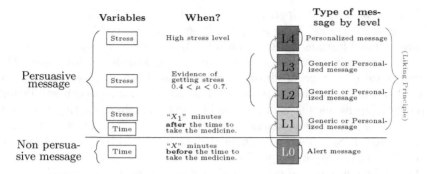

Fig. 1. Strategy for delivering adaptive persuasive messages

because it is easier to obtain changes of attitude, by using personalized messages at all persuasiveness levels. We consider that these messages, emitted by people that care-giver knows and likes, will be more friendliness for the care-receiver to improve his/her medical adherence.

The mobile application emits an alert message (non persuasive message) "X" minutes before for alert to user that is time to take the medicine. "X_1" minutes after to take the medicine the mobile application will emit persuasive messages, which can be generic or personalized.

Figure 1 illustrates how the variables of stress and time are used as main inputs for rendering messages with different levels of persuasiveness. For instance, if a high stress level is detected, then a level 4-persuasive message is rendered. Whereas having a medium stress level, messages of level 2 or level 3 can be emitted.

We use fuzzy theory for representing the Stress level as a linguistic variable. The Fig. 2(a) shows the graphic of this function and the values of our sigmoidal membership function is defined as Fig. 2(b).

Where $x \in [-1; 8]$, this interval of values corresponds to the scale of the EDA (Electro Dermal activity) sensor (using E4-Wristband). The unit is measured in microSiemens (μS). According to Ollander [10], the presence of stress is considered when the EDA value is $\geq 4.5\,\mu S$.

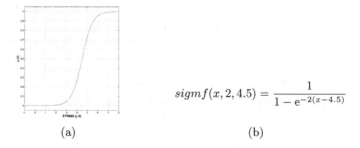

$$sigmf(x, 2, 4.5) = \frac{1}{1 - e^{-2(x-4.5)}}$$

(a)   (b)

Fig. 2. (a) Graphic of membership function. (b) Sigmoidal membership function for Stress linguistic variable.

In order to adapt the persuasiveness level and time interval, we design an inference engine based on the Adaptive Resonance Theory (ART) [11]. ART is an unsupervised learning method that allow to retain previously learned knowledge and simultaneously integrate new discovered knowledge. Moreover, ART compared to other type of classifiers require less training effort (usually less than 20 epochs) [12]. Thanks to the ART algorithm, our approach will be able to render adaptive persuasive messages by using as main input the outcome of the sigmoidal membership function defined for the stress. This way, we avoid that messages become monotonous for the user (care-receiver) by changing the level of persuasiveness and type of messages.

Therefore, our messages catalog is classified by persuasiveness level and type of messages (i.e. generic and personalized). The generics will be given by default and the personalized messages are those messages, whose content is defined by care-givers (i.e. family member). The Table 1 illustrates some examples of persuasive messages.

Table 1. Persuasiveness messages catalog.

Level	Type	Action
L4: *Authority*	Personalized	1. Emit Message: *"Mom should take the pill for you're well."* 2. Send a text message to the phone of doctor or relatives close with authority, indicating that the patient is not in compliance with the prescription
L3: *Commitment*	Generic personalized	Emit Message: *"Remember that improve your health is your goal."* Emit Message: *"Grandma should take your pill remember that you committed to improving your health."*
L2: *Consensus*	Generic personalized	Emit Message: *"All people care about their health and you too!."* Emit Message: *"Grandma takes her pill every want that you are well."*
L1: *Scarcity*	Generic personalized	Emit message: *"Your health could worsen if not take their medicines."* Emit message: *"Grandma takes her medicine for that you can still visit her friends."*
L0: *Notification*	Non persuasive	Emit message: *"It's time to take the pill."*

3   Adaptive Persuasive Mobile Application Architecture

The Fig. 3 depicts the architecture and main components of the persuasive mobile application. On the left side, there is the care-receiver, who would wear a E4 wristband, an smartphone with the application running on it, and, optionally, a bluetooth wearable speaker hanging on the lapel or any other suitable place according to user conditions. The wristband has several sensors embedded that provides readings about stress measures (EDA), heart rate (Photoplethysmography), and physical activity (3-axis accelerometer) and skin temperature (Infrared thermopile). The data gathered in run-time is submitted to the smartphone via bluetooth.

The application basically consists of a messaging interface that is able to (i) make use of the feedback user interface to render persuasive messages and reinforcing feedback to care-receiver; and (ii) push messages targeted at care-givers. The rendering of messages can be done in text and/or in audio form, depending on a format header associated to each message.

On the right side, there are the different service layers to support the working application. The primary service layer is the one responsible for the direct communication with the application. It basically contains a messaging gateway, which is able to reach recipients (e.g. care-givers and care-receivers) and deliver messages. The Scheduler controls when messages should be delivered and re-transmitted again provided by the Feedback service. The messages are configured following the persuasiveness strategy described above, which is implemented by the services in the Management layer. This also uses the Context layer, which maintains the relevant context data for users, including the historical information.

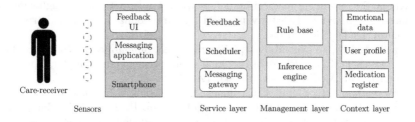

Fig. 3. Persuasive mobile application architecture

4   Conclusion and Future Work

In this paper we present the architectural design of an adaptive persuasive mobile application for stimulating the medication adherence. The purpose of the application is to provide the most effective reminder service by means of using adaptive persuasive messages. We argue that this adaptation is possible by exploiting physiological data in order to adjust the different persuasiveness levels at run-time. Based on the six principles of persuasion proposed by Cialdini, we have defined a persuasion strategy by identifying four different persuasiveness levels and proposing a catalogue of types of messages; which can be generic and personalized. Another important contribution of our approach are the evaluation rules defined for determining the stress and the persuasiveness levels, as well as the decision rules for selecting the most appropriate persuasive message (management layer). As part of our future work, we are going to validate the prototype of our adaptive persuasive application in two different stages. First, we plan to conduct a series of simulation-based experiments to assess our inference rules. Then, we plan to conduct a single case-base experiment for evaluating the effectiveness of persuasive messages delivered by our prototype application. Our case is a patient with hypertension (83 years old), who will use the wearable and wireless E4 Wristband device for collecting real-time data in her daily life and long-term settings.

Acknowledgment. We would like to thank the reviewers and Alejandro Catala for their valuable comments.

References

1. World Health Organization: Adherence to Long-term Therapies: Evidence for Action. World Health Organization, Geneva (2003)
2. Gonzales, M.J., Riek, L.D.: A sociable robotic aide for medication adherence. In: Proceedings of 5th International Conference on Pervasive Technologies Related to Assistive Environments, PETRA 2012, pp. 38:1–38:4. ACM, New York (2012)
3. Kamal, A.K., Shaikh, Q.N., Pasha, O., Azam, I., Islam, M., Memon, A.A., Rehman, H., Affan, M., Nazir, S., Aziz, S., Jan, M., Andani, A., Muqeet, A., Ahmed, B., Khoja, S.: Improving medication adherence in stroke patients through short text messages (SMS4Stroke)-study protocol for a randomized, controlled trial. BMC Neurol. **15**(1), 1–9 (2015)
4. Walsh, J.M.E., McDonald, K.M., Shojania, K.G., Sundaram, V., Nayak, S., Lewis, R., Owens, D.K., Goldstein, M.K.: Quality improvement strategies for hypertension management. Med. Care **44**, 646–657 (2006)
5. Viswanathan, M., Golin, C.E., Jones, C.D., Ashok, M., Blalock, S.J., Wines, R.C., Coker-Schwimmer, E.J., Rosen, D.L., Sista, P., Lohr, K.N.: Interventions to improve adherence to self-administered medications for chronic diseases in the United States. Ann. Internal Med. **157**, 785 (2012)
6. Cialdini, R.: Influence: Science and Practice. Allyn and Bacon, Boston (2001)
7. Ibrahim, N., Shiratuddin, M., Wong, K.: Persuasion techniques for tourism website design. In: Proceedings of International Conference on E-Technologies and Business on the Web (EBW 2013) (2013)
8. IJsselsteijn, W., Kort, Y., Midden, C., Eggen, B., Hoven, E.: Persuasive technology for human well-being: setting the scene. In: IJsselsteijn, W.A., Kort, Y.A.W., Midden, C., Eggen, B., Hoven, E. (eds.) PERSUASIVE 2006. LNCS, vol. 3962, pp. 1–5. Springer, Heidelberg (2006). doi:10.1007/11755494_1
9. Kaptein, M., De Ruyter, B., Markopoulos, P., Aarts, E.: Adaptive persuasive systems: a study of tailored persuasive text messages to reduce snacking. ACM Trans. Interact. Intell. Syst. **2**, 1–25 (2012)

10. Ollander, S.: Wearable sensor data fusion for human stress estimation. Ph.D. thesis, Linkoping University, Linkoping, Sweden (2015)
11. Jain, B.L.L., Ugur, H.: Innovations in ART Neural Networks. Studies in Fuzziness and Soft Computing. Physica, New York (2000)
12. Jones, M.: Artificial Intelligence: A Systems Approach. Jones and Bartlett Publishers, Sudbury (2009)

Interactive Advertisements in an IoT Era

Vassilis Javed Khan[1(✉)], Dion Bonné[2], and Suleman Shahid[2,3]

[1] Eindhoven University of Technology, 5612 AZ Eindhoven, The Netherlands
v.j.khan@tue.nl
[2] Tilburg University, Warandelaan 2, 5037 AB Tilburg, The Netherlands
{d.a.e.bonne,s.shahid}@uvt.nl.com
[3] Lahore University of Management Sciences, Lahore 54792, Pakistan

Abstract. The Internet has profoundly changed the nature of ads by making them interactive. We are currently observing an evolution to the Internet of Things (IoT) and it is inevitable that interaction designers will utilize IoT for creating a new ilk of interactive ads. In this paper, we present evidence that the attitude towards a TV ad interacting with a robot is positive when compared to the absence of interaction. Furthermore, we sketch the interaction space of TV ads and generally TV content with smart objects.

Keywords: Interactive advertisement · Human robot interaction · IoT

1 Introduction

The extension of the viewer's experience of content on the TV has been researched and has proven to have market success in the near past. One of the first well-known examples of such an extension, which was brought to the market with quite some success, is that of Philips' AmbiLight TV. The device itself was extended with several LED lights in its edges. Moreover, the TV was also able to recognize certain color patterns in the played content and based on that content it turns on the LED lights to create an extension to the experience in the ambiance of the room. Microsoft researchers have recently extended that idea with the IllumiRoom project [6].

Enabling interconnectedness among devices – anytime and anywhere - is called the Internet-of-Things. Due to the Internet-of-Things (IoT) paradigm, several devices can be connected to a (smart) TV and this enables cross-media interaction [5]. This entails that a TV can also be extended, by connecting it to several devices. One of these inventions is the ability to remotely control a TV system through a smartphone. These forms of interactive television also offer the ability to create interactive advertisements. For example, Durex was the first to introduce a dual-screen advertisement, which provides an extra layer to the story through a mobile app [6].

Although advertisements have been used for centuries the advent of the Internet and mobile technology has driven ads to become more personalized and more interactive. The ultimate goal of ad designers has been to make them effective. With the new Internet-of-Things (IoT) paradigm, new forms of ad interactivity will arise. With all of the new forms of interactive ads, attracting the viewers' attention to the ad has become more important. The Interactive Advertising Model (IAM) [8] has examined the unique

© ICST Institute for Computer Sciences, Social Informatics and Telecommunications Engineering 2017
R. Poppe et al. (Eds.): INTETAIN 2016, LNICST 178, pp. 106–111, 2017.
DOI: 10.1007/978-3-319-49616-0_10

attributes of the Internet and the way they impact the experience of ads. The primary aspects are "interactivity and virtual reality". The advertiser-controlled aspects in IAM state several "Ad-Formats" that extend Internet ads compared to print ads, such as: banner, pop-up, hyperlink, etc. As was the case with the Internet, in an IoT era we would expect the concept of ad interactivity to extend to other dimensions. For example, smart objects in the viewers' environment (e.g. robots or smart toys) could extend the ad's interaction space.

In the area of robotics, an increasing number of robots are designed for personal use. Robots are a unique opportunity to create new systems to cooperate in reaching better living conditions [4], even within a living room environment. The design of such personal robots extends the use of simple, mundane tasks -e.g. robotic vacuum cleaner and lawn mowing- to entertainment purposes -e.g. Sony's robotic singing Elvis [3]. Thus, robots can actively change the environment by performing actions and offer the possibility of richer interaction with humans. Recent research on social and personal robotics has shown that these robots are already accepted in a living room environment [2].

Thinking along this line of extending media content around the output device we envision a TV ad in which the characters involved can interact with physical robots in the proximity of the TV. Based on previous research that has shown that interactive ads are more engaging and that robots in the living room environment can be engaging social partners, we hypothesize that this form of interaction will lead to an enriching user experience when compared to its absence. For example, one might imagine a simple interaction in which the characters in the TV ad might wave to the side of the robot and the robot might wave back, to more complex interactions such as the physical robot actively being part of the content in the TV whether that is an ad, an animated movie or a computer game. Although similar ideas have been already proven successful in mass-entertainment venues, such as Disney world and 4D films [1], no one has yet explored them in a home setting and in relationship to ads.

2   Method

We conducted a between subjects experiment (N = 70). One group (N = 35 - control group) watched a short (8 min) TV documentary with an ad (40 s) and the robot next to the TV but without the robot actually moving at all. The other group (N = 35 - experimental) watched the same movie and ad only in this case the robot also moved in combination to the advertisement that was playing on the TV.

2.1   Material and Setting

The documentary was eight-minutes and it was about the KMA - the military academy in Breda, the Netherlands. Halfway through the video, we included an ad, about LEGO Mindstorms (Fig. 1). The ad features LEGO Mindstorms, a robotic platform for teenagers. The ad was specially produced for our research. Before the production, a brainstorm session with the production crew, comprising of five students (background

Fig. 1. Left: Position of the researcher (left arrow), two participants at a time (right arrow) and the robot (top arrow) are highlighted, as well as the movement of the robot. Right: A frame of the TV ad featuring the snake-figure of LEGO Mindstorms. The same toy-robot was placed next to our lab's TV. The experimental group saw the robot actually interacting with the TV ad.

in media design) was held. Five ideas/scenarios were elaborated on storyboards and we picked one scenario, named "Bedtime stories" (Fig. 1) which conveyed the best relationship between the ad and the robot. The story of the ad depicts a young boy who is sleeping on his bed and wakes up when his sister drives with a remote control the snake figure of the LEGO Mindstorms to scare him off. Since there were several robot-figures one could build with the kit of LEGO Mindstorms that we had, we chose the snake figure that fitted best the ad's storyline. Since this was a new concept for our participants, we were particularly careful about choosing an interaction that would not seem accidental or random. That is why our main criterion for choosing an idea to produce the ad was the one that better conveyed the interaction between the robot and the ad.

The interaction of the robot with the ad was pre-programmed with LEGO's Mindstorm software platform. The interaction was programmed to mimic part of what was presented in the ad itself. We used the snake figure, as it was in the ad (Fig. 3). The robot moved on the TV table when the snake moved in the ad (Fig. 2). Finally the snake-robot did an attack move and played a snake-rattle sound at the same time when this was shown in the ad. The installed program on the robot itself was triggered through the researcher's computer that was connected through Bluetooth to the robot.

A room at our university was transformed to resemble a typical living room. A TV, couch, chairs, plants and coffee table were strategically placed to make the setting as realistic as possible. The researcher sat behind the participants, primarily for launching the robot's movement and secondarily for observing.

2.2   Measurement Instrument

When the viewing session finished, participants were asked to fill out two questionnaires. The first one measures the general attitude towards the ad, found in the marketing scales handbook [4]. It is a six item, seven-point Likert-type scale that measures a person's reaction to an advertisement he or she has been exposed to. The second one is about Human-Robot Interaction [7]. It is a fourteen item, seven-point Likert-type scale that measures the negative attitude toward communication robots in daily life. This scale is divided into three subscales: (1) the negative attitude toward situations of interaction with robots, (2) the negative attitude toward social influences of robots, and (3) the negative attitude toward emotions in interaction with robots. Since the robot was an integral part of the interaction we wanted to find out whether there is any negative perception of it being part of a living room leisure activity. Next to the questionnaire, eight structured interviews (four control group and four experimental) were conducted to get a more detailed insight into participants' views about the general concept. The interviews were audio recorded and transcribed.

3 Results

For the first questionnaire, the general attitude towards the ad was significantly higher $t(68) = -2,687$, $p < .01$, in the experimental group (M = 4.30) than in the control group (M = 3.61). For the second questionnaire, for subscale 1, the participants' attitude toward situations of interaction with the robot was not statistically significant for the two groups $t(68) = 1.668$, $p = 0.10$ (control group M = 3.63, experimental group M = 3.23). For subscale 2, the participants' attitude toward social influences of robots was not statistically significant as well, $t(68) = 1.740$, $p = 0.086$ (control group M = 4.94, experimental group M = 4.11) and the). For subscale 3, the participants' attitude toward emotions in interaction with robots was also not statistically significant, $t(68) = 1.756$, $p = 0.084$ (control group M = 4.48, experimental group M = 3.94).

When asked about the interaction between robot and advertisement our participants had a very positive opinion about it. Most interviewees agreed that it would also help to make TV advertisements more effective. Participant 2 (female, 25) described it as follows: *"normally, you look at advertisements, but you do not really see them. It is like you shut yourself down until the seven minutes are over and you can continue watching your movie or TV show. Something like this (the interaction with the robot) really grabs your attention."*

On the issue of attention, there was the concern expressed that one will only be able to focus on the robot once it starts moving around during advertisements. Participant 3 (male, 22) said the following about it: *"the main problem has to be how to divide the attention (between the advertisement and the robot). For example, if the robot would walk behind my couch, I would turn around and focus on the robot, because I tend to find a robot more interesting that an advertisement. This means that placement and timing are extremely important, because it could also be distracting."*

Finally, participants saw an opportunity for this concept to be specifically addressed to children. This might be due to the use of LEGO Mindstorms as the robot itself. Participant 7 (male, 21) was one of those interviewees who mentioned: *"I believe that this robot interaction could have a greater effect on children, because I think that they would be more sensitive to something like this."*

4   Discussion and Conclusion

This study extends the current line of research by showing that smart objects –toys- can be used for extending TV experience. Our study clearly shows that this is a promising direction for designing such interactions and investigating its effects. We found a statistically significant difference for the ad that includes interaction with a robot. Our second measurement was about negative attitude towards robots of which we found no evidence when comparing the two conditions –a result that is also positive when designing such types of interactions in a living room setting. Our results are in line with the previous studies where it has been shown such an extension adds to the user's experience [6] and shows a clear potential for further research.

In terms of further research, the possible movements of a robot can be thought of in relation to the: (1) TV content; (2) TV as a device (Table 1). In our study the movement was synchronous replicating the content but we can imagine other scenarios. An example of synchronous that extends the content is when the robot would interact with the virtual character in the TV – in a simple scenario waving back to the virtual character. An example of asynchronous would be a movement that does not necessarily directly relate to the TV content. We can imagine an abstract movement during a TV ad that has as purpose just the aesthetic enhancement of the ad.

Table 1. The possible robot's movements that we envision.

	Movement		
	Synchronous		Asynchronous
In relation to TV content	Replicating the content	Extending the content	
In relation to the TV (as device)	Attached		Detached

In relation to the TV as a device, the movement can take place either attached to the device or detached from the TV. In the case of our study, the movement was detached from the TV. We envision more rich movements such as the robot actually moving behind the TV –"disappearing" from the physical world while appearing on the virtual - or even moving on top of the TV in the case of drones. Further, we envision robots that could actually be physically extended parts of a TV and could move in the periphery or on top of the actual screen of the TV. In that case movement would be actually attached on the TV itself.

Since attitude is a precursor to behavior [1] we expect that this interaction will actually positively affect the overall ad experience of users. Nevertheless, more research is required to further investigate behavioral aspects such as purchasing or social recommendations. This study was particularly focused on ads only. We do envision other media types such as animated movies, documentaries, talk shows, and even educational programs to take advantage of this novel way of extending the TV content. For future research we will explore a robot and type of TV ad are applicable to an even broader audience.

References

1. Ajzen, I.: The theory of planned behavior. Org. Behav. Hum. Decis. Process. **50**(2), 179–211 (1991)
2. Angulo, C., Pfeiffer, S., Tellez, R., Alenya, G.: Evaluating the use of robots to enlarge AAL service. J. Ambient Intell. Smart Environ. **7**(3), 301–313 (2015)
3. Beer, J., Prakash, A., Mitzner, T., Rogers, W.: Understanding Robot Acceptance (2011). http://hdl.handle.net/1853/39672
4. Bruner II, G.C.: Scale #51: Attitude Toward the Ad (General). Marketing Scales Handbook. GCBII Productions, Carbondale (2009)
5. Jensen, J.: Interactive television: new genres, new format, new content. Paper presented at Proceedings of 2nd Australasian Conference on Interactive Entertainment, Sydney, Australia (2005)
6. Jones, B.R., Benko, H., Ofek, E., Wilson, A.D.: IllumiRoom: peripheral projected illusions for interactive experiences. In: Proceedings of SIGCHI Conference on Human Factors in Computing Systems, pp. 869–878. ACM (2013)
7. Nomura, T., Kanda, T., Suzuki, T.: Experimental investigation into influence of negative attitudes toward robots on human-robot interaction. AI Soc. (2005). doi:10.1007/s00146-005-0012-7
8. Rodgers, W., Thorson, E.: The interactive advertising model: how people perceive and process interactive ads. J. Interact. Adv. **1**(1), 42–61 (2000)

Exertion Games

Cooperative Tetris: The Influence of Social Exertion Gaming on Game Experience and Social Presence

Danića Mast[✉] and Sanne de Vries

Research Group Healthy Lifestyle in a Supporting Environment,
The Hague University of Applied Science, Johanna Westerdijkplein 75,
2521EN The Hague, The Netherlands
{d.mast,s.i.devries}@hhs.nl

Abstract. This paper presents the primary results of a study that examined the difference between exertion vs. non-exertion in game experience and social presence. This study aims to gain more insight in the influence of body movement in a cooperative game on social presence and game experience, to be better able to design interactive technology that helps people to adopt a healthy lifestyle and to connect people socially. The study was performed among 336 adults (age range: 16–64 years) who played a two-player exertion (n = 167) or a non-exertion (n = 169) version of cooperative Tetris. Analysis of an extended version of the Gaming Experience Questionnaire showed that although participants who played the exertion version of the game found themselves less competent, there was no significant difference between the two groups (exertion players and non-exertion players) in game experience or social presence.

Keywords: Gaming · Exertion interface · Exertion gaming · Physical interface · Game experience · Body movement · Social interaction · Social presence · Physical activity

1 Introduction

Technology is increasingly becoming part of all aspects of everyday life [1, 16]. This has many consequences, such as an increased inactive lifestyle [5] and decreased and shallower face-to-face social interaction [1, 16]. As researchers and designers of new technology we should study how technology in can help people gain an active lifestyle and stimulate social interactions.

Exertion games and exertion interfaces are increasingly being used to encourage people to be physically active in a fun and accessible way. These games and interfaces focus on individual activities or have a competitive goal, while many sports activities are collective [11] and not necessarily competitive.

Knowledge on the relationship between social and physical exertion play is still limited [4]. If we want to be able to design social exertion interfaces and games that invoke social interaction and encourage physical activity, we need to understand which factors play a role in the relationship between cooperation, exertion, game experience and social interaction.

© ICST Institute for Computer Sciences, Social Informatics and Telecommunications Engineering 2017
R. Poppe et al. (Eds.): INTETAIN 2016, LNICST 178, pp. 115–123, 2017.
DOI: 10.1007/978-3-319-49616-0_11

2   Related Work

Bianchi-Berthouze et al. found that body movement positively affects engagement when playing Guitar Hero [2, 15] when playing with a guitar-like controller vs. a dual-shock controller. In addition, Lindley et al. have found a relation between body movement, social interaction and game experience when playing Donkey Konga with a conga-controller (requiring more natural body movement) [10]. Segura and Mueller et al. have also shown that physical and exertion interfaces (interfaces that deliberately require physical effort [11]) have a positive influence on game experience and social connection between players [13, 15].

Social and physical forms of play have many similar effects: higher engagement, arousal and positive emotions [15]. Combining both these types of play might increase these effects.

3   Goal

Previous research into the effects of body movement in games and interfaces have mainly addressed multiplayer games in which players are competing against each other [2, 9, 11] while in many traditional sports activities players have to cooperate to achieve a certain goal.

Research into cooperative exertion games [14], where people have to work together to achieve goals is still limited and further research is needed to gain insight into the influence of cooperation in exertion games on game experience and social interaction.

Our study aims to gain more insight in the influence of body movement in a cooperative game on social presence and game experience to be better able to design interactive technology that stimulates people to adopt a healthy lifestyle and interact socially.

4   Research Question

What is the difference in game experience and social presence between playing a cooperative game with and without exertion?

5   Method

In this study, adults were recruited at the 2016 Lowlands festival in the Netherlands (visited by >48.000 people). Bypassers were either randomly invited to participate or volunteered themselves after seeing other people play. All participants played once and voluntarily over a period of three days; the non-exertion and exertion condition were alternately played. Participants did not know in advance which version they would play.

Participants were asked to play a modified version of Tetris that required cooperation of both players to control the game. The left player was responsible for moving the bricks to the left; the right player was responsible for moving the bricks to the right.

An action by both players simultaneously caused the brick to rotate clockwise (Fig. 4). In the non-exertion version the players played by pressing buttons (Figs. 1 and 5), in the exertion version players played by jumping while wearing an accelerometer belt (Figs. 2 and 6).

Fig. 1. Non-exertion

Fig. 2. Exertion

After an explanation of the experiment and game, participants gave their written consent. Next, participants were invited on stage to play. They were told which version of two-player Tetris they were going to play and the controls were explained to them. All duos played for four minutes. When finished playing, the participants were asked to fill in a questionnaire about their game experience and social presence in an area next to the stage were they played the game (Fig. 3).

Fig. 3. Participants filling in questionnaires

6   Participants

A convenience sample of 336 adults (180 males, 156 females, mean age: 25,3 years, SD = 7,3) participated in this study. We included all 336 participants who filled in the questionnaire in this study.

Condition 1 – non-Exertion. (Figure 1) The non-exertion version of the game was played by 169 participants (70 females (41,4 %) and 99 males (58,6 %)), with an average age of 24,7 years (SD: 7,0).

Condition 2 – Exertion. (Figure 2) The exertion version of the game was played by 167 participants (86 females (51,5 %) and 81 males (48,5 %)), with an average age of 25,9 years (SD: 7,6).

7   Materials and Measurements

7.1   Game

For this study we developed a multiplayer version of Tetris (based on an existing Tetris game written in Processing [6]). We chose Tetris because it is fun to play, well known and intuitive; we expected most people to have prior experience with and under-standing of the mechanics and the goal of the game. Tetris' original gameplay allowed it to be modified into an exertion and non-exertion cooperative two-player version without losing the goal or affordances of the original version. While playing, players can still communicate and it is possible to hold a similar posture in both the exertion and non-exertion condition.

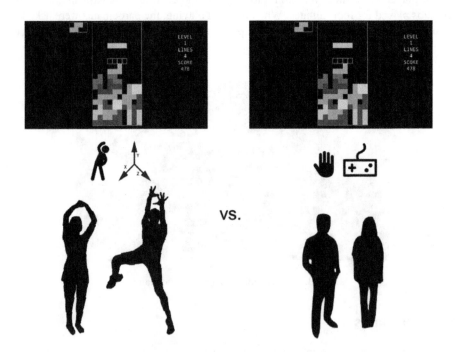

Fig. 4. Exertion vs. Non-exertion cooperative Tetris

7.2   Controllers

Condition 1: Non-exertion. The input device for the non-exertion version of our experiment was a wooden box with two arcade buttons that controlled the game (Fig. 5). This controller was custom made (Arcade buttons connected to a Adafruit 5 V 16 MHz Pro Trinket for keyboard output), avoiding possible effect of familiarity with the input device [1].

Condition 2 – Exertion. The input device for the exertion version of our experiment was a custom-made belt (Fig. 6) (Adafruit MMA8451 Triple-Axis Accelerometer connected to an Adafruit 5 V 16 MHz Pro Trinket) that allowed us to send keyboard input based on the players body movements. Players had to jump to send keyboard output.

Fig. 5. Button controller for Non-exertion condition

Fig. 6. Accelerometer controller for exertion condition

7.3   Screen and Stage

The game was projected on a large screen in front of the players (Fig. 7). Participants played standing on a slightly elevated stage in front of the screen, visible for other festival-visitors.

Fig. 7. Screen and stage used for gameplay

7.4 Questionnaire

To measure Game Experience and Experienced Social Presence we used revised versions of the Core and Social Presence Modules of the Game Experience Questionnaire by IJsselsteijn et al. [8] and de Kort et al. [9] with a 5-points Likert Scale. Items unrelated to our type of game (Sensory and Imaginative Immersion; Psychological Involvement - Negative Feelings) were removed. We included relevant questions from a previously used social questionnaire [12] to the Social Presence Module to gain more insight into the social interaction between players. In addition, background variables were gathered such as age, gender, how well participants knew the other player, exercise and gaming frequency.

7.5 Video

Besides the questionnaire responses, videos of all games played were gathered. This data will be analyzed in a next phase of this study.

7.6 Analysis

The answers to the Core and Social Presence Module of the Game Experience Questionnaire were coded (Not = 1; a Little Bit = 2; Somewhat = 3; Quite = 4; Very = 5). To compare the exertion and non-exertion condition of our experiment, we checked if the results were normally distributed and calculated the mean scores and standard deviation for each component and individual questions, followed by a t-test (two-tail, two-sample, unequal variance). To avoid the risk of a type-1 error we performed a post hoc Holm-Bonferonni [3, 7] correction.

8 Results

8.1 Game Experience

Participants who played the exertion version (M = 2.55, SD = 0.84) of cooperative Tetris felt significantly (t(334) = −4.51, p = <0.0001, Holm-Bonferonni correction: p' = <0.0001) less competent than participants who played the non-exertion version (M = 2.97 SD = 0.86) (Fig. 8). On the other constructs of game experience (Flow, Annoyance, Challenge, Negative Affect, Positive Affect) no significant differences were found.

8.2 Social Presence

The results for the constructs that measure social presence (Empathy and Behavioral) do not show a significant difference between the exertion and non-exertion condition.

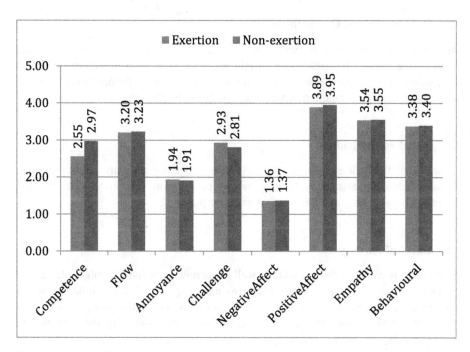

Fig. 8. Means of all components of the core and social presence module of the game experience questionnaire.

9   Conclusion, Discussion and Further Work

Previous work shows a relationship between exertion games, user experience and social play. Our results show a difference in perceived competence between the exertion and non-exertion version of cooperative Tetris. We could however not find a quantifiable difference in other aspects of user experience and in perceived social engagement between the exertion and non-exertion version of two-player cooperative Tetris, even though participants found the exertion version more difficult and challenging to play.

9.1   Gender, Familiarity, Exercise and Gaming Frequency

The exertion condition (86 females (51,5 %)) was played by more women than the non-exertion condition (70 females (41,4 %)). Furthermore, other variables were measured (How well players knew each other, Exercise and Gaming frequency) in our questionnaire, that we did not include in our current analysis. Further analysis will have to show if these variables had an influence on the outcome of our questionnaire.

9.2   Cooperation vs. Competition

Our study compared two conditions where players had to play together to achieve the goals of the game. To gain more insight into the role of cooperation on social engagement and game experience, in future work we will look further into the role of cooperating with or competing against each other when playing.

9.3   Social vs. Individual

To see what the influence is of playing a game together on game experience, we consider extending this study with a one-player exertion version to look into the difference between social vs. individual exertion play.

9.4   Effect of Novelty

What previous research doesn't address well is the novelty value that might play a role in game experience. Is a new type of gameplay more engaging than a familiar game and is a new controller more exciting than a familiar controller? In this study we used two novel controllers to avoid any influence caused by controller-novelty and we designed novel gameplay for both conditions.

9.5   User Research Methods

For this paper we relied on self-report for our analysis. We have however used a mixed-methods data collection (questionnaire and video) and will improve our study with a mixed-methods analysis approach [12]. We will improve this study by including video analysis to be able to keep track of verbalizations, speech, utterances, non-verbal behavior, instrumental gestures and empathic gestures while playing [10].

Acknowledgments. We would like to thank all participants in this study, Joey van der Bie for his technical support and assistance and Else ten Broeke, Thijs Heemskerk, Susan Hombergen, Kristel Kerstens, Michiel Krijger, Max Longarini, Renee Maurits, Peter Volken Smidt and Mariska van der Vegt for their assistance during the Lowlands festival.

References

1. Baym, N.K.: Personal Connections in the Digital Age. Wiley, Hoboken (2015)
2. Bianchi-Berthouze, N.: Understanding the role of body movement in player engagement. Hum.-Comput. Interact. **28**(1), 40–75 (2013)
3. Gaetano, J.: Holm-Bonferroni sequential correction: an EXCEL calculator-ver. 1.2 (2013)
4. Gibbs, M.R., Frank, V.: Designing for social and physical interaction in exertion games. In: Nijholt, A. (ed.) Playful User Interfaces. Gaming Media and Social Effects, pp. 227–251. Springer, Singapore (2014)

5. Hallal, P.C., Andersen, L.B., Bull, F.C., Guthold, R., Haskell, W., Ekelund, U., Lancet Physical Activity Series Working Group: Global physical activity levels: surveillance progress, pitfalls, and prospects. Lancet **380**(9838), 247–257 (2012)
6. Hiner, K.: Tetris OpenProcessing, 25 August 2011
7. Holm, S.: A simple sequentially rejective multiple test procedure. Scand. J. Stat. **6**(2), 65–70 (1979)
8. IJsselsteijn, W.A., De Kort, Y.A.W., Poels, K.: The Game Experience Questionnaire: Development of a self-report measure to assess the psychological impact of digital games. Manuscript in Preparation (2013)
9. de Kort, Y.A.W., IJsselsteijn, W.A., Poels, K.: Digital games as social presence technology: development of the social presence in gaming questionnaire (SPGQ). In: Proceedings of PRESENCE, pp. 195–203 (2007)
10. Lindley, S.E., Le Couteur, J., Berthouze, N.L.: Stirring up experience through movement in game play: effects on engagement and social behaviour. In: Proceedings of the SIGCHI Conference on Human Factors in Computing Systems. ACM (2008)
11. Mueller, F., Agamanolis, S., Picard, R.: Exertion interfaces: sports over a distance for social bonding and fun. In: Proceedings of the SIGCHI Conference on Human Factors in Computing Systems, pp. 561–568, 5 April 2003
12. Mueller, F.: Exertion interfaces: sports over a distance for social bonding and fun. Massachusetts Institute of Technology. Media Arts and Sciences thesis (2005)
13. Mueller, F., Bianchi-Berthouze, N.: Evaluating exertion games. In: Bernhaupt, R. (ed.) Game User Experience Evaluation, pp. 239–262. Springer International Publishing, Heidelberg (2015)
14. Sato, A., Yokokubo, A., Siio, I., Rekimoto, J.: Collaborative digital sports systems that encourage exercise. In: Kurosu, M. (ed.) HCI 2014. LNCS, vol. 8512, pp. 332–340. Springer, Heidelberg (2014). doi:10.1007/978-3-319-07227-2_32
15. Segura, E.M., Katherine, I.: Enabling co-located physical social play: a framework for design and evaluation. In: Bernhaupt, R. (ed.) Game User Experience Evaluation. Human–Computer Interaction Series, pp. 209–238. Springer International Publishing, Heidelberg (2015)
16. Turkle, S.: Alone Together: Why We Expect More from Technology and Less from Each Other. Basic Books, New York (2012)

Distributed Embodied Team Play, a Distributed Interactive Pong Playground

Robby van Delden$^{(\boxtimes)}$, Steven Gerritsen, Dennis Reidsma, and Dirk Heylen

Human Media Interaction, University of Twente,
P.O. Box 217 Enschede, The Netherlands
{r.w.vandelden,d.reidsma,d.k.j.heylen}@utwente.nl,
steven.gerritsen@gmail.com

Abstract. This paper presents work in the field of distributed exertion games, which are controlled by moving the body. People play these games together while being located at different places in the world. The novel contribution of this paper is the introduction of *distributed team play* in which both collocated and distributed players participate. In our Distributed Interactive Pong Playground (DIPP) players bounce a ball towards a goal by moving, walking, and running around in a 5.3 by 5.3 m interactive playground. We investigate whether we can increase coordination in movement between players by changing the game to enforce teamwork. This was done by letting the players in a team control one end each of a shared paddle, as opposed to both players having separate paddles. Although the results should be taken with care, the comparisons do indicate that we could steer the amount of coordination between players in this way. Furthermore, we investigated the effect of distributed team play on the level of coordination. The results indicate that coordination goes down if the teammate is at another location. In this distributed team setting, enforced team work through a connected paddle still leads to a higher level of measured coordination. In contrast, our current analysis of self-reported social presence did not show a clear difference, not favoring enforced team work nor a particular team distribution. With the DIPP and this study we provide a new direction for distributed exertion games with a focus on aspects of team play.

Keywords: Play · Interactive playground · Embodied interaction · Exertion games · Pong · Coordination · Social presence · Collocated · Distributed · Team play

1 Introduction

Computer entertainment can help people fulfilling a happy, pleasant and perhaps even a meaningful life [3,23]. Physical exertion and playing together with other people are a large part in this. *Distributed games* build upon the rise of broadband internet gaming technology. They allow computer entertainment to better include

---

This paper builds on Steven Gerritsen's Master's thesis work [5].

© ICST Institute for Computer Sciences, Social Informatics and Telecommunications Engineering 2017
R. Poppe et al. (Eds.): INTETAIN 2016, LNICST 178, pp. 124–135, 2017.
DOI: 10.1007/978-3-319-49616-0_12

the social-relatedness factor, even when the people whom we want to play with are physically far away. *Exertion games* (or exergames) target intense physical effort to play the game [16], which can result in enjoyment but also has other benificial effects. For instance, the high prevalence of obesity in western countries could be targeted with these exergames, as these games have been proven to increase energy expenditure [21]. The combination of the two leads to *distributed exertion games* [16], which allow one to play intense physical games, together with other people, over a geographical distance. Mueller et al. created several games and sport experiences that can be enjoyed with people on the other side of the world, including *table tennis for three, jogging over a distance,* kicking a ball against a wall (*break out for two*) and *airhockey over a distance* [18].

Although these games target interaction with distributed players, they do not allow for concurrent interaction with collocated players. In our research we thus investigate an extension on these distributed exertion games in which players are distributed as well as collocated, using our Distributed Interactive Pong Playground (DIPP). This allows us to investigate social connectedness and team interactions in a distributed exertion game. The game is played in teams of 2 vs. 2. Players control their paddle in order to bounce the ball into their opponents' goal by stepping, walking and running around an interactive space. To play this game we use an interactive camera-projection system based on the Interactive Tag Playground [9]. Our current system shows the same game visuals at two different locations. The interactive space of 5.3 by 5.3 m tracks players based on the depth streams of four Kinects and a real-time tracking algorithm. Subsequently our game incorporates these positions and uses two projectors to provide appealing visualizations on the floor. Two of these interactive spaces were linked to each other in combination with a microphone array and Skype connection to create the DIPP.

Our current study explores how people play together in the DIPP. An important part of people's interaction is how they coordinate their movements and how present they feel the other is [1,19]. We try to change and measure this coordination between players. We propose and try-out five different configurations of the game. We vary whether the two players in one team control one paddle together or if each player in the team has his/her own paddle. We also vary whether each team is collocated at one location (with the opponents being at the other location) or whether the members of the teams are distributed over the two locations (physically sharing that location with one person from the opponent team). In order to compare this to non-distributed play we use also observed play in a totally collocated game of interactive pong.

2   Related Work

Several distributed exertion games have been introduced in the last decade [18]. Almost all of them build upon an existing game, activity or sport. *Breakout for two*, is an interactive wall on which targets have to be hit with a ball, while an opponent player is simultaneously shown on the same wall but is playing from another location. The game is a combination 'of soccer, tennis and the popular computer game Breakout' [10, p. 4]. The targets are shared between the players and have to be hit several times before they break out, and only when the last hit is delivered a point is awarded to that player. *Table tennis for three*, is similar to *break out for two* but is based on table tennis instead of soccer and tennis. The players see their two opponents and hit similar targets on an upstanding part at the end of a table tennis table [17]. Here two players can decide to play 'together' against one. *Airhockey over a distance*, is a distributed game that builds on the table game of air hockey [15]. Players again can view their opponents projected at the half of the table. Players have to slide a puck into the goal of the opponent, by hitting the puck with a small round bat. Half-way (under the 'wall') a system detects the position and velocity of the hit puck where it disappears in a small slot. A 'canon' at the other location then shoots a puck with similar velocity and from approximately this position towards the goal of the opponent. This opponent defends its goal and attempts to score by hitting the puck back again. *Shadow Boxing*, is an installation where players can kick, punch and use their bodies to hit the opponents' shadow, which is projected on a 'touch sensitive' mattress-like wall [14]. *Tug of war*, is a system where the well known game of rope pulling is used as a starting point for a distributed game [2]. The game provides distributed haptic feedback, it is played by pulling a small rope that is connected to a servo motor which provides a pulling force based on the opponent pulling force. The game unlike the previous games is played in a cooperative way, by pulling or releasing the rope the players control a shared basket on the screen that can be used to collect falling objects.

Several of these systems have also been used to show that (distributed) embodied gaming can have positive effects on play experience and relation between players. Playing with *Tug of war*, when compared to a variation where there was no physical feedback of the other user, resulted in an increase of several dimensions from social presence of the distributed player [2]. Playing with *break out for two* when compared to a keyboard alternative, made the players feel they knew one another better and became better friends, increased fun, and unexpectedly resulted in increased perceived quality of the audio and video [11]. Participants playing with the *table tennis for three* reported that they could imagine it would help to increase rapport, and forgot the world around them [18]. Exertion games, also when not distributed but still compared to non-embodied interaction styles, can indeed have an effect on social interaction, trust, emotional experience, role-taking, competition, and connectedness [12]. Exertion games as well as similar movement-based social immersive media including camera-projection systems, can be designed in various ways to encourage emotional responses, deal with appropriate game-play time, competition etc. [20], can be designed to steer or change player interactions [8,22], and a wide set of guidelines have been created to aid in development of such games [7].

Many benefits of the developed distributed exertion games and distributed games have been linked to how players play together with another player. Although two players playing a game together was seen in tug-of-war and it was

 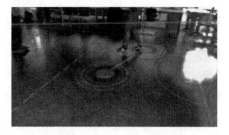

Fig. 1. The Distributed Interactive Pong Playground (DIPP). In this configuration, two opposing players are collocated and have distributed teammates, the paddle can be seen between the distributed team of green (L) and yellow (R). (Color figure online)

also welcomed for local players to team up during the *Breakout for two* games to increase throughput, to our knowledge there are not yet team distributed exertion games [10,18].

3   Design of DIPP

We propose our team distributed exertion game DIPP that includes two players on each team, two players on two location, a virtual ball and two virtual goals, see Fig. 1. Each player is represented with a unique colored circle projected at their position. The players control a paddle by moving around the play-field, the paddle can be used to bounce the ball in their opponents goal. The game is played for 7.5 min after which it will automatically stop.

3.1   The System

The system consists of duplicate setups at two locations communicating over the (university's) network using the UDP protocol. Both setups have four top-down oriented depth sensors (Kinect), a tracker PC (transforming depth information to tracks of players), a visualization PC and two projectors, see Fig. 2. One 'game' PC, the master, gathers the track information and transforms these to game coordinates. These game coordinates are used to run the game, the master sends the game information to another 'game' PC at the second location. This second PC simply visualizes the game objects at the second location. This setup forces the game to be deterministic. This is unlike the setup of what seems to be the first distributed embodied game, arm wrestling over a phone-line, in which both players could win at their end of the game [13][1]. Mueller et al. pointed out that the audio channel is the premium communication channel (in a distributed game) [18]. In order to let players communicate verbally we set-up a Skype call between the two locations using two additional Kinects, allowing communication in the entire playing field without letting the players wear microphones.

---

[1] Introduced in 1986, idea by Doug Black and Norman White, http://v2.nl/archive/works/telephonic-arm-wrestling, last visited 27-2-2016.

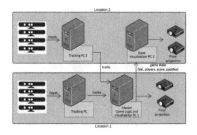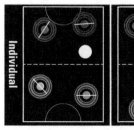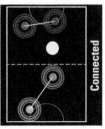

Fig. 2. The setup of the DIPP. On the left the system layout, at 2 locations we installed 4 Kinects and 2 projectors, and we use two tracker PCs sending tracks of players (ID and position), and by processing this info a master PC sends game info (ball, players, score and paddles) to a slave PC. On the right the two game variations are shown.

3.2 The Variations in Game and Distribution

Our contribution focuses on cooperative team play and the mix between collocated and distributed players. We are interested to see how players will play in different distributions and if we can increase coordination between players by changing the game play. Ideally, such an increase in coordination could also lead to an increased social presence of the other players.

We made two game variations, see Fig. 2. In the *individual* mode players are assigned an individual paddle. They still play in a team but each paddle is controlled by one player. The paddle rotates towards the ball until the distance is below a certain threshold (approximately 1.5 m). In this way players can bounce the ball in different directions by approaching the ball in different angles. In the *connected* mode players in a team each control one end of a connected paddle. Players can also rotate this paddle by moving around the other player. When the players are too far apart (approximately 1.5 m, twice the size of an individual paddle) the paddle breaks (disappears). While both forms require teamwork, we try to encourage closer coordination between players with the connected version. Especially once the game is distributed we still want the players to still pay attention to the (other) distributed players.

We also vary the way players are distributed. Players can either have their teammate at the same location, or have their teammate distributed and have an opponent at the same location. This leads us to 5 conditions to investigate: (#1) collocated$_{individual}$, (#2) collocated$_{connected}$, (#3) distributed-opponent$_{connected}$, (#4) distributed-team$_{individual}$, and (#5) distributed-team$_{connected}$. A possible sixth condition, distributed-opponent$_{individual}$, was played only once, deemed least interesting and was omitted from analyses due to a lack of participants.

We expect (1) that the coordination will be higher if we steer towards a more *connected* game than with an *individual* game (*coordination in #1 > #2*), (2) distributing a connected team still has a detrimental effect on their coordination in movement, thus in distributed play the coordination will be higher for collocated teams than for a distributed teams (*coordination in #3 > #5*),

(3) that if we have distributed teams the connected version will still have a higher coordination (*coordination in #5 > #4*).

4   User Study

4.1   Procedure

The experiment consists of groups of four participants that know each other, playing only one of the five conditions in order to reduce the threshold (time) to participate. The two setups are both located at our university, in different buildings 400 m apart. Participants were recruited in groups of four players that knew each other at the university. Participants were told that they would play a game of Interactive Pong, were informed about the game and had to give written consent. Participants were then asked to fill in a digital pre-experiment questionnaire, including questions regarding familiarity with each other and a baseline for the 'including Other In the Self' (OIS) scale by Aaron et al. [1]. We let the participants choose the teams, so there was no influence from us in this creation. Based on which distribution type the group had to play in, we took the participants to the associated locations.

Once the players arrived at the other location we tested the communication channel. We had to omit the Skype connection in one game from #4 due to technical difficulties. In another game from #5 we switched to a speaker phone. We first let the participants play the game as long as they needed to get used to the game (about 1 min). This was done in order to remove any difference in pre-knowledge people may have in playing interactive games and/or previous versions of the pong game. We then started a 7.5 min session where we let them play uninterrupted. At the end of the session, participants answered a questionnaire including the OIS-scale, and questions regarding the social presence of the other players including six different constructs [6]. This particular questionnaire was chosen as it fitted the intended measure, had proven internal consistency, its development based on existing theory seemed appropriate and it was applied successfully in the context of the *Tug of war* game. After finishing the questionnaire we asked the participants to share their thoughts on the game. We also saved the real-world positions of the players during the games, this data of the tracker allowed us to investigate the physical coordination between the players.

4.2   Participants

In total we had 80 participants, equally divided over the four conditions, 62 were male and 19 were female. All participants were between 19 and 34 years of age (23 on average), most were studying at our university. Two participants had an autism spectrum disorder (in #2 and #5). Seven participants had physical discomforts/limitations (back-ache, motor disorder, low energy levels etc.) most were unnoticeable in play-behavior with our direct observations, and spread over all conditions, although 3x in #5 and 2x in #3.

4.3 Results

Observations and Interviews. Some players in the distributed opponent configurations thought they were part of a Turing test. We were explicitly asked this question a couple of times (seemingly more often in #3). Players immediately had several ideas how to improve the game, like restricting the time one stands close to the goal. Nonetheless, most players indicated to us they liked the game very much, and we heard utterances such as *'This is so strange, this is so cool!'* (in #4). During the games several players were cheering and booing, giving high fives if they scored, and some made exaggerated movements like jumping in the air when (almost) scoring. These behaviors all seem to be qualitative indications of players being immersed in the game.

Questionnaire. Similar to Beelen et al. we performed comparisons on the social presence constructs between players in the different conditions [2]. However, as we are performing more exploratory investigations in this new type of setup, in our study this resulted in two-tailed tests on 13 different hypotheses regarding the effect of distributions and game variations on the social presence. A detailed description of each test or even hypothesis is outside the focus for this current paper as it would require too much space for explanation, instead we only discuss some interesting (condensed) 'results'.

The analyses of these 13 hypothesis on 6 constructs plus the difference in pre- and post-test in the OIS-scale, resulted in 91 comparisons, thus requiring a Bonferroni correction $(0.05/91 = 0.00054)$. Reliability for the six constructs is known [6] and internal consistency for this study was good to excellent, Cronbach's α in the range of 0.74–0.92 for all player comparisons for each of the constructs. Due to non-normal distributions we used the two-tailed version of the Mann-Whitney U test and all with $n_1 = n_2 = 16$. With the uncorrected significance level **only 21 of the 91 comparisons would have been significant** $(p < 0.05)$.

None of the social presence constructs or the IOS scale indicated a difference for teammates in the distributed teams conditions comparing *connected* (#4) and *individual* paddles (#5), (7x n = 16, $p > 0.05$). Furthermore, **no effect is seen for teammates if we compare the collocated version (#1 and #2)**, (7x n = 16, $p > 0.05$). Although not significant, there were even indications that **aspects of social presence (PAU/PMU) of the remote opponent might even increase with individual paddles (#4) instead of connected paddles (#5)**. PMU did not differ significantly (#4, Mdn = 3.33 vs #5, Mdn = 2.67), $U = 61.5$, $z = -2.52$, $\frac{0.05}{91} < p < 0.05$. Nor did PAU differ significantly (#4, Mdn = 2.92 vs #5, Mdn = 2.00), $U = 53.5$, $z = -2.82$, $\frac{0.05}{91} < p < 0.01$).

We did find a significant difference for teammate-OIS during enforced distributed play, between having a teammate distributed (#5, Mdn = 0.0) or collocated (#3, Mdn = 2.0), $U = 35$, $z = -3.56$, $p < \frac{0.05}{91}$). PMU was not significantly different (#5, Mdn = 3.25, #3, Mdn = 4.17), $U = 44$, $z = -3.18$, $\frac{0.05}{91} < p < 0.001$), nor was PAU (#5, Mdn = 2.33, #3, Mdn = 3.42), $U = 67$,

$z = -2.31$, $\frac{0.05}{91} < p < 0.05$. All (trends) were in the direction of **decrease of OIS/PMU/PAU for the connected distributed teammate (#5) compared to a connected collocated teammate(#3)**.

Coordination Between Players. One measure for coordination between people is their correlation in movement[2] [19]. For our exploratory study we see speed as an appropriate measure for movement. If players are coordinating their play-behavior more, we should be able to see an increase in correlation between player speeds. If over the game both players have high speeds and low speeds at the same moments in time, we see this as form of coordination.

Implementation of Coordination Measurement with Players' Speed. To investigate this form of coordination we filtered and transformed the position data. Using Matlab 2012a we did this as follows. Our tracker provided 'lines' of raw position data with a time stamp $(t(i))$, id, and x,y positions. The interval with which the tracker provides information is not constant (varying around 12.5 to 28 fps). For every first time stamp $(t(0) = ts_0)$ we encountered, we looked for position data within a time slot of 50 ms $(\pm \, {}^1/_{fps})$ or less $((t(i) \leq (ts_0 + 50))$, and saved all available position data for all players. When more than one positions is given for a player id within this time slot we only used its latest value. We continued until position data with a time stamp outside this time slot was found $(t_i \geq (ts_j + 50), \rightarrow ts_{j+1} = t(i))$.

We then interpolated the empty slots for each player with the x and y positions that were available. For values that had many consecutive missing values $(\geq 10, \geq 500$ ms) we kept the slots empty instead. We then calculated the speeds between slots and used a median filter (5 values, ≥ 250 ms) to filter out noise/outliers. We averaged the existing values over a period of 10 slots $(\geq 500$ ms). We threshold these values to a realistic maximum value of 11.61 km/h (top 0.05%), in order to minimize impact of extreme values for which Pearson's r is sensitive. We then correlated these average speeds between players.

Correlations. The correlations of teammates can be seen in Table 1. If teammates correlate their movement most, this allows one to attempt to automatically recognize teams using the optimal scores of correlations between player combinations from the correlations matrices. This optimum correlation combination resulted in 19 out of 20 proper combinations (one mismatch in the collocated versions #1), where the baseline would be 7.

Feeling slightly more confident in the applicability of the used correlations, we investigated our three expectations regarding coordination with the explained method. We expected (1) correlation values in *#1 > #2*, (2) correlation values

---

[2] Ramseyer and Tsacher also incorporated Pearson's r as a core part in their automatic measurement of synchrony [19]. They used temporal correlations and nifty corrections for random correlations. For our study we will keep to correlating (windowed) average concurrent speeds over entire sessions.

Table 1. Pearson's correlations (r) of teammates in the different configurations. L1 or L2 labels Location 1 or 2. Each session (s#) has two teams shown left and right in the table. * *Not the optimal combination, r optimal non-team: .10 and .20.*

	Condition									
	#1 co.$_{ind.}$		#2 co.$_{con.}$		#3 dis.-opp.$_{con.}$		#4 dis.-team$_{ind.}$		#5 dis.-team$_{con.}$	
	r_{L1L1}	r_{L1L1}	r_{L1L1}	r_{L1L1}	r_{L1L1}	r_{L2L2}	r_{L1L2}	r_{L1L2}	r_{L1L2}	r_{L1L2}
s1	.15	.15	.57	.49	.45	.52	0.16	0.07	0.31	0.17
s2	.14	.15	.40	.45	.34	.56	0.11	0.24	0.38	0.33
s3	.13*	.10*	.48	.47	.44	.47	0.18	0.07	0.32	0.16
s4	.11	.13	.6	.43	.49	.30	0.10	0.12	0.30	0.33
Avg.	.14		.47		.45		.13		.28	

in #3 > #5, (3) correlation values in #5 > #4 but due to the exploratory state of the research we also test for differences in the other direction using two-tailed test. Pearson's r is known to have a non-normal distribution and a Fisher z-transformation can be applied to transform towards a normal distribution [4]. Knowing the known non-normal distribution of Pearson's r we simply performed the more well known non-parametric two-sided Wilcoxon rank-sum test, all with $n_1 = n_2 = 8$.

In the collocated game, the used speed values have a significantly different Pearson's r correlation between teammates when their paddles are connected (#2 Mdn = .47) compared to individual paddles (#1 Mdn = .14), $W_r = 36$, $z = -3.36$, $p < 0.001$. This difference is in the expected direction of **higher coordination in movement of teammates if teammates are *connected*, when they are playing a collocated game**, #2 > #1.

With connected paddles the Pearson's r correlation of the the used speed values significantly changes between teammates being collocated (#3 Mdn = 0.46) or teammates being distributed (#5 Mdn = .31), $W_r = 42$, $z = -2.73$, $p < 0.01$. The difference is in the expected direction of **an increase in coordination of teammates if they are *collocated*, when they are playing distributed play where they are connected to their teammate**, #3 > #5.

In this distributed playground with distributed teams the Pearson's r correlation of the transformed and filtered speed values significantly changes between teammates when they are connected (#5 Mdn = .31) instead of having their individual paddle (#4 Mdn = .12), $W_r = 41$, $z = -2.84$, $p < 0.01$. This difference is in the expected direction of **an increase in coordination in movement of teammates if the teammates are *connected*, when they are playing with a distributed teammate**, #5 > #4.

5 Discussion

The method of correlation that we used seems usable to investigate the difference between distribution and enforcing team work. Our results suggest that forcing people to work together, to control/share an element together, increases a form of coordination. It would be interesting to investigate if these results would generalize to other games. It is important to realize that the FPS and the recognition seem to differ between locations. As the temporal character, linear interpolation and linear correlation are intertwined in the analysis results should be considered carefully. The collocated version did not suffer from these problems and still showed similar tendencies, larger correlation between teammates and especially larger when they are enforced.

Regarding the analysis of social presence it seems we set out a too broad investigation. More focused attention to aspects of interactive distributed play and core factors influencing social presence would be worthwhile in the future. The current reported values of the social presence are also leaning towards cherry picking results of such a questionnaire and show the shortcomings of having many hypothesis in an exploratory state of research. Nonetheless, there is a suggested trend towards a decrease in social presence constructs once teammates get distributed, asking for further investigations of these effects and possible ways to mitigate this decrease.

The game was enjoyed by many players. We think the collocated aspect in combination with distribution and the novelty of such a system were important reasons for this. The game itself could be improved, as suggested by some players, to trigger other more risky types of game play and providing a richer game play. For instance, adding a ball that speeds up or restricting the time that a player can be near to the goal. We found the idea of doing a Turing test with distributed interactive exertion games very interesting. Perhaps as a first step, future distributed exertion games could even become a combination of collocated players, distributed players, and computer players.

6   Conclusion

We reported on what to our knowledge is the first distributed embodied game with a focus on teams with collocated and distributed play at the same time, the Distributed Interactive Pong Playground (DIPP). We investigated if we could increase coordination, measured as correlation between speed of players, by more strictly enforcing teamwork in the game. This was done by letting both players control one end of a shared paddle (the main game object), as opposed to both players having separate paddles. Although the results should be taken with care, the comparisons strongly indicate that we could steer coordination between players in this way. Furthermore, we investigated the effect of distributed team play on the level of coordination. The results indicate that coordination goes down if the team mate is at another location. In this distributed team setting, enforced team work through a connected paddle still leads to a higher level of measured coordination. In contrast, our current analysis of self-reported social presence did not show a clear difference for either enforced team work or team distribution. Nonetheless, the combination of distributed and collocated games seems to be an interesting new avenue for distributed embodied play.

Acknowledgements. This publication was supported by the Dutch national program COMMIT.

References

1. Aron, A., Aron, E.N., Smollan, D.: Inclusion of other in the self scale and the structure of interpersonal closeness. J. Pers. Soc. Psychol. **63**(4), 596–612 (1992)
2. Beelen, T., Blaauboer, R., Bovenmars, N., Loos, B., Zielonka, L., Delden, R., Huisman, G., Reidsma, D.: The art of tug of war: investigating the influence of remote touch on social presence in a distributed rope pulling game. In: Reidsma, D., Katayose, H., Nijholt, A. (eds.) ACE 2013. LNCS, vol. 8253, pp. 246–257. Springer, Heidelberg (2013). doi:10.1007/978-3-319-03161-3_17
3. Desmet, P., Hassenzahl, M.: Towards happiness: possibility-driven design. In: Zacarias, M., Oliveira, J.V. (eds.) Human-Computer Interaction: The Agency Perspective. SCI, vol. 396, pp. 3–27. Springer, Heidelberg (2012). doi:10.1007/978-3-642-25691-2_1
4. Field, A.: Discovering Statistics Using SPSS, 3rd edn. SAGE Publications, Thousand Oaks (2005)
5. Gerritsen, S.: Using teamwork to enhance the social presence on a distributed playground. Master's thesis, University of Twente, Enschede, The Netherlands (2015)
6. Harms, C., Biocca, F.: Internal consistency and reliability of the networked minds measure of social presence. In: Proceedings of the 7th Annual International Workshop on Presence (2004)
7. Isbister, K., Mueller, F.: Guidelines for the design of movement-based games and their relevance to HCI. Hum.-Comput. Interact. **30**(3–4), 366–399 (2015)
8. Landry, P., Pares, N.: Controlling and modulating physical activity through interaction tempo in exergames: a quantitative empirical analysis. J. Ambient Intell. Smart Environ. **6**(3), 277–294 (2014)
9. Moreno, A., van Delden, R., Poppe, R., Reidsma, D., Heylen, D.: Augmenting playspaces to enhance the game experience: a tag game case study. Entertain. Comput. **16**, 67–79 (2016). http://www.sciencedirect.com/science/article/pii/S1875952116300106
10. Mueller, F., Agamanolis, S.: Sports over a distance. Comput. Entertain. **3**(3), 1–11 (2005)
11. Mueller, F., Agamanolis, S.: Sports over a distance. Pers. Ubiquit. Comput. **11**(8), 633–645 (2007)
12. Mueller, F., Bianchi-Berthouze, N.: Evaluating exertion games. In: Bernhaupt, R. (ed.) Evaluating User Experience in Games. Human-Computer Interaction Series, pp. 187–207. Springer, Heidelberg (2010)
13. Mueller, F.F.: Long-distance sports. In: Computers in Sports, pp. 1–27. WIT Press, UK (2008)
14. Mueller, F.F., Agamanolis, S., Gibbs, M.R., Vetere, F.: Remote impact: shadowboxing over a distance. In: Extended Abstracts on Human Factors in Computing Systems, CHI 2008, pp. 2291–2296 (2008)
15. Mueller, F.F., Cole, L., O'Brien, S., Walmink, W.: Airhockey over a distance: a networked physical game to support social interactions. In: Proceedings of the 2006 ACM SIGCHI International Conference on Advances in Computer Entertainment Technology, ACE 2006, p. 70. ACM Press (2006)

16. Mueller, F.F., Edge, D., Vetere, F., Gibbs, M.R., Agamanolis, S., Bongers, B., Sheridan, J.G.: Designing sports: a framework for exertion games. In: Proceedings of the 2011 Annual Conference on Human Factors in Computing Systems, CHI 2011, pp. 2651–2660 (2011)
17. Mueller, F.F., Gibbs, M.: A physical three-way interactive game based on table tennis. In: Proceedings of the 4th Australasian conference on Interactive Entertainment, IE 2007, pp. 1–7 (2007)
18. Mueller, F.F., Vetere, F., Gibbs, M.: The design of networked exertion games. JVRB - J. Virtual Reality Broadcast. **5**(13) (2008). doi:10.20385/1860-2037/5.2008.13
19. Ramseyer, F., Tschacher, W.: Nonverbal synchrony in psychotherapy: coordinated body movement reflects relationship quality and outcome. J. Consult. Clin. Psychol. **79**(3), 284–295 (2011)
20. Snibbe, S.S., Raffle, H.S.: Social immersive media: pursuing best practices for multi-user interactive camera/projector exhibits. In: Proceedings of the Conference on Human Factors in Computing Systems, pp. 1447–1456 (2009)
21. Sween, J., Wallington, S.F., Sheppard, V., Taylor, T., Llanos, A.A., Adams-Campbell, L.L.: The role of exergaming in improving physical activity: a review. J. Phys. Act. Health **11**(4), 864–870 (2014)
22. van Delden, R., Moreno, A., Reidsma, D., Poppe, R., Heylen, D.: Steering gameplay behavior in the interactive tag playground. In: Proceedings of European Conference on Ambient Intelligence, pp. 145–157 (2014)
23. Delden, R., Reidsma, D.: Meaning in life as a source of entertainment. In: Reidsma, D., Katayose, H., Nijholt, A. (eds.) ACE 2013. LNCS, vol. 8253, pp. 403–414. Springer, Heidelberg (2013). doi:10.1007/978-3-319-03161-3_30

A Throw Training System Utilizing Visual and Sound Effects

Kaoru Sumi[✉] and Yuki Tsukamoto

Future Universiyu Hakodate, Hakodate, Japan
kaoru.sumi@acm.org

Abstract. This study introduces a throw training system that aims to improve the athletic performance of children who see themselves as not good at sports. The lack of exercise among children has become more severe in recent years, the main causes being fewer opportunities and environments in the neighborhood that enable children to play outside and engage in sports activities. The authors of this study have developed a throw training system that utilizes visual and sound effects. The system is designed for use in elementary school physical education (PE) classes and allows for enjoyable use, training, and learning. The effectiveness of the system was evaluated by elementary school students who participated in a set of experiments in a PE-class setting.

Keywords: Visual effect · Sound effect · Throw training

1 Introduction

The lack of exercise among children has given rise to declining athletic performance in recent years in Japan. The average record of a softball throw declined by 5.2 m among boys and 3.4 m among girls in the 2012/2013 school year compared to the mid-1980s. The widening gap between children who exercise and those who do not has become a social issue. While the frequency of exercise is an important factor to maintain a healthy level of fitness, many children who consider themselves not good at sport or physical activity in fact like to exercise but have fewer opportunities to engage in physical activity because they do not want to be made to feel incompetent in comparison to their peers. The goal of this study was to develop a training system that would improve children's perceptions of physical competence and provide them with an intrinsic motivation to become more involved in physical activity.

In related studies, sample movement and a first-person perspective for effective motion training [1] and anticipation in tennis were examined using realistic film simulations, movement-based response measures, and a portable eye movement recording system [2]. In sports, learning every part of the movement involved in a physical action is an effective training procedure [3]. Recent years have seen a wide range of studies on sports, exercise, and the applications of motion capture. These studies form the basis for support systems aiming to improve sports skills and attitudes toward exercise. In a study [4], a system that learns the movements of a user's dominant hand is developed. The system then uses these movements to make a mirror image, which the user can utilize to acquire motor skills with their non-dominant hand effectively. A system using

© ICST Institute for Computer Sciences, Social Informatics and Telecommunications Engineering 2017
R. Poppe et al. (Eds.): INTETAIN 2016, LNICST 178, pp. 136–145, 2017.
DOI: 10.1007/978-3-319-49616-0_13

the Kinect motion-sensing device to learn how to throw darts accurately focuses on darts, which is an activity that requires very consistent movements, aims to improve a user's throwing mechanics by clarifying how the user's throwing motion differs from an ideal throwing motion [5]. In a study [6], the authors introduced a devised inter-action method using an acceleration sensor and a noren-turned-screen, which uses the surface of a split shop curtain (noren) to project video images. These enabled more accurate representations of pitches thrown, by accommodating a wider range of ball behavior and the throwers' body movements.

Recent years have seen a rise in learning tools and methods that involve games, such as serious games [7–9] and gamification [10–12]. Serious games are computer games that aim less to offer entertainment than to solve social problems, and they are used in areas such as education and medicine to advance learning, practical experience, and the arousing and development of interest. The current study's training system is similar to serious games in that it aims to improve performance in physical activity and to enable enjoyable training through the use of a system. There is increasing attention being turned toward the educational applications of games, such as serious games and gamification.

Leveraging the power of serious games and other games, this study succeeded in developing a throw training system that motivates users through the use of visual and sound effects.

2 A Throw Training System Utilizing Visual and Sound Effects

Our research group has been implementing system-based throw training programs in PE classes in schools [13]. Our past studies have shown that by using visual and sound effects in the feedback provided by the system that records the student' throws, students can improve their throwing distance while enjoying the practice. This study takes a closer look at the training system and examines the effectiveness of each set of visual and sound effect.

Microsoft Kinect was used to record each student's throwing motion, which was then evaluated and scored based on an ideal throwing motion (Fig. 1). Unity 5 was used to develop the entire system. The system is made up of three main segments, which can be defined by user-interface screens: the Start Screen, the Training Screen, and the Special Effect Screen.

When the Training Screen appears after the Start Screen, the student is asked to do three throwing motions, each of which is given a score. The Training Screen segment of the system is made up of a session for learning through observation and a practice session (when the student does the throwing motions). One practice session involves three sets of three throws, providing nine chances to do throwing motions in total. The practice only involves the motion, or gesture, of throwing a ball, without actually throwing it. The reason is that by doing the throwing motions while looking at the ideal throwing motion, the student can pay more attention to and hence improve their motion. The Training Screen displays the ideal throwing motion together with a pro-jected image of the student's motion (Fig. 2).

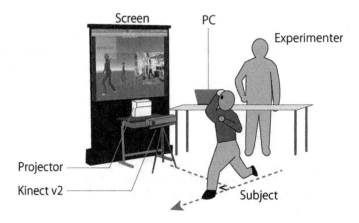

Fig. 1. System settings.

Fig. 2. Training screen.

The ideal throwing motion was based on the motion of a college student with five or more years of experience in baseball. This throwing motion was shot using Opti-Track's Motive. The projected image of the student was laid over the college student's ideal throwing motion to help the thrower (student) understand their motion. The display with the image was placed in a position such that the student could see where they were throwing and the image at the same time.

Throwing motion was broken down into three stages, each of which was subject to evaluation, according to the pitching biomechanics [14].

1. First half of cocking: In this stage, the evaluation is based on whether the arm is pulled back fully and whether the position of the hand is lower than the elbow.
2. Second half of cocking: The evaluation of this stage is based on whether the elbow is raised high enough and on the position of the elbow relative to the shoulder.

3. Acceleration: The evaluation of this stage is based on whether the thrower is taking a stride forward as they throw and on how big the stride is relative to the distance between their feet at stage 1.

The scores for the evaluations of the three stages were added up (one point per stage) for each of the three throwing motions done by a thrower in a set, and the next Special Effect Screen was determined and displayed based on this total score for the set (out of a maximum of nine points). Scores took into account whether the timings of the stages of the throwing motion by the student were in line with those of the ideal throwing motion. Each student received a total of nine scores for the nine throws that were graded (three scores per set). The Special Effect Screen provided the student with feedback, communicating how well the student was able to imitate the ideal throwing motion.

The special effect was designed to appear after the Training Screen. The system's camera device could follow a ball's trajectory as instructed by the student who threw a ball. As feedback, a student was shown one of three special effects: SE_Poor, SE_Good, and SE_Excellent. SE_Poor was shown when the throwing motion was done poorly, and SE_Excellent was shown when the throwing motion was done very well. A student was shown one of the three special effects based on the total score of the three throwing motions recorded while on the Training Screen: SE_Poor for 1–3 points, SE_Good for 4–7 points, and SE_Excellent for 8–9 points.

In this study, we prepared three types of special effects to see whether performance and behavior during practice would vary depending on the special effect used. The three kinds of special effects involved: manga "speed lines" (Fig. 3), cheering voices (Fig. 4), and a "flashy" animation (Fig. 5).

Fig. 3. Special effect screen (speed lines, SE_Excellent). The animation of a ball in a straight line accompanied by the sound of a thrown a ball.

Fig. 4. Special effect screen (cheering voices, SE_Excellent). The animation of a ball in a straight line along with people shouting and applauding, accompanied by the sound of a thrown ball, and cheering and applause.

Fig. 5. Special effect screen (flashy, SE_Excellent). The animation of a flying phoenix accompanied by the sound of flaring up.

3   Experiment 1

We divided 80 sixth graders (39 boys and 41 girls) into six groups to examine the effects of training and special effects. The students' scores in the nationwide sports test that the students took while in fifth grade (the "Shin-tairyoku test") were taken into account when deciding the groups. For this experiment, each student did three minutes of training using our system. The six groups are the following.

Group 1: Control group, Group 2: Special effects-only group, Group 3: Training-only group, Group 4: Training-and-speed-lines group, Group 5: Training-and-cheers group, Group 6: Training-and-flashy group.

Group 1 served as the control group to gauge the effectiveness of the system. Group 1 members did the throwing motion ten times as they saw themselves projected on the screen, without using the training features of our system. Group 2 members were shown special effects at predefined intervals as they did the throwing motions. Group 3 members did the throwing motion ten times while using the training features. Members of Groups 4, 5, and 6 were shown their respective special effects in addition to using the training features.

The purpose of Group 2 was to see whether scores improve just by seeing special effects. The purpose of Group 3 was to see the effectiveness of the training features of our system. The purpose of Groups 4, 5, and 6 was to examine differences in how scores improve after seeing the respective special effects after using the training features.

At the start of the experiment, the students were explained about the different user-interface screens, using the training manual. The following are the guidelines for the softball throw in the Shin-tairyoku test, which were largely followed in the experiment.

Use a "Type 1" softball (with a circumference of 26.2–27.2 cm and a weight of 136–146 grams) and a tape measure. A circle with a diameter of 2 m is drawn on flat ground. A mat is placed on the ground, with one end at the center of the circle, orienting it in the direction in which the ball should be thrown, so that students could all throw in roughly the same direction.

The rules when doing a throw were that: (1) the thrower must stay inside the circle to throw the ball, (2) the thrower must not step on or outside the circle both while and after throwing the ball, and (3) the thrower may only leave the circle after coming to a complete stop after releasing the ball. A speed gun was used at a certain distance away from the circle to take measurements. Each measurement was rounded to the nearest kilometer/hour. Five sets of throws and measurements were recorded. All measurements were documented and kept.

As for additional notes: 1. There is no set way one must throw, but throwers are encouraged not to throw underhand, 2. To enable equal conditions, supervisors were asked not to provide advice or practice after making the measurement before treatment.

As a result, improvement was quantified by calculating an improvement rate based on a score before treatment and a score after treatment. An analysis of variance was then carried out in order to compare the improvement rates between the groups. The analysis showed that the differences in improvement rates were not significant (F $(5,74) = 2.11$, n.s.). T-tests were carried out to see whether there were significant differences between the improvement rate of Group 1 (control group) and those of the other groups. A significant difference was found for Group 1 and Group 6 ($t = -1.75$, $df = 17$, $p < .05$), suggesting that Group 6's treatment was an effective training method.

4 Experiment 2

Experiment 2 was designed to study the impression one receives when shown the special effect used in Group 6 of Experiment 1. We asked 13 people (12 male and 1 female) from a University to participate in a survey to evaluate impression. We aimed to use the results of this impression evaluation survey to obtain a quantitative understanding of the special effects used in our system. We hypothesized that the impression made by the special effects with speed lines and cheers would be different from the impression made by the special effect with a flashy animation. In the survey, a participant was shown a special effect after doing a throwing motion. The participant was then asked to associate their impression of the special effect with a number (on a scale of 1 to 5) in terms of eight impression variables (these were the same variables as those used in Sect. 5).

A factor analysis (exploratory factor analysis and Promax rotation) was conducted for the eight variables. Eight factors had at least one variable for which the factor loading was 0.40 or more (Table 1). Two factors were chosen based on the magnitude of the initial eigenvalue and eigenvalues after rotation (3.919, 1.141, and 1.065). The first factor was interpreted to be the "Success" factor, and the second factor to be the "Evaluation" factor. The results are shown below. Factor scores were calculated for the two factors and were averaged in terms of "Display" (content displayed on the Special Effect Screen), as shown in Table 2. The values were then used to perform a cluster analysis, the results of which are shown in a dendrogram (Table 4).

The mean factor scores for Displays show that the special effects with "speed lines" and "phoenix" scored high on the "Success" factor while the display with SE_Poor (Display A) was characterized by a weak "Success" factor" (Table 3). The special effect with cheers had a strong "Evaluation" factor while the special effects with "block destruction" and "phoenix" had a weak "Evaluation" factor. The results supported the hypothesis that "the impression made by the special effects with speed lines and cheers

Table 1. Factor loadings.

Variable/adjective	Factor 1	Factor 2
Powerful (distance thrown)	0.88	−0.04
Cool	0.85	−0.04
Pleasant/delightful	0.84	0.18
Fast	0.82	−0.03
Flashy	0.76	−0.28
Natural	−0.03	0.69
Praiseful	0.48	0.55
Light/casual	0.39	−0.55
Rotation sums of squared Loadings (a)	3.89	1.31

Table 2. Variables and interpretation of factor meanings.

Factor	Variable	Rotation sums of squared loadings (a)	Interpretation of factor meaning
1	Powerful, cool, pleasant/comfortable, fast, flashy	3.89	Success
2	Friendly, natural, light	1.31	Evaluation

Table 3. Mean factor scores.

	"Success" factor	"Evaluation" factor
Display A (SE_Poor)	−1.73	0.19
Display B (SE Good)	0.06	0.34
Display C (speed lnes)	0.59	0.17
Display D (cheers)	−0.15	0.95
Display E (block destruction)	0.24	−0.57
Display F (phoenix)	0.99	−1.07

Table 4. Dendrogram.

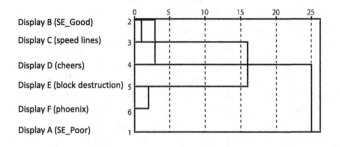

would be different from the impression made by the special effect with a flashy animation." The results therefore suggest that the special effects with flashy animations used in the group that experienced improved performance can be characterized by a strong "Success" factor and a weak "Evaluation" factor.

5 Discussion

Our experiments showed that effective training was achieved in the group that used our training features and a special effect with a flashy animation (Group 6). Students in this group showed signs of continued engagement in practice and seemed to be enjoying the practice as well. The use of a special effect that has elements to draw attention and arouse interest may have played a role to achieve continued practice and improved athletic performance. A special effect that introduces a sense of newness or originality to the practice seems to have enabled the students to practice continuously. However, the standard deviation of the improvement rates in this group was larger than in other groups, implying a large gap between those who were improving and those who were not. This disparity in improvement suggests that the training method may have been difficult to understand for some members. Future efforts should therefore be directed toward adjusting the training method so that all users may improve scores and performance.

No significant difference was found between the improvement rates of the control group and the group that did training only without special effects. Some members of this group found the training too monotonous and lost the motivation to continue. A significant difference was also not found between the improvement rates of the control group and the group that only used special effects without using the training features. The group members seemed to be enjoying the practice but were not able to improve their scores. They may have enjoyed the special effect itself but may not have been able to utilize the enjoyment for the improvement of their scores. No significant differences were found between the improvement rates of the control group and the "training-and-speed-lines" group (Group 4) and between the improvement rates of the control group and the "training-and-cheers" group (Group 5). The behavior of the students in these groups suggested that seeing these special effects during practice had no effect on sustaining the motivation to practice. This may be because the special effects were not appealing or interesting enough. The behavior of the students in these groups suggested that they had lost the motivation to continue practicing, and some students stopped doing the throwing motions in the middle of practice. This may account for the decline in scores after treatment compared to before treatment.

The impression survey administered to college students showed that the special effects that improved performance were those that scored high on impression variables that were associated with the "Success" factor extracted through factor analysis (i.e., powerful, cool, pleasant, fast, and flashy) and scored low on impression variables that were associated with the "Evaluation" factor (i.e., praiseful, natural, and light).

The flashy special effect may have caused an extrinsic motivation during practice. Human behavior based on extrinsic motivation is motivated by external factors such as evaluation, reward, punishment and coercion, while behavior based on intrinsic motivation is motivated by motives that occur from within, such as interest, enthusiasm, and desire. While extrinsic motivation is generally considered to have a temporary effect that does not necessarily lead to character development, behavior that is initially based on extrinsic motivation may eventually give rise to interest and enthusiasm and hence lead to intrinsic motivation-based behavior. This suggests that, while practice based on the training system we developed alone may not improve performance, the concurrent use of special effects may enable the user to engage in continued practice, which may in turn lead to improved performance.

6 Summary

We developed a training system that utilizes visual and sound effects. Results of experiments involving elementary school children showed a group of students who experienced improved athletic performance. A survey to evaluate the impression of the special effect that caused improved athletic performance showed that the effective special effect/could be characterized more by "Success" (associated with the impressions of powerful, cool, pleasant, fast, and flashy) than by "Evaluation" (associated with the impressions of praiseful, natural, and light).

References

1. Yang, U., Kim, G.J.: Implementation and evaluation of "just follow me": an immersive, VR-based, motion-training system. Presence 111(3), 304–323 (2006)
2. Williams, M., Ward, P., Knowles, J.M., Smeeton, N.J.: Anticipation skill in a real-world task: measurement, training, and transfer in tennis. J. Exp. Psychol. Appl. 8(4), 259–270 (2003)
3. Grosser, M., Neumaier, A.: Techniktraining. Theorie und Praxis aller Sportarten. BLV Buchverlag GmbH & Co., Munich (1996)
4. Ishii, K., Soga, M., Taki, H.: Proposal and development of reversal motion skill leaning support environment. In: 2011 International Conference on Information Technology Based Higher Education and Training (ITHET), Kusadasi, Izmir, pp. 1–6 (2011)
5. Nagata, Y., Hashiyama, T., Tano, S., Ichino, J.: A novice support system for the darts throwing. In: 28th Fuzzy System Symposium, pp. 572–573. Japan Society for Fuzzy Theory and Intelligent Informatics (SOFT)
6. Iyoda, A., Kimura, H., Takei, S., Kakiuchi, Y., Xiaodong, D., Fujii, S., Masuda, Y., Masuno, D., Miyata, K.: A VR application for pitching. J. Soc. Art Sci. 5(2), 33–44 (2006)
7. Abt, C.: Serious Games. The Viking Press, New York (1970)
8. Aldrich, C.: The Complete Guide to Simulations and Serious Games, p. 576. Pfeiffer, San Francisco (2009). ISBN 0-470-46273-6
9. Reeves, B., Reed, J.L.: Total Engagement: Using Games and Virtual Worlds to Change the Way People Work and Businesses Compete. Harvard Business School Publishing, Boston (2009)
10. Zichermann, G., Cunningham, C.: Introduction. In: Gamification by Design: Implementing Game Mechanics in Web and Mobile Apps, 1st edn., p. xiv. O'Reilly Media, Sebastopol (2011). ISBN 1449315399

11. ab Huotari, K., Hamari, J.: Defining gamification - a service marketing perspective. In: Proceedings of the 16th International Academic MindTrek Conference 2012, Tampere, Finland, 3–5 October (2012)
12. Deterding, S., Dixon, D., Khaled, R., Nacke, L.: From game design elements to gamefulness: defining gamification. In: Proceedings of the 15th International Academic MindTrek Conference, pp. 9–15 (2011)
13. Yuki, T., Kaoru, S.: Study of a system for training in pitching form to improve throwing distance using kinect. In: The 28th Annual Conference of the Japanese Society for Artificial Intelligence, JSAI 2014 (2014)
14. Sakakibara, N.: Pitching biomechanics. http://www.chiro-journal.com/wp-content/uploads/2014/02/sportschiro_09.pdf

Play with Me! Gender-Typed Social Play Behavior Analysis in Interactive Tag Games

Alejandro Moreno[1($\boxtimes$)], Ronald Poppe[2], and Dirk Heylen[1]

[1] Human Media Interaction, University of Twente, Enschede, The Netherlands
{a.m.morenocelleri,d.k.j.heylen}@utwente.nl
[2] Interaction Technology Group, Utrecht University, Utrecht, The Netherlands
r.w.poppe@uu.nl

Abstract. Promoting social behavior is one of the key goals in interactive games. In this paper, we present an experimental study in the Interactive Tag Playground (ITP) to investigate whether social behaviors reported in literature can also be observed through automated analysis. We do this by analyzing players' positions and roles, which the ITP logs automatically. Specifically, we address the effect that gender and age have on the amount of tags and the distance that players keep between them. Our findings largely replicate existing research, although not all hypothesized differences reached a level of statistical significance. With this proof-of-concept study, we have paved the way for the automated analysis of play, which can aid in making interactive playgrounds more engaging.

Keywords: Interactive playgrounds · Social behavior analysis · Children's play · Ambient entertainment

1 Introduction

Studies have shown that play is essential for the development of children [1,2], of their physical capabilities [3], cognitive processes [4], and social understanding [5]. Playgrounds, parks, or, in general, spaces that allow children to move and interact with other children freely, have been the typical settings for play. Nowadays, children spend a significant amount of time consuming online digital media, and a considerable part of this time is dedicated to digital gaming [6]. Most young people play video games at least occasionally, and many, especially boys, play them on a daily basis [7,8]. The consequences of these changes in children's play habits are increasingly becoming apparent. There is an alarming trend of children playing "together and apart", playing games with others but not directly interacting with them [9].

To counter this trend, interactive technology is being used to design games that aim to bring players closer together and trigger social interactions amongst them [10]. This can be achieved by implementing games where multiple players play together, such as interactive playgrounds [11,12], or by explicitly designing

© ICST Institute for Computer Sciences, Social Informatics and Telecommunications Engineering 2017
R. Poppe et al. (Eds.): INTETAIN 2016, LNICST 178, pp. 146–157, 2017.
DOI: 10.1007/978-3-319-49616-0_14

interactive installations that target social interactions such as competition [13] or collaboration [14]. To evaluate whether these games achieve their specified goals, questionnaires, observational studies, and interviews are typically used [15,16]. This leaves room for improvement as these measurement techniques are usually subjective and their application in analyzing play behavior is often time-consuming. Considering that there are fundamental differences in social play behavior between boys and girls [17,18], being able to measure and act upon these differences in-game could help make interactive play more engaging.

This paper addresses this scenario by investigating whether players' social behavior can be objectively measured and analyzed automatically in the Interactive Tag Playground (ITP). The ITP is an interactive game installation that uses sound, sensor and projection technology to enhance the traditional game of tag [19,20]. It has been designed to retain the essence of the original game while making it possible to introduce novel gameplay elements easily. The ITP tracks players and displays a colored circle underneath them. The color of the circle indicates the role of the player: orange for taggers, blue for runners. To facilitate the tracking of the players, instead of physically touching other players to tag them, the tagger has to get his circle to overlap with a runner's circle. The ITP can automatically measure cues that can aid in the analysis of social behavior, such as the distance between players or the number of times a player is tagged.

This paper is structured as follows: Sect. 2 presents literature related to gender-typed behavior, typical behavior exhibited specifically by boys and girls, and how it affects how children play together. In Sect. 3 we describe our experimental setup and the user study that we conducted to analyze gender-typed behavior. In Sect. 4 we present and discuss the results of our study. Finally, in Sect. 5, we summarize our findings.

2 Age and Gender Effects on Social Play Behavior

Children prefer to interact with other children of the same gender [21–24]. This tendency starts very early in childhood, and lasts well until children reach puberty. A study of children between one and twelve years old showed that, although this behavior is already shown at an early age, it is more evident as children grow older [25]. This is due to the fact that they become more conscious of, and grow into, their own gender as time goes by. Moreover, the behavioral patterns exhibited by these groups differ between genders. Boys prefer to interact in larger groups, leading to many "shallow" relationships, whereas girls prefer smaller groups, typically of only a couple of "best" friends [21,26]. Differences in behavior that are typically attributed to gender are called gender-typed behavior.

Gender-typed behavior is not only limited to everyday social interactions, but it can also be observed during play. Boys, for instance, often prefer to play in public spaces such as streets, whereas girls usually get together in private homes or yards [17]. Maccoby and Jacklin showed that boys usually play in groups, whereas girls play mostly with one or two best female friends [18]. Although children most often play with children of the same gender, cross-sex play is also seen in children's play. Often this is due to external factors such as limited availability in playing partners [27].

Preference towards certain play activities that children engage in, and the manner in which the activities are carried out, also differs between genders. Pellegrini observed that rough-and-tumble play is not only seen more often in boys than in girls, but it is also related to the social standing amongst boys [28]. Archer also presented several studies where boys engaged in more active play than girls [29]. Eccles and Harold found that gender plays a big part in the attitude of children towards certain sports [30]. Interestingly, they mentioned that the preference was not so much about their aptitude towards the sport itself, but more related to gender-role socialization. In other words, the more they saw sports as being appropriate for their gender, the higher they rated their abilities. Cherney and London considered not only sports, but also toys, computer games, TV shows and outdoor activities differences for kids between five and thirteen years old. They found gender to be a significant factor [31]. Boys preferred to spend more time doing sports, playing video games and watching television, whereas girls preferred only to watch television. Also, the activities they preferred became more gender-typed with age.

Since the ITP automatically collects players' positions and roles, this paper serves as an experimental validation of whether this information can be used to analyze social behavior. We are especially interested in whether gender and age change the way in which players behave during interactive tag games. In the next section, we present how the data obtained from tracking players in the ITP can be used to analyze social behavior automatically during games.

3   Objective Analysis of Social Behavior in the ITP

To test if we can measure differences in gender-typed social behavior in the ITP, we conducted a user study with children of different ages and genders playing interactive tag. Each session consisted of four children, two boys and two girls, of the same age group. The playing area was $6\,\mathrm{m} \times 5\,\mathrm{m}$. This arrangement was designed to bring forth differences in play behavior, as seen in the literature. The user study was approved by the university's ethical committee. Our hypotheses and the cues that we measure are explained in Sects. 3.1 and 3.2, respectively.

3.1   Hypotheses and Operationalization

We define social engagement as the construct to analyze how children's social play behavior differs between genders and age groups. Social engagement refers to how socially active players are during the game. We identified in the literature three different approaches that are normally followed when studying gender-typed social engagement: the analysis of differences between same-gender interactions (i.e. boy-boy versus girl-girl), differences between mixed-gender and same-gender interactions (i.e. boy-girl and girl-boy versus boy-boy and girl-girl), and differences between interactions of children of different ages.

For same-gender interactions, differences have been observed between boys and girls. Specifically, boys tend to play in larger groups than girls [18], which leads to many, but superficial, relationships [21,26]. On the other hand, girls play in smaller groups, which leads to fewer, but more intense, relationships. We believe this will be reflected in the ITP by (a) girls interacting with (tagging) girls more often than boys interacting with boys, and (b) girls staying closer to other girls than boys stay from other boys. This leads to the first set of hypotheses:

Hypothesis 1a (H1-Tg). The average number of tags between girls is higher than between boys.

Hypothesis 1b (H1-Dt). The average distance between boys is bigger than the distance between girls.

In regards to same-gender versus mixed-gender interactions, researchers have suggested that children usually form groups made up of children of the same gender [22,24], and that children mostly play with children of the same gender [27]. We believe this will lead to (a) players preferring to tag players of the same gender over those of the opposite gender, and (b) players staying closer to players of the same gender. We thus formulate a second set of hypotheses:

Hypothesis 2a (H2-Tg). Players of the same gender will tag each other at a higher rate than players of the opposite gender will.

Hypothesis 2b (H2-Dt). The average distance between pairs of the same gender is smaller than the distance between pairs of opposite genders.

Finally, gender-typed behavior is exhibited from a very young age up until the teen years. Studies have shown that this type of behavior becomes more evident as children age [25]. We believe that this will manifest itself in the form of greater differences between the measurements of behavioral cues for young and older children. Our final set of hypotheses is as follows:

Hypothesis 3a (H3-Tg). The number of tags between players of the same gender will be higher for the older children.

Hypothesis 3b (H3-Dt). The distance between pairs of the same gender will be smaller for the older children.

3.2   Behavioral Cues

To investigate our hypotheses, we use two behavioral cues derived solely from the position and role information of each player. The first cue, Tg, is the average number of tags between players per session. By analyzing whom a player tags the most, we should be able to find if there is a preference to interact with players based on their genders. The ITP keeps track of the roles of the players and, by counting the number of times the tagger role switches, we can measure the number of times a player has tagged someone. We consider the gender of a player when counting the number of tags. Therefore, we look at the number of tags between male players, female players, and players of the opposite gender.

The second cue, Dt, is the average distance between players. By calculating the distance to other players, we expect to find preferences related to whom they want to be close to and, therefore, interact with more. Since the ITP tracks players and logs their position during the game, we calculate Dt by averaging, over the entire game duration, the distance between any two given players. This means that, inherently, Dt is a pairwise cue. When analyzing this cue, we specifically look at pairs of players, taking into consideration their genders. As such, we analyze the distance between pairs of male players, female players, and players of the opposite gender. Dt is measured in meters.

3.3   Experimental Design

In this study, we specifically look at how children's social engagement is affected by gender and age. For the first variable, *gender*, we designed each session in such a way that the same number of players from each gender played together. For our second variable, *age*, we had players of 6–8 years old playing together (A-Y), and players of 9–10 years old playing together (A-O). We will refer to these two groups as younger and older children, respectively.

Thirty two children from two different schools were invited to our university over the span of two days. The children took part in many activities, including playing tag in the ITP. The children were divided into groups of four players, which led to a total of eight groups. Sixteen of the children were boys, and half of those sixteen were 6–8 years old. This means that we had eight young boys, eight young girls, eight old boys and eight old girls. The consent forms that we used only asked whether we could record and analyze the data of the children. Therefore, there are no pictures or video recordings of the game sessions.

3.4   Experimental Procedure

Once the children arrived at the university, they were shown all the possible activities they could partake in. After this, they were allowed to move around and participate in any activity they wished. For each session, two boys and two girls were chosen randomly from the pool of available children. This meant either choosing children who were at the ITP or, if needed, asking children who were at other stations if they wanted to play a game of tag.

Once the children were selected, the game was explained to them. Afterwards, they were asked to stand on specific colored stars located in the corners of the playground (Fig. 1). Girls were asked to stand on the red stars, whereas boys were asked to stand on the yellow ones. Using this method, we could know which players were male and which females at the start of each game session. Each group played the game for one minute and a half. After each session, players were asked to participate in a very brief feedback session.

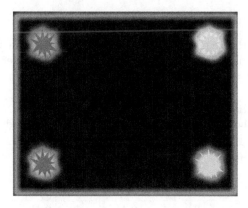

Fig. 1. Projected image before every tag game session in the ITP. (Color figure online)

Manual Annotation of Data. Although the performance of ITP's tracker is good (on average, two track switches per game session) [32], occasionally, the label assigned to each player by the ITP changes when players run too close to each other. For this study, we had to ensure that the labels assigned to the players at the beginning of the game were maintained throughout the entire session, as a player's starting position indicates its gender. Therefore, the track information provided by the ITP was manually revised and corrected.

The manual correction was carried out by saving unprocessed depth images from the game sessions. These images were watched next to a visual representation of the ITP's tracker output on a frame-by-frame basis. Although we could not identify players from the depth images, their contours provided sufficient information to distinguish them from each other when in close proximity. Whenever labels were incorrectly assigned, they were corrected. When a player was lost by the tracker, its position was annotated. After the manual correction, we ran a median filter with a window of 1/3 of a second on the position data to smooth it. By manually correcting the label assignment process, we made sure that the analysis of behavior could be carried out not only at the group level but also at the individual level. Nonetheless, this process significantly increases the time needed to analyze behavior.

4 Experimental Results

To evaluate social engagement, we study in detail the pairwise interactions between the players. We specifically look at how the distance between pairs of players (Dt) and the number of tags (Tg) differ between genders and age groups. A total of eight play sessions were analyzed: four play sessions in the A-Y condition, and four in the A-O condition. Each session consisted of two boys playing with two girls in the same age group.

4.1   Average Number of Tags per Player

We first calculate the tagging ratio of the players based on their gender. We count the times a player tagged children of a specific gender, and divide this value by the player's total number of tags. Results are shown in Table 1.

Table 1. Tagging ratio based on a player's gender and age. Male-Male represents tags from a boy to other boys. Female-Female represents tags from a girl to other girls.

Tagging ratio	Male-Male	Female-Female	Average
A-Y	0.33	0.30	0.32
A-O	0.37	0.44	0.41
Average	0.35	0.37	

Considering that every game session consists of two boys and two girls, for any given player, the baseline ratio of tagging a player of the same gender is 0.33, and 0.67 for a player of the opposite gender. We can see that only the older children show a preference to tag other players of the same gender (0.41). In the A-Y condition, we can see that the tagging ratio between boys is 0.33, which means there is no preference. For the girls, this value is 0.30, which is also close to the baseline value. However, when we look at the A-O condition, we can see that the tagging ratio for boys increases to 0.37, and the ratio of girls tagging other girls increases to 0.44.

To get a better picture of how tagging behavior changes between conditions, we also calculate the number of tags between players. Since there are two players of each gender, we normalize the number of tags between players of opposite genders by dividing them by two. Results are shown in Table 2.

Table 2. Average number of tags between players based on their gender and age. The number of tags between players of opposite genders has been normalized.

Normalized average number of tags between players per session	Male-Male	Male-Female	Female-Female	Female-Male
A-Y	1.75	1.81	1.63	1.81
A-O	1.88	1.50	2.25	1.56
Average	1.81	1.66	1.94	1.69

The average number of tags between girls (1.63) is lower than for boys (1.75) when considering the A-Y condition, but in the A-O condition the average number of tags per player for girls (2.25) is higher than for boys (1.88). This means that, apparently, the age of the children has an influence on tagging preferences. Also, it seems that girls prefer to interact with girls more often than boys do with boys, at least for the older group of children.

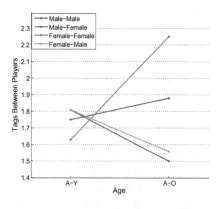

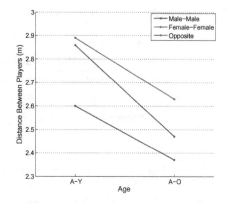

Fig. 2. Average number of tags between players based on age and gender.

Fig. 3. Average distance between players based on age and gender.

The average number of tags between players of the same gender increases in the A-O condition when compared to the A-Y condition. Consequently, the average number of tags between players of the opposite gender decreases. The difference is more marked for girls, which changes from −0.18 (1.63–1.81) to 0.69 (2.25–1.56). For boys, the difference in tagging preference from A-Y to A-O changes from −0.06 (1.75–1.81) to 0.38 (1.88–1.50).

The interaction between Tg, gender and age can be seen in Fig. 2. The graph shows an important increase in the number of tags between girls when going from the A-Y to the A-O condition. There is also an increase in the number of tags between boys, but it is considerably smaller than the one seen for girls. The number of tags between players of opposite genders decreases in the A-O condition. Notice that the younger girls have the lowest number of tags between players of the same gender, but the older girls have the most.

To evaluate H1-Tg and H3-Tg, we run a 2-way factorial ANOVA to find the effect of gender and age on the number of tags between players. There was no statistically significant interaction between the effects of gender and age on the number of tags per player ($F(1, 28) = 0.415, p = ns$). To assess H2-Tg, we run a set of 1-sample t-tests against the baseline tagging ratio for players of the same gender (0.33). We found no statistically significant differences in any of the four tests (number of tags between males and number tags between females for the younger and older children).

4.2 Average Distance to Other Players

In Table 3 we can see that for both the A-Y and A-O conditions, the distance that girls keep between them is shorter than the distance boys keep. When looking at A-Y, we can see that the distance between boys (2.86 m) is larger than the distance between girls (2.60 m), but is almost the same as the distance between players of opposite genders (2.89 m). This means that boys did not show

Table 3. Average distance to other players based on their gender and age.

Average distance to other players (m)			
	Male-Male	Female-Female	Opposite gender
A-Y	2.86	2.60	2.89
A-O	2.47	2.37	2.63
Average	2.67	2.49	2.76

a marked preference in staying close to players of the same gender. Girls, on the other hand, already show gender-typed behavior in the young group.

When looking at the A-O sessions, the distances between all the players shrink, and boys start to exhibit a preference to stay close to other boys. This can be seen in the 2.47 m they keep from each other, in comparison to the 2.63 m that players keep to players of the opposite gender. Girls do not really change their behavior, and prefer to stay even closer to other girls (2.37 m). The graph with the interactions between the variables can be seen in Fig. 3.

To test H1-Dt, H2-Dt and H3-Dt, we conducted a 2-way factorial ANOVA to measure the effect of gender and age on the distance between players. The test shows a statistically significant decrease in Dt for the older children ($F(1, 42) = 11.78, p < 0.05$). We also found that gender has a statistically significant effect on Dt ($F(2, 42) = 4.215, p < 0.05$). After running a post-hoc test on gender, we found that the distance between girls was significantly lower than the distance between players of different gender ($p < 0.05$). However, there was no statistical difference in Dt between boys and girls, nor for boys and opposite gender pairs. Finally, the interaction between age and gender did not show a statistically significant effect on Dt ($F(2, 42) = 0.275, p = ns$).

4.3 Discussion of Social Engagement Results

The results show that there are some differences in social engagement with respect to gender and age in the ITP. For the number of tags between players, Tg, we only found small differences. From these differences, the most noticeable one was found for girls in the A-O condition, which had the highest number of tags between them when compared to tags between boys or between mixed gender pairs. Also, the difference in tagging behavior between the girls in the younger group and the older group was the most pronounced. Nonetheless, neither the 2-way factorial ANOVA nor the 1-sample t-tests we ran showed statistically significant differences in tagging ratios or number of tags per player. Consequently, we reject H1-Tg, H2-Tg and H3-Tg.

When looking at the distance between players, Dt, we found the largest differences for girls in the A-O condition. In this case, the older girls kept the shortest distance between them when compared to the distance between boys or players of opposite genders. The biggest difference between age groups was seen for the boys. We found a statistically significant difference in the distance between girls in comparison to the distance between players of different genders. However, since there was no significant difference between girls and boys, or boys and pairs of children of opposite genders, we reject H1-Dt and H2-Dt. In regards to H3-Dt, we found a statistically significant decrease in the distance between players when going from A-Y to A-O, which confirms this hypothesis.

One possible limitation in our current study is that, by explicitly telling boys and girls to stand on specific corners to start the game, we may be priming them into thinking about their gender and enhancing their awareness of it. Moreover, studies suggest that gender segregation is more evident when situations have not been structured by adults [17], which could mean that by forcibly arranging mixed gender play groups, children may feel pressured to adapt their playstyle to fit the situation. We have no evidence to suggest that either happened, but it would be better if the children themselves chose who they wanted to play with.

This relates to another limitation in our experiment: the number of children that took part in the experiment. Since we only had eight mixed gender sessions, the number of observations was quite low. This could be one of the reasons why some of the observed differences were not found to be statistically significant. With a larger sample size, the variance of the measurements may diminish.

Lastly, since the children that played together knew each other, we may be overlooking the effect that their social relationships have on their playing preferences. Since each group was composed of randomly selected children, this effect might be mitigated. Nonetheless, future studies could be carried out with children that do not know each other to see if the behavior changes.

5   Conclusions

In this paper, we have addressed the automated analysis of gender-typed social play behavior in the ITP. We have conducted a user study with children of different age groups and genders playing interactive tag. We have analyzed these play sessions using two behavioral cues that were measured unobtrusively by the ITP: the number of tags and the distance between players. Our results generally follow what we expected based on the existing literature on children's play. Our analyses show that age has an effect on the distance that players keep to each other during interactive tag. More specifically, older children tend to stay closer to each other when compared to younger children. We also found that the distance between girls is significantly shorter than the distance between players of opposite genders. Other measurements hint at the presence of gender-typed social play behavior, but the differences were not statistically significant.

These results convey that certain gender-typed behavior is exhibited during interactive tag games, and that it can be measured in the ITP. This is important because it allows us to evaluate game interventions that target specific aspects of social play. For instance, a game intervention that encourages isolated players to interact with other children could be evaluated based on the distance between players. An intervention to steer passive players to engage other players could be evaluated based on the number of times the player tags others. Although these interventions and the results of this study might be specific to this particular type of game, we consider this study a first step towards the automated analysis of social behavior in interactive playgrounds.

Acknowledgments. This publication was supported by the Dutch national program COMMIT.

References

1. Barnett, L.A.: Developmental benefits of play for children. J. Leis. Res. **22**(2), 138–153 (1990)
2. Pellegrini, A.D.: The Role of Play in Human Development. Oxford University Press, Oxford (2009)
3. Pellegrini, A.D., Smith, P.K.: Physical activity play: the nature and function of a neglected aspect of play. Child Dev. **69**(3), 577–598 (1998)
4. Sutton-Smith, B.: Play and Learning. Gardner Press, New York (1979)
5. Christie, J.F., Johnsen, E.: The role of play in social-intellectual development. Rev. Educ. Res. **53**(1), 93–115 (1983)
6. Blumberg, F., Blades, M., Oates, C.: Youth and new media. Z. Psychol. **221**(2), 67–71 (2013)
7. Desai, R.A., Krishnan-Sarin, S., Cavallo, D., Potenza, M.N.: Video-gaming among high school students: health correlates, gender differences, and problematic gaming. Pediatrics **126**(6), 1414–1424 (2010)
8. Ferguson, C.J., Olson, C.K.: Friends, fun, frustration and fantasy: child motivations for video game play. Motiv. Emot. **37**(1), 154–164 (2013)
9. Turkle, S.: Alone Together: Why We Expect More from Technology and Less from Each Other. Basic Books, New York (2011)
10. Courtney, R., Scarlatos, L.L.: Mind reader: designing for more intimate social play in video games. In: Extended Abstracts of the Conference on Human Factors in Computing Systems, pp. 1211–1216 (2015)
11. Moreno, A., van Delden, R., Poppe, R., Reidsma, D.: Socially aware interactive playgrounds. IEEE Pervasive Comput. **12**(3), 40–47 (2013)
12. Poppe, R., van Delden, R., Moreno, A., Reidsma, D.: Interactive playgrounds for children. In: Nijholt, A. (ed.) Playful User Interfaces, pp. 99–118. Springer, Singapore (2014)
13. Fogtmann, M.H., Grønbæk, K., Ludvigsen, M.K.: Interaction technology for collective and psychomotor training in sports. In: Proceedings of the International Conference on Advances in Computer Entertainment Technology, pp. 13:1–13:8 (2011)
14. Parés, N., Durany, J., Carreras, A.: Massive flux design for an interactive water installation: water games. In: Proceedings of the International Conference on Advances in Computer Entertainment Technology, pp. 266–269 (2005)
15. Bakker, S., Markopoulos, P., de Kort, Y.: OPOS: an observation scheme for evaluating head-up play. In: Proceedings of the Nordic Conference on Human-Computer Interaction, pp. 33–42 (2008)
16. Staiano, A.E., Calvert, S.L.: The promise of exergames as tools to measure physical health. Entertain. Comput. **2**(1), 17–21 (2011)
17. Maccoby, E.E.: Gender and relationships: a developmental account. Am. Psychol. **45**(4), 513–520 (1990)

18. Maccoby, E.E., Jacklin, C.N.: The Psychology of Sex Differences. Stanford University Press, Stanford (1974)
19. Moreno, A., van Delden, R., Poppe, R., Reidsma, D., Heylen, D.: Augmenting traditional playground games to enhance game experience. In: Proceedings of the International Conference on Intelligent Technologies for Interactive Entertainment, pp. 140–149 (2015)
20. Moreno, A., van Delden, R., Poppe, R., Reidsma, D., Heylen, D.: Augmenting playspaces to enhance the game experience: a tag game case study. Entertain. Comput. **16**, 67–79 (2016)
21. Eder, D., Hallinan, M.T.: Sex differences in children's friendships. Am. Sociol. Rev. **43**(2), 237–250 (1978)
22. Thorne, B.: Girls, boys together... but mostly apart: gender arrangements in elementary schools. In: Wrigley, J. (ed.) Education and Gender Equality, pp. 117–132. The Falmer Press, London (1992)
23. Maccoby, E.E.: The Two Sexes: Growing Up Apart, Coming Together. Harvard University Press, Cambridge (1998)
24. Archer, J., Lloyd, B.: Sex and Gender. Cambridge University Press, Cambridge (2002)
25. Ellis, S., Rogoff, B., Cromer, C.C.: Age segregation in children's social interactions. Dev. Psychol. **17**(4), 399–407 (1981)
26. Waldrop, M.F., Halverson Jr., C.F.: Intensive and extensive peer behavior: longitudinal and cross-sectional analyses. Child Dev. **46**(1), 19–26 (1975)
27. Maccoby, E.E., Jacklin, C.N.: Gender segregation in childhood. In: Reese, H.W. (ed.) Advances in Child Development and Behavior, vol. 20, pp. 239–287. JAI (1987)
28. Pellegrini, A.D.: Boys' rough-and-tumble play, social competence and group composition. Brit. J. Dev. Psychol. **11**(3), 237–248 (1993)
29. Archer, J.: Childhood gender roles: social context and organization. In: McGurk, H. (ed.) Childhood Social Development: Contemporary Perspectives, pp. 31–61. Lawrence Erlbaum Associates Ltd. (1992)
30. Eccles, J.S., Harold, R.D.: Gender differences in sport involvement: applying the eccles' expectancy-value model. J. Appl. Sport Psychol. **3**(1), 7–35 (1991)
31. Cherney, I.D., London, K.: Gender-linked differences in the toys, television shows, computer games, and outdoor activities of 5- to 13-year-old children. Sex Roles **54**(9–10), 717–726 (2006)
32. Moreno, A., Poppe, R.: Automatic behavior analysis in tag games: from traditional spaces to interactive playgrounds. J. Multimodal User Interfaces **10**(1), 63–75 (2016)

Game Studies

Deep Learning for Classifying Battlefield 4 Players

Marjolein de Vries and Pieter Spronck[✉]

Tilburg Center for Cognition and Communication,
Tilburg University, Tilburg, Netherlands
mdv@marjoleindevries.com, p.spronck@tilburguniversity.edu

Abstract. In our research, we aim to predict attributes of human players based on observations of their gameplay. If such predictions can be made with sufficient accuracy, games can use them to automatically adapt to the player's needs. In previous research, however, no conventional classification techniques have been able to achieve accuracies of sufficient height for this purpose. In the present paper, we aim to find out if deep learning networks can be used to build accurate classifiers for gameplay behaviours. We compare a deep learning network with logistic regression and random forests, to predict the platform used by Battlefield 4 players, their nationality and their gaming culture. We find that deep learning networks provide significantly higher accuracies and superior generalization when compared to the more conventional techniques for some of these tasks.

Keywords: Deep learning · Computer games · Player classification

1   Introduction

In recent years, research into gaming and how people interact with games has received much interest. That interest stems partially from the advent of so-called "serious games", i.e., games used for educational purposes [5]. While most serious games use a "one size fits all" approach to their users, adapting a game to a user's personality, skills, and needs, has the potential to make the games more effective [10]. Developers have thus shown interest in modeling the characteristics and behaviours of game players [11].

Games tend to form a rich environment of interaction, from which much knowledge about a player can be gleaned. Previous research has, for instance, focused on modeling a player's personality [3,7], demographics [6], and national culture [1].

While it is relatively easy to gather data on players and their in-game behaviour, attaching meaning to this data is problematic as only player actions can be observed, and not the motivation behind those actions. As a consequence, deriving higher-level interpretations of the observations that allow the game to actually draw conclusions on the player, so that it can adapt effectively to the

© ICST Institute for Computer Sciences, Social Informatics and Telecommunications Engineering 2017
R. Poppe et al. (Eds.): INTETAIN 2016, LNICST 178, pp. 161–166, 2017.
DOI: 10.1007/978-3-319-49616-0_15

player's needs, is a tough challenge. Basically, a model is required that is highly accurate in classifying aspects of a player's characteristics. Previous research has shown that player models can be constructed using regular classification techniques, but that such models do not make predictions of sufficient accuracy.

Recently, a resurgence of interest in neural network research has occurred, driven by the increase in computational power and the high availability of data. "Deep learning networks", i.e., neural networks with dozens of layers of high numbers of neural nodes, can be trained to perform classification tasks that have not been handled successfully before. Deep learning has demonstrated its power in classifying images [9], general gameplaying [4] and in recognizing patterns in challenging board games [8].

Our research is driven by the question whether deep learning networks can also be used to classify attributes of game players from observations of their game-play behaviour. The present paper describes our initial research in this respect, where we train a deep learning network with observations of around 100,000 Battlefield 4 players, in an attempt to classify their gaming platform, their nationality and their gaming culture. We chose gaming platform as target variable as it is known for all players, only a limited number of platforms is possible, and because we felt that gaming platform might have subtle interactions with other player features. Nationality was chosen, as previous research [1] has also shown a relation between nationality and gaming behaviour. Moreover, we created a third target variable by dividing the nationalities over five clusters, to reduce the number of target values compared to nationality on its own. We compare the accuracy of our results with the accuracies achieved using logistic regression and random forests.

2   Data

We built a data set of gameplay behaviours of Battlefield 4 players, as such data can be derived easily online. We used a web crawler to acquire the data of about 100,000 Battlefield 4 players from the website *www.bf4stats.com*. As Battlefield 4 can be played on five different platforms (PC, PS3, PS4, Xbox 360, and Xbox One), we made sure to get data for each of those platforms for about 20,000 players.

The web crawler started by retrieving names from the leaderboards, thus making sure that we were mainly gathering data from players who were actually involved with the game. Then we retrieved information on each of those player-names, consisting of statistics such as kill/death ratio, objective scores, scores for different game modes, scores for different roles within the game, and the usage of different weapons. Retrieved statistics concerned the performance of a player up until the moment of retrieval. All player features which are time-dependent were divided by the total playing time. Finally, the dataset was centered and scaled with the R package `caret`, i.e. the mean of every feature was removed to have an average mean of zero and every feature was divided by its standard deviation. During the preprocessing several records were removed, for reasons such as a player having zero playtime, or a playername simply being inaccessible. The resulting dataset contained 99,912 training examples and 159 features. All features were checked to not have a strong correlation with the target variable platform, which they did not. The distribution of the training examples among the five platforms is shown in Table 1.

Table 1. Platform distribution of the dataset

Platform	PC	PS3	PS4	X360	XOne
Nr of examples	19,839	20,007	20,010	20,021	20,035
Percentage (%)	19.86	20.02	20.03	20.04	20.05

Nationality was known for only 10,665 out of the 99,912 players. 155 different nationalities were present in the dataset. We selected only countries with 50 or more representatives, resulting in a dataset consisting of 9,770 training examples with 33 different nationalities. The most common nationality was American, with 1,897 players. k-Means clustering with $k = 5$ was performed on the averages for each country, resulting in the five different clusters as shown in Table 2. An ANOVA on the effect of cluster on each of the six Hofstede dimensions [2] was performed. Cluster 2 was left out in this analysis, as it consisted of only one nationality. A significant effect at $p < 0.05$ level of cluster on the dimensions Power Distance ($F(3,28) = 9.34, p < 0.001$), Individualism ($F(3,28) = 15.25, p < 0.001$), Long Term Orientation ($F(3,28) = 4.28, p = 0.013$) and Indulgence ($F(3,28) = 8.14, p < 0.001$) was found. A significant effect was found between every pair of clusters, except for cluster 3 and 5. As Hofstede's cultural dimensions are clearly distinguishing the clusters we found, we may assume that the clusters can be regarded as a representation of culture.

Table 2. k-Means clusters with $k = 5$

Nr	Size	Members
1	934	China, Chech Republic, Russia, South Korea, Turkey, Ukraine
2	101	Saudi Arabia
3	3612	Australia, Belgium, Britain, Canada, France, Poland, USA
4	1071	Argentina, Brazil, Chile, Mexico
5	4052	Austria, Denmark, Finland, Germany, Italy, Japan, the Netherlands, New Zealand, Norway, Portugal, Spain, South Africa, Sweden, Switzerland

3   Data Analysis Models

We used three different data analysis models: (1) logistic regression, (2) random forest, and (3) deep learning network.

Multinomial Logistic regression with regularization is a widely used model for data analysis. It is an adaption of the Linear Regression model in order to make it usable for classification. There are different methods for subset selection for this model, for which the standard is the shrinkage method, by which a penalty is given on large weights in order to prevent overfitting. We used the R package `glmnet` for logistic regression.

A Random Forest is a collection of decision trees, where the output of all decision trees is combined into one classification label. We used the R package `randomForest` to implement this classifier.

A deep learning network is a neural network that may have many layers, and a great many nodes per layer. For training the network we use standard backpropagation, using the Python `Keras` library, which is built onto the `Theano` library.

Each model has different parameters which need to be optimized. To do so, we divided the dataset into a training, validation, and test set before learning the models for predicting platform. The training set consists of $60,000$ examples, the validation set consists of $20,000$ examples and the test set consists of the remaining $19,912$ examples. The different models are trained on the training set and their error percentage is evaluated on the validation set in order to determine the best parameter(s) for each model. The test set is used to determine the final accuracy of the model. Because of the smaller size of the dataset for nationality and cluster culture, we used 10-fold cross-validation instead of a seperate training and validation set. The cross-validation set for this approach consists of $8,000$ examples, and the test consists of the remaining $1,770$ examples. All models use the same division of training examples among the sets for each type of target variable.

4   Results

The results for all four models are shown in Table 3.

For the logistic regression, we used different values for α and λ.

For the random forest, we tested different numbers of trees (ranging from 10 to 5,000) and different numbers of minimum leaf node sizes (ranging from 1 to 500). In total, we compared 56 different configurations. However, these results are in all cases worse than those for logistic regression.

For the deep learning network, we considered a perceptron network with one hidden layer and with two hidden layers, and for classifying platform also with three hidden layers, with different numbers of hidden nodes in each layer. The number of hidden units varied within the values $(128, 256, 512, 1024)$. Moreover, the values $(0.01, 0.001, 0.0001)$ were considered for the learning rate. As the outcome of a neural network is dependent on the start weights, we built each model five times with different random start weights. The final error percentage for a set of parameters was calculated by averaging over these five networks.

The error percentage on validation set for classifying platform was 18.99 for one hidden layer, 17.69 for two hidden layers and 17.24 for three hidden layers.

The best performing neural network for classifying platform has three layers with 1024 hidden nodes each. Due to the diminishing returns of adding more layers, we did not test what adding a fourth layer would do.

The table shows that neural networks show a significant better performance than other models when classifying platform. For classifying nationality and cluster culture, they show similar performance as logistic regression. This is not surprising, as the dataset used for nationality and cluster culture consisted of only 10 % of the examples for platform, and neural networks perform better on large datasets.

From the table it can also be seen that the results for almost all models are slightly better on the test set than on the validation set. This demonstrates that they all generalize well.

An analysis of the confusion tables for the neural networks on platform showed that identifying a PC player is most easy. Xbox One players are sometimes confused with PS4 players, and Xbox 360 players are sometimes confused with PS3 players. Evidently, the generation of the console has more impact on playstyle than the type of console.

Table 3. Error percentage on validation and test sets

Model	Platform		Nationality		Cluster	
	Validation	Test	Validation	Test	Validation	Test
Baseline	79.49	79.79	80.48	81.07	58.64	58.02
Logistic regression	20.39	20.33	55.88	55.93	39.46	39.77
Random forest	23.37	22.99	60.24	60.17	43.59	42.77
Neural network	17.24	16.43	56.10	55.75	39.67	39.31

5   Conclusion

Our research goal was to investigate to what extent a deep learning neural network can derive players' characteristics from their gaming behaviour. We remark that a neural network with three layers is a fairly simple deep learning network, but the gain in accuracy between two and three layers in the present setup did not warrant adding more layers. However, even the three-layer neural network has proven to perform significantly better than conventional approaches for classifying platform, with a classification accuracy of 83.57%. On a much smaller dataset, neural networks perform similar to logistic regression to classify nationality and culture, with a classification accuracy of 55.75% for nationality and of 39.31% for cluster culture. We are currently investigating whether using a larger dataset improves the neural network performance for this task.

We have shown that neural networks, by their strong performance, are a viable modeling approach to player attribute classification, and thus have the potential to open the road to actual automatic game adaptation based on player observations. However, improved accuracy could definitely be achieved when we use more extensive feature sets. In this research, all the features were snapshots of statistics at a specific time. Previous research has shown that far better results can be achieved by including features that express behaviour change over time [6]. Naturally, we also need to investigate predicting different player attributes.

Note: A white paper with many details on the experiments described in this paper is available from the authors on request. The dataset is also available from the same source.

References

1. Bialas, M., Tekofsky, S., Spronck, P.: Cultural influences on play style. In: Proceedings of the 2014 IEEE Conference on Computational Intelligence in Games, pp. 271–277. IEEE Press (2014)
2. Hofstede, G., Hofstede, G.J., Minkov, M.: Cultures and Organizations: Software of the Mind, revised and expanded 3rd edn. McGraw-Hill, New York (2010)
3. Van Lankveld, G., Spronck, P., Van den Herik, J., Arntz, A.: Games as personality profiling tools. In: 2011 IEEE Conference on Computational Intelligence in Games, pp. 197–202. IEEE Press (2011)
4. Mnih, V., Kavukcuoglu, K., Silver, D., Rusu, A.A., Veness, J., Bellemare, M.G., Graves, A., Riedmiller, M., Fidjeland, A.K., Ostrovski, G., Petersen, S., Beattie, C., Sadik, A., Antonoglou, I., King, H., Kumaran, D., Wierstra, D., Legg, S., Hassabis, D.: Human-level control through deep reinforcement learning. Nature **518**, 529–533 (2015)
5. Prensky, M.: Digital Game-Based Learning. McGraw-Hill, New York (2001)
6. Tekofsky, S., Spronck, P., Goudbeek, M., Plaat, A., Van den Herik, J.: Past our prime: a study of age & play style development in battlefield 3. IEEE Trans. Comput. Intell. AI Games **7**(3), 292–303 (2015)
7. Tekofsky, S., Spronck, P., Plaat, A., Van den Herik, J., Broersen, J.: PsyOps: personality assessment through gaming behavior. In: Proceedings of the 2013 Foundations of Digital Games Conference (2013)
8. Silver, D., Huang, A., Maddison, C.J., Guez, A., Sifre, L., Van den Driessche, G., Schrittwieser, J., Antonoglou, I., Panneershelvam, V., Lanctot, M., Dieleman, L., Grewe, D., Nham, J., Kalchbrenner, N., Sutskever, I., Lillicrap, T., Leach, M., Kavukcuoglu, K., Graepel, T., Hassabis, D.: Mastering the game of Go with deep neural networks and tree search. Nature **529**, 484–489 (2016)
9. Simonyan, K., Zisserman, A.: Very deep convolutional networks for large-scale image recognition. In: Proceedings of the ICLR 2015 (2015)
10. Westra, J., Dignum, F.P.M., Dignum, M.V.: Organizing scalable adaptation in serious games. In: Proceedings of the 3rd International Workshop on the uses of Agents for Education, Games and Simulations (2011)
11. Yannakakis, G.N., Spronck, P., Loiacono, D., André, E.: Player modeling. In: Artificial and Computational Intelligence in Games. DFU, vol. 6, pp. 45–59. Dagstuhl, Germany (2013)

Do Warriors, Villagers and Scientists Decide Differently? The Impact of Role on Message Framing

J. Siebelink[1(⊠)], P. van der Putten[1], and M.C. Kaptein[2]

[1] Media Technology, Leiden University, Leiden, The Netherlands
siebelink.jorrit@gmail.com,
p.w.h.v.d.putten@liacs.leidenuniv.nl
[2] Tilburg University, Tilburg, The Netherlands
m.c.kaptein@uvt.nl

Abstract. The role people play in real or virtual environments can have an influence on how we make decisions. Furthermore, it has been suggested that stimulating analytic or impulsive information processing can influence framing effects. In this study we combine these previous results and examine whether virtual role-playing influences the strength of the effect of message framing. Participants were subjected to an experiment in which they played different characters in a computer game. Within the game, the effects of different types of message framing where measured. The results suggest that susceptibility to attribute framing increases when role-playing an impulsive character. The current study contributes to the existing literature both by demonstrating a novel effect virtual role playing has on our information processing, as well as by introducing games as a novel medium for studying the effects of message framing.

Keywords: Behavioral economics · Framing effect · Proteus effect · Role-playing · Avatars · Serious gaming

1 Introduction

Ever since its demonstration by Tversky and Kahneman [1], the so-called 'framing effect' has been a well-researched phenomenon in the field of decision-making and behavioral economics. The framing effect is a cognitive bias, it assumes that choices between logically equivalent alternatives can be influenced by framing the problem in different ways. It is claimed to be one of the strongest cognitive biases in human decision-making. As such, the presence of the framing effect is often used as evidence for irrational or impulsive decision making. In this paper a study is presented which investigates whether the effect size of different variants of the framing effect can be influenced by playing a specific role or avatar in a virtual environment. We hypothesize that by playing a distinct role different types of information processing can be primed, and subsequently influence the strength of the framing effect. Thus, the goal of the study was to show the influence of digital persona on cognitive processes related to decision making. In particular, the focus of this research is the question: "Does playing

© ICST Institute for Computer Sciences, Social Informatics and Telecommunications Engineering 2017
R. Poppe et al. (Eds.): INTETAIN 2016, LNICST 178, pp. 167–177, 2017.
DOI: 10.1007/978-3-319-49616-0_16

an analytic or impulsive character, respectively, influence the susceptibility to the framing effect?"

This research can be seen as a proposal for how virtual role-playing environments can be used to produce novel and interesting insights, especially in the field of behavior psychology and decision-making. Where most of the research on framing is conducted in a lab-setting and by using questionnaires, the present research shows how a game can be used as an alternative medium to gather data in situ. Even though games are virtual, they may provide a more natural environment in which psychological experiments may be concealed, as well as provide some increased motivation to win by all means, thus reducing observer effects such as the Hawthorne effect. Whilst the main interest of the authors is in biases in decision making in general, this kind of research can also contribute to the use of gaming for serious, non-entertainment purposes.

The remainder of this paper is structured as follows: First, a background section will provide an overview of the literature regarding the framing effect and serious gaming, as well as explaining the different variants of the framing effect. Second, an overview of studies on video-games and behavioral change is given. Third, the method used for the research is discussed, as well as its merits in comparison to methods used in other framing studies. Finally, the empirical results are presented and reviewed.

2 Background

In this section a more detailed explanation of the framing effect and the types of framing, is given.

2.1 The Framing Effect Explained

The classic understanding of the framing effect is often called the 'risky-choice framing effect'. An example of the risky-choice framing effect is the 'Asian Disease Problem' as described by Tversky and Kahneman [1]. The 'Asian Disease Problem' is an experimental setup in which two groups of participants are proposed the situation of a hypothetical outbreak of an Asian disease that infected 600 patients. For this outbreak the participants need to choose one out of two treatments. For each of the two treatments a different description is given, either describing a sure outcome or a gamble. E. g. the first treatment would be described as "Treatment A will save 200 patients" while the second treatment would be described as "With treatment B, there is a 1/3 probability that everyone will be saved, and a 2/3 chance that nobody will be saved." For both groups a similar description is given. However, the difference in the descriptions for each of the groups is that net results of each of the options is either described as a gain (positive frame) or a loss (negative frame). For example, instead of the example descriptions as given above (the positive or gain-frame), in the second group the medicines would be described as: "With treatment A, 400 people will die" vs. "With treatment B, there is a 1/3 probability that nobody will die, and a 2/3 chance that everyone will die" (a negative or loss-frame). Note that the description in both groups is logically the same; for both groups the expected net results of either option is 200.

Although logically equivalent, the different frames have a profound effect on the choice preference of the participants in each group. Kahneman & Tversky observed that most participants avoided risks when presented with a positive frame, while seeking risks when presented with a negative frame. Even more, they found the effect to be as strong as to induce an almost symmetric reversal of choice preference in both groups; in the 'positive framing' group 72 % choose for the sure option while only 22 % chose for the sure option in the 'negative framing' group (and vice versa).

Apart from the risky framing effect other variants of framing can be distinguished, namely attribute framing and goal framing. In the case of attribute framing a choice shift is caused by describing the attributes of an object, or a procedure, in either a positive way or in a (equivalent) negative way. The effect of the attribute framing is then measured by the willingness to do the action or the evaluation of the product. For example, consumers are more likely to rate a piece of meat positively when it is described as 25 % lean instead of 75 % fat [2].

Lastly, goal framing entails the effect that is caused by describing either the positive or negative consequences of doing an action or avoiding to do that action. For example, women are more apt to participate in breast self-examination when they are presented with the negative consequences of not engaging in the procedure than when presented with information stressing the positive consequences of doing the procedure [3].

2.2 Causes of and Influences on the Framing Effect

Although the framing effect has been proven to be consistent and strong, several influences on the magnitude and presence of the framing effect have been found. For example, when one is presented with a risky framing problem and is asked for a rationale for the decisions, the framing effect seems to disappear [4]. Even more, the framing effect seems to (dis)appear when a participant is respectively asked to *'think like a scientist'* or *'choose using their gut feeling'* before a framing experiment [5].

Due to the supporting research, the causes of the framing effect have often been related to dual process theories, which roughly state that our cognitive information processing system is divided into two separate systems, namely a system concerned with intuitive judgments and an analytic or rational system [6].

2.3 Role-Playing, Avatars and Behavioral Change

The influence of virtual characters on human behavior is often related to video-games. For example, the research by Konijn et al. [7] suggests that when adolescent boys identified with a violent game character, they show increased aggression while playing against other players. An earlier study by Nowak et al. [8], suggest that playing aggressive video games can increase aggressive behavior outside the virtual world. Even more, a study by Yoon and Vargas [9], more specifically researching *types* of avatars, showed that the specific type of avatar can have a profound influence on the behavior of a subject outside the virtual environment. In their experiment the subjects played either a hero or a villain. After their play-through they were asked to pour either chili-sauce or chocolate sauce on a dish which was said to be for the next participant. Ultimately, the results showed that the participants who played as a villain not only chose to pour chili-sauce more often, but did so in considerably higher amounts than the participants who played the hero avatar. A study by Happ et al. [10], relating avatars to (pro) social behavior, showed similar results.

Although the relation between avatars and behavioral change has been demonstrated multiple times, studies concerning the relation between virtual role-playing and the framing effect are lacking. This is especially surprising since the framing effect could provide interesting insights in the cognitive processes of players playing a specific kind of avatar.

3   Method

The goal of the present research was to answer the question: "Does playing an analytic or impulsive character, respectively, influence the susceptibility to the framing effect?" In this section the design and procedure of the experiment is discussed. Furthermore, the rationale for using a digital environment is given.

3.1   Experiment Design

The experiment utilizes a 'mod' made for the well-known video role-playing game called Skyrim.[1] A mod or modification is an addition to an existing game, changing the content or the game-play mechanics of the game. In this research a self-developed mod was used to modify Skyrim so that it was usable for the experiment.

Out of a group of 86 participants, each participant was randomly given a specific role and had to play a small scenario. More specifically, 29 played as a 'Warrior' character, 29 played as a 'Scientist' character and 28 as a 'Neutral' character. The reason for including the neutral character was that it functioned, more or less, as a 'control group' character. For example, it was expected that players playing the warrior role showed the highest susceptibility to the framing effect, players playing the scientist role the lowest, while a moderate effect was expected for the players playing the neutral character.

Each of the roles had certain abilities which let the player manipulate the world in certain ways. For example, the warrior had the possession over a sword and a shield, allowing him to defeat enemies by force. The scientist had the ability to activate certain puzzle elements in the game. The neutral character had no specific abilities. In this research a combination of visual cues and character traits are given to manipulate the concept of "role". In the research we added a number of manipulation checks to assess whether our role manipulation was successful.

During the gameplay, the participants were presented with four framing tasks in either a positive framing or a negative framing. The tasks the participants received were

---

[1] See https://cognitiveroleplaying.wordpress.com/ for screenshots and http://bit.ly/1mdfsre for user feedback and downloading the mod.

two risky framing tasks, one attribute framing task and one goal framing task. The framing for each separate task was randomly assigned. As such, this experiment utilized a 3 (role) x4 (task) x2 (valence) mixed-subject design with role and valence as between subject factors, and task as a within subject factor. Most participants were subjected to the experiment by face-to-face contact; the participants met the researchers in 'real-life' and were instructed by the researchers directly. A sub group of 26 of the participants were found on internet fora and were instructed how to conduct the experiment through online media. Of 66 out of the 86 participants the age is known, which averaged around 25 years old (median = 25.5).

3.2 Procedure

The players were asked to take place behind a laptop and were given a small explanation of the research. However, the explanation did not include any references to the framing effect itself. Instead the participants were told that "they partook in a study regarding role-playing and behavior". The participants were asked to play through a small introduction level to get acquainted with the mechanics and the controls. After the introduction level, the main story of the game was explained. Finally, participants were *given* one specific role and were presented with a small background story of their character. Again, as a means of avoiding any bias of the participant for (non) risky behavior, the characters were described simply by their occupation and origin. References suggesting whether the characters themselves would or wouldn't take risks were avoided.

The main premise of the game consisted of finding a cure for an outbreak of a mysterious disease, in a supposed abandoned research facility. Throughout their exploration they were presented with two challenges. For the first challenge the player had to find a way past a guarded gate, either by using force, solving a puzzle or using dialogue. The second challenge consisted of a group of enemies which the player had to evade by using force or triggering a trap. However, if player was the neutral character, the player would be allowed to cross without the need for any interaction. The purpose of these challenges for the research was to prime the players to 'get in character' and roleplay.

In the game the player met a non-playing-character (NPC) which guided the player through the use of dialogue. The reason for including this character was threefold: first, through this character more story-elements were given to the player. Second, through the interaction with the character the player was able to role-play his or her character by giving answers during the dialogue. Lastly, through the answers on the dialogue, data was generated by which could be deduced whether the player was giving answers like the character (the participant was playing) would. On a similar note, the actions performed during the challenges were also recorded for the same reason. After going through the level, a code was generated which contained the data of the experiment, namely the choices as well as the role-playing actions performed by the player. A full play-through from begin till end, for either online or offline participants, averaged around 20 min.

Framing tasks: Throughout the play-through each player was presented with four framing tasks:

Task 1 (Goal framing task): In the starting dialogue with the NPC, the player is told that there are several items present in the research facility. After this dialogue, the framing message is given in either a positive or negative frame. In the positive frame the message was as follows: "If you take these valuable items, you might receive a reward in the end". The negative frame read: "Don't leave these items, since you might miss out on a reward in the end". At the end of the experiment the amount of valuable and non-valuable items the player picked up were measured.

Task 2 (First risky framing task): After the first challenge the player encounters a chest which initiates the task. The player is told that there is an amount of 400 gold pieces in the chest. Two options are given in either a positive or negative frame. In the positive frame the two options were described as follows: either the player could gain exactly 100 gold pieces for sure, or the player would have a $1/4^{th}$ chance to gain all gold pieces while having a 3/4th chance of gaining none. In the negative framing the two options were described as follows: either the player could lose exactly 300 pieces (from the 400) for sure, or the player would have a 1/4th chance to lose none of the gold pieces while having a 3/4th chance to lose all the gold pieces.

Task 3 (Attribute framing task): During dialogue with the NPC, the player is told about a medical procedure one of the patients in the research facility had to undergo. An attribute or characteristic of the procedure is described, namely the success or mortality rate. In the positive frame the procedure was being described as "2/3th chance of being successful". In the negative frame the mortality rate was being described, which was 1/3th. After, the player was asked whether he or she would or wouldn't have done the procedure.

Task 4 (Second risky framing task): At the end of the play-through the players find a medicine cabinet with ingredients to make the final cure. However, they are being told that they can make only one cure out of two possible cures. This task is essentially the classic 'Asian disease experiment'. In the positive frame both cures were described as follows: The first cure saves exactly 300 out of 900 patients while the second cure has a 1/3th chance of saving all patients and a 2/3th chance of saving none. In the negative frame the cures were described as follows: The first cure lets exactly 600 out of 900 patients die, while the second cure has a 1/3th chance of letting no patients die and a 2/3th chance of letting all patients die.

3.3   Rationale for Using a Digital Medium

The main reason for using a digital environment was that the researchers were essentially able to 'catch the subjects in the act' (roleplaying while being subjected to framing research). Furthermore, by using a digital medium instead of using a more traditional approach to framing research is that it's escaping the controlled and sometimes more unrealistic circumstances of the lab. Although not all framing research is conducted using this setting, often the classic framing research method is to provide participants with hypothetical situations and simple A/B choices on questionnaires. However, 'real-life' choices are often made in more subtle contexts in variable circumstances. Therefore, by providing the participants with a digital video-game, a game similar to games they play at home as well, the present research can be considered somewhat of a field-research instead. An interesting observation, acquired by informal interviews after the experiment, supporting this claim was that during the experiments the players actually thought there was something at stake; that by answering the questions they could eventually 'win' the game. It was strongly believed that, since they were presented with a game, a reward and punishment system existed. This provided the advantage that the players really took the experiment seriously. Therefore, one could argue that the results of the research present a more realistic picture. Especially, in comparison with classic risky framing research it might be that the participants felt more involved. In the classic risky framing experiment, participants were asked to imagine the hypothetical outbreak. Instead, in the research as presented by this article, participants (implicitly) thought that their actions had an impact, since that's normally how a game works.

3.4   Results

In this section the main results of each framing task are given. This means that for the attribute framing and risky framing tasks the choice preference of the participants for that task are evaluated. For the goal framing, the amount of valuable was measured. Although all of the framing tasks are evaluated, graphs are shown for key results only.

During the play-through the role-playing actions of the subjects were measured on specific control tasks to determine whether the player behaved like a warrior, scientist or neutral character in terms of choices made, based on the randomly assigned role. Based on the amount of these actions it was determined whether the player acted according to his or her role. For example, if a participant receiving the warrior role would chose the warrior option at all five moments, that participant would receive a score of 5 for 'playing according to their role'. Based on the average amounts of correct actions done according to role per participants for each group (War: M = 2.8; Sci: M = 3.6; Neu: M = 3.6), we can conclude that for the warrior and scientist group the role manipulation worked as participants receiving those roles, mostly chose the options according to their given role. Hence, there was a positive association between the role, and the actions selected by the participants indicating that our role manipulation was successful.

Attribute framing task: In Fig. 1. (figure in the right-corner) the results of the attribute framing for all the participants, independent of the role they played, are shown. A significant effect of attribute framing was found with X2 = 4.54; df: 1; p = 0.033. These results suggest that, overall, attribute framing had a significant effect on the choices made by the participants.

The main graph of Fig. 1. represents the choice preferences of participants playing the different roles. Since the different role-groups were relatively small, a fisher-exact test was used for producing more powerful results. Comparing the three different groups, interacting with attribute framing, no difference between each of the groups could be demonstrated (p = 0.075) > 0.05. However, a "trend" indicating the warriors being affected more strongly by the framing effect was shown. Using a fisher-exact test

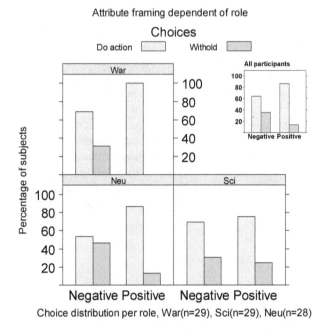

Fig. 1. Choice distribution for attribute framing task (for all participants and per role).

a difference between the two frames in the warrior group was found (p = 0.047). Since no differences were found in either the scientist group (p = 1) or the neutral group (p = 0.192), these results suggest that participants playing the warrior character were indeed influenced by attribute framing, while participants playing the other roles weren't being affected.

Risky framing task 1: From looking at the results independent of role (Fig. 2. right-corner), there was no indication that there was a framing effect. The results as divided by role showed a more noticeable difference in the warrior group. However, using a fisher-exact test a p-value of 0.264 was found, indicating that there was no statistical difference between the two framing groups. Also, in all other groups no difference was found (fisher-exact test, Sci: p = 0.682; Neu: p = 1). Comparing the three roles, no difference between the groups could be demonstrated (p = 0.176).

Risky framing task 2: The results independent of role, didn't suggest there was a framing effect present. Moreover, from a role-specific perspective no big differences can be distinguished. A fisher-test found a p = 1 for the warrior group, p = 0.390 for the scientist group and p = 0.705 for the neutral group. Also, there was a difference in preference for choosing either the risk or certain options among roles in general. For example, the participants playing the warrior role preferred the risky option despite the framing. Instead, both the neutral and the scientist group preferred the certain option. Lastly, no difference between the three role-groups could be demonstrated (p = 0.134).

Goal-framing: At the end of the play through the amount of valuable items, that were picked up by the players, was measured. The mean scores of picked up valuable

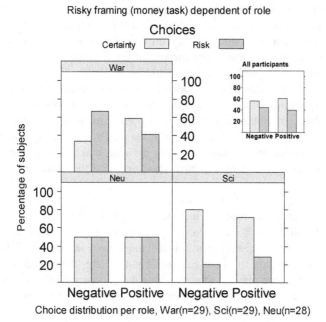

Fig. 2. Choice distribution for first risky framing task (for all participants and per role).

items for the three class groups under both valence conditions, were respectively: War (positive): M = 8.92, SE = 0.33; War (negative): M = 12.43, SE = 0.35; Sci (positive): M = 9.43, SE = 0.42; Sci (negative): M = 9.54, SE = 0.40; Neu (positive): M = 9.64, SE = 0.30; Neu (negative); M = 9.73, SE = 0.42.

For determining whether there was a main effect for either the role or framing, an ANOVA test was used. However, no main effect was found for either role, F(2, 72) = 0.330, p = 0,720, or framing, F(1, 72) = 0.625, p = 0.432. These non-significant results suggest that framing and class, overall, have no impact on the amount of valuable items that the participants picked up (or that the study was underpowered to demonstrate the effect). Moreover, using a two-way ANOVA it was found that there is no interaction between the role participants played, and the framing of the message on the measured amount of valuable items, F(2, 72) = 0.554, p = 0.577.

4   Discussion

The results as presented by this research bring some interesting implications to light. First, since the framing effect has often been regarded as one of the stronger cognitive biases, the fact that the results as presented in the current didn't show the framing effect convincingly in most tasks raises some interesting questions. For example, it is of interest to see whether the current manipulation and measurement contained too much variation (or whether merely the sample was too small) to replicate earlier studies. Most importantly, it raises the question whether the framing effects found in previous studies would be present when those studies would utilize different environment. When using a digital medium amounts to the disappearance of the framing effect, one could doubt whether current framing methodologies should be revised.

The results suggest that using a video-game as the medium may have been an influence on the absence of the framing effect in most cases. However, this immediately raises the problem of immersion. When is a participant really involved in a video game? And, can use of a game as a medium, if the player isn't feeling immersed, result in the player behaving more rational in their decision making? Furthermore, can the fact that the player may or may not have identified with the character influenced the results?

Some of these concerns can be addressed by evaluating the experimental results in detail. For example, in the research included multiple control tasks to check whether the player assumed his or her role correctly. These checks showed that most players acted according to their role. However, this still might have left the possibility open that the player acted according to his or role while not feeling 'connected' with the character. Even though some players, after finishing the experiment, did mention that they felt immersed more thorough measurements of immersion or the 'emotional involvement' of the player, could be provide some interesting insights.

Most importantly, the current results not only shed some light on current framing methodologies, but can be seen as an argument for using digital media, such as role-playing games, for more serious research topics. Often, videogames are considered to be meant for more playful or entertaining purposes. However, these results clearly show that research into video games combined with more serious topics can shed some interesting, new insights and yield results which are against established findings.

5 Conclusion

In this research an answer was sought to the question whether playing an impulsive or analytic character respectively induces or reduces the framing effect. In our in situ experiment a main effect of attribute framing was found. Furthermore, it was found that the group playing the warrior character was influenced strongly by the attribute framing effect while the other groups were not. The results, however, did not show a strong effect of risky-choice framing or goal framing: in our in situ experiments the effects of these manipulations were apparently small. However, even in these conditions results indicated that players adopting the warrior role seemed more prone to the effects of framing. Hence, we conclude that while a study with more power is certainly worthwhile, the current study at least provides initial evidence that the "warrior" — and hence impulsive — role is more prone to framing effects. Furthermore, our presented method using immersive gaming introduces a novel methodological paradigm to study human decision making: we hope this approach can benefit future studies.

References

1. Tversky, A., Kahneman, D.: The framing of decisions and the psychology of choice. Science **211**(4481), 453–458 (1981)
2. Levin, I.P., Gaeth, G.J.: How consumers are affected by the framing of attribute information before and after consuming the product. J. Consum. Res. **15**(December), 374–378 (1988)
3. Meyerowitz, B.E., Chaiken, S.: The effect of message framing on breast self-examination attitudes, intentions, and behavior. J. Pers. Soc. Psychol. **52**(3), 500–510 (1987)
4. Fagley, N.S., Miller, P.M.: The effects of decision framing on choice of risky vs certain options. Organ. Behav. Hum. Decision Process. **39**, 264–277 (1987)
5. Thomas, A.K., Millar, P.R.: Reducing the framing effect in older and younger adults by encouraging analytic processing. J. Gerontol. Ser. B: Psychol. Sci. Soc. Sci. 1–11 (2011)
6. Kahneman, D.: A perspective on judgment and choice: mapping bounded rationality. Am. Psychol. **58**(9), 697–720 (2003)
7. Konijn, E.A., Bijvank, M.N., Bushman, B.J.: I wish I were a warrior: the role of wishful identification in the effects of violent video games on aggression in adolescent boys. Dev. Psychol. **43**(4), 1038–1044 (2007)
8. Nowak, K.L., Kromar, M., Farrar, K.M.: Examining the relationship between violent video games, presence, and aggression. Presence, 139–146 (2006)
9. Yoon, G., Vargas, P.T.: Know thy avatar: the unintended effect of virtual-self representation on behavior. Psychol. Sci. **25**(4), 1043–1045 (2014)
10. Happ, G., Melzer, A., Steffgen, G.: Superman vs. BAD man? The effects of empathy and game character in violent video games. Cyberpsychol. Behav. Soc. Netw. **16**(10), 774–778 (2013)

The Effect of Gender, Native English Speaking, and Age on Game Genre Preference and Gaming Motivations

Shoshannah Tekofsky[1(✉)], Paul Miller[1], Pieter Spronck[1], and Kevin Slavin[2]

[1] Tilburg University, Warandelaan 2, 5037 AB Tilburg, The Netherlands
{S.Tekofsky,P.Spronck}@uvt.nl, PaulM@ieee.org
[2] Massachusetts Institute of Technology,
77 Massachusetts Ave, Cambridge, MA 02139, USA
Slavin@media.mit.ed

Abstract. Gender, native English speaking, and age significantly effect game genre preference and gaming motivations. Ordinary Least Squares (OLS) regression shows they explain 5 %–10 % of the variance in game genre preference and up to 7 % in gaming motivation. Gender coefficients show males prefer the competition-based First Person Shooter (FPS) games while females prefer the immersion-based Massively Multiplayer Online Role Playing Games (MMORPG). Native English speaking coefficients show native English speakers prefer the text-heavy MMORPGs, while non-Native English speakers prefer the text-light Multiplayer Online Battle Arenas (MOBA) and FPS games. Age coefficients show younger players prefer MOBAs, while older players prefer FPS games. When it comes to gaming motivation, males are more driven by competition, while females are more driven by immersion and social motivations. Native English speaking only factors into two motivations related to immersion. Age coefficients show that gaming motivation decreases across the board as players grow older.

Keywords: Gender · Age · English · Video games · Motivation

1 Introduction

Video games have grown into a mainstream pastime, with half the American public engaging in the activity on a weekly basis [1]. As video games have gained more traction with the general public, they have also grown as a field of academic inquiry. An expanding body of work has emerged that seeks to uncover who plays video games, how they engage with video games, and why they feel driven to pursue video game play as a pastime [2–4].

To ensure reliable and robust research results on such complex issues, the effect of potential confounds such as gender, native English speaking, and age should be determined. Currently the video game literature shows mixed effects of these confounds on the behavioral and cognitive processes underlying, perpetuating, and resulting from video game play. For instance, in a meta-review of

© ICST Institute for Computer Sciences, Social Informatics and Telecommunications Engineering 2017
R. Poppe et al. (Eds.): INTETAIN 2016, LNICST 178, pp. 178–183, 2017.
DOI: 10.1007/978-3-319-49616-0_17

35 research reports, Anderson et al. [5] determined that gender is not a significant confound on aggression resulting from video game play. Conversely, seminal research by Yee et al. [6] on gaming motivation, as well as extensive work by Mitchell & Savill-Smith [7] on the role of video games in education have shown that gender significantly confounds the appeal and impact of video game play in their research.

To shed more light on the strength of potential confounds in video game research, we look at the effect of three common confounds on the most basic aspects of video game play: what people play, and why. The potential confounds in question are gender, native English speaking, and age. The what and why of play are instantiated as an individual's game genre preference and their gaming motivations. If the confounds significantly impact game genre preference and gaming motivation, then the case is strengthened for controlling for these confounds to ensure robust results in future video game research.

2 Methods

To test the effect of gender, native English speaking, and age on game genre preference and gaming motivation, we collected data from participants online. Data consisted of gender, age, country of residence, English skill level, a survey of gaming motivation [6,8,9], and a valid game account in at least one of four games: World of Warcraft (WoW), League of Legends (LoL), Battlefield 4, and/or Battlefield: Hardline. Battlefield 4 and Battlefield: Hardline are functionally identical games. For that reason, the players of these two games are grouped and jointly referred to as 'Battlefield' (BF) players for the remainder of this paper. Each game represents one of the most popular online multiplayer games and supports an active player base of at least 10 million players. World of Warcraft represents the fantasy themed, third-person, cooperative/competitive, story and exploration driven genre of Massively Multiplayer Online Role Playing Games (MMORPG). League of Legends represents the fantasy themed, third-person, team-based competitive, match-structured genre of Multiplayer Online Battle Arena games (MOBA). Battlefield represents the realistic military shooter, first-person, team-based competitive, match-structured genre of First-Person Shooter games (FPS). The survey of gaming motivation was compiled by using a short form of 13 motivational factors validated by Yee et al. [6], Hilgard et al. [8], and Sherry et al. [9]. The short forms are reliable as they correlate with the original long forms with effect sizes over .9. The 13 motivational factors are listed in Table 1.

Before analysis, the data was filtered on four criteria. First, data from minors (age < 18) was excluded from the sample, resulting in the inclusion of 2817 players. Secondly, 28 players were excluded as outliers for showing no univariate variance in their responses. Thirdly, 19 participants were excluded as outliers for indicating the gender value "other" while all remaining participants indicated either "male" or "female" for gender. Lastly, 363 participants were excluded for indicating an English skill level other than "Advanced" or "Native". Both

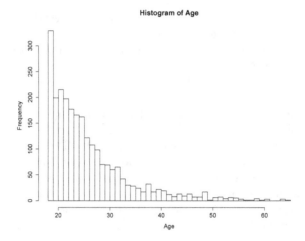

Fig. 1. Age distribution

advanced and native speakers of English are expected to fully understand all survey items. Therefore, native English speaking became a proxy for culture (Anglosphere cultures versus non-Anglosphere cultures).

The characteristics of the remaining sample are as follows. It contained 2400 participants, including 2073 males and 327 females, of which 943 were advanced English speakers and 1457 were native English speakers. The average age was 26.17 (std = 7.72), with a zero-inflated distribution around the minimum age of 18 (see Fig. 1). Most participants played World of Warcraft (n = 1181), followed by League of Legends (n = 919) and Battlefield (n = 824). In total, 436 participants indicated playing two of the aforementioned games, and 44 participants indicated playing all three games.

3   Results

Ordinary Least Squares (OLS) regression showed that gender, native English speaking and age are significant confounds to game genre preference. They explain 5 %, 10 % and 9 % of the variance in preference for playing World of Warcraft, League of Legends, and Battlefield, respectively. Table 1 shows the results of the regression. The gender coefficients reveal that women show a mild preference for MMORPG and MOBA games, while males show a pronounced preference for FPS games. The native English speaking coefficients reveal that native English speakers are biased toward (the more text-heavy) MMORPG genre, while advanced English speakers show a slight preference for (the less text-heavy) MOBA and FPS genres. The age coefficients reveal that age is not a confound for MMORPG play, while age is negatively related to MOBA play and positively related to FPS play. The age coefficients seem low compared to the gender and native English speaking coefficients, but this is due to the value range

Table 1. OLS regression of the predictors gender, native English speaking, and age on the outcome variables game genre preference and gaming motivation. Game genre preferences are binary and gaming motivations are continuous variables. Gender is (M)ale or (F)emale. Native English speaking is (A)dvanced or (N)ative. Age is a value from 18–65. * indicates that $R^2 < .01$. All models are significant at $\alpha = .05$. Coefficients are listed when $R \geq .01$ for the relevant model and $p \geq .05$ for the relevant coefficient.

	Gender 1 = M, 2 = F		English 1 = A, 2 = N		Age 18–65		Model Fit
	β	t	β	t	β	t	R^2
Game genre preference							
MMORPG: WoW	.18	6.22	.19	9.30			.05
MOBA: LoL	.08	2.85	−.12	−6.31	−.02	−14.24	.10
FPS: BF	−.33	−12.08	−.08	−4.11	.01	8.76	.09
Gaming motivation							
Competition	−.40	−6.90			−.02	−9.09	.06
Challenge							*
Fantasy	.22	3.79	.23	5.48	−.02	−5.87	.03
Arousal					−.01	−5.15	.01
Story	.22	3.70			−.02	−8.12	.03
Escapism	.27	4.50	.24	5.65	−.01	−3.51	.02
Loss aversion							*
Customization	.65	11.20			−.02	−8.06	.07
Grinding/completion	.40	6.76					.02
Autonomy/exploration							*
Socializing							*
Relationships	.39	6.57			−.01	−5.21	.03
Team work							*

of each variable. For instance, the reasonably large difference between males and females on Battlefield ($\beta = -.33$) would be equaled by a 33 year difference in age ($\beta = .01$) on the same game.

Gender, native English speaking, and age explain up to 7 % in the variance in gaming motivations. The coefficient values for gender, native English speaking, and age for the outcome variables related to gaming motivations are conceptually in line with the coefficient values for game genre preference. They show that men prefer competition, such as can be found in FPS games, while women prefer Fantasy, Story, Escapism, Customization, Grinding/Completion, and Relationships, such as can mainly be found in MMORPGs. Native English speaking is only weakly related to gaming motivation. The notable exception is that native English speakers show a preference for Fantasy and Escapism motivations that are in line with their preference for MMORPG games. Age is negatively related to half the gaming motivations, showing either a cohort effect and/or that people progressively lose interest in gaming as they grow older.

4   Discussion and Conclusion

Gender, native English speaking, and age have been shown to be significant confounds for game genre preference and gaming motivation. The variance explained by the confounds is between .01 and .10. Although these values are too low to form a predictive model, they are considerable in the context of confounding variables. They indicate that when the confounds are not controlled for, research results may incur an *additional* error of 1%–10%. Translated to effect sizes in correlational studies, this can lead to the misattribution of .1 to .32 of the effect sizes of variables that are influenced by gender, native English speaking, and/or age.

We wish to point out that the (already considerable) effects of gender in the realm of gaming might be more pronounced than found in this study. Additionally, interaction effects were not explored, even though it is plausible that, for instance, gaming motivation develops differently with age for males than for females. Due to the recruitment method of using anonymous online volunteers, the sample became biased towards male gamers, with a male-female ratio of around 5:1. This ratio is common in the field of video game research [6], and does not actually reflect the gender distribution among gamers. In their 2015 rapport on the gamer demographic in America, the Entertainment Software Association reports an almost 50–50 ratio of males to females [1]. Presumably, females are less vocal in sharing their gaming interest and engaging in the video game culture online where most game research samples are drawn from. This gender bias in the research samples can be remedied by specifically recruiting females. Hilgard et al. [8] and Sherry et al. [9] follow this approach in their studies. However, in order to verify and recruit an even gender distribution, it is necessary to resort to offline recruitment, such as is common at college campuses. This in turn strengthens the sample bias toward native English speaking and age, as most participants are college age individuals who are predominantly from one culture.

All in all, the results of this study show that gender, native English speaking, and age have a considerable effect on what (game genre preference) and why (gaming motivations) people play video games. Therefore, they underline the importance of controlling for these variables in video game related studies. Future work should endeavor to minimize sample biases on these three variables, as well as further explore how they interact with more detailed game behaviors and related cognitions.

References

1. Entertainment Software Association: 2015 Sales, Demographics and Usage Data. Essential Facts About the Computer and Video Game Industry (2015)
2. Ryan, R.M., Rigby, C.S., Przybylski, A.: The motivational pull of video games: a self-determination theory approach. Motiv. Emot. **30**(4), 344–360 (2006)

3. Yannakakis, G.N., Maragoudakis, M.: Player modeling impact on players entertainment in computer games. In: Ardissono, L., Brna, P., Mitrovic, A. (eds.) UM 2005. LNCS (LNAI), vol. 3538, pp. 74–78. Springer, Heidelberg (2005). doi:10.1007/11527886_11

4. Yee, N.: The demographics, motivations, and derived experiences of users of massively multi-user online graphical environments. Presence **15**(3), 309–329 (2006)

5. Anderson, C.A., Bushman, B.J.: Effects of violent video games on aggressive behavior, aggressive cognition, aggressive affect, physiological arousal, and prosocial behavior: a meta-analytic review of the scientific literature. Psychol. Sci. **12**(5), 353–359 (2001)

6. Yee, N.: Motivations for play in online games. CyberPsychology Behav. **9**(6), 772–775 (2006)

7. Mitchell, A., Savill-Smith, C.: The Use of Computer and Video Games for Learning: A Review of the Literature. Learning and Skills Development Agency, London (2004)

8. Hilgard, J., Engelhardt, C.R., Bartholow, B.D.: Individual differences in motives, preferences, and pathology in video games: the gaming attitudes, motives, and experiences scales (GAMES). Front. Psychol. **4**, 608 (2013)

9. Sherry, J.L., Lucas, K., Greenberg, B.S., Lachlan, K.: Video game uses and gratifications as predictors of use and game preference. Playing Video Games: Motives Responses Conseq. **24**, 213–224 (2006)

Measuring Affective, Physiological and Behavioural Differences in Solo, Competitive and Collaborative Games

Daniel Gábana Arellano[1]([⊠]), Laurissa Tokarchuk[1], and Hatice Gunes[2]

[1] Electronic Engineering and Computer Science, Queen Mary University of London,
Mile End Road, London E1 4NS, UK
{d.gabanaarellano,laurissa.tokarchuk}@qmul.ac.uk
[2] Computer Laboratory, University of Cambridge,
William Gates Building, 15 JJ Thomson Avenue, Cambridge CB3 0FD, UK
hatice.gunes@cl.cam.ac.uk

Abstract. In this paper, we aim to measure affect and behaviour indicators of players to understand how they feel in different play modes and how games could be improved to enhance user experience, immersion and engagement. We analyse the affective states in sets of two users playing a Wii video game in three play modes: solo, competitive and collaborative. We measured their physiological signals and observed the nonverbal behaviours to infer their affective states. Although other studies have looked at these signals in gaming, this work focuses on the differences between the three play modes aforementioned. Our results show that: (1) Players experience similar levels of arousal during both solo and collaborative play modes; (2) players' heart rates are significantly correlated during the competitive mode but not during the collaborative one; and (3) heart rate variability is a good indicator of engagement when playing video games.

Keywords: Affective gaming · Physiological signals · Non-verbal behaviour

1 Introduction

User affective states play a major role in immersive and engaging game experiences by influencing user experience and satisfaction [1]. As the present focus of game design is to increase the degree of immersion, enjoyment or simply to provide a pleasurable experience to the player, it is important to understand how players feel when interacting with the game and how different game events change their affective states. The recognition of the player's affective states brings exciting possibilities to gaming, from controlling games using physiological signals (biofeedback) to adapting it according the player's emotions (affective feedback) [2,3]. Gilleade et al. [1] propose that affective gaming should be used to keep the player engaged and motivated to play. For example, if the player gets bored,

© ICST Institute for Computer Sciences, Social Informatics and Telecommunications Engineering 2017
R. Poppe et al. (Eds.): INTETAIN 2016, LNICST 178, pp. 184–193, 2017.
DOI: 10.1007/978-3-319-49616-0_18

the game should increase the difficulty level to keep him engaged, but if he gets frustrated or too stressed, the game should be easier or give hints about how to progress. Current research in affective gaming is mainly focused on affective feedback, trying to enhance user experience by adapting the game to the player's affective state. However, not many studies have explored the effects evoked by video games in different play modes such as competitive, collaborative or solo.

This study is interested in investigating how collaborative and competitive game modes affect the player interactions and whether we can assess this by measuring players' physiological and behavioural signals in different play modes. We present a pilot study which explores the physiological and behavioural differences between sets of two co-located users playing a Wii video game in three play modes: solo (one-vs-computer), competitive and collaborative. Our analysis show that (1) heart rate is a good measure for assessing arousal and heart rate variability for assessing player engagement; (2) competitive play evokes higher arousal than the other two play modes; and (3) players experience a similar arousal level when playing solo and collaboratively.

2   Related Work: Affective and Multiplayer Gaming

The recognition of affective states is key for any affective computing application. The classification of affect can be a challenging task due to subjective cognitive and physiological reactions to external stimulus, since not everybody responds in the same way to different events. The most common classification approach is the two-dimensional arousal-valence [4]. The first dimension, arousal, maps the activation level and can be measured through the physiological modality such as cardiac activity, using electrocardiogram (ECG), or sweating level, measured with Galvanic Skin Response (GSR) [3,5]. The second one, valence, describes the degree of pleasantness of the affective state, frequently measured by looking at the visual or audio modality, including facial expressions, non-verbal and verbal behaviour [2]. Savva and Bianchi-Berthouze [6] used a motion capture system to analyse the affective states of the users playing a Wii tennis game. Using a Recurrent Neural Network algorithm, they grouped the affect into four different categories: happiness, concentration and low and high intensity negative emotion. The results showed recognition accuracy of 57 %.

The physiological signals related to the player's affective state have been mostly used in affective gaming in two different ways, either to directly control the game (biofeedback) or to indirectly adapt it to the player (affective feedback) [2,3]. *Relax-to-win* [7] is a biofeedback game where the player's arousal, measured by the GSR, controls the speed of a racing dragon, decreasing the dragon's pace when the arousal level increases so the player who relaxes more quickly wins the race. The game *Left 4 Dead 2* [8] was transformed into an affective feedback game, where the player's stress level was monitored by measuring arousal through heart rate. The game automatically adapted to the player's affective state, changing certain elements such as music loudness if the player is too stressed.

The objective of co-located competitive and collaborative leisure games is to encourage social interactions between players [9]. Collaboration is defined as the behaviour shown when multiple people work together towards a shared goal [10]. Collaborative and competitive games have been studied, often separately, looking at the affective states and behaviours they evoke. Different groups of researchers have investigated whether competitive games promote negative affective states but results are controversial. Some studies affirm they promote aggressive behaviour [11] while others argue that these games can also promote positive affect (if the player's motivation is winning, s/he might experience stress as positive affect) [12]. Kivikangas et al. [10] explored gender differences in emotional responses in collaborative and competitive games. The results revealed that males experienced more positive emotions during competitive than collaborative games whereas female participants evidenced no discernible difference.

Table 1. A summary of studies in affective gaming for solo and multiplayer games

Ref.	Play mode	Sensors	Self-rep. labels	Behaviours	Measured labels
[9]	Solo & Comp.	ECG, GSR, EMG & Resp.	Boredom, Engag. & Fun	N/A	Arousal
[10]	Collab. & Comp.	ECG, GSR, EMG	SAM & SPGQ	N/A	Valence & Arousal
[3]	Solo	ECG, GSR, EMG & Resp.	SAM		Valence & Arousal
[7]	Comp.	GSR	N/A	N/A	Arousal
[8]	Collab.	ECG	N/A	N/A	Arousal
[13]	Collab. & Comp.	ECG, GSR, EMG & Resp.	GEQ	N/A	Social interaction & Presence
Ours	Solo, Comp. & Collab.	ECG, GSR	GEQ & IQ	Non-verbal	Arousal

Notes: SAM: Self-Assessment Manikins. SPGQ: Social Presence in Gaming Questionnaire. GEQ: Gaming Engagement Questionnaire. IQ: Immersion Questionnaire

Collaborative games have been shown to lead to engagement, social interaction and positive emotions (i.e., enjoyment [9]). Mandryk and Inkpen [9] investigated the physiological changes in competitive and solo games (see Table 1). The study showed a significant increase in the sweating level (GSR) during the competitive mode, which correlated with a higher level of fun [9]. These results were confirmed correlating the physiological signals with the self-reported data gathered. However, this experiment did not look into differences between competitive and collaborative play modes. Chanel et al. measured the physiological compliance, defined as *the correlation between the physiological signals of a dyad* [13], in competitive and collaborative games both in co-location and remotely. They concluded that physiological compliance is higher in competitive games, with minor differences related to the location. In this paper we present a study where we measured the affective, physiological and behavioural indicators in solo, competitive and collaborative gaming in order to understand how players feel in these play modes and the differences in behaviour they exhibit in each mode.

3   The Study

Participants played a video game for Nintendo's Wii[1] console called *Boom Blox: Bash Party* (Fig. 1), a physics-based puzzle video game designed by Steven

---

[1] Nintendo's Wii console: http://www.wii.com/.

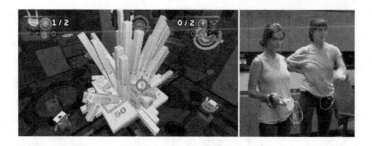

Fig. 1. Screenshot of Nintendo's Wii game *"Boom Blox: Bash Party"*

Spielberg. The game consists of knocking down a structure made of blocks by throwing balls against it using the Wii Remote controller as if it were the ball itself. Each block has a number drawn on it that indicates how many points it gives. We had to slightly modify the collaborative play mode in order to allow both players to play simultaneously without time limit. No prior experience was required to participate in this study, except both players within a pair had to know each other before the experiment to increase the chances of collaboration between them [14].

3.1   Tasks and Measurements

The players had to play *Boom Blox: Bash Party* in three play modes. In *solo*, players play alone and get points by knocking down the structure. In *competitive*, two players compete to get as many points as possible knocking down the blocks. In *collaborative*, two players play together to break the structure with as few throws as possible. The number of throws were counted for both players, so they had to talk and think about how to do it in the most efficient way. The duration of each play mode lasted 4–7 mins and the play order was randomised for every pair to avoid bias.

Subjective (self-reported) and objective (continuous and physiological) data was recorded from all players in every play mode. Table 2 summarises the data gathered and the features extracted. An electrocardiogram (ECG) to measure the heart's electrical activity was used, sampled at a rate of 512 Hz. We extracted the Heart Rate (HR), Inter-Beat Interval (IBI) and Heart Rate Variability (HRV). We also used a Galvanic Skin Response (GSR), which measures the activity of the sweating glands. The electrodermal activity is associated with stress and anxiety, an indicator of emotional arousal [5]. This sensor was placed in the hand holding the game controller and sampled at 51 Hz. The GSR sensor used also had an accelerometer incorporated to record the movements of the hand holding the controller. Baseline activity levels were recorded for all physiological signals to normalise individual differences.

Three questionnaires were designed using 5-point Likert scales: pre-experiment (PRE), post-play (PPQ) and post-experiment (POST) questionnaire. PPQ were given after each play with questions about player engagement [15] and immersion [16]. Questions were randomised to avoid any bias due to

Table 2. Objective (continuous) and subjective (self-reported) data recorded.

Measure	Sensor/method	Features	Type of data
ECG	Shimmer ECG sensor	Heart Rate (HR): mean & SD Inter-Beat Interval (IBI): mean Heart Rate Variability (HRV): Root Mean Square of Successive Differences (RMSSD)	Quantitative
GSR	Shimmer GSR sensor	Skin Conductance Level (SCL): mean & SD Skin Conductance Response (SCR): mean & SD	Quantitative
Motion	Accelerometer	Number of throws (peaks), quantity of motion, highest peak (velocity throw)	Quantitative
Video	Front-facing camera	Gestures, body position, spatial behaviour, number of gazes, positive and negative facial expressions...	Quantitative and qualitative
Self-report	PRE, PPQ & POST	Engagement, immersion, frustration, stress, enjoyment, effort, boredom	Quantitative

repetition of the questionnaire after each play mode. Finally, a video camera placed at one side of the monitor displaying the game recorded the experiment for observational analysis and qualitative data extraction.

3.2   Data Pre-processing and Feature Extraction

As all the physiological data was recorded using the same software, all the data was recorded at the same sampling rate. Data from all sensors was plotted to check if it was correct. The GSR data was extremely noisy since it was placed in the hand holding the controller, which was constantly moving and shaking while playing. We applied different filters such as lowpass or moving average filter to remove the noise, making the data considerably smoother although it was still too noisy to use in this analysis. ECGTools[2] was used to analyse the ECG and extract the R-peaks, which corresponds to individual heart beats. We then calculated the HR and IBI values per second and extracted the (HRV), which measures the variation of the frequency of heart beats over time.

The mean Quantity of Motion (QoM) of the Wii controller was computed from the accelerometer data. Using a peak detection algorithm, we extracted the number of throws of each player per play mode. Video recordings were manually annotated to determine the predominant facial expressions in each play mode as well as the non-verbal behaviours such as gestures, body positions and spatial behaviours (i.e.: moving around the room).

4   Analysis

4.1   Analysis Between Play Modes

Eight players (four pairs) took part in the experiment with a mean age of 30.88 (SD: 4.28). Half of the players preferred playing video games alone, three

---

[2] http://www.ecgtools.org/.

Table 3. Paired T-tests among play modes

Param.	Mean	SD	t(df)	Sig.
Mean HR	10.67	5.25	5.38 (6)	.002
Num. throws	20.75	7.50	9.03 (7)	.000
Mean QoM	1.07	.56	5.35 (7)	.001
Fastest throw	.50	.78	1.83 (7)	.109

Note: SD = Standard Deviation. df = degrees of freedom.

Table 4. HR correlations.

	Pair 1	Pair 2	Pair 3	Pair 4
Comp.	.509**	.165**	−0.066*	.200**
Collab.	.021	.034	.061	.022

Note: Significance of Spearman's rho: $*p < .05$; $**p < .01$.

collaboratively and only one competitively. Four out of the eight players reported in the POST questionnaire to have enjoyed the collaborative mode the most, three preferred playing competitively and one the solo mode. Players reported to be equally engaged with their colleagues during the collaborative (M: 3.88, SD: 0.99) and the competitive play mode (M: 3.25, SD: 1.16). No significant differences were found in the immersion level.

In order to analyse whether there was significant differences among play modes in the continuous features, we carried out various paired t-tests, specially between the competitive and collaborative play modes (Table 3). One of the players who reported neither enjoyment nor engagement in any of the play modes and whose physiological signals did not vary much across play modes, was removed in the HR paired t-test, which would just mean as if he would not have taken part on the experiment. The mean HR and the mean IBI showed very significant ($p < 0.01$) statistical difference between the competitive and collaborative modes, with a mean variation of 10.67 in the HR (SD: 4.09) and −100.24 in the IBI (SD: 63.35). Participants experienced a higher HR of 10 Beats Per Minute (BPM) average in the competitive play mode.

The accelerometer showed some significant ($p < 0.01$) differences, particularly in the number of throws and the mean QoM. The statistical difference of number of throws had a mean of 20.85 (SD: 7.01), meaning that players made on average 20 throws more in the competitive than in the collaborative play mode. This high difference is caused not only by the nature of the collaborative mode where players had to make as few throws as possible, but also due to the turn-taking strategy all pairs followed when playing together. The mean QoM of the hand holding the controller was higher in the competitive mode (see Table 3).

4.2 Physiological Analysis Within Pairs

In this section we compare the behavioural and physiological responses between the players within each pair, investigating the correlations in the continuous signals of the two players. Due to the intrinsic auto-correlation of the ECG signal, it is not possible to perform a simple cross-correlation with this data as it is biased [17]. One way to overcome this problem is to make a 1 s interpolation of the HR values in order to have an evenly spaced continuous data. Then a

Table 5. Spearman's correlations between continuous and self-reported data

Param.	Depend. var.	Rho	Sig.
Mean QoM	Norm. Mean HR	.413	.052
Mean QoM	Norm. Mean IBI	−.462	.053
Effort	Norm. Mean HR	.584	.001
Engage w/Partner	Norm. Mean HRV	−.535	.001
Enjoy w/Partner	Norm. Mean HRV	.265	.211
Enjoy w/Partner	Norm. Mean HR	.122	.571
Flow	Norm. Mean HR	−.157	.497

Table 6. Spearman's correlations between play modes at individual level

Play mode	Param.	Depend. var.	Rho	Sig.
Competitive	Effort	Engagement	.756	.030
	Effort	Immersion	.571	.139
	HRV	Fun w/partner	.639	.088
Collaborative	Effort	Engagement	−.103	.808
	Effort	Immersion	.130	.759
	HRV	Fun w/partner	.041	.923
	Mean Norm. HR Solo	Mean Norm. HR Collab	.929	.001

non-overlapping window of 3 s was generated for every single participant and play mode. Once the data was windowed, we were able to perform a normal Spearman's correlation between members of a pair in each play mode separately.

As shown in Table 4, all players experience a statistically significant higher correlation in HR when playing competitively than collaboratively. We think that the higher correlation of pair 1 during competitive mode might be due to their increased motivation levels as player 2 of this pair was the only one reporting to prefer playing competitively. This important detail might explain an emotional contagion between players. However, the low (and in some cases) negative correlation in the collaborative play mode can be again explained by the turn-taking strategy followed by all the pairs. In the collaborative mode, whilst one player experienced arousal while playing, the other player was more relaxed. For example, pair 3 in competitive mode have a very small negative HR correlation due to the lack of engagement, immersion and even enjoyment of the second player reported in the POST questionnaire. Therefore, player 1 was more activated than player 2 as their HR differ considerably.

4.3 Analysis Across Play Modes and Pairs

This analysis focused on the relation between continuous and self-reported data of all players. Prior to this analysis, we had to normalise the physiological data of each player to mitigate individual differences. Each player's ECG data was normalised according to his/her own baseline. In order to normalise the physiological data of each play mode, we divided the mean of the baseline by the mean of each mode, getting the percentage of increase for a particular play mode. For example, if the mean resting HR of one player was 73 BPM and the mean HR for this same person was 96 BPM in the competitive play mode, we can say that the HR increased by 131 % in that particular mode.

Once all the physiological data was normalised, it was correlated with objective (QoM) and subjective measures such as effort or enjoyment (Table 5). The mean QoM had a moderate positive correlation with the normalised HR (r .413, $p < .05$) and, at the same level, was negatively correlated with the IBI (r −.462, $p < .05$). This correlation between QoM and HR is probably related to the significant correlation (r .584, $p < .01$) of the mean HR with the effort reported in the questionnaires. These correlations are meaningful, since the BPMs increased with the required movement and effort needed to achieve a good performance.

The normalised mean RMSSD (Root Mean Square of Successive Differences) of the HRV showed a strong significant but negative correlation with engagement with the partner (r $-.535$, p $< .01$). This correlation demonstrates that the HRV is lower when the player is more engaged. Previous studies have demonstrated that HRV decreases with mental effort [9], meaning that when the subject is more focused, the body tends to be more relaxed and the heart activity settles down without much fluctuations.

4.4   Individual Analysis Between Play Modes

Since we are interested in how players experience each play mode at both a physiological level and through self-reports, we looked at each individual's data in the different play modes (Table 6). We examined the Spearman's correlations of effort with engagement and immersion. The rho coefficient in the competitive mode is clearly higher, which means that a higher effort leads to higher level of immersion and engagement.

The normalised mean HR in the solo and collaborative modes were also correlated, looking for relations in the physiological responses in these play modes. This analysis evidenced an extremely significant and very strong correlation (r $.929$, p $< .01$). Thereby, we can affirm that when a player is relaxed playing alone, s(he) will calm down at the same level when playing collaboratively.

4.5   Behavioural Analysis

The analysis in this section focuses on the video observations of the facial expressions, gestures, body positions and spatial behaviour of players. We manually labelled the facial expressions into 3 groups: positive (smiling or laughing), negative (frustrated or angry) or neutral. We also described spatial behaviour or movement as the activity of one individual moving through the surrounding environment (the room).

We divided each recorded video into three equal parts and annotated the predominant facial expressions for each part. The most common expressions in the competitive mode were negative as the players tried to win but not always got the expected results (getting stressed and even angry). Positive facial expressions were also present in this play mode, usually appearing at the end of the game when both players got more relaxed and talked about their performance. Some participants had recurrent 'specific' expressions such as biting their lower lip, sticking out the tongue or frowning, which displayed their frustration or engagement. The collaborative play mode elicited more positive facial expressions and laughters, and neutral faces were the most frequent in the solo mode.

When labelling body positions, gestures and spatial behaviour of players, we looked at their reactions and behaviours over the whole play mode. Overall, players had a more relaxed behaviour and body posture during the collaborative and solo play modes than when competing (Fig. 2), displaying a greater spatial

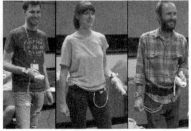

Fig. 2. Participants playing competitive (left) and collaboratively (right).

movement and more gestures such as head nods or moving arms around their body. Players changed their body position more often in this play mode, normally after each throw, and had more social interactions, conversations and mutual glances. In the competitive play mode, players were more static, barely moving their body or legs, and rarely speaking to each other until the game was over.

5   Results and Conclusions

In this paper we looked at the physiological signals and non-verbal behaviour indicators in solo, competitive and collaborative play modes for co-located gaming. The significant correlation of HR between players during the competitive mode, plus the significant mean HR difference compared to the other two modes, demonstrate a clear arousal increase when playing competitively. The strong correlation of the normalised mean HR in the solo and collaborative modes show that the arousal level in these modes are related. HRV is also an interesting cardiac feature to measure engagement [3], evidenced by a significant negative correlation with the self-reported engagement with partner. Video observations also revealed that competition evoked a tense behaviour in players, whereas playing collaboratively players were more relaxed and positive (Fig. 2).

However, HR must be interpreted carefully in gaming. While an increase in HR, caused by the cardiac sympathetic activity, is associated with affective arousal, a slow HR inflicted by the cardiac parasympathetic activity is related to attentional engagement [18]. Since video games can evoke both states simultaneously, HR alone might not be a good measure of arousal in games. Although skin conductance is a good and unambiguous indicator of arousal [2], it is very prone to noise. For this reason, GSR is not appropriate for experiments where the players have to constantly move their hands.

The results presented from this study are indicative of the affective states and behaviours players manifest in different play modes. Further research will investigate how affective states can be measured using non-invasive sensors and how this data can be used to enhance user experience in competitive and collaborative gaming. Also, it would be interesting to look at how certain game events have an impact on the player's affective states in the three play modes.

References

1. Gilleade, K., et al.: Affective videogames, modes of affective gaming: assist me, challenge me, emote me (2005)
2. Saari, T., et al.: Emotional regulation system for emotionally adapted games. In: FuturePlay (2005)
3. Tijs, T., Brokken, D., IJsselsteijn, W.: Creating an emotionally adaptive game. In: Stevens, S.M., Saldamarco, S.J. (eds.) ICEC 2008. LNCS, vol. 5309, pp. 122–133. Springer, Heidelberg (2008). doi:10.1007/978-3-540-89222-9_14
4. Gunes, H., Schuller, B.: Categorical and dimensional affect analysis in continuous input: current trends and future directions. Image Vis. Comput. **31**, 120–136 (2013)
5. Christy, T., Kuncheva, L.: Technological advancements in affective gaming: a historical survey. GSTF J. Comput. **3**, 32 (2014)
6. Savva, N., Bianchi-Berthouze, N.: Automatic recognition of affective body movement in a video game scenario. In: Camurri, A., Costa, C. (eds.) INTETAIN 2011. LNICSSITE, vol. 78, pp. 149–159. Springer, Heidelberg (2012). doi:10.1007/978-3-642-30214-5_17
7. Sharry, J., et al.: Relax to win treating children with anxiety problems with a biofeedback video game. Eisteach **2**, 22–26 (2003)
8. Bouchard, S., et al.: Using biofeedback while immersed in a stressful videogame increases the effectiveness of stress management skills in soldiers. PloS ONE **7**, e36169 (2012)
9. Mandryk, R., Inkpen, K.: Physiological indicators for the evaluation of co-located collaborative play. In: Proceedings of ACM CSCW (2004)
10. Kivikangas, J., et al.: Gender differences in emotional responses to cooperative and competitive game play. PloS ONE **9**, e100318 (2014)
11. Adachi, P., Willoughby, T.: The effect of video game competition, violence on aggressive behavior: which characteristic has the greatest influence? Psychol. Violence **1**, 259 (2011)
12. Vorderer, P., et al.: Explaining the enjoyment of playing video games: the role of competition. In: Proceedings of Conference on Entertainment Computing (2003)
13. Chanel, G., et al.: Physiological compliance for social gaming analysis: cooperative versus competitive play. Interact. Comput. **24**, 306–316 (2012)
14. Bengler, B., Bryan-Kinns, N.: Designing collaborative musical experiences for broad audiences. In: Proceedings of ACM Conference on Creativity & Cognition (2013)
15. Brockmyer, J., et al.: The development of the game engagement questionnaire: a measure of engagement in video game-playing. J. Exp. Soc. Psychol. **45**, 624–634 (2009)
16. Jennett, C., et al.: Measuring and defining the experience of immersion in games. J. Hum. Comput. Stud. **66**, 641–661 (2008)
17. Dean, R., Bailes, F.: Time series analysis as a method to examine acoustical influences on real-time perception of music. Empir. Musicol. Rev. **5**, 152–175 (2010)
18. Ravaja, N.: Contributions of psychophysiology to media research: review and recommendations. Media Psychol. **6**, 193–235 (2004)

Novel Applications and Tools

The Oculus Rift Film Experience: A Case Study on Understanding Films in a Head Mounted Display

Hannah Syrett, Licia Calvi$^{(\boxtimes)}$, and Marnix van Gisbergen

Academy for Digital Entertainment, NHTV University of Applied Sciences,
Breda, The Netherlands
hannah_e_syrett@hotmail.com,
{calvi.l,gisbergen.m}@nhtv.nl

Abstract. The purpose of this research was to determine the level of narrative comprehension in films when watched in a virtual reality headset (Oculus Rift). A 360-degree live-action film was created and was shown to participants after which the level of comprehension of various literary aspects as well as the feeling of distraction and enjoyment were measured using questionnaires and interviews. Revealing how increased freedom to view a movie in virtual reality has an effect on storyline understanding, provided a framework to start a discussion on whether and how to utilize virtual reality as a means for storytelling through films.

Keywords: Oculus rift · Virtual reality · Film · Storytelling · Narrative comprehension

1 Introduction

Films provide a brief escape from reality. They provide distraction, add action, love and fear and in doing so change a person's mood [1]. Films absorb viewers in a storyline in which case viewers might forget time and place. In recent years advanced virtual reality technologies have been developed that might enhance a film experience, shifting feelings from absorption to immersion. Immersion can be described as the "psychological state characterized by perceiving oneself to be enveloped by, included in, and interacting with an environment that provides a continuous stream of stimuli" [2]. Virtual reality (from here on abbreviated as VR) devices, which made use of head-mounted displays, were created as early as the nineteen fifties. A device created by Sutherland and Sproull in 1968, which made use of a stereoscopic display and a mechanical tracking system, is considered as one of the first head-mounted VR devices [3]. However recent progresses related to display improvements, positional tracking possibilities, new interaction options, audio improvements (such as built-in interactive 3D audio) and viewer comfort (lower weight, better ergonomics) increased the attention for using VR as a means to experience a film. A successful example of a head-mounted VR device is the Oculus Rift (OR). The OR was initially created for 3D gaming in 2012 and the company behind OR achieved global success, which is

© ICST Institute for Computer Sciences, Social Informatics and Telecommunications Engineering 2017
R. Poppe et al. (Eds.): INTETAIN 2016, LNICST 178, pp. 197–208, 2017.
DOI: 10.1007/978-3-319-49616-0_19

demonstrated in the $10 million deal acquired via crowdfunding campaigns and the $2 billion acquisition deal with Facebook in March 2014. The success is related to being the first to introduce a relative low cost and technologically advanced head-mounted (large field of view) display that created true feelings of immersion without feeling nauseous [4].

Since the introduction of VR and the OR there are 'believers' that are looking for possibilities to use VR for films, wanting to utilize the expected advantages of an increased experience. There are however also 'challengers' that prefer possibilities in 'traditional media', such as cinema, that provide more control over the narrative. Heilig, who created the famous VR device 'Sensorama' in 1962, already described in his paper "The cinema of the future" (1955) how film critics were sceptical about new 3D and other VR related developments, as it could have a negative effect on story perception [5]. The same discussion continues today, see for instance online articles by Conditt (2016) and Franklinn-Wallis (2016), leading to the question whether the freedom to look around in a 360-degree virtual world increases a film experience or decreases the experience due to a lack of control and comprehension of how a story unfolds [6, 7].

Despite criticism and scepticism, the OR has gained popularity as a medium for film since the Sundance Film Festival in 2012 [8]. Films for the OR might have started small but quickly received a lot of attention. An important development was the establishment of the new Oculus company called 'Story Studio'. The main goal of this company is to build truly immersive cinematic experiences and is lead among others by a former Pixar director [4]. The growing interest in VR films is also demonstrated in new investments, such as the $66 million investment in VR start-up Jaunt by among others The Walt Disney Company. Other examples that reveal a rising attention for VR as a medium for film, relate to an increase in available content (see for instance new VR films shown at the 2016 Sundance film Festival) and available channels that release new VR channels (such as YouTube) or are present in VR environments (such as Netflix and Hulu).

Many small independent companies and enthusiasts came up with an idea for an OR film. More often tips and tricks are shared on how to create a VR movie [9, 10]. However a mere three years ago 'pioneers' had no guidelines concerning how to make a film that could engage as well as immerse viewers in VR without losing grip of the story and needed to learn by doing [11]. In the Netherlands the Creative Lab at the NHTV University of Applied Sciences, created one of the first short films for the Oculus Rift called 'Dyskinetic'. The film allowed the viewer to experience being a helpless coma patient while your family is discussing whether or not they should end your life [12]. The Media Lab Amsterdam, together with the company WeMakeVr, created a live-action movie, which was one of the first interactive films in the Netherlands [13]. Both films were well received. However as the OR (DK1) was only accessible for developers, audience reach was low. The first OR for consumers, with many improvements, however has recently been released (March 28th) which will open doors to a larger audience and will stimulate the creation of more VR films [8].

Creating a story based immersive film in VR is not an easy-to-reach goal and often confusion arises whether content should be regarded as a film or more as a different kind of experience. A horror film created by The Sid Lee Collective for example did allow viewers to "experience a 360-degree nightmare". This film however lacks a storyline and might therefore be perceived not as a 'film' but an experience.

Films in the OR seem to provide a different viewing experience compared to traditional film viewing. Using the OR seems to reduce the possibilities a director has to guide the audience. It is the viewer who seems in charge of deciding what to look at, where to look and for how long. For this reason, traditional perceptions of and rules for filmmaking cannot simply be applied when using VR technologies. As VR films are relatively new, little research is available on the subject. Hence the need to study what aspects of a film's storyline could be understood without enforcing the director's vision on the viewers by making use of traditional film techniques such as restricting the amount of freedom to look in a virtual reality environment.

The objective of this research is to understand the viewers' experience of a VR film in terms of immersion and comprehension and in how far these effects are determined by the storytelling techniques adopted. In particular, we focused on the storyline to determine what aspects of a film's storyline can be comprehended in VR and whether viewers find it pleasurable to watch a film in a head mounted display such as the OR. In doing so we provide new insights to be used to answer the question whether or not it is possible to create a story that can easily be comprehended in virtual reality while generating an immersive experience. Insights that will enable further development ideas on how to create a movie in VR and in doing so stimulate future endeavours in VR filmmaking. In order to study the viewers' experience and understanding of an OR film, a film had to be created that could serve as a case study. A film called 'The Prism' (see Sect. 3.3 for a full description) was created specifically for this research and was one of the first of its kind. This film was a detective themed live-action film shot in 360-degrees. The viewer was part of the story having the actors speaking to them and looking at them for guidance, however as this was not an interactive film the viewer could not interact with the actors. The film can be viewed via YouTube (https://www.youtube.com/watch?v=oIqXdtkFKDg).

In the next sections we provide a brief outline concerning the challenges of creating a VR film in connection to film comprehension challenges. Next, we discuss how the research was conducted and provide the research results. Finally, we discuss future research recommendations and avenues for creating films in VR.

2 Oculus Rift Filmmaking

Throughout the years, many proposals have been created on how on screen data is converted into a story world and how viewers perceive this. Scholars have identified the most important elements in a film as being script, setting, technology, performance, conflicts, camera shots, style, plot and narration, which combined can be described as the literary aspects of a film [14]. In traditional filmmaking, directors function as narrators and use various techniques to tell the story on screen. They for example use shot sequences, editing and unify functional diegetic time and space to guide the audience's attention [15]. The abovementioned techniques however are hard to apply to VR films, as they might break that feeling of immersion [9]. When watching a VR film the viewer needs to feel like being part of the film. By editing the film and changing shot sequences as in traditional filmmaking, the viewer could be ripped out of the current situation and forced to acclimatize themselves to a new surrounding or a new angle which could be confusing as well as disturbing. In a certain sense, the viewer takes over the role of the director within a VR film, as they are able to look around and can determine what they want to look at, when they want to look at it and how (often) they want to look at it. This means they can direct their own attention, instead of having particular items, feelings or people being focused on for them. This provides the viewer with an extra sense of freedom. However it is still unclear whether this freedom has a positive or negative result on the viewing experience. Without having the certainty of the viewer's attention for objects, actors or emotions, important parts of the film can for instance be missed, resulting in a 'reduced experience'. Style, which represents the director's vision and attitude towards the film, is also limited in a VR film. Directors see the style of a film as a way to add value to it by giving the film their own distinct signature through the use of camera shots and editing. But in VR films this is for a large part absent due to the primacy of the viewer. Technical aspects of filming need to be given considerable attention when making a film for the VR. Not only because of the viewer's freedom but also because a 360-degrees view means that there is no place to hide. However, script, plot and narration are aspects from traditional filmmaking that should and can still be taken into account when creating a VR film. The assumption behind this is that viewing a film in VR creates a better experience when storyline, or any of the aforementioned narrative elements, are taken into account and kept intact as much as possible. Therefore, comprehension of the narrative elements and storyline is taken as the key focus of the current study when watching a VR film.

3   Method

We were interested in the viewer's understanding of a film when watched in the Oculus Rift (OR). The focus was on the literary aspects of a film, in particular the aspects of characterization, plot and mood. Our hypothesis was that the viewers would be able to recognize and understand the literary aspects of a VR film, despite the lack of story control due to more freedom and possibilities in how to view the film content. The study took place in April 2015 at two different locations. A survey was conducted at the Go Short International Short Film Festival in Nijmegen (Fig. 1). A qualitative research by means of face-to-face interviews was conducted at the NHTV University of Applied

Fig. 1. Participants viewing the film at the Go Short International Film Festival

Sciences in Breda. The literary aspects were examined in the survey as well as the interviews. Whereas the survey identified what literary aspects where understood, the interviews gave an indication to why these aspects were (not) understood. In both locations participants viewed the film while sitting at a table, which mirrored the seating situation in the film (see Sect. 3.3). An Oculus Rift Development Kit 2 was placed on their head with a Sennheiser HD202 over-ear headphone. The film played on a Micro-Star International (MSI®) Gaming Series laptop that ran on Windows 8.

At the Go Short Film Festival, participants were given a multiple-choice questionnaire after they watched the film. The interviews were conducted a week later with a different group of participants. Interviews were conducted a few minutes after viewing the movie.

3.1   Participants

The Oculus Rift is not advised for children under the age of 13 or for any adults who suffer with heart conditions or epilepsy [8]. Sixty-three participants were recruited via convenience sampling and all matched the target group of the film and had never seen the movie before. Thirty-three participants were female, with two thirds of the sample being between the ages of 18–30 years old. All participants were inexperienced VR users. Almost 70 % of the participants had never used a VR device before. Participants that already used a VR device had only experienced this once with an older version of the OR. This high number of inexperienced users was expected because of the newness of the product; no consumer edition of the OR was available and the Development Kit 2 had just been released (in July 2014).

Nine semi-structured interviews were conducted with a separate group of participants between 18–30 years old (five males and four females). After the ninth interview it became apparent that conducting more interviews would not provide the research with any new information and therefore the amount of interviews was considered sufficient. Seven participants had no experience with VR. The remaining participant used the OR a few times before this study was conducted.

3.2   Measurements

A questionnaire was used to understand the participants' comprehension of the storyline. The questionnaire mainly consisted out of five-point Likert scale questions with a few nominal questions to allow participants to choose the answer 'other' and to answer freely. Frequency of distribution was used to determine the overall level of agreement for the descriptive statistics. Themes and patterns were sought throughout the interviews to bring more meaning to the information as well as to explain and support the quantitative data. In order to understand plot comprehension, characterization and mood as specific narrative elements in an OR film, we adopted methods used for traditional film analysis.

Story Comprehension. Several studies have been conducted that measured the comprehension of film narratives and images all having a different focus. Bordwell discussed measurements of narration in fiction film [16], Turtola focused on the literary, theatrical and cinematic approaches within drama comprehension [17] and Branigan discussed narrative comprehension and film in general [14]. A widely accepted way to measure the level of plot comprehension in films is the three-R scale [18]. The three R's are used as a direct method to access memory, as they measure Recognition, Recall and recognition, with the latter sometimes being replaced by Recounting [19]. Recognition is the quicker and simpler way to access information in the memory, as you can compare information provided now with information you learnt in the past, but all three are important [20]. The three R's combined determine the level of comprehension the viewers had of that particular film [21]. The questions addressing recognition of the storyline are multiple-choice questions in which the participant can read more options and determine which answer they recognize to be correct for the film they watched. For recall and recognition, open questions were used to allow participants to recreate the story in their mind on their own with the information they remember (not recognize). This type of questions allowed participants to recall the main storyline of the film and reconstruct all surrounding parts to make up the whole story. By having the participants recognize, recall and reconstruct the storyline after watching the film in the OR, comprehension of the storyline could be assessed.

Characterization Comprehension. Whereas the three R's are specifically suited for plot analysis and comprehension, there is no agreed upon scale to distinctively measure how viewers understand characterization in a film. Characterization is described as a way for the writer to reveal the personality of a character. The mnemonic device of STEAL (Table 1) is frequently used to explore characterization in a film as it includes all of the aspects of indirect characterization [22].

Table 1. Mnemonic device of STEAL [22].

Speech	What does the character say? How does the character speak?
Thoughts	What is revealed through the character's private thoughts and feelings?
Effect on others toward the character	What is revealed through the character's effect on other people? How do other characters feel or behave in reaction to the character?
Actions	What does the character do? How does the character behave?
Looks	What does the character look like? How does the character dress?

These aspects of STEAL can be applied to VR film as they rely on the film's storyline and not on the technology showing the film.

Mood Measurements. Finally, to determine the mood of the film, a mood measure grid was used which was inspired by Russell's cognitive structure of affect [23]. Russell's cognitive structure of affect summarizes representations of affect covering the level of pleasure-displeasure and those of arousal-sleep. Different moods from each part of this structure were used to describe the feelings of mood experienced by the participants when watching the OR film.

Interview Topics. The approach used for the mixed method was connecting data, which is when a dataset is analysed and then used to inform the subsequent data collection [24]. Firstly, the quantitative data was analysed, which gave an indication as to which topic needed a higher level of understanding. These topics were then used to create the questions for the qualitative data. Participants were asked to reconstruct the storyline. The interviews allowed the participants to go back and forth through the film's storyline, recalling the overall storyline in order to be able to answer elaborately [14]. The participants were given neutral questions such as "What can you tell me about the characters in the film?" which were formulated in such way to not influence or persuade the interviewee [25]. By not mentioning a specific character it was up to the participant to recall the characters they saw in the film and reconstruct the story surrounding that character.

Frequency of distribution was used to determine the overall level of agreement for the descriptive statistics. Themes and patterns were sought throughout the interviews to bring more meaning to the information as well as to explain and support the quantitative data.

3.3 Material

The film that was created for the research was called 'The Prism' (Fig. 2). The film was created to entertain as well as to make it possible to measure comprehension of specific literary aspects of the film. The film was shot with four Canon 5D cameras, on which fish eye lenses were attached allowing for a full 360-degree coverage. The film lasted 7 min in which the viewer was given numerous cues about why they were sitting in the interrogation room and what information about the crime to investigate was known.

Fig. 2. Screenshot from 'The Prism' showing the point-of view of the viewer

The story was about a police interrogation. The viewer (participant) experienced the film from the perspective (viewpoint) of the police officer (the interrogator) in the storyline and was being spoken to by police officer 'Winters' and by the interrogatee 'Emma Garner'. The story was set in an interrogation room with a one-way mirror with the police officer (the viewer) as well as the interrogatee sitting at a table. Information was spread out on the table in front of the police officer to give the viewer more clues about the storyline.

The characters Emma Garner and a second officer were present in the room and were speaking to the viewer as if the viewer was the other interrogator. Additionally, a second officer (Bell), who was sitting behind the one-way mirror and therefore not visible to the viewer, spoke to officer Winters and the viewer via a headpiece and in doing so provided the viewer with more information on the case. The two-sided conversation, headset information and visual clues allowed the viewer to understand the literary aspects.

4 Results

The usage of the newest OR version helped to create a positive experience: 94 % of the participants and almost all interviewees did not suffer with any health problems whilst watching the film. For those that had some complaints, this was related to dizziness or eyestrain problems. The film was perceived positively with just under 90 % admitting to enjoying watching a film in the Oculus Rift and over 90 % of both samples agreeing to expecting a future for films in head mounted displays. Over 60 % of the participants felt that being able to look around during a film felt like a distraction, however the interviews made clear that the feeling of distraction was also due to the newness of the product/experience. Many participants mentioned that as this was their first encounter with the Oculus Rift they were more interested in the features of the display than in what was actually being shown. In addition only a weak correlation was found ($r = -0.29$) for the enjoyment of watching the OR between first-time users and users who had used the Oculus Rift before. Both equally enjoyed the experience. The interviews revealed that even for the more experienced users VR still felt new (especially the DK2) and that they never experienced a film in VR before.

Characterization of the interviewee Emma Garner and officer Winters. Descriptive statistics were used in the questionnaire relative to the questions formulated by using the mnemonic device of STEAL. When watching the film in the Oculus Rift the participants frequently mentioned body language and the fact that they were evidently reading the body language of the people in their surroundings. They also mentioned the feeling of empathy towards the characters as the participants felt part of the story with the characters pleading for their help. Finally, the feeling of intimidation bestowed upon by the police officer as he circled around the participants and got in their personal space was also frequently mentioned, a fact that is not possible with regular film.

More than 60 % of the participants correctly acknowledged that the police officer was not experienced nor in charge of the interrogation and more than 80 % correctly read Emma Garner's body language and tone of voice as saying she was insecure and losing control.

Plot. Simple nominal questions were used to confirm whether the participants could recognize and recall factors of the film's storyline. The distribution of responses were analysed showing that for each statement over 65 % of the participants selected the correct answer, therefore confirming they understood the plot of the story. One of the facts mentioned on numerous occasions in the film was the brother and sister relationship between the interviewee and the suspect. However, surprisingly, 14 % claimed to have no clue about this relationship proving that the Oculus Rift did distract some participants a lot more than others. Readable facts placed on the table in front of the participant were noted by nearly all. However, they could not be read easily, limiting the amount of small details possible for films. The participants of both the questionnaires and interviews confirmed that they received most information from audible clues. Overall the participants comprehended the film's plot correctly. However some of the smaller details were overlooked or overheard. The participants were able to recall and reconstruct the film's plot when asked about what happened. They also experienced no difficulties in describing what happened prior to the beginning of the film moving back and forth through the film's story [14].

Conflict. Most participants understood the conflicts in the film: 81 % of the participants understood that the internal struggle of betrayal and protection was a reoccurring theme. Participants inferred these themes mainly using visible cues 'reading' the interaction between the police officer and the interviewee as well as the internal struggle displayed within the characters.

Setting and Mood. Being fully immersed in the setting helped the participant feel part of the film. The feeling of tenseness was recorded by 70 % of the participant. They mentioned in the interviews that this feeling of tenseness was evoked by the storyline and by the aggression the police officer displayed. Being surrounded in an interrogation environment did contribute to the storyline comprehension but did not seem to increase feelings or mood experiences.

Distracting Elements. Besides the literary aspects there were a few noticeable distracting elements, which were frequently mentioned throughout the interviews. Especially the unexpected immersion and point of view was a reoccurring topic in the interviews. Many participants mentioned they felt being part of the film and yet they also mentioned that they felt slightly confused with the point of view of this film, which differed from a regular film. Participants did not expect and are not used to being part of the story in a film, let alone that the characters acknowledge the presence of the viewer. Or as one participant explained: "It took me a while to understand that I was part of the story". Especially as a character was staring at the participant as if waiting for a response, viewers missed the option to interact as if in a game: "It made me feel kind of stupid". This increased the distraction and therefore decreased story comprehension.

5   Discussion and Conclusion

The research showed that viewers liked the experience of a VR film. Although the key features of a VR device do distract the viewer, the overall story comprehension remains intact. When watching a film in the OR participants felt distracted by the freedom the device provided. Being able to look around during the film, even when a character was looking directly at or talking to them was a different viewing experience and added a new feature to film viewing. As such the research showed that important factors of a storyline are missed and this must be taken into account when creating a story in VR.

Although the results make clear that it is a challenge for a director to guide viewers' attention in VR, the difficulty to do so is also related to the unexpected point of view and the newness of the medium. The newness factor created a wow feeling that stimulated the viewing behaviour, which might not reflect the viewing behaviour when more VR movies have been seen. The participants were trying to experience all of the features possible in the OR and were less interested in following the actual storyline. It is to be expected that when the device becomes more accessible the newness will wear off and the viewers will pay more attention to the content instead of the technology and environment context. Once viewers become more experienced in viewing films in VR, they might better understand the intention of a director and feel less inclined to test all movement possibilities. That could also result in viewers noticing more and thus following cues given by the director such as what and where to look at in a specific moment. Even so, increased viewing experience is still no guarantee that a viewer will be looking in the direction the director wishes. The challenge remains to produce a story that fits into the VR world created and takes into account the (higher) need for an experience.

However even though the experience was new and exciting and participants wanted to test what was possible, this did not negatively affect the level of comprehension of the film. The majority of the participants had not been in contact with the OR before, but surprisingly they were still able to comprehend the film's storyline even though they had to get used to the technology whilst watching the film. The participants were able to recognize the characterization and conflict within the film; as well as being able to easily recall factors, which supported their level of comprehension of these aspects [19].

There were several limitations in this research mainly due to the lack of previous research. For this reason research conducted on general films had to be used. However due to the large differences in regular films and 360-degree OR films, not all research could simply be adopted. Due to the lack of pre-existing research it was also difficult to find supporting data. The most challenging part of this research however was the creation of a 360-degree film. Without any guidelines and with timing issues and restrictions, some unexpected effects were stimulated, among which the point-of-view used that made viewers want to interact with the characters as if being in a game. However, overall the results provided positive insights into films for the OR and indications on how to achieve better results, which is very insightful for future research. Elements, which were not comprehended as much, were mood and setting. It became apparent in the interviews that these elements were not felt sufficiently as they received insufficient attention from the filmmakers. The room was extremely bare and did not project any feeling to the participants. The participants felt as if they were in the room, however there was nothing in the room to give them a certain feeling or mood, which a more exciting genre could have made better use of.

A genre that relies heavily on mood and that could profit from the OR is horror as the genre tries to provoke the feeling of tenseness and scariness in viewers. Especially the use of darkness could benefit in the horror genre as the OR allows for a viewer to look around and search for what might scare them. The question of what happened next in 'the Prism' arose by numerous participants, fuelling their desire to know more, however this desire was only limited. Reason being that the detective genre and storyline lacked tension and an attractive setting to get the viewers excited.

Frequently mentioned in the interviews as well as in personal conversations was the need for more. Participants wanted to interact with their surroundings, picking up items, moving and speaking to the characters, thus showing a preference towards interactive films over non-interactive films for the OR.

More research should be conducted on comprehension of a storyline within the Oculus Rift. The results from this study provided insights into acquiring more adept results from a more detailed and elaborate survey. Films of different genres should be examined and results compared to this current research to provide more insightful information. The film we studied was perceived as very immersive. However any technical issue, such as small editing errors or little glitches would break this feeling of immersion as it would remind the viewer that it was not a real-life experience. It is therefore of high importance that when creating a film for the OR, it is technically of a high quality to minimize distractions and maximize the feeling of immersion.

This research was not about whether VR is a better means than traditional cinema to create a film. With this research we wanted to see whether a film experience could be created that takes into account possible benefits of a more immersed experience as well as possible drawbacks of a decreased comprehension due to less control. Although hard to conclude based on one research using one movie (genre), that has not been optimally created for VR, the results seem to indicate that it is possible to tell stories in VR by means of a film. As such we tend to join the ambassadors and advocate VR to be used for films. VR devices such as the Oculus Rift offer a lot of potentials for the film industry by creating new viewing experiences.

Acknowledgements. We would like to thank the Creative Lab team for providing the facilities to create this movie as well as Anneliene van den Boom for the production of the movie.

References

1. Tannenbaum, P., Gaer, E.: Mood change as a function of stress of protagonist and degree of identification in a film-viewing situation. J. Pers. Soc. Psychol. **2**(4), 612–616 (1965)
2. Witmer, B.G., Singer, M.J.: Measuring presence in virtual environments: a presence questionnaire. Presence Teleoperators Virtual Environ. **7**(3), 225–240 (1998)
3. Earnshaw, R.A. (ed.): Virtual Reality Systems. Academic Press, London (2014)
4. Rubin, P.: The inside story of oculus rift and how virtual reality became reality. Wired (2014). http://www.wired.com/2014/05/oculus-rift-4/. Accessed 26 Jan 2015
5. Heilig, M.L.: El cine del futuro: the cinema of the future. Presence Teleoperators Virtual Environ. **1**(3), 279–294 (1992)
6. Condit: Virtual reality is not the (immediate) future of film. Engadged (2016). http://www.engadget.com/2015/03/16/virtual-reality-film-gaming/. Accessed 25 Mar 2016
7. Franklinn-Wallis: Virtual reality will transform cinema in 2016. Wired (2016). http://www.wired.co.uk/news/archive/2016-01/27/virtual-reality-breaks-fourth-wall. Accessed 1 Mar 2016
8. OculusVR (2016). https://www.oculus.com/en-us/rift/. Accessed 5 Jan 2015
9. Yao, R., Heath, T., Davies, A., Forsyth, T., Mitchell, N., Hoberman, P.: Oculus VR Best Practices Guide (2014). http://treyte.ch/oculus/tools/0.4.2/documentation/OculusBest Practices.pdf. Accessed 9 Jan 2015

10. Watercutter: 6 Rules for making movies in the VR age. Wired (2015). http://www.wired.com/2015/08/6-rules-making-movies-vr-age/. Accessed 3 Jan 2016
11. Tanak, N.: Interactive Cinema Guide (2015). http://medialab.hva.nl/wp-content/uploads/2015/01/InteractiveCinema_Guideline_v5.pdf. Accessed 20 Feb 2015
12. Dyskinetic (2014). http://www.imdb.com/title/tt3686216/. Accessed 25 Mar 2015
13. Bogers, L.: Interactive Cinema – MediaLAB Amsterdam. http://medialab.hva.nl/blog/project/interactive-cinema-2/. Accessed 15 April 2015
14. Branigan, E.: Narrative Comprehension and Film, p. XI. Routledge, London (1992)
15. Film Reference (2015). http://www.filmreference.com/encyclopedia/Independent-Film-Road-Movies/Narrative-CLASSICAL-REALISM.html#ixzz3Y1dYzWTZ. Accessed 2 April 2015
16. Bordwell, D.: Narration in the Fiction Film. Routledge, London (1986)
17. Turtola, P.E.: Literary, theatrical and cinematic approaches to drama. Yale-New Haven Teachers Institute (2015)
18. Sauro, J.: The 3 R`s of Measuring Design Comprehension (2013). http://www.measuringu.com/blog/measuring-comprehension.php. Accessed 2 May 2015
19. Brown, A.: Recognition, reconstruction, and recall of narrative sequences by preoperational children. Child Dev. **46**(1), 156–166 (1975)
20. Mandler, J., Johnson, N.: Remembrance of things parsed: story structure and re-call. Cogn. Psychol. **9**(1), 111–151 (1977)
21. Pyrczak, F.: Objective evaluation of the quality of multiple-choice test items designed to measure comprehension of reading passage. Read. Res. Quaterly **8**(1), 62–71 (1972). Wiley
22. Straker, D.: Changing Minds: In Detail. Syque, Crowthorne (2010)
23. Russell, J.: A circumplex model of affect. J. Pers. Soc. Psychol. **39**(6), 1161–1178 (1980)
24. Creswell, J., Clark, V.: Designing and Conducting Mixed Methods Research, 2nd edn. SAGE Publications, Thousand Oaks (2011)
25. Merton, R., Fiske, M., Kendall, P.: The Focused Interview; A Manual of Problems and Procedures, 2nd edn. The Free Press, New York (1990)

WWoW: World Without Walls Immersive Mixed Reality with Virtual Co-location, Natural Interactions, and Remote Collaboration

Ramesh Guntha[✉], Balaji Hariharan, and P. Venkat Rangan

Amrita Center for Wireless Networks and Applications,
Amrita School of Engineering, Amritapuri Campus,
Amrita Vishwa Vidyapeetham University, Clappana, India
{rameshg,balajih}@am.amrita.edu, venkat@amrita.edu

Abstract. Communicating and sharing knowledge through teleconferencing systems is a common phenomenon now a days. But the traditional remote collaboration systems lack naturalness and are not very immersive. Though existing mixed reality systems support natural interactions, many of them use 3D avatars to represent remote users, hence do not reflect finer movements and emotions of the remote users, and a number of them are quite cumbersome to setup and calibrate. We present our remote collaborative mixed reality environment which provides virtual co-location and gestural interactions using Kinect user image masks and skeletons and is simple to setup. The resulting system is both immersive and natural, gives a feeling to participants that they are in the same physical location, communicating and sharing knowledge objects through natural gestural controls and speech [1].

Keywords: Mixed reality environment · Virtual co-location · Remote collaboration · Kinect user mask streaming · Audio conference · Gestural control

1 Introduction

Communicating and sharing knowledge through teleconferencing systems is a common phenomenon now a days. But the traditional video conferencing and eLearning systems like Skype and Vidyo lack naturalness and are not very immersive. They require users to adopt un-natural interaction mechanisms through keyboard and mouse, resulting in interruptions to the communication flow and thought process. The existing eLearning systems present each knowledge-object such as video, whiteboard, document and 3D models in separate components, hence the users need to focus on multiple parts of the screen(s) simultaneously, resulting in loss of concentration and subsequently loss of interest. In the case of video-conferencing systems the video of each location is presented in a separate window with their native backgrounds. Because of that there is never a feeling of co-location as the remote users are always seen to be separated by virtual walls.

R. Poppe et al. (Eds.): INTETAIN 2016, LNICST 178, pp. 209–219, 2017.
DOI: 10.1007/978-3-319-49616-0_20

Though there are mixed reality systems which try to solve the above problems of lack of immersion and naturalness, many of them require a lot of equipment, setup and calibration [2–4]. Some of the mixed reality systems try to solve the co-location problem through creation of 3D avatars to represent the remote participants, but the 3D avatars do not reflect finer bodily movements and facial emotions of the remote users.

In this paper we introduce the World Without Walls (WWoW). It is a virtually co-located, naturally interactive, and remote collaborative knowledge sharing and conferencing system which would address the above mentioned issues and it is quite simple to setup and does not require any calibration. WWoW system allows users from remote locations to interact through 3D content as if they are in the same room. The Kinect extracts user mask images and these are streamed into the mixed reality environment, which is shared across all the clients in real-time. As the user masks get assembled against the common background of the mixed reality environment, it appears as though the users are in the same location and interacting with the local 3D objects (Fig. 1).

Fig. 1. Remote user performing rotation gesture on 3D object.

Apart from extracting user masks, Kinect also extract skeleton joint locations of the tracked users. The relative locations and movements of the joint locations can be used to derive various natural gestures which are used to load, move, rotate, zoom in/out and unload the 3D objects. All the interactions are replicated to all the clients in real-time. The streaming and rendering of image masks against common background, natural gestural interactions with content, replicating it in real-time to all the clients result in immersive and engaging experience.

The rest of the paper contains related work, architecture, testing and data analysis, applications and conclusions.

2 Related Work

Research on mixed reality environments has been going on for decades, as it provides tremendous immersion and user engagement. According to [5] mixed reality is based on the basic principles of immersion, interaction and user involvement. These qualities make it a perfect fit for entertainment games and serious games. Reference [6] developed a collaborated game of ball passing using mixed reality with physics engine. They use Kinect to track user skeletons to identify ball passing and ball catching gestures. The remote users are represented only through skeleton joint frame and hence it does not provide immersive co-location experience.

Reference [7] presents a thorough study of how virtual reality evolved over the period and how it is applied in the fields of education and health. Their study acknowledges the inconvenience of wearing virtual reality helmets and goggles for extended period for ergonomic reasons. In WWoW system users do not have to wear any equipment on them. Reference [8] points out that a player's real world gaming experience consists of physical, social, mental and emotional parts. Our WWoW system provides physical experience through the use of natural gestures to control the 3D objects, best social experience as users feel that they are in the same location and can interact with each other, provides mental experience through immersion and interaction and finally emotional experience through problem solving and learning with 3D objects. Reference [9] states that the future mixed reality system should satisfy the conditions of telepresence, interactivity, connectivity and synthesis. The WWoW system enables telepresence through real-time streaming of audio and video (image masks) of all the users, provides interactivity through gestural control of the 3D objects and connectivity through remote collaboration and synthesis through rendering content and users on the mixed reality environment and sharing it across all the clients in real-time. Reference [10] concludes that a co-located environment which provides freedom to interact with content freely and allows movement of people around the content enables for better collaboration and learning. Reference [3] achieves co-location by developing 3D model of the remote user in real-time using Kinect. This system is quite laborious to setup and needs 6 Kinects to be connected and calibrated precisely, which makes this system not so easy to use.

Mixed reality concepts are applied for learning as well [2, 4, 11, 12]. Reference [11] observes that immersion in a digital environment can enhance education by allowing multiple perspectives, situated learning, and transfer. In the WWoW system, the users can use rotation and movement gestures to interact and see multiple perspectives of 3D content, and in future, solve puzzles and quizzes under the supervision of other participants. Reference [2] proposes an elaborate mixed reality collaboration system around physical artifacts by using virtual reality glasses and pocket computer per participant, 2 Kinects, webcam, computer per location, and a central server, to project 3D avatars of remote participants in the augmented space. We believe this system is too cumbersome and costly to implement and because the remote users are represented as static 3D model avatars their real-time finer emotions and body movements are not represented and another limitation of this system is that only local participants can control the physical artifacts directly, the remote participants can only have indirectly control through requesting the local participants. On the contrary, the WWoW system needs much less hardware and almost no setup, the finer physical moments and emotions of the remote participants are reflected through the user image masks and since the participants control the virtual artifacts, all the participants can control them directly. Reference [4] developed a system that created avatars for remote participants using Second Life. Participants are able to view remote participants through head mounted displays and interact with digital objects. But this system has the same limitation of avatars mentioned above and also requires an identical physical environment to that of virtual environment, which would be cumbersome to achieve for every user. Gestural and speech based controlling of the electronic artifacts is another challenging area. The gestures have to be natural and effective at the same time. Reference [13] studies that direct free-hand manipulation gestures are good for selection, rotation and moving the objects, whereas indirect multimodal gestures perform better for scaling the objects. Reference [14] developed and studied the effectiveness of tracking bare hands to detect natural gestures for picking, moving and releasing objects on the tabletop digital surface and achieved comparable results to that of real world activity. Reference [15] developed a system to interact with and manipulate the objects in virtual world through hand gestures. Users found their system to be very natural and easy to use. In WWoW system, the users use their bare hands to control the 3D objects.

3   Setup and Architecture

WWoW system requires minimum hardware and is very simple to setup. Each client should have a Windows PC with Kinect and the server can run Linux or Windows operating system. The Adobe Media Server (AMS) should be installed on the server (Fig. 2).

The Connection manager on the AMS keeps track of all the connected clients, synchronizes the connection status, and automatically tries to re-establish the lost connections to achieve the fault-tolerance and recovery. The collaboration manager maintains the lifecycle of the shared objects with the help of connection manager to make sure that they get reconnected in the event of connection restoration. Client system also has the corresponding stubs for the connection manager, collaboration manager and shared objects and has the Flare 3D virtual environment to host the image masks and 3D objects and to enable the interactions (Fig. 3).

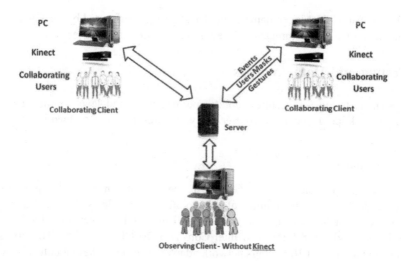

Fig. 2. System setup.

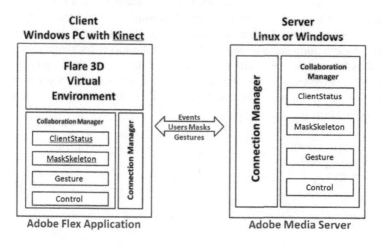

Fig. 3. System architecture.

The shared objects synchronize various data elements across the connected clients to achieve remote collaboration. Each shared object contains data in the form of key-value pairs. When a client modifies the data in a shared object, the changes get propagated to all the shared objects at the connected clients. ClientStatus shared object synchronizes the connection status. The key is clientName and the value is client's status. Control shared object synchronizes the userId of the control user. The key is "ControlUser", the value is the concatenated string of clientName & Kinect userId of the user who has the control over 3D object. MaskSkeleton shared object synchronizes the user mask image and skeleton joint positions of the users. The key is the concatenated string of clientName & Kinect userId and the value contains user mask image and the skeleton object. It is updated with the user mask and skeleton as they are provided by Kinect at 30 frames per second. Gesture shared object synchronizes the current gesture and the related details such as position and rotation angle. The value of the "GestureName" key is the name of the latest gesture performed by the control user and the value of the "GestureDetails" key is the gesture details object (Fig. 3).

4   Testing and Data Analysis

The system is tested for gesture stability, performance, and level of immersion as compared to Skype through a pilot user study. The results are presented below.

4.1   Performance

We have tested the system to analyze how the performance metrics like fps, latency, and bandwidth vary with the number of collaborating users. We used three client nodes and a server, which are connected over 1 GB Ethernet LAN network. Each of the clients have Windows 8.1 PC with Intel Core i7-3770 CPU and 3.4 GHz processor with 8 GB memory and 100 Mbit/s network adapter. The server has Ubuntu 12.0.4 OS with 12 core processor and 16 GB memory.

The FPS start at 22 frames per second, and stay around 15 till 4 collaborating users and comes down to 5 when 8 users are collaborating, similarly the average latency starts at 30 ms from client to client and goes up to 200 ms with 8 users. The average bandwidth consumption starts around 100 Mbps at the server for single user and goes to 250 Mbps for 8 users, the reason it is not growing linearly with the number of users is because fps is reducing as the number of users go up. Similarly the average client bandwidth consumption per transmitted frame is around 5 Mbps for single user and goes up to 33 Mbps for 8 users (Fig. 5).

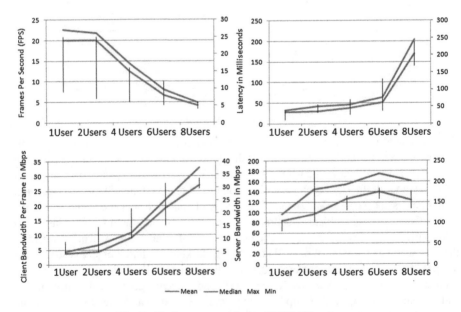

Fig. 5. Performance analysis of WWoW system.

Overall the system seems to be stable and within the limits of acceptable fps and latency for a smooth collaborative and interactive session.

4.2 Gesture Stability

While positioning the 3D Object based on the hand coordinates it is noticed that the 3D object is shaky, even though the user is keeping the hands as still as possible. The xyz coordinates of the left and right hand joints are analyzed to assess the variations (Fig. 4). The measurements are taken for the duration of 10 s after the user is in

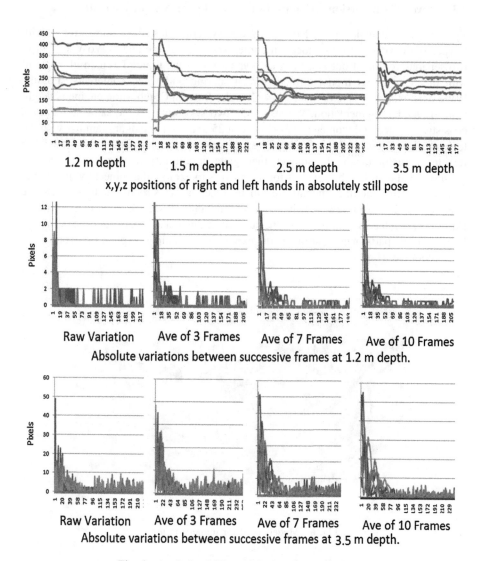

Fig. 4. Analysis of Kinect joint position variations.

absolutely still position. The top row presents the variations of xyz coordinates of both hands; while it takes few seconds stabilize in the beginning, they become quite stabilize with some jitter. The jitter seems to increase as the user moves away from Kinect. The second and third rows show the plot of the moving average of variations between subsequent frames at the depth 1.2 and 3.5 m respectively with. It is noted that both 7 and 10 frame moving averages show much less variations compared to raw and 3 frame ones. So we chose 7 frame moving average as a balance between stability and responsiveness.

4.3   Level of Immersion - Comparison with Skype: A Pilot User Study

The level of immersion provided by WWoW system is tested by comparing it with Skype. We have setup a two location conference with Skype and WWoW system in two separate rooms of our lab. For the Skype session, the topic of Windmill is taught with the help of 3D model through screen sharing and video conference. For the WWoW session the topic of 4-Stroke 4-Cylinder Internal Combustion engine is taught with 3D model augmentation. We tested the two sessions with the same set of users consisting of men and women of ages between 25 and 30, none of are familiar with the topics taught. Same method of teaching and testing is used for both the sessions; The remote instructor taught the subject, then gave opportunity for the students to ask questions and then left the students for themselves to explore the subject by interacting with the system, later the students are called to the teacher's room one by one and are interviewed. The interview questions are both qualitative such as level of immersion, learning experience and difficulty of the subject etc., and also specific questions such as locate various parts, name various parts, explain the principle, explain the working of the system etc. (Fig. 6).

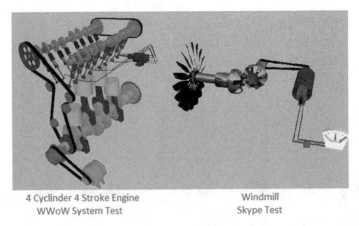

4 Cyclinder 4 Stroke Engine   Windmill
WWoW System Test   Skype Test

Fig. 6. Models used for immersion test.

Even though the topic in WWoW system is much more complex and took much more time to teach, the students exhibited lot of interest and asked a lot of questions to the teacher and also spent much more time in interacting and exploring with the system and among themselves. As the results suggests that WWoW system performed better than Skype in qualitative terms by providing much more engaging and immersive experience with lot of student-to-student and student-to-teacher interaction (Table 1).

The students have done equally well in answering subject specific questions in both the methods of teachings, but they preferred learning though WWoW system as they found it much more interesting to see the 3D object augmentation on the remote teacher's image, and to interact with the 3D model through natural hand gestures.

During the post-test discussion the students mentioned that there is a lot of potential to the WWoW concept if we can improve it by implementing more natural and smooth gestures and improve the video quality and gaze alignment.

Table 1. Level of immersion test results.

Test criteria	Skype	WWoW
Lecture duration	3 min	15 min
Number of questions by students	0	7
Student's exploration duration	2 min	18 min
Complexity of the subject	Medium	High
Level of immersion	Medium	High
How other students spent time during interview	On smart phone	Discussing and playing with system
Students explanation of principles	Excellent	Excellent
Number of subject questions asked in the interview	9	12
Average percentage of questions answered	100 %	100 %
Level of immersion	Medium	High
Preference to learn complex topics through the system	Medium	High
Overall experience	Medium	High

5 Applications

WWoW system has many applications in education, meetings and panel discussions, trainings, demos, and presentations.

In education it can be used for teaching of complex engineering, medical and science subjects with engaging and interactive multi-media content, it can be used for quizzes, to test the assembly of various engineering components, it can be used for virtual labs, e.g., students can learn to operate various machinery in mechanical engineering labs, students can learn to make various circuits or electronic boards in electrical and electronics labs, in medical labs, students can experiment various medical equipment to examine body parts.

The meetings in WWoW can be refreshing to see the distant participants in the same virtual room, interacting with power point presentations or presenting latest design models by controlling rotations and zoom, all with through using only natural gestures.

Engineers and marketing personnel in the industry can present and interact with various 3D models of components or products and see how they look by altering various physical properties such as color and sizes of these models in run time.

6 Conclusions

This work needs to expand to include many more gestures to control variety of multimedia content. The resolution of the image masks can be improved greatly if we use KinectV2 as it provides HD resolution image masks. User masks can be replaced with 3D textures of users built from point clouds in real-time, such 3D representations of the users can be used to interact with mixed reality environment much more intimately. Much more work needs to go in to the positioning of user's masks in the mixed reality environment, so that there is proper gaze alignment to bring even more naturalness in conversations, as the current system shows only the frontal view of all the participants to each other, which is ideal for instruction and demo scenarios, but it is not quite suited for a discussions and round table meetings, where each participant should be presented with different angular perspectives of the remote users.

References

1. https://www.youtube.com/watch?v=1Lv9A2pnnEE&feature=youtu.be
2. Weigel, J., Viller, S., Schulz, M.: Designing support for collaboration around physical artefacts: using mixed reality in learning environments. In: 2014 IEEE International Symposium on Mixed and Mixed Reality (ISMAR), pp. 405–408. IEEE, September 2014
3. Maimone, A., Bidwell, J., Peng, K., Fuchs, H.: Enhanced personal autostereoscopic telepresence system using commodity depth cameras. Comput. Graph. **36**(7), 791–807 (2012)
4. Kantonen, T., Woodward, C., Katz, N.: Mixed reality in virtual world teleconferencing. In: 2010 IEEE Virtual Reality Conference (VR), pp. 179–182 (2010)
5. Pinho, M.S.: Realidade Virtual. PUC, Rio de Janeiro (2004)
6. Tang, T.Y., Winoto, P., Wang, Y.F.: Alone together: a multiplayer mixed reality online ball passing game. In: Proceedings of the 18th ACM Conference Companion on Computer Supported Cooperative Work & Social Computing, pp. 37–40. ACM, February 2015
7. Carvalho, B., Soares, M., Neves, A., Soares, G., Lins, A.: The state of the art in virtual reality applied to digital games: a literature review. In: 5th International Conference on Applied Human Factors and Ergonomics AHFE 2014, July 2014
8. Nilsen, T., Linton, S., Looser, J.: Motivations for mixed reality gaming. Proc. FUSE **4**, 86–93 (2004)
9. Lau, H.F., Lau, K.W., Kan, C.W.: The future of virtual environments: the development of virtual technology. Comput. Sci. Inf. Technol. **1**, 41–50 (2013)

10. Church, T., Hazelwood, W.R., Rogers, Y.: Around the table: studies in co-located collaboration. In: Adjunct Proceedings of the 4th International Conference on Pervasive Computing (2006)
11. Dede, C.: Immersive interfaces for engagement and learning. Science **323**(5910), 66–69 (2009)
12. Marzouk, D., Attia, G., Abdelbaki, N.: Biology learning using mixed reality and gaming techniques. Environment **2**, 3 (2013)
13. Piumsomboon, T., Altimira, D., Kim, H., Clark, A., Lee, G., Billinghurst, M.: Grasp-Shell vs gesture-speech: a comparison of direct and indirect natural interaction techniques in mixed reality. In: 2014 IEEE International Symposium on Mixed and Mixed Reality (ISMAR), pp. 73–82. IEEE, September 2014
14. Figueiredo, L., Dos Anjos, R., Lindoso, J., Neto, E., Roberto, R., Silva, M., Teichrieb, V.: Bare hand natural interaction with augmented objects. In: 2013 IEEE International Symposium on Mixed and Mixed Reality (ISMAR), pp. 1–6. IEEE, October 2013
15. Tecchia, F., Avveduto, G., Carrozzino, M., Brondi, R., Bergamasco, M., Alem, L.: Interacting with your own hands in a fully immersive MR system. In: 2014 IEEE International Symposium on Mixed and Mixed Reality (ISMAR), pp. 313–314. IEEE, September 2014

My Drama: Story-Based Game for Understanding Emotions in Context

Xiaoyu Shen[✉] and Emilia I. Barakova

Eindhoven University of Technology,
P.O. Box 513, 5600 MB Eindhoven, The Netherlands
x.shen@studnet.tue.nl, e.i.barakova@tue.nl

Abstract. This paper presents *My Drama*, a story-based game application that helps to understand emotions in context. The game was developed for young people with autism, who usually have trouble understanding the non-verbal expression of emotions. We combined elements of drama therapy and mobile game design to let players experience taking perspectives by assuming the role of the cartoon character and practice context-dependent recognition of expressed emotions in the story, and collecting of related to the story emotional expression photographs n in a known environment. The outcomes of a pilot test indicate that *My Drama* is a promising and engaging training tool for emotion understanding while collecting of emotional expression photographs increased the communication. Long-term research on its effectiveness is needed.

Keywords: Interactive game design · Drama therapy · Emotion understanding · Design for children with autism · Educational applications for adolescents with ASD

1 Introduction

Deficits in emotion recognition [1] and empathy [2] in children with Autism Spectrum Disorders (ASD) may lead to isolation from their peers and difficulties to integrate into education and everyday life situations. It was shown that drama training can promote self-efficacy and greater awareness and sensitivity towards others [3]. Drama therapy [4] can provide context for the participants to tell their stories, set goals and solve problems, express feelings, or achieve catharsis. Through drama therapy, the depth and breadth of inner experience can be actively explored, and the ability to establish interpersonal relationships can be enhanced. Participants can expand their repertoire of dramatic roles to increase confidence in interaction in real life encounters. This therapy has shown to be both fun and educational.

One example of an application of drama therapy is *Social Emotional NeuroScience Endocrinology (SENSE)* Theatre [5]. It was proposed that the "active practice" of reciprocal social interaction, video modeling, and role-playing might facilitate social awareness and perspective taking. During the evaluation, participants showed improvements in emotion recognition and empathy [5].

Mobile applications about emotion development that are related to our method were reviewed. Among the existing apps, demonstrative but not interactive ones are

© ICST Institute for Computer Sciences, Social Informatics and Telecommunications Engineering 2017
R. Poppe et al. (Eds.): INTETAIN 2016, LNICST 178, pp. 220–230, 2017.
DOI: 10.1007/978-3-319-49616-0_21

prevalent. For instance, *Model Me Kids* [6] demonstrates social skills by modeling peer behavior in videos. *Autism Emotions* [7] models behaviors in photographic story-boards. Mobile applications like *Between the Lines* [8] and *Look at Me* [9] combine context modeling with tasks. The tasks in these apps are independent of each other and are mainly categorized by topics and difficulty.

The current study aims to improve the interaction and playfulness of emotion training tools. Instead of using independent behavior modeling materials, we test whether embedding tasks into a consistent story will help users to perform better in role transformation and contexts awareness. Furthermore, playful elements were also added to keep children with ASD motivated and engaged in the training.

2 Design of the Experimental Tool

The current study aims to design a novel tool for children with ASD to develop abilities of emotion understanding in context. We combine theatrical intervention [5] with mobile game application methods.

The theatrical intervention [5] features role-play and contextual stimuli, which can create a safe space to work through individual issues. However, it is hard to make a large-scale theatrical intervention, because of high demands on sites, facilities, and trainers. To decrease the expense, we propose a mobile application on the digital devices. The affinity of children with ASD with digital devices is well established [13] while the mobile apps provide conditions for privacy and own tempo of training [14].

With this game we aim to train the children with ASD to recognize emotions, to switch perspectives and learn to gain empathy with others. It aims to demonstrate the importance of the skills of reading and using social cues during interpersonal interaction.

To increase the engagement, we included playful elements in the training. Inspired by the *Look At Me* app [6], rich interactions, reward system, visual/sound effects, etc. were implemented to let the child learning with fun.

Also, familiarity with the context was shown to give very positive effects on training children with ASD [11]. That is the reason to look for popular cartoon movies as the basis of the drama script in this game application.

2.1 Background Information

The song of the sea is a 2014 Irish animated fantasy film by Cartoon Saloon, which is about a little girl who departs on an adventure with her brother, Ben, to save the spirit world and other magical beings like her. The story line of the game *My drama* was adapted from this film. To stay consistent, all the images and music of this game were reproduced from the original movie.

The game was initially designed on Keynote. Links and animation effects were used to make the game interactive. Music and audio effects were added to create a more immersive experience. Then, the game was exported as an HTML file and uploaded on the Internet so that everyone can access it.

2.2   My Drama

My drama is a story-based game application that can be used on a tablet. A cartoon movie *The Song of the Sea* has been adopted as the story background in *My Drama*. The script of the game is adapted from the original story to make the tasks fit into the storyline smoothly. The tasks are related to emotion recognition, understanding, and expression. While emotion recognition has been a subject of many studies, the more complex skill of emotion understanding has not received enough attention in studies of using technologies for autism training. Emotion understanding has been defined by Saarni [19] (p. 106) as the *'ability to discern and understand others' emotions, using situational and expressive cues that have some degree of cultural consensus as to their emotional meaning'*. Emotion understanding encompasses a range of behaviours. For example, Denham [20] describes nine areas of emotion understanding. These include the ability to identify situations that might elicit specific emotions, and the ability to understand more complex emotions, such as confusion, shocked, boredom, guilt, pride, or empathy. A story line as *The Song of the Sea* provides opportunities to identify situations and contexts in which an emotion emerges, and to suggest causal relations between an event and the triggered emotion [18].

Tasks that intend to help understanding of emotional states were divided into four increasingly complex levels and embedded in the storyline. These are (1) emotion learning, (2) facial expression recognition, (3) context dependent emotion expression recognition and (4) social interaction with the people in the child's environment.

Considering that boys to girls ratio among the children with ASD is close to 6:1 [15], the story is presented from the perspective of a male character (Ben) that is also the role the player takes.

In the story, Ben's sister, Sanneke, was caught by an evil witch who stole emotions from fairies and turned them into stones. On the way to save Sanneke and the fairies, Ben went through a tunnel where emotion diamonds could be collected and used for defeating the evil witch later.

Collecting emotion diamonds is the first task of emotion learning (Fig. 1). It aims to help the player understand the emotions in different facial expressions. A certain emotion will be introduced when the player succeeds in collecting an emotion

Fig. 1. Task 1 – The player learns about the basic emotions by collecting emotion diamonds. Emotions are presented as a combination of facial expression and context.

diamond. The basic emotions like happiness, anger, sadness, fear and complex emotions like confused, shocked, bored were used. Because the complex emotions are more related to the contextual cues, examples of situations that trigger an emotion were presented (e.g. "When something unexpected happens you will feel shocked.").

At the end of the tunnel, Ben ran into an old fairy who knows everything. To get his trust, Ben must prove he was not a spy from the evil witch by showing his emotions were not stolen. The task given by the old fairy was to recognize the right facial expression for a limited time across a range of increasingly complex levels (Fig. 2). The goal of this task is to review the learning outcomes of the first stage.

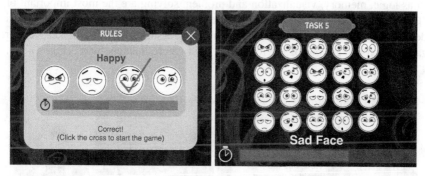

Fig. 2. Task 2 - Facial expression recognition. The player needs to find the right facial expression in a limited time across a range of increasingly complex levels.

With the help of the old fairy, Ben finally found the evil witch. However, the sly witch tried to seduce Ben to give up his emotions and then steal them. To stop her, the player must place right emotion diamonds into memory pieces, such as "Sanneke was taken by Macha's owls" and "fairies sacrificed themselves to protect you".

The third task requires the player to express emotion appropriately in different contexts (Fig. 3). This assignment aims to develop the ability of appropriate emotion expression. The contexts were selected from the previous story line. The facial

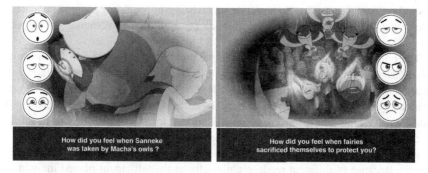

Fig. 3. Task 3 – Context-dependent recognition of expressed emotions. The player needs to choose the right emotions for different contexts selected from the previous story line.

expressions in the main pictures were removed, so that player needs to recall the whole story and find the right emotion for each context.

In the end, Ben found Sanneke half-stoned. To save her and defeat the evil witch, the player needs to take photos of specific facial expressions. The final task aims to encourage social interactions. By taking photos of others' face with certain emotion, players will be encouraged to communicate and experience how people express emotions in daily life.

Learning with fun was shown to be more effective [16]. According to the study of Alan Amory and his colleges, game elements could provide sufficient stimulation to engage learners in knowledge discovery and skill development and game elements such as logic, memory, visualization and problem solving are the most important ones [17]. Therefore, except for the tasks directly related to emotion recognition and understanding, fun elements related to story progression are added to keep children engaged, such as "get out of the room" or "find where Sanneke was" (Fig. 4), etc.

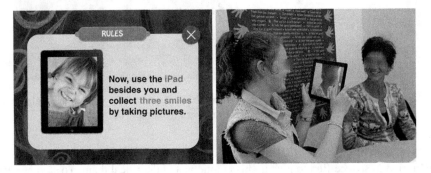

Fig. 4. Task 4 - Social interaction with the people in the player's environment. In the photo of pilot user test, the female participant was taking a smiling photo of her therapist.

3 Pilot User Test

We piloted the design with Royal Dutch Kentalis [10] expertise center, which is a national organization in the Netherlands specializing in providing diagnostic, care and educational services to people with communication problems, including young people with ASD accompanied by severe speech and language difficulties.

The pilot user test was performed with one therapist and two 15-year-old teenagers with ASD (one male and one female), who both have much lower development in communication and social interactions skills than their age group. The female partic-ipant has Attention Deficit Hyperactivity Disorder (ADHD), and she could be dis-tracted easily. This pilot test took place at Kentalis, location Velp. Before conducting the pilot test, informed consent was obtained from the parents of the participants.

Participants played the same game one by one accompanied by their therapist (Fig. 5). Because of different reading ability, the male participant played the game on his own, while the female participant asked help from the therapist to read the scripts

Fig. 5. Two examples of game elements: 1. The player needs to click on the items and find a way to get out of the room; 2. The player needs to click on the possible locations where the target person was hidden.

for her. After playing the game, participants were asked to fill in the questionnaire individually, which reflected his or her attitude towards the game. Then he/she could talk about their feelings while playing the game. The therapist filled another questionnaire at the end of the test and gave comments from the perspective of a psychologist.

The questionnaire for therapist consisted of six statements (e.g., 'I think *My Drama* is an effective training tool to develop ability on emotion recognition and expression') and the questionnaire for the participants consisted of nine statements (e.g., 'It is more fun to have facial expression training on *My Drama* than in the regular treatments.'). All statements were rated on a 5-points Likert Scale with a range from 1 (strongly disagree) to 5 (strongly agree). About the difficulty of the game, the participants rated the perceived difficulty of each task with a range from 1 (very easy) to 5 (very difficult). Finally, the last question of the questionnaire was: 'My final score for *My Drama* is…' where the therapist and participates could choose a score ranging from 1 to 10.

4 Results

The male participant spent 25 min to finish the game, and the female participant spent 45 min. During the game, participants were especially excited and interested while the music or some audio effects started to play or they succeeded in passing a task. Both participants performed more concentrated during the game compared to their daily learning activities, as observed by the therapist. This effect was especially strong on the female participant who used to be easily distracted. The male participant passed all the tasks smoothly and quickly without any mistake. The female participant expressed her anxiety at the beginning of the test, but relaxed as the test proceeded. She felt a little nervous and asked for help when she could not finish a task or find the solution. She passed emotion recognition task with two attempts and contextual emotion expression task also with two attempts.

Figure 6 shows the data gathered from the participants' questionnaire. The participants reported the facial expression training on *My Drama* as more fun than the

Fig. 6. A snapshot of the male participant playing *My Drama* on a tablet. A therapist was present at the test.

regular training ($Q_{11} = 5$, $Q_{21} = 4$). They reported to have learnt how to recognize and use facial expressions in this game ($Q_{12} = 4$, $Q_{22} = 4$). Quoted from the male partic\-ipate, "What I really like is when the game is close to the end, you have to recall the story and choose the right emotional faces. And that's exactly the game is saying, 'you have to pay attention.'" The instructions in the game are reported as clear ($Q_{13} = 4$, $Q_{23} = 4$). Both participants felt they were the main character in the story ($Q_{14} = 4$, $Q_{24} = 5$). They liked to play *My Drama* on a tablet ($Q_{15} = 5$, $Q_{25} = 4$). All participates expressed their willingness to play the game with others ($Q_{16} = 5$, $Q_{26} = 4$). Moreover, the story was reported as attractive and educational ($Q_{17} = 5$, $Q_{27} = 4$). And more stories were desired on *My Drama* ($Q_{18} = 4$, $Q_{28} = 5$).

Finally, *My Drama* scored 9 out of 10 in the overall evaluation session ($Q_1 = 9$, $Q_2 = 9$).

Figure 7 shows the result of perceived difficulty of each task in *My Drama*. The first task (Collect emotion diamonds) and the last one (Collect emotions in daily life) were both considered as easy ($Q_{11} = 2$, $Q_{21} = 2$; $Q_{14} = 2$, $Q_{24} = 2$). Moreover, the second task (Find the right facial expression) ($Q_{12} = 3$, $Q_{22} = 4$) and third task (Place emotions in the contexts) ($Q_{13} = 4$, $Q_{23} = 3$) were both considered as more difficult.

Figure 8 shows the data gathered from the therapist's questionnaire. The therapist reported that she considered *My Drama* as an effective training tool for emotion development ($Q_1 = 4$).

From the perspective of a psychologist, she suggested putting more training materials into the story. "The story in the game is quite long, but there are only four times when the participant has to do something with the emotions. So I would like to advise you to put more emotion recognition (training) into the game" (Fig. 9).

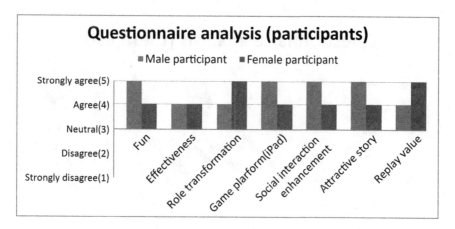

Fig. 7. Evaluation by the participants

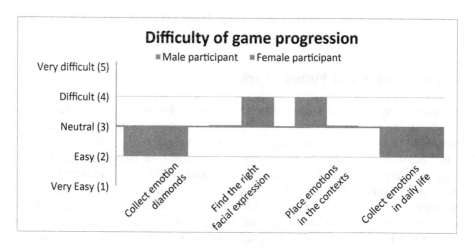

Fig. 8. The perceived difficulty of each task

The therapist liked the story in the game ($Q_2 = 4$), and enjoyed very much playing the game with the two participants ($Q_3 = 5$). As an observer and company to the participants, the therapist said both participants are able to concentrate on the game. "They were quite into the game. Although the female participant with ADHD can get quickly distracted, she was able to concentrate well on the game. I think that makes it a good game."

On the other hand, she stays neutral about the statement "The game is worth playing more than once" ($Q_4 = 3$). She mentioned that, "If they go through the same emotion (game) again and again, then it will be very easy." In the test, there was only one story in the game. It will be more appreciated, if there are more stories available on *My Drama* platform ($Q_5 = 5$). And she was willing to pay for stories if they are available ($Q_6 = 5$).

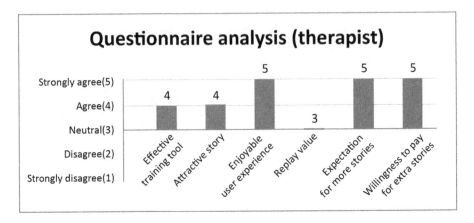

Fig. 9. Evaluation by the therapist

Finally, the therapist rated the overall acceptability and effectiveness of the training with *My Drama* as positive (Q = 8).

5 Conclusions and Future Work

The results of the pilot user test indicate that *My Drama* has a good potential to become an educational support in developing abilities to understand emotions in context. Embedding tasks into one consistent story encourages players to stay focused and think within the different contexts. The indication for that was the engagement of the participants while recognizing and imitating emotions, which was mentioned by the therapist. As mentioned by the male participant, the emotion recognition part made him pay attention to the whole story and recall the scenarios while doing the task. For the female participant the playfulness eliminated the anxiety of being trained, but retained the effect of learning and prolonged training time. The reported feeling of being the main character in the game, *My Drama* could help children and adolescents with ASD develop empathy, which is one of the previously reported benefits of drama therapy [3].

Regarding the game design, audio effects, rich interactions, animations and instant feedbacks were observed to intrigue curiosity and interest of players. Because some individuals with autism are not good at reading text, audio scripts should be added in the future redesign.

Higher game levels were expected to be perceived as more difficult than the lower ones. Based on their perceived difficulty and actual error rate, the difficulty of the first three tasks was found appropriate. However, the final task of collecting emotions in daily life was experienced to be easier than the previous two tasks. This may result from the limitation of the test conditions: In the test room, the participants can ask the therapist or the experimenter to help them finish the last task. Since the rules were available to the therapist and the experimenter, the participants got the final pictures of emotions from them with no effort. The game is actually designed for situations where players are encouraged to interact with people who do not know the game. This way the game encourages communication and social interaction skills to finish the task.

In this pilot study *My Drama* was evaluated from the perspective of usability and user experience. As suggested by the therapist, a good balance between story and training parts should be further considered and improved. The effect on the development of emotion recognition and empathy needs to be validated by a controlled study with more participants. Further improvements of the game are needed for long-term training, as suggested in [12]. The present study only provides one example story with a limited number of emotional contexts, which is not sufficient to support a long-term training. More stories and training approaches need to be developed on *My Drama*.

Finally, to our knowledge, this is the first design that combines the benefits of *Drama therapy* with the positive engagement effects of game design. Different from the majority of existing applications and games in this domain, it embeds the training elements into one consistent story. The understanding of emotions is trained in a context of this story. The affinity of the children with cartoon stories and especially with a familiar story is an extra element that helps the children enjoy the game and learn better.

References

1. Hobson, R.P., Ouston, J., Lee, A.: Emotion recognition in autism: coordinating faces and voices. Psychol. Med. **18**(04), 911–923 (1988)
2. Happé, F.G.: An advanced test of theory of mind: understanding of story characters' thoughts and feelings by able autistic, mentally handicapped, and normal children and adults. J. Autism Dev. Disord. **24**(2), 129–154 (1994)
3. Peter, M.: Drama, narrative and early learning. Br. J. Spec. Educ. **30**(1), 21–27 (1994)
4. Johnson, D.R.: Developmental approaches in drama therapy. Arts Psychother. **9**(3), 183–189 (1982)
5. Corbett, B.A., Gunther, J.R., Comins, D., Price, J., Ryan, N., Simon, D., et al.: Brief report: theatre as therapy for children with autism spectrum disorder. J. Autism Dev. Disord. **41**(4), 505–511 (2011)
6. Model Me Kids. http://www.modelmekids.com/
7. Autism Emotion. https://itunes.apple.com/us/app/autism-emotion/id550027186?mt=8
8. Between the Lines. http://www.hamaguchiapps.com/between-the- lines.html
9. The *Look at me* project. http://pages.samsung.com/ca/lookatme/English/
10. Royal Dutch Kentalis. http://www.kentalis.nl/
11. Gruarin, A., Westenberg, Michel, A., Barakova, Emilia, I.: StepByStep: design of an interactive pictorial activity game for teaching generalization skills to children with autism. In: Anacleto, Junia, C., Clua, Esteban, W.,G., Silva, Flavio, S.,Correa, Fels, S., Yang, Hyun, S. (eds.) ICEC 2013. LNCS, vol. 8215, pp. 87–92. Springer, Heidelberg (2013). doi:10. 1007/978-3-642-41106-9_10
12. Barakova, E.I., Bajracharya, P., Willemsen, M., Lourens, T., Huskens, B.: Long-term LEGO therapy with humanoid robot for children with ASD. Expert Syst. **32**(6), 698–709 (2015)
13. Goldsmith, T.R., LeBlanc, L.A.: Use of technology in interventions for children with autism. J. Early Intensive Behav. Interv. **1**(2), 166–178 (2004)

14. Franko, O.I., Tirrell, T.F.: Smartphone app use among medical providers in ACGME training programs. J. Med. Syst. **36**(5), 3135–3139 (2011)
15. Wing, L.: Sex ratios in early childhood autism and related conditions. Psychiatry Res. **5**(2), 129–137 (1981)
16. Lepper, M.R., Cordova, D.I.: A desire to be taught: instructional consequences of intrinsic motivation. Motiv. Emot. **16**(3), 187–208 (1992)
17. Amory, A., Naicker, K., Vincent, J., Adams, C.: The use of computer games as an educational tool: identification of appropriate game types and game elements. Br. J. Educ. Technol. **30**(4), 311–321 (1999)
18. Barakova, E.I., Gorbunov, R., Rauterberg, M.: Automatic interpretation of affective facial expressions in the context of interpersonal interaction. IEEE Trans. Hum.-Mach. Syst. **45**(4), 409–418 (2015)
19. Saarni, C.: The Development of Emotional Competence. Guilford, New York (1999)
20. Denham, S.: Emotional Development in Young Children. Guilford, New York (1998)

Building Game Scripting DSL's with the Metacasanova Metacompiler

Francesco Di Giacomo[1]([✉]), Mohamed Abbadi[1], Agostino Cortesi[1],
Pieter Spronck[2], and Giuseppe Maggiore[3]

[1] Universita' Ca' Foscari, Venice, Italy
{francesco.digiacomo,mohamed.abbadi,cortesi}@unive.it
[2] Tiburg University, Tilburg, The Netherlands
p.spronck@uvt.nl
[3] Hogeschool Rotterdam, Rotterdam, The Netherlands
maggg@hr.nl

Abstract. Many video games rely on a Domain Specific Language (DSL) to implement particular features such as artificial intelligence or time and synchronization primitives. Building a compiler for a DSL is a time-consuming task, and adding new features to a DSL is hard due to the low flexibility of the implementation choice. In this paper, we introduce an alternative to hand-made implementations of compilers for DSLs for game development: the Metacasanova metacompiler. We show the advantages of this metacomplier in terms of simplicity of designing and coding requirements, and in terms of performance of the resulting code, whose efficiency is comparable with hand-made implementations in commercial general purpose languages.

1 Introduction

In video games development it is often the case that *Domain Specific languages* (DSL) are used, as they provide ad-hoc features that simplify the coding process and yield to more concise and readable code when dealing with time management, synchronization, and AI thanks to their little CPU and memory overhead [1,8,16]. A typical synchronization problem arises when waiting for an event to happen, for instance when the short distance of a player from a door enables him to open it. These scenarios usually happen in a heavily concurrent system, where possibly hundreds of entities perform such interactions within the same update of the game. In order to tackle these problems, as a valuable alternative to the use of Threads, Finite state machines, or Strategy patterns, developers make use of Domain specific languages, like JASS [3], Unreal Script [14], or NWScript [2].

A first approach is implementing a DSL by building an interpreter within the host language abstractions, such as monads in a functional programming language [9,10,13]. Unfortunately the performance of an interpreted DSL built with monads is not as high as that achieved by compiled code, as monads make a large use of anonymous functions (or lambda expressions) which are often

© ICST Institute for Computer Sciences, Social Informatics and Telecommunications Engineering 2017
R. Poppe et al. (Eds.): INTETAIN 2016, LNICST 178, pp. 231–242, 2017.
DOI: 10.1007/978-3-319-49616-0_22

implemented with virtual method calls. Moreover functional languages are rarely employed in game developments as games are highly stateful programs.

Another typical approach is to design a hard-coded compiler for the DSL. This is a hard and time-consuming task, since a compiler is made of several components which perform transformations from the source code into machine code. The steps performed in this transformations are often the same, regardless of the language for which the compiler is being implemented, and they are not part of the creative aspect of language design [4]. This is why metacompliers come into the scene, with the ability to treat programs as data [5].

In this paper we present a novel solution to ease the development of a compiler for a game DSL by developing a metacompiler, called Metacasanova, producing code that is both clear and efficient, especially designed for games development. We show that, with this approach, the code to generate the compiler is 5 times shorter than a hard-coded compiler.

In this work we briefly describe the most common techniques used to build DSL's for game and their drawbacks (Sect. 2). We then propose a novel approach by introducing Metacasanova as a tool to develop a DSL (Sect. 3) and by re-emplementing Casanova DSL (Sect. 4). We then evaluate the result in terms of time performance and code length (Sect. 5) and draw the conclusion.

2 The Challenges of Building a Game DSL

In this section we introduce the general architecture of a game. We then present an example of common timing and synchronization primitives used in DSL's for games and we show some techniques typically used to implement them. For each technique we list the main drawbacks. Finally we present our solution to the problem of developing a DSL for games.

2.1 Preliminaries

A game engine is usually made of several interoperating components. All the components use a shared data structure, called *game state*, for their execution. The two main components of a game are the *logic engine*, which defines how the game state evolves during the game execution, and the *graphics engine*, which draws the scene by reading the updated game state. These two components are executed in lockstep within a function called *game loop*. The game loop is executed indefinitely, updating the game state by calling the logic engine, and drawing the scene by using the graphics engine. An iteration of the game loop is called *frame*. Usually a game should run between 30 to 60 frames per second. This requires both the graphics engine and the logic engine to be high-performance. In this paper we will only take into account the performance of the logic engine, as scripting drives the logic of the game loop.

2.2   A Time and Synchronization Primitive

A common requirement in game DSL's is a statement which allows to pause the execution of a function for a specified amount of time or until a condition is met. We will refer to these statements as `wait` and `when`. Such a behaviour can be modelled using different techniques: (*i*) *Threads* are used in game engines to parallelize the tasks of the single components [15], like the logic engine, but they are not suitable to implement those behaviours individually because of the memory overhead: the default stack size is 1 MB [12], which would mean allocating 1 MB per script in games with hundreds of thousands of entities running at least one script. (*ii*) *Finite State Machines* are high performance but the code logic is lost inside a `switch` structure, (*iii*) *Strategy pattern* uses polymorphism to represent the language constructs but it is inefficient due to the extensive use of virtuality, (*iv*) *Monadic DSL's* use monads to model the waiting or synchronization behaviour but extensively use virtuality as well due to lambda expressions, (*v*) *Compiled DSLs* are the most common solution, are high performance, but they require to implement a compiler or an interpreter (Table 1).

Table 1. Pros and cons of script implementation techniques

Technique	Readability	Performance	Code length
Monadic DSL	✓	✗	✓
Strategy pattern	✗	✗	✓
Finite state machines	✗	✓	✗
Hard-coded compiler	✓	✓	✗

In this work we propose another development approach in building a game DSL by using a metacompiler, a program which takes as input a language definition, a program written in that language, and generates executable code.

Given these considerations, we formulate the following problem statement:

PROBLEM STATEMENT: Given the formal definition of a game DSL our goal is to automate, by using a metacompiler, the process of building a compiler for that language in a (*i*) short (code lines), (*ii*) clear (code readability), and (*iii*) efficient (time execution) way, with respect to a hand-made implementation.

3   The Metacasanova Metacompiler

In this section we show how `wait` and `when` can be expressed with type and semantics rules. We show how these rules are implemented in a hard-coded compiler. We then introduce the idea of the metacompiler, explaining the advantage over a hard-coded compiler. We then give an overview of how a program in Metacasanova is written.

3.1   Type and Semantics of Wait and When

Usually the type and semantics rules of language elements are represented by rules that resemble those of logic models. Each rule is made of a set of *premises* and a *conclusion*. The conclusion is true if all the premises are true. According to this model, the type rules for wait and when are the following ($E \vdash x : T$ means that x has type T in the environment E):

$$\frac{E \vdash t \;:\; \texttt{float}}{E \vdash \texttt{wait } t \;:\; \texttt{void}} \qquad\qquad \frac{E \vdash c \;:\; \texttt{bool}}{E \vdash \texttt{when } c \;:\; \texttt{void}}$$

while their operational semantics is (with $\langle expr \rangle$ we mean "evaluating *exp*", with; a sequence of statements, and with dt the time difference between the current frame and the previous):

$$\frac{\langle t - dt > 0 \rangle \;\Rightarrow\; \texttt{true}}{\langle \texttt{wait } t; k\ dt \rangle \;\Rightarrow\; \langle \texttt{wait } t - dt; k\ dt \rangle} \qquad \frac{\langle t - dt > 0 \rangle \;\Rightarrow\; \texttt{false}}{\langle \texttt{wait } t; k\ dt \rangle \;\Rightarrow\; \langle k\ dt \rangle} \qquad \frac{\langle c \rangle \;\Rightarrow\; \texttt{true}}{\langle \texttt{when } c; k\ dt \rangle \;\Rightarrow\; \langle k\ dt \rangle}$$

$$\frac{\langle c \rangle \;\Rightarrow\; \texttt{false}}{\langle \texttt{when } c; k\ dt \rangle \;\Rightarrow\; \langle \texttt{when } c; k\ dt \rangle}$$

3.2   Implementation in a Hard-Coded Compiler

The semantics rules of wait and when can be implemented into the type checker module of a compiler written in a general purpose language. The rules are evaluated by means of a recursive function. In the case of a wait statement, we first type check its argument. If the argument is a float then we return the node in the type-checked Abstract Syntax Tree (AST) corresponding to the type-checked wait. If the argument has another type then we raise an exception since the argument has an invalid type. In the case of a when statement we do the same, but this time we check that the argument has boolean type. The code generation part requires to output code according to the semantics rules defined above. In this step the compiler can, for example, generate state machines described in Sect. 2.2.

3.3   Motivation for Metacasanova

From the discussion above we observe that, regardless of the implemented language, the process of type checking and implementing the operational semantics in a hard-coded compiler, is repetitive. Indeed, building the type checker and the code generator of a hard-coded compiler is a single, fixed translation of these rules into the general purpose language that was chosen for the implementation. This process can be summarized by the following behaviour: (*i*) find a rule which conclusion matches the structure of the language we are analysing, (*ii*) recursively evaluate all the premises in the same way, (*iii*) when we reach a rule with no premises (a base case), we generate a result (which might be the type of the structure we are evaluating or code that implements its operational semantics).

Our goal is to take this process and automate it, starting only from the specifications which the hard-coded compiler would implement. In order to achieve this we propose to use Metacasanova metacompiler. In what follows we show how a Metacasanova program is defined.

3.4   General Overview

A Metacasanova program is made of a set of **Data** and **Function** definitions, and a sequence of rules. A data definition specifies the constructor name of the data type (used to construct the data type), its field types, and the type name of the data. Optionally it is possible to specify a priority for the constructor of the data type. For instance this is the definition of the sum of two arithmetic expressions:

```
Data Expr ->"+" -> Expr : Expr  Priority 500
```

A function definition is similar to a data definition but it also has a return type. For instance the following is the evaluation function definition for the arithmetic expression above:

```
Func "eval" -> Expr : Evaluator => Value
```

In Metacasanova it is also possible to define polymorphic data in the following way:

```
Value is Expr
```

In this way we are saying that an atomic value is also an expression and we can pass both a composite expression and an atomic value to the evaluation function defined above.

A rule in Metacasanova, as explained above, may contain a sequence of function calls and clauses. In the following snippet we have the rule to evaluate the sum of two floating point numbers (`$ f` is **Data** type for floating point values):

```
eval a => $f c
eval b => $f d
<<c + d>> => res
-------------------------------
eval (a + b) => $f res
```

Note that if one of the two expressions does not return a floating point value, then the entire rule evaluation fails. The code between angular brackets specifies C# code that can be embedded in Metacasanova, allowing to perform the arithmetic operations with .NET operators. Metacasanova selects a rule by means of pattern matching in order of declaration on the function arguments. This means that both of the following rules will be valid candidates to evaluate the sum of two expressions:

```
...                       ...
---------------           ----------------------
eval expr => res          eval (a + b) => res
```

Finally the language supports expression bindings with the following syntax:

```
x := $f 5
```

4   Case Study: A Language for Game Development

In this section we will briefly introduce the Casanova language, a domain specific language for games. We then show a re-implementation, which we call Casanova 2.5, of the Casanova 2 language hard-coded compiler as an example of use of Metacasanova.

4.1   The Casanova Language

Casanova 2.5 is a language oriented to video game development which is based on Casanova 2 [1]. A program in Casanova is a tree of *entities*, where the root is marked in a special way and called *world*. Each entity is similar to a *class* in an object-oriented programming language: it has a constructor and some fields. The fields do not have access modifiers because they are not directly modifiable from the code except with a specific statement. Each entity also contains a list of *rules*, that are methods that are ticked in order with a specific refresh rate called dt. Each rule takes as input four elements: dt, this, which is a reference to the current entity, world that is a reference to the world entity, and a subset of entity fields called *domain*. A rule can only modify the fields contained in the domain. The rules can be paused for a certain amount of seconds or until a condition is met by using the wait statement. It is possible to modify the values of the fields in the domain by using the yield statement which takes as input a tuple of values to assign to the fields. When the yield statement is executed the rule is paused until the next frame. Also the body of control structures (if-then-else, while, for) is interruptible. In the following section we show the implementation of Casanova 2.5 in Metacasanova.

4.2   Casanova 2.5

The memory in Casanova 2.5 is represented using three maps, where the key is the variable/field name, and the value is the value stored in the variable/field. The first dictionary represents the global memory (the fields of the world entity or *Game State*), the second dictionary represents the current entity fields, and the third the variable bindings local to each rule.

The core of the entity update is the tick function. This function evaluates in order each rule in the entity by calling the evalRule function. This function executes the body of the rule and returns a result depending on the set of statements that has been evaluated. This result is used by tick to update the memory and rebuild the rule body to be evaluated at the next frame. The result of tick is a State containing the rules updated so far, and the updated entity and global fields. Since a rule must be restarted after the whole body has been evaluated, we need to store a list containing the original rules, which will be restored when evaluation returns Done (see below). At each step the function recursively calls itself by passing the remaining part of original rules (the rules which body was not altered by the evaluation of the statements) and modified rules (which body has been altered by the evaluation of the statements) to be

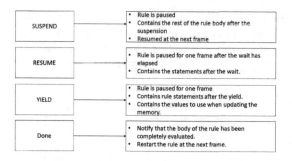

Fig. 1. Casanova 2.5 rule evaluation

evaluated. The function stops when all the rules have been evaluated, and this happens when both the original and the modified rule lists are empty.

Interruption is achieved by using *Continuation passing style*: the execution of a sequence of statements is seen as a sequence of steps that returns the result of the execution and the remaining code to be executed. Every time a statement is executed we rebuild a new rule whose body contains the continuation which will be evaluated next.

The possible results returned by the `tick` function are the following: (*i*) `Suspend` contains a `wait` statement with the updated timer, the continuation, and a data structure called `Context` which contains the updated local variables, the entity fields, and the global fields. The function rebuilds a rule which body is the sequence of statements contained by the `Suspend` data structure. (*ii*) `Resume` is returned when the timer must resume after the last waited frame. In order not to skip a frame we must still re-evaluate the rule at the next frame and not immediately. In this case the argument of `Resume` is only the remaining statements to be executed. (*iii*) `Yield` stops evaluation for one frame. We use the continuation to rebuild the rule body. Memory is updated by `evalRule`. (*iv*) `Done` stops the evaluation for one frame and rebuilds the original rule body by taking it from the original rules list.

For brevity we write only the code for `Suspend`. A full implementation can be found at [7]. You can see a schematic representation of the tick function in Fig. 1.

```
evalRule (rule dom body k locals delta) fields globals => Suspend (s;cont) (Context newLocals newFields
    newGlobals)
r := rule dom s cont newLocals dt
tick originals rs newFields newGlobals dt => State updatedRules updatedFields updatedGlobals
st := State (r::updatedRules) updatedFields updatedGlobals
-------------------------------------------------------
tick (original::originals) ((rule dom body k locals delta)::rs) fields globals dt => st
```

The function `evalRule` calls `evalStatement` to evaluate the first statement in the body of the rule passed as argument. The result of the evaluation of the statement is processed in the following way: (*i*) if the result is `Done`, `Suspend` or `Resume` then it is just returned to the caller function. We omit the code for this case, since it is trivial; (*ii*) if the result is `Atomic` it means that the evaluated statement was uninterruptible and the remaining statements of the rule must be re-evaluated immediately; (*iii*) if the result is `Yield` then the fields in the domain are updated recursively in order and then the updated memory is encapsulated in the `Yield` data structure and passed to the caller function.

```
evalStatement b k ctxt dt => Atomic z c
evalRule (rule dom z nop c dt) => res
--------------------------------
evalRule (rule dom b k ctxt dt)  => res
```

```
evalStatement b k (Context locals fields globals) dt => Yield ks values context
updateFields dom values context => updatedContext
------------------------------------------------------
evalRule (rule dom b k locals dt) fields globals => Yield ks values updatedContex
```

Note that, in case of a rule containing only atomic statements, we will eventually return `Done` after having recursively called `evalStatement` for all the statements, and the rule will be paused for one frame.

The `evalStatement` function is used both to evaluate a single statement and a sequence of statements. When evaluating a sequence of statements, the first one is extracted. A continuation is built with the following statement and passed to a recursive call to `evalStatement` which evaluates the extracted statement. If the existing continuation is non-empty, then it is added before the current continuation. If both the continuation and the body are empty (situation represented by the `nop` operator) then it means the rule evaluation has been completed and we return `Done`.

```
a != nop                                  ------------------------
--------------------                      addStmt nop nop => nop
addStmt a b => a;b

addStmt b k => cont
evalStatement a cont ctxt dt => res       -------------------------------------
--------------------------------          evalStatement nop nop ctxt dt => Done ctxt
evalStatement (a;b) k ctxt dt => res
```

We will now present, for brevity, only the evaluation of the `wait` and `yield` statements. Both the evaluation of the control structures and the variable bindings always return `Atomic` because they do not, by definition, pause the execution of the rule.

The `wait` statement has two different evaluations, based on the rules defined in Sect. 2: (*i*) the timer has elapsed: in this case we return `Resume` which contains the code to execute after the `wait` statement, or (*ii*) the timer has not elapsed: in this case we return `Suspend` which contains the `wait` statement with the updated timer followed by the continuation.

```
<<t <= dt>> == false
------------------------------------
evalStatement (wait t) k ctxt dt => Suspend wait <<t - dt>>;k ctxt
<<t <= dt>> == true
------------------------------------
evalStatement (wait t) k ctxt dt => Resume k ctxt
```

The `yield` statement takes as argument a list of expressions whose values are used to update the corresponding fields in the rule domain. The evaluation rule recursively evaluates the expressions and stores them into a list passed as argument of the `Yield` result. Those arguments are used later by `evalRule` to update the corresponding fields.

```
eval expr ctxt => v
evalYield exprs ctxt => vs
-----------------------------------------    -----------------------------
evalYield (expr :: exprs) ctxt => v :: vs     evalYield nil ctxt => nil
```

5   Evaluation

In this section we provide an implementation of a patrol script for an entity in a game. The sample is made up of an entity, representing a guard, and a couple of checkpoints. The guard continuously moves between the two checkpoints. We choose this sample because this is a typical behaviour implemented in several games, where the user is able to set up a patrol route for a unit. We show the comparison between the sample implemented in Casanova 2.5 and an equivalent implementation in Python with respect to the running time. We then show a comparison between the hard-coded compiler of Casanova 2.0 and the implementation of Casanova 2.5 in Metacasanova with respect to the code length.

5.1   Chosen Languages

We compared the running time of the sample in metacompiled Casanova with an equivalent implementation in Python. This language was chosen based on its use in game development: Python has been used extensively in several games such as Civlization IV [6] or World in Conflict [11] because of the native support for coroutines. We deliberately ignore C++ and C# implementations, although they are widely used in the industry, because we knew in advance [1] that the

Table 2. Patrol sample evaluation

Casanova 2.5

Entity #	Average update time (ms)	Frame rate
100	0.00349	286.53
250	0.00911	109.77
500	0.01716	58.275
750	0.02597	38.506
1000	0.03527	28.353

Python

Entity #	Average update time (ms)	Frame rate
100	0.00132	756.37
250	0.00342	292.05
500	0.00678	147.54
750	0.01087	91.988
1000	0.01408	71.002

Table 3. Meta-compiler vs standard compiler

Casanova 2.5 with Metacasanova

Module	Code lines
Data structures and function definitions	40
Query Evaluation	16
While loop	4
For loop	5
If-then-else	4
When	4
Wait	6
Yield	10
Additional rules for Casanova program evaluation	40
Additional rules for basic expression evaluation	201
Total: 300	

Casanova 2.0 compiler

Module	Code lines
While loop	10
For-loop and query evaluation	44
If-Then-Else	15
When	11
Wait	24
Yield	29
Additional structures for rule evaluation	63
Structures for state machine generations	754
Code generation	530
Total: 1480	

current version of the code generated by the meta-compiler would not match the high performance of these languages: the main goal of this work is to reduce the effort of writing a compiler for a DSL for games while having acceptable performance.

5.2   Performance

The performance results are shown in Table 2. We see that the generated code has performance on the same order as Python. This is mainly due to the fact that the memory, in the metacompiled implementation of Casanova, is managed through a map, and because of the virtuality of the implemented operators. Each time Casanova accesses a field in an entity this must be looked up into the map.

To this we add the complexity of dynamic lookups when we must deal with polymorphic results into the rules.

From Table 3 we see that the implementation of Casanova 2.0 language in Metacasanova is almost 5 times shorter in terms of lines of code than the previous Casanova implementation in F#. We believe it is worthy noticing that structures with complex behaviours, such as *wait* or *when*, require hundreds of lines of codes with a standard approach (the code lines to define the behaviour of the structure plus the support code to correctly generate the state machine), while in the meta-compiler we just need tens of lines of codes to implement the same behaviour. Moreover we want to point out that the previous Casanova compiler was written in a functional programming language: these languages tend to be more synthetic than imperative languages, so the difference with the same compiler implemented in languages such as C/C++ might be even greater.

The readability with respect to the hard-coded compiler code is also improved: we managed to implement the behaviour of synchronization and timing primitives almost imitating one to one the formal semantics of the language definition (see the semantics rules in Sect. 3 and their implementation in Sect. 4). In the hard-coded compiler implementation for Casanova 2.0 the semantics are lost in the code for generating finite state machines.

6   Conclusion

In this work we proposed an alternative technique to implement a DSL for games by using a metacompiler called Metacasanova. As a case study we re-implemented the Casanova language, a DSL for game development, in Meta-casanova. Our results show that the code required to re-implement Casanova in Metacasanova is (*i*) shorter, and (*ii*) more readable with respect to the existing hard-coded compiler for the same language. Moreover we showed that the language behaviour can be expressed in a way that directly mimics the formal semantics definition of the language. Adding the layer of the meta-compiler to the language affects the performance of the generated code so that we cannot achieve the same performance as with the manual implementation. Despite this, we managed to achieve performance similar to Python, a language typically used as a scripting language to define the game logic in several commercial games.

References

1. Abbadi, M., Giacomo, F., Cortesi, A., Spronck, P., Costantini, G., Maggiore, G.: Casanova: a simple, high-performance language for game development. In: Göbel, S., Ma, M., Baalsrud Hauge, J., Oliveira, M.F., Wiemeyer, J., Wendel, V. (eds.) JCSG 2015. LNCS, vol. 9090, pp. 123–134. Springer, Heidelberg (2015). doi:10.1007/978-3-319-19126-3_11
2. Bioware. Nwscript api reference (2002). http://www.nwnlexicon.com/
3. Blizzard Entertainment. Jass api reference (1999). http://jass.sourceforge.net/doc/
4. Book, E., Shorre, D.V., Sherman, S.J.: The cwic/360 system, a compiler for writing and implementing compilers. SIGPLAN Not. **5**(6), 11–29 (1970)

5. Czarnecki, K., Eisenecker, U.W.: Generative Programming: Methods, Tools, and Applications. ACM Press/Addison-Wesley Publishing Co., New York (2000)
6. Games, F.: Civlization iv scripting api reference, October 2008. http://wiki.massgate.net/Our_Python_files_and_Event_Structure
7. Di Giacomo, F.: Casanova 2.5 source code (2016). https://github.com/vs-team/metacompiler/tree/master/Sources/Content/Content/CNV3
8. Kelly, J.P., Botea, A., Koenig, S.: Offline planning with hierarchical task networks in video games. In: AIIDE (2008)
9. Maggiore, G., Bugliesi, M., Orsini, R.: Monadic scripting in f# for computer games. In: TTSS 115th International Workshop on Harnessing Theories for Tool Support in Software, p. 35 (2011)
10. Maggiore, G., Spanò, A., Orsini, R., Bugliesi, M., Abbadi, M., Steffinlongo, E.: A formal specification for casanova, a language for computer games. In: Proceedings of the 4th ACM SIGCHI Symposium on Engineering Interactive Computing Systems, EICS 2012, pp. 287–292. ACM, New York (2012)
11. Massive Entertainment. World in conflict script reference, September 2007. http://civ4bug.sourceforge.net/PythonAPI/
12. Microsoft Corporation. Msdn. https://msdn.microsoft.com/en-us/library/windows/desktop/ms686774(v=vs.85).aspx
13. Sheard, T., Benaissa, Z., Pasalic, E.: Dsl implementation using staging and monads. In: Second Conference on Domain-Specific Languages DSL 1999, pp. 81–94. ACM (1999)
14. Sweeney, T., Hendriks, M.: Unrealscript Language Reference. Epic MegaGames Inc., Cary (1998)
15. Tulip, J., Bekkema, J., Nesbitt, K.: Multi-threaded game engine design. In: Proceedings of the 3rd Australasian conference on Interactive Entertainment, pp. 9–14. Murdoch University (2006)
16. van Deursen, A., Klint, P., Visser, J.: Domain-specific languages: an annotated bibliography. SIGPLAN Not. **35**(6), 26–36 (2000)

Interaction Design Tools for Autism

Andrea Di Salvo[(✉)] and Paolo Marco Tamborrini

Dipartimento di Architettura e Design, Politecnico di Torino,
Viale Mattioli 39, 10125 Turin, Italy
{andrea.disalvo,paolo.tamborrini}@polito.it

Abstract. Children with Autism and Asperger Syndrome, though they are very different according to the broad spectrum of the criteria used for diagnosis, can be greatly supported by the use of new digital technologies in their daily lives, at school, at home, with their families. The paper shows the design approach to an interactive application for high-functioning children aged 14 to 18 in order to generate independence in the children, to ensure their safety, to create a network of aware and careful people regarding the Autism themes in order to better support families. The design of the application involves families, patients and educators.

Keywords: Interaction design · Autism · Asperger Syndrome · Social inclusion

1 Introduction

Digital technologies induced great interest in the families of patients with Autism Spectrum Disorders (ASD) and especially they have high expectations in these tools. One of the main reasons concerns the great accessibility of devices like smartphones, tablets and nowadays wearables. The paper aims to present the first results of the research project called "Interaction Design 4 Autism" in collaboration between the Department of Architecture and Design at the Politecnico di Torino and the C.A.S.A. Clinic (Centro Autismo e Sindrome di Asperger, specialised in Child Neuropsychiatry) based in Mondovì (Cuneo - Italy). The research process firstly describes the scenario of the Autism children and the contribution that technologies can give to the patients. Then a group of application is analysed with a set of heuristics in order to underline potentialities and criticalities. The meta-design part explores the user-needs taking into account the literature and the data obtained from families, patients and educators. The article concludes with the description of the project that contains a new application that aims to generate independence in the autistic children not only at home and at school but also during the movements on the outside.

2 The Research Process

The criteria for identifying the Autism Spectrum Disorder are very complex, as various as the patients are, to the point that every person with autism is almost different from the others. That is why the word *spectrum* is used. Some individuals may also be

© ICST Institute for Computer Sciences, Social Informatics and Telecommunications Engineering 2017
R. Poppe et al. (Eds.): INTETAIN 2016, LNICST 178, pp. 243–253, 2017.
DOI: 10.1007/978-3-319-49616-0_23

influenced by the context and show variable behaviours and characteristics depending on the situation [1]. Basically autistic children and adults show, although with varying degrees, the following symptoms: impairment in social interaction, verbal and non-verbal communication; stereotypical or repeated behaviours, interests and activities; an extreme need for consistency and predictability in the routine of daily life [2]; challenges with establishing joint attention [3]. Autism is a neurological disorder that is diagnosed in the first three years of life and causes, even in the less severe cases, difficulties interacting with other people. This happens because social rules, facial expressions and a series of abstract languages commonly used as metaphors and irony, are not understood [4]. These symptoms are effectively summarized in the Wing's Triad [5]. Some patients with Asperger Syndrome (the "high-functioning" end of the spectrum) can often have a certain degree of independence in their life. Their cognitive faculties and their intelligence can enable to establish themselves professionally even if an high propensity to anxiety and limited social skills still persist. In fact, they have to memorize and to reproduce socially correct behaviours considering that they are unable to "naturally" interpret continual signals.

2.1   Digital Technologies and Autism: Devices, Tablet, Robots

Digital technologies have proven to be a great help in the treatment of Autism. Devices such as PCs, tablets, and robots have, in fact, positive intrinsic aspects able to adapt to the characteristics of autism. This is due to: the components and their functionalities, like geolocalization sensors or speech-generation that empower people capabilities and continuously generate useful data; the opportunity of designing an environment and an interaction system that suit the needs of autistic children; the possibility of having a sort of continuous treatment even without the direct observation of medical or professional staff. If the interaction with individuals presenting repetitive behaviours can be difficult and frustrating, that does not happen with specifically designed software. An application can: create a familiar and predictable environment, reward correct actions through visual cues, offer advices and eliminate the complexities due to social interaction, work as one-to-one essential tool to teach even simple tasks. Below a list of uses and main collected results to this day is presented. Desktop systems with dedicated programs and voice output communication devices establish a communication channel between autistic children and, for example, classmates rather than teachers and parents. Some of these devices, including the first PDA, were very resistant and specifically designed to solve the problem of, for example, speech generation. However, they had some issues such as the weight, the size and the high cost, combined with a lack of product availability and assistance services. Tablets and smartphones immediately turned out to be much more flexible tools, cheaper than their predecessors, multi-functional and above all, thanks to their spread, they are more inclusive and socially accepted as a medium of communication [6]. These technologies have been tested mainly in the educational field in which, from the outset, the improvements were evident in terms of attention, motivation and retention of vocabulary during the class [7]. Within the familiar sphere, instead, the majority of applications tried to structure some fragments of communication in a more agile way, the same ones that previously needed visual-interactive supports made of paper. However the ease and immediacy in the interaction can become a critical issue and a way to be more isolated if applications and use modalities are not specifically designed. In any case, every single action requires extensive training and ongoing assistance especially with low-functioning children. Given the complexity of the theme, a large corpus of scientific evidences that quantify the benefits of using smart devices is not yet available in the literature, but the number of researches is still rising. The first results show that some improvements are possible from the point of view of communication and of behaviours while data are too limited and noisy as regards the social skills [8]. This category is still too difficult to deal with, considering the differences between cases and the extreme difficulty that these subjects show. The study conducted by Hourcade et al. [9], in particular, compares similar activities made with or without an app on a tablet. The results show that the 8 involved children responded very positively to the use of the app by increasing: the number of spoken phrases, the verbal interactions, the physical involvement and somehow the support comments. Beyond the technological tool, which is undoubtedly able to sustain a design action, each subject is able to interact with the application according to three factors: the individual capabilities (that can be motor, sensory and cognitive); the device architecture (the way the display is organised and the interaction modalities); the specific communication requirements [10]. These factors have to be then connected to the specific context of use. This categorization highlights the large number of variables to assess the scalability of each project action. There are also numerous experiences that relate to the interaction between autism and robotics. In the more complex projects, humanoid robots are used to facilitate an interaction comparable to the human-human one. The main difference, compared to a system based on PC or tablet, is the ability to have a direct interaction including all classes, from direct manipulation to multimodal stimuli and feedback. The target of robotics thus relates to design an interaction that is specifically configured on the subject, easily controlling and generating core social interactive behaviour such as: eye gaze, turn taking, joint reference or imitation [11]. Establishing a relationship of direct manipulation with tangible interfaces is important for children with learning disabilities because they can discover a strong correlation between a physical action and a digital feedback, they can obtain the effect of positive reinforcement and their motivation increases in the interaction [12]. Some projects also show that it is also possible to create face-to-face interaction by using, for example, LEGO [13]. The role of digital technology described in this section is a way to emphasize the support that they can provide to children, families and educators. As tools, technologies cannot substitute the human-to-human interaction. On the contrary every device and application is designed to empower autistic children, engage them and to reduce their gap in communication.

2.2 Definition of the Heuristics and Critical Analysis of Related Works

There is a large number of applications designed for autistic children in literature and on the on-line stores: applications to create social stories and task analysis; specific applications for AAC (Augmentative Alternative Communication, a form of communication that substitutes, complements, enhances oral verbal language through pictures, gestures, symbols, and anything that can help users to express their thoughts in an alternative way); apps that use PECS (Picture Exchange Communication System); apps exploiting the ABA method (Applied Behaviour Analysis); apps to reinforce the visual channel (with images, drawings, photographs, symbols, music, sounds, words, objects) or to draw and colour; to produce and listen to music. All these applications offer rehabilitation and educational tools that are very stimulating and can be presented singly or in groups of functions within the same package. The research team chose and analysed 16 applications in order to get a map of the criticalities about usability. The applications have been chosen according to these criteria: a previous analysis or use in the clinic, the creation of independence should be one of the main goals, the availability on the on-line stores. This last criterion has been adopted to get data not only from usability experts but also from common users. Even if those apps may not come from a scientific research, quantitative data, like comments that come from personal use, can be considered useful to have the big picture of the actual scenario. The creation of independence, instead, is one of the most important needs that the team has found and will be discussed in the next section. In this way the team created a system, including quantitative and qualitative data, to evaluate the apps using the heuristics of Nielsen [14]. For each heuristic, the research team assigned a rating on a scale from 1 to 5 (5 = perfectly coherent with the heuristic) in order to identify criticalities and strong points to be taken into account during the project. The evaluation considers both the qualitative rates given by three usability experts of the team (with a review by the staff of the clinic) and the quantitative data harvested from reviews of the users. The reviews have been collected through the app-stores and also in the web sites that are worldwide considered as a reference for families for autistic children. Quantitative data have been considered as a feedback from the real world and have been used to average the ratings given by the experts or to highlight malfunctionings. Some differences have been applied to the original heuristics because autistic children have different perception and degree of attention during the interaction. For example "User control and freedom" cannot be applied because autistic subjects need to follow well-defined paths. The heuristic should be changed by referring to the persuasive technique called tunneling by Fogg [15]. For the same reason "Flexibility and efficiency of use" cannot be considered. Design for flexibility means in this case the need to customize the paths and, where possible, take advantage of this to improve the level reached in communication and interaction. The analysed apps are: Tools For Autism, FTVS HD - First Then Visual Schedule Hd, Autism Emotion, Immaginario, TOUCHforAUTISM, Able AAC Free, Upper Case - Autism Series, Autism & PDD Associations, AutisMate, Zac, Autism iHelp - Toys, Io Parlo, Emotions, Proloquo2go, Autism Speaks, Teens With Autism. Figure 1 shows that very important heuristics like for example visibility, aesthetic and minimalism are not well considered in the majority of the evaluated app. The research team used these criticalities to better implement the graphic visualization and the interaction design of the app.

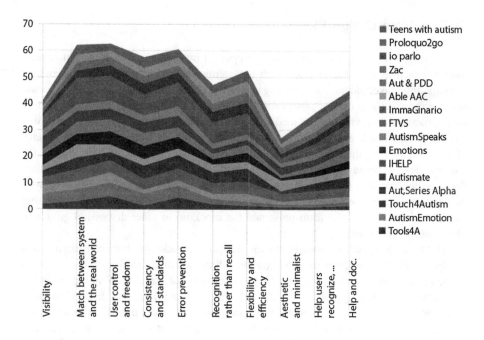

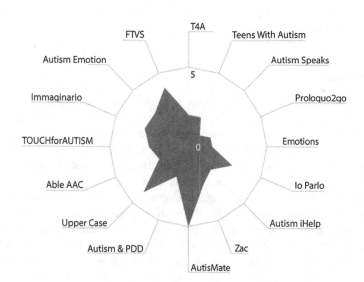

Fig. 1. Comparison between apps (above) and focus on the visibility heuristics (below).

3 The Meta-Design Phase

In this project the design research team, supported by the expertise of the clinic staff, tried as much as possible to think with a systemic design approach [16], to connect participating stakeholders, to build engaging interactive modes. In this way the team firstly conducted a period of observation of the activities in the clinic, then proposed semi-structured interview to the medical staff. After that the team participated to discussion groups inside events in which the autism's problems were discussed by parents of autistic children, their familiars and educators, to explore user's needs. Before the concept design phase the team checked user's needs coherence in literature, then designed the app and the interactions following an iterative design process both with the medical staff of the clinic and a group of educators. Approximately one year after the start of the project, the team presented the mock-up to other discussion groups to obtain useful feedback.

The described path is peculiar to the design methodology but, considering that children with Autism Disorder show greater difficulties in some characteristic aspects of the interaction, the interaction design team acted also as an aid tool in the project to collect heterogeneous approaches to the problem that come from very different fields of research and practices. Assistant teachers anecdotes, for example, often describe the effectiveness of self-made tools and teaching strategies that have been developed day by day trying to adapt general knowledge to custom-tailored intervention. It is not simple at all to create a system starting from these several needs, as well as the full replicability of any test on an autistic child can be quite difficult because of the many differences within the spectrum.

3.1 User's Needs

One of the main postulates of Interaction Design is the importance of involving stakeholders in the process and iteratively verifying the output with the users, but applying this concept to the case of autism becomes critical. It is rather rarely possible to reconstruct at least the needs or the feelings of the subject itself, precisely because of its communication difficulties. The concept itself of Human Centred Design in this case relies more on the observation and the comments of therapists and parents obtaining ex-post data. Recently, some research has attempted to collect the needs of the three more important involved actors like family members, teachers and subjects through series of questionnaires. The first results show that the needs are an improvement of: social and communication skills, academic skills, the development of a greater capacity for flexible organization [17]. In particular, most of the obtained answers regards the possibility of creating independence. These answers are quite the same that the team obtained during the discussion groups. Even in front of these responses it should be emphasized that expectations for achievable results should be proportionate to the real possibilities of the children that differ according to the spectrum. Although the percentage of people with autism that can live independently in adulthood remains low [18, 19], it can be assumed that, through a structured and early intervention, good results can be achieved in terms of independence. At the present time as the enthusiasm derived from the first application has encouraged the spread of smart devices, such as tablets, they are mostly used with educational or communication purposes but not for the creation of independence.

The generation of anxiety is one of the biggest problem that parents and educators usually underline. This phenomenon occurs in more than half of people with autism, especially in those who have higher cognitive skills. Anxiety is usually due to the inadequacy in dealing with unexpected social situations and changes and can be approached in several ways. The ones that are most closely related to the Interaction Design include aspects such as the hands-on tasks, visual supports and modulated integration of personal strengths and interests of the subject [20, 21]. Some anxiety-perceived tasks, if they are gradually addressed, can be achieved in the course of time in a more relaxed way increasing the level of independence in daily life [22].

4   The Design Project

The project is developed in cooperation with the C.A.S.A. clinic that has worked closely with the design team during all the phases. Among the many initiatives of the centre there is a project that includes activities inside the clinical, in the form of rehabilitation laboratory, using touch technologies. Consequently the medical staff has already experienced treatments using smart digital devices. According to the needs that emerged in the research phase, the team focused on the concepts of: creating independence in the autistic children aged 14 to 18 during the movements on the outside; ensuring the safety of children; creating a network of aware and careful people regarding the Autism themes in order to better support families; using inclusive common smart devices as smartphones. The main goal regarding the autistic child is to help him reaching a series of pre-defined places in autonomy and assisting him in case of emergency or anxiety. At the same time both parents and members of the community must be informed of a possible emergency in order to intervene immediately and reassure the child. The designed application has three access mode: one for the autistic child, one for the parent, and one for the users belonging to the community. Every user can operate different functions. The first step of the project concerns the design of a further aid that has to meet the demands for independence, security and daily life, especially in children. Some high-functioning children may in fact also begin to move outside on their own. This percentage may reach the 20 % of cases. This decision aims to fill the current shortage of applications that support individuals and families not only in protected and well-known environments, as a house, but that can become also portable. As it happens with able-bodied children, the fears of parents considerably increase when they cannot assist their sons doing tasks that until that moment were faced in protected environments, but interactive digital tools allow them to create an opportunity. The same application is accessible from two users, the parents and the child. The two users are connected to the same service to get different information. Four options are presented to the autistic child: "communicate my position", "call parent", "talk for me" and "where I'm going". The first in order of importance, therefore regarding shape and colours, allows the child to communicate its position in the event of emergency (using the built-in GPS module) to 4 pre-set contacts.

This message will appear on the smartphone of the parent who can easily get to the child. Considering the importance of this function it can be activated at any time through the tangible help button that corresponds to the volume command on the smartphone side. This aspect is still undergoing study, especially from the point of view of the code and the constraints that some operating systems impose in application projects. "Call parent" allows the child to directly communicate with the parent, or with other reliable person, via a shortcut button. This does not necessarily imply an emergency but it is useful if the child needs to be reassured by a friendly voice or a face, if video call is set by default. The third button is the "talk for me". This feature is designed for non-verbal children that need to ask for help. A voice message can be earlier recorded and it can be played to anyone around the child. The last key is the "where I'm going". This is a simplified navigator that helps the child to autonomy follow a path and to reach the destination. After the choice of the point of departure and of arrival, simple screens made of brief texts instructions and photographs come in succession. This feature has been designed starting from the configuration used for social stories; autistic children are used, in fact, to perform tasks step by step, reading simple instructions. It is assumed, therefore, that the path and the images have been previously configured with the help of a parent. The parent can instead contact the child, identify its location, have access to settings that will have an impacting also on the settings of the child's app (like destinations or preset phone numbers) but mainly adds the functionality of the "Find close friend". This function integrates in the app the key part of the community of people interested in and attentive to the issue of autism. In case of difficulty, in fact, the application is able to send a message to all the holders of the app that are located close to the child. This feature allows the parents to ask for help to the community in case of danger; the goal is to create a network of informed people about autism in contact with each other. An autistic child caught by anxiety can indeed make gestures and behaviours that are socially misinterpreted. People who are part of the community can help him or at least explain the situation and ask for help by themselves. Regarding the interface and the wireframe of the app, two main working environments have been created, one for the autistic subject and one for the parents. The requirements are in fact very different. The child with autism should stay focused on the task until its conclusion. The number of interactive elements in the user interface has been reduced both to become minimal and because, especially on pages where he needs to make choices, it is more likely to make mistakes. A uniform and consistent grid has been created in order to gather non-interactive elements as much as possible in defined areas. The interactive areas of buttons and their perceptibility were increased to correctly support also the children with motor disabilities. The chosen colours are suitable for a children to be attractive and friendly; they differ in sections while maintaining a narrow range of colours. Great care has been taken to ensure a high level of contrast in order to maintain high legibility and to highlight the differences between interactive and non-interactive areas. Once the activity starts, the screen modulates avoiding deviations from the path and hiding, for example, system bars or panels. The fonts has been examined to address the possible reading difficulties which some autistic patients may present. Often children with autism have difficulty learning to read and write; it is a issue that has been also observed in subjects suffering from the dyslexia. Appropriate fonts were then analysed [23] to ensure high readability, with highly irregular features (that is without symmetry between letters that could be confused) with evident ascents and descents. The chosen font, TestMe, has then be adapted by increasing line-spacing and kerning, using words and phrases as short as possible and avoiding interruption between lines. The illustrations were not the subject of a redesign because the clinic uses them for many years and they have proven their effectiveness in communication. This application is also part of a larger project that integrates an awareness and communication campaign made through a video and a payoffs printable on, for example, t-shirts and other objects typical of a teenager (Fig. 2).

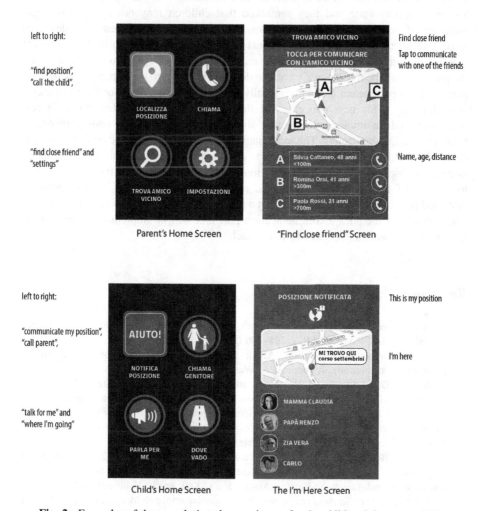

Fig. 2. Examples of the new designed screen's app for the child and the parent [24].

5   Conclusion and Future Work

The paper tried to demonstrate how interaction designers can design tools to improve social inclusion of autistic children and of their parents, through technologies that today are accessible and sustainable from the economical and social point of view. After the first year of research, the team presented the app to discussion groups and dedicated events for obtaining feedback about the goal and the interaction of the app. The application has been positively evaluated, the main criticality underlined by the groups was the trustability both of the app and of the community. They imagined their children lost in a anxiety state and they remarked that children may not operate the right sequence of actions. In this case the touch interface, even if it has been designed respecting all the usability criteria, seems to be not so appropriate in case of some mobility impairments summed to an increasing anxiety. One solution discussed with the parents could be the use of a wearable device connected to the app, in order to track physiological parameters and automatically communicate the need for help to parents or community. This new concept, and the first results, needs a test phase in real conditions and an implementation that should solve some of the coding problems related to the OS constraints. The team planned to test the app connected to a wearable device with at least 5 children in the next months in a defined area in order to obtain more data observing the children behaviours and the perception of their parents. The trustability of the community is instead related to the creation of a community of informed people, while today there is not a proper communication about autism. In this case the project includes a communication part that will be implemented and can be used in the dissemination part of the research.

References

1. Lopez, B., Leekam, S.R.: Do children with autism fail to process information in context? J. Child Psychol. Psychiat. **44**(2), 285–300 (2003)
2. American Psychiatric Association (APA): Diagnostic and Statistical Manual of Mental Disorders (text revision), 4th edn. APA, Washington (DC) (2000)
3. McArthur, D., Adamson, L.B.: Joint attention in preverbal children: Autism and developmental language disorder. J. Autism Dev. Disord. **26**(3), 481–496 (1996)
4. Howlin, P.: Children with Autism and Asperger Syndrome: A Guide for Practitioners and Carers. Wiley, Chichester (1998)
5. Wing, L.: The Autistic Spectrum. Constable, London (1996)
6. Sennot, S., Bowker, A.: Autism, AAC, and Proloquo2Go. In: SIG 12 Perspectives on Augmentative and Alternative Communication, December 2009, vol. 18, pp. 137–145. American Speech-Language-Hearing Association (2009). doi:10.1044/aac18.4.137
7. Moore, M., Calvert, S.: Brief report: vocabulary acquisition for children with autism: teacher or computer instruction. J. Autism Dev. Disord. **30**(4), 359–362 (2000)
8. Logan, K., Angus, T., Smith, C.: Creating 'App'ortunities for learning using touch technologies: how iPads can facilitate learning, communication, social skills and positive behaviour in children with autism across the spectrum. Presented at Autism Spectrum Australia's Research Conference, 4 April 2013

9. Hourcade, J.P., Williams, S.R., Miller, E.A., Huebner, K.E., Liang, L.J.: Evaluation of tablet apps to encourage social interaction in children with autism spectrum disorders. In: Proceeding CHI 2013, Proceedings of SIGCHI Conference on Human Factors in Computing Systems, pp. 3197–3206. ACM, New York (2013)

10. Light, J., Wilkinson, K., Drager, K.: Designing effective AAC systems: research evidence and implications for practice. ASHA (2008)

11. Robins, B., Dautenhahn, K., te Boekhorst, R., Billard, A.: Effects of repeated exposure to a humanoid robot on children with autism. In: Proceedings of 2nd Cambridge Workshop on Universal Access and Assistive Technology. Springer, Cambridge (2004, forthcoming)

12. Keay-Bright, W., Howarth, I.: Is simplicity the key to engagement for children on the autism spectrum? Pers. Ubiquitous Comput. **16**(2), 129–141 (2012). Springer

13. Farr, W., Yuill, N., Raffle, H.: Social benefits of a tangible user interface for children with autistic spectrum conditions. Autism **14**(3), 237–252 (2010)

14. Nielsen, J.: Heuristic evaluation. In: Nielsen, J., Mack, R.L. (eds.) Usability Inspection Methods. Wiley, New York (1994)

15. Fogg, B.J.: Persuasive Technology: Using Computers to Change What We Think and Do. Morgan Kaufmann Publishers, San Francisco (2003)

16. Bistagnino, L.: Systemic Design, Designing the Productive and Environmental Sustainability/Design Sistemico, progettare la sostenibilità produttiva e ambientale, 2a ed. (ebook). Slow Food Editore, Bra (Cuneo) (2011)

17. Putnam, C., Chong, L.: Software and technologies designed for people with autism: what do users want? In: Assets 2008, Proceedings of 10th International ACM SIGACCESS Conference on Computers and Accessibility, pp. 3–10, ACM, New York (2008)

18. Billstedt, E., Gillberg, C., Gillberg, C.: Autism after adolescence: population-based 13- to 22-year follow-up study of 120 individuals with autism diagnosed in childhood. J. Autism Dev. Disord. **35**(3), 351–360 (2005)

19. Eaves, L.C., Ho, H.H.: Young adult outcome of autism spectrum disorders. J. Autism Dev. Disord. **38**(4), 739–747 (2008)

20. Drahota, A., Wood, J.J., Sze, K.M., van Dyke, M.: Effects of cognitive behavioral therapy on daily living skills in children with high-functioning autism and concurrent anxiety disorders. J. Autism Dev. Disord. **41**, 257–265 (2011)

21. Lang, R., Regesterm, A., Lauderdale, S., Ashbaugh, K., Haring, A.: Treatment of anxiety in autism spectrum disorders using cognitive behaviour therapy: a systematic review. Dev. Neurorehabilit. **13**, 53–63 (2010)

22. McNally Keehn, R.H., Lincoln, A., Brown, M., Chavira, D.: The Coping Cat program for children with anxiety and autism spectrum disorder: a pilot randomized controlled trial. J. Autism Dev. Disord. **43**(1), 57–67 (2013)

23. Iacopino, A.: Progettazione di una font per dislessici, Torino (2011)

24. Bertot, F., Tamagnone, M.: Design for autism. Interaction design a supporto della progettazione per ragazzi autistici, Torino (2013)

Poème Numérique: Technology-Mediated Audience Participation (TMAP) Using Smartphones and High-Frequency Sound IDs

Fares Kayali[1(✉)], Christoph Bartmann[1], Oliver Hödl[1],
Ruth Mateus-Berr[2], and Martin Pichlmair[3]

[1] Vienna University of Technology,
Argentinierstrasse 8/187, 1040 Vienna, Austria
{fares,oliver}@igw.tuwien.ac.at, cbartmann@gmx.at
[2] University of Applied Arts Vienna,
Oskar-Kokoschka-Platz 2, 1010 Vienna, Austria
ruth.mateus-berr@uni-ak.ac.at
[3] IT University of Copenhagen, Rued Langgaards Vej 7,
2300 Copenhagen, Denmark
mpic@itu.dk

Abstract. In this paper we discuss a setup for technology-mediated audience participation using smartphones and high-frequency sound IDs. Drawing from the insights of a research project on audience participation in live music we describe a setup for playful music interaction composed of smartphones. In this setup the audience needs to install a smartphone app. Using high-frequency sound IDs music samples and colors can be triggered on the audience's smartphones without the need to have an internet connection. The resulting soundscape is determined by the samples and parameters selected by the artist as well as by the location audience members choose in the performance space.

Keywords: Technology-mediated audience participation · TMAP · Live music · Smartphones · High-frequency sound Ids

1 Introduction

This article presents a specific method for technology-mediated audience participation (TMAP) using smartphones. Audience members can use their own smartphones to join in a performance. Music samples and different color schemes can be triggered by the performing artist on all participating smartphones. The resulting soundscape consists of shifted and overlapping samples, which create new rhythmic and melodic patterns dependent on how participants group themselves in the performance space. The presented approach does not require the phones to have an internet connection as control signals are sent from the artist using high-frequency Sound IDs. The music for the proposed demo has been composed by Austrian electronic music artist Electric Indigo [1]. The performance that will build on the described technology is part of the art-based research project Breaking The Wall [2], which discusses audience participation from

© ICST Institute for Computer Sciences, Social Informatics and Telecommunications Engineering 2017
R. Poppe et al. (Eds.): INTETAIN 2016, LNICST 178, pp. 254–258, 2017.
DOI: 10.1007/978-3-319-49616-0_24

the perspective of the involved creative processes. The presented technical development was part of a master thesis at the Vienna University of Technology [3].

Audience participation goes back to as far as Mozart (1756-1791), who allegedly composed the parts of the *"Musikalisches Würfelspiel"* [4] (musical dice game minuet). He made a quite conscious game design decision. He recognized chamber music as a participatory musical form in the need for an interactive diversion for the audience. Thus he introduced two dice, thrown to determine one of many possible combinations of musical segments of waltz music played afterwards. It's a minuet with 16 measures with the choice of one of eleven possible variations (11^{16}), each possibility selected by a roll of two dice, with literally trillions of possible mirror combinations.

One of the core challenges in designing musical gameplay for entertainment was – also due to marketing reasons - to make music accessible to people who do not necessarily play an instrument or are literate in musical notion. This gaming approach seemed to represent the very antithesis of compositional strategies [5].

In Mozart's case he succeeded to make music more varied and introduced a participative mechanic. While this game mechanic is purely based on luck it still involves the audience and makes the musical result feel more personal and unique. For this purpose Mozart abstracted waltz music from continuous pieces of music to smaller segments, which can be rearranged freely. The common denominator of many works in the field of sound art and music-based games [6], is that they make aspects of playing music and composition accessible to the audience by abstracting from its original complexity. In the case of technology-mediated audience participation the process of abstraction is even more delicate. On the one hand there is a need to reduce and abstract complexity to make music easily accessible to the audience, on the other hand the complexities and intricacies of musical play must not be lost. Mazzini also presents metrics to describe and evaluate the characteristics of participatory performances [7].

The presented technology allows an audience to participate seamlessly using their own smartphones. A lot of control remains with the artist, who is able to trigger the samples played back on the smartphones and the colors of their screens. The audience can shape the resulting soundscape and their own experience by moving around in the performance space.

2 Project Context: Breaking the Wall

The field of audience participation has a rich history of custom-built instruments and devices, and ways to facilitate collaborative performances. The artistic potential of audience participation both for musicians as well as their audiences is very high. Recent advancements in sensor and interface technology have further increased this potential. While research on audience participation shows both practical as well as theoretical perspectives, a structured creative and evaluated approach to fully explore the artistic potential is missing so far. Thus the art-based research project Breaking The Wall addresses the central research question "Which new ways of artistic expression emerge in a popular form of music performance when using playful interfaces for audience participation to facilitate interactivity among everybody involved?"

To answer this important question and to shed light on the artists' creative practice we develop, document and evaluate a series of interfaces and musical performances together with popular music artists. The focus is on providing playful game-like interaction, facilitating collaborative improvisation and giving clear feedback as well as traceable results. The interfaces will be deployed in three popular music live performances at one event. The art-based research approach uses mixed methods, including a focus group and surveys as well as quantitative data logging and video analysis to identify parameters of acceptance, new ways of artistic expression, composition and musical experience. The evaluation will allow to present structured guidelines for designing and applying systems for audience participation.

The project team is comprised of popular music artists, and researchers covering diverse areas such as media arts, computer science, human-computer-interaction, game design, musicology, ethnomusicology, technology and interface design.

The results of the project will be situated at the interdisciplinary intersection of art, music and technology. It will present structured and evaluated insights into the unique relation between performers and audience leading to tested and documented new artistic ways of musical expression future performances can build on. It will further deliver a tool-set with new interfaces and collaborative digital instruments.

3   Implementation

The technical basis of Poem Numérique is the use of high-frequency sound IDs to trigger events on the audience's smartphones. The use of high-frequency sound or "Ultra Sound Communication" for audience participation has first been documented in [8]. In this approach frequencies above the average human hearing spectrum are transmitted by dedicated speakers and are used to quasi silently trigger events. An app that has to be downloaded before the performance listens for these sound IDs using the smartphone's microphone. Figure 1 shows the full setup with a computer used to send the sound triggers to a sound system and the audience's smartphones, which listen for these triggers using a cross-platform Android/iOS app. The cross-platform app has been implemented using Xamarin Forms [9].

Each Sound ID is composed of two distinct frequencies between 18 kHz and 20,7 kHz. Two speakers are used to transmit the two frequencies simultaneously. The IDs always are played back for three seconds. Much smaller playback timeframes are theoretically possible, but our application does not need to allow for fast sequences of triggers. Within the above frequency range we managed to implement 15 unique IDs. To reduce false positives and faulty recognition we used one of these for a Sync ID sent before an actual Sound ID. This Sync ID prompts the phone to listen for a Sound ID for nine seconds. After the Sync ID we introduced the option of sending what we called a Change ID used to allow a second bank of triggers. After that the actual Sound ID is transmitted. By this means the system at present supports 26 unique Sound IDs. A PD (Pure Data) [9] patch is used to play back the high-frequency Sound IDs and thus is the central hub for controlling the distributed performance. The PD patch can itself be controlled through any network protocol including MIDI or OSC.

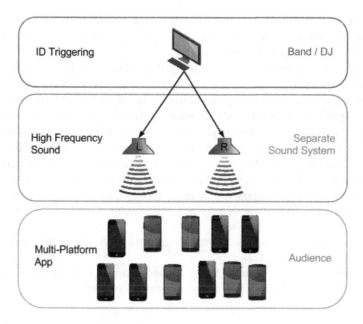

Fig. 1. The technical setup of using high-frequency sound IDs.

4 Setup and Outlook

To demo the setup at the conference little infrastructure and no dedicated performance space is needed. The technical and creative aspects can be demoed in an ado setting where visitors pass by a small performance hub and either just listen to the soundscape or take part using a provided or their own smartphone. The authors will provide a laptop and a minimum of ten smartphones. The app also is available for download for free for both Android and iOS platforms. The authors will also bring speakers, which

Fig. 2. A test of the system with students during a lecture.

are able to emit the frequencies needed to control the smartphones. One consideration when demoing Poème Numérique is that it produces a certain (but not very high) level of noise, which might disturb other exhibitors.

Figure 2 shows a test performance using the system at a lecture at the Vienna University of Technology with informatics students. The test performance showed that the transmission of high-frequency sound IDs is mostly robust, but that recognition problems might occur with untested smartphones and with increasing distance from the sound source. Also some Android mods (e.g. Cyanogen) block microphone access due to privacy settings. Further tests will determine the acceptance and creative possibilities of such a system from an artist and an audience perspective. Poème Numérique has been designed building on a series of workshops with the performing artist Electric Indigo. The design of the system will be refined iteratively based on the evaluation of the test performance and on future tests in a live setting.

Acknowledgements. "Breaking The Wall" is a project funded by the Funded by the Austrian Science Fund (FWF), AR 322-G21.

Project team: Geraldine Fitzpatrick, Simon Holland, Susanne Kirchmayr, Johannes Kretz, Ulrich Kühn, Peter Purgathofer, Hande Sağlam, Thomas Wagensommerer.

References

1. http://indigo-inc.at
2. http://www.piglab.org/breakingthewall
3. Bartmann, C: Exploring audience participation in live music with a mobile application. Master thesis, Vienna University of Technology (2016)
4. Mozart, W.A.: Anleitung so viel Walzer oder Schleifer mit zwei Würfeln zu componiren so viel man will ohne musikalisch zu seyn noch etwas von der Composition zu verstehen, J. J. Hummel, Berlin-Amsterdam (1793)
5. Zbikowski, L.M.: Conceptualizing Music. Cognitive Structures Theory, and Analysis. Oxford University Press, Oxford (2002)
6. Pichlmair, M., Kayali, F.: Levels of sound: on the principles of interactivity in music video games. In: Proceedings of the Digital Games Research Association 2007 Conference Situated play (2007)
7. Mazzanti, D., Zappi, V., Caldwell, D., Brogni, A.: Augmented stage for participatory performances. In: Proceedings of the International Conference on New Interfaces for Musical Expression, pp. 29–34 (2014)
8. Hirabayashi, M., Eshima, K.: Sense of space: the audience participation music performance with high-frequency sound ID. In: Proceedings of the NIME 2015 International Conference on New Interfaces for Musical Expression. LSU, Baton Rouge, LA (2015)
9. http://xamarin.com/forms
10. Puckette, M.: Pure data: another integrated computer music environment. In: Proceedings of the Second Intercollege Computer Music Concerts, Tachikawa, Japan (1996)

Workshop: Playable Cities

From Playable to Playful: The Humorous City

Chamari Edirisinghe[⊠], Anton Nijholt, and Adrian David Cheok

Imagineering Institute, Anchor 5, Mall of Medini, no 4, Lebuh Medini Utara,
Medini Iskandar, 79200 Iskandar Puteri, Johor, Malaysia
{chamari,anton,adrian}@imagineeringinstitute.org

Abstract. This writing is focusing on the concept of play in the city. In pursuit of ideal city, the concept of play has been neglected, pushed to labelled corners, assigned to certain age bracket. Playable city movement has brought the play in to the dialogue on city, the contemporary smart city, underlining the factors such as humor, spontaneity and pleasure. This paper introduces taking the playable city a step further towards a playful city, where play is a continuous process of city living, seamlessly integrated into the smart structure of the city, where citizens can reinvent the infrastructure for humorous purposes.

Keywords: Playable · Playful · Humor · Urban spaces · Smart city

1 Introduction

Until Industrial Revolution, the city was considered as an image of the society rather than a distinctive form of social living [1]. Sennett considers city as a "… one of the oldest artifacts of civilized life" [1]. Today, 54 % of the world population are living in urban areas and expected to rise to 66 % by 2050 according to the 2014 UN report on Urbanization. Although the city is expected to be permanent and stable, it is a constantly changing entity. Mumford [2] believed that the city is a facet of human potentials and social actions. Jane Jacobs [3] has underlined the capability and flexibility of both city and its people to create change, emphasizing on the inclusiveness.

According Lefebvre [4] spaces are created socially through interactions. Thus, a city is not merely about policy and planning but also what varied interactions have created, freely or intentionally. The global communication, powers of multi-national corporations and increased mobility define the primary functions of the contemporary city, making distance and place inconsequential. Although some argued that the smart city, Information Communication Technology (ICT) integrated urban solutions, is an affixation of a label to a city [5], people are part of the system by means of their interactions [6] and communication devices.

The contemporary city is hyper-connected, over populated, divided, polluted and socially active, and still connected through mutual practices, such as friendship, sociality and pleasure. Mumford's "theater of social action" [2] or Jacobs's street dance [3] is in essence an emphasis on these mutual practices, and Lefebvre's social production of space is a discussion on experiencing the city through these mutual practices. Play is a practice of experiencing pleasure and grounded on sociality, humor and freedom. Play is not new to the city or vice versa. Cities are centers for playing various

© ICST Institute for Computer Sciences, Social Informatics and Telecommunications Engineering 2017
R. Poppe et al. (Eds.): INTETAIN 2016, LNICST 178, pp. 261–265, 2017.
DOI: 10.1007/978-3-319-49616-0_25

games, such as conventional marathons, extreme bull runs or hilarious *La Tomatina,* the tomato throwing festival. Through playing, the city becomes the center of participation, producing pleasurable spaces of humor and play. According to Jane Jacobs [3] 'casual social interactions' create public trust, thus strengthening the activities, and enhancing the experience and joy.

Every city has designated places for play, a clearly drawn out borders, frequently associated with children rather than adults, neither encouraging Jacobs's 'casual social interactions', nor evoking spontaneous humor. Play is associated with that specific space, within those specific boundaries, with clearly expressed interpretation of what play should be. With the city planning employing networks and sensors to create a systemic smartness within city living, play signifies a practice that makes city a joyful and humorous experience, spontaneous and unpredicted. The objective of this writing is to understand the concept 'play' in the city and how a city can be a playful and humorous space, encouraging spur-of-the-moment joy, unexpected experiences and participation.

2 City as a Playroom

In the contemporary city, governments and tech corporations are conjoining to make cities 'smart'. While the city is going through this digitizing process, citizen dialogue, and the engagement with the city is increasingly becoming impeded [5] due to perhaps the nature of the technological smartness of the city [7]. Play and humor are suggested as an extension to the smart city, an alternative to the lack of human-centric approach and citizen engagement with the city. It is being suggested to combat the impending distress of inhabitants over the alienating city. Smart city has redefined the 'right to the city', the right to change the city and change ourselves within the city, and play as part of the city falls within this claim, especially when the play is being discussed in a holistic manner.

There are number of perspectives as concerns, when discussing city as a playroom. Firstly, play needs to be a seamless integrated to the cityscape and infrastructure and be part of the city activities. Human Pacman [8], a wearable interactive entrainment system, that transits between virtual and real world in an urban setting, is an attempt at this compelling to scale the cityscapes and create and share. Shadowing [9], a project that makes the city lights alive by giving it a memory of people that passed by as shadows, and then reflecting them on passers-by, is a an integration of play into night time cityscape.

Secondly, humor and fun is an important factor when considering a city as a playground. Nijholt [10] has extensively discussed the advantage of integrating humor into digital environment and internet of things, especially utilizing technology to generate humor. Humor has a tendency to lighten up an environment, create unexpected sense of balance in interactions, and gives pleasure that even in retrospective brings a smile. In 2012, 25 years old Singaporean artist Samantha Lo, decided to spray paint the streets of Singapore with messages, and attached stickers on roadside crossings, creating a nationwide controversy [11]. Her musings were humorous and her play with the smart structure of the city is by evoking satire of the smartness itself.

With Singapore's strict laws on street art, the artist was promptly arrested. However, the citizens found this humorous as an act of play that should be encouraged and allow citizens to reinvent and hack the infrastructure for their own humorous purposes.

As the third point in this discussion in city as a playroom, is the arbitrary and involuntary participation which promotes the qualities of freedom and choice. Jane Jacobs [3] recounting a successful city, underlined the idea that there should be a clear separation of public and private spaces. It is similar with play in a city; the participation needs to be arbitrary and involuntary, neither forced nor unfairly manipulated. The Smart Car Company has started an initiative to make pedestrians mindful of traffic through entertaining them while waiting for the red light to turn green, discouraging them from crossing across a red traffic light [12]. This initiative used humor, in the form of red manikin dancing in its small window, and voluntary participation by providing the dance moves to the manikin, thus evoking public participation and a joyful experience.

3 From Playable to Playful

Play is not supposed to be a formalized activity. It should be open, free, impulsive, humorous and joyous. In the city with sensors and actuations systematizing, monitoring and controlling activities, and city planning and policy methodically mapping the city while erasing urban histories and memories, play is an approach to recapture the city.

The 'Playable' city movement explaining their objectives stressed the need for city infrastructure to be part of connections: both interpersonal and person to city connections. Thus, it encourage to create spaces of interactions while integrating with the city's infrastructure, making 'playable' city an extension of the digital city, with joy, humor, and play as leading themes. At this juncture, after deliberating on the city as a playroom and objectives of playable city, the authors would like to enquire why playable city not becomes an everyday experience, an everyday interaction that is part of the city itself. De Lange [5] has mentioned that the playful city is a city that stimulate citizens with play while the playable city is a city that becomes smart at infrastructure and institutional level, thus indicating certain dependency. However, the authors would like to avoid providing definitions to differentiate playable and playful city, with the knowledge that definitions will constrain its flexibility as a practice, putting it in to a certain framework. Since play is described according to the context, the authors would like the playful city to be understood by stakeholders according to the city context.

The 'Playable' city movement has already established the importance of play being part of the contemporary city. It established that the playable city is, to a certain level, a bottom-up endeavor and also established that city can be playable, spatially and through social interactions. However, there arises the question why the city is considered only as a place appropriate to play, rather than city itself is a play. The shift from playable to playful may possibly appear to be rhetorical, yet it reveals certain realities in contemporary smart city living. One aspect is the safety of the existing security measures in city infrastructure. To contemplate creating playful spaces in a smart city as an everyday experience, without obstructing the everyday functions of the city, needs careful planning, because our discussion here is not about conventional spaces for play, but involving digital sensors and actuators. Nijholt [10] was discussing the integration of humor into this digital environments as a community initiation; nonetheless this concept needed essentially to be part of city planning for seamless integration and security.

However, the concept of playful city being absorbed into the policy and planning will signify certain constraints on somewhat bottom-up approach enjoyed by the playable city and particularly pleasing and popular experiences, such as spontaneity and unexpected joy. Nonetheless, as Lefebvre has stated, human interactions create social spaces, thus the top-down playful city will be appropriated by individuals who interact with its playful arrangements, creating new playful experiences. The perception of the city as a playful city will encourage individuals to be humorous and create their own play environs on smart city platforms.

Another aspect of playful city concept is understanding the limitations of play. The playable city is experimenting with the notion of city as a possible playroom to improve the everyday experiences of city life, thus it undeniably has limitations on play and joy of impulsive participation. Conversely, playful city requires maintaining the playful ideals. The city itself is play, thus presenting complex concerns such as new interpretations to certain concepts such as humor, spontaneity, participation and plays itself. Humor and spontaneity will be interpreted by the participants to suit the context of their choosing. Those interpretations will be user-centric, which will seamlessly flow with the rest of the city's trappings.

This writing is not a proposal for playable city vs playful city, but considering the notion of changing the perception of the city as a place that could play to a place that is engaged in the play in a continuous process, as part of its psyche. As Lefebvre [5] expressed space is produced through social interactions, thus any initiation on play, whether it is bottom-up or top-down, will be interpreted, changed, modified, and adjusted with societal interactions. Thus, a continuous process of play or playfulness in a city will continue to grow with participation and interactions of people. Playable city conducts to playful living, but playful city will be part of the living experience.

4 Conclusion

In the quest for ideal city, the concept of play has been neglected, pushed to designated corners, assigned to certain age bracket. Playable city movement has brought the play into the dialogue on city, the contemporary smart city, underlining the factors such as humor, spontaneity and pleasure. This paper is introducing taking the playable city a step further towards a playful city, where play is a continuous process of city living, seamlessly integrated into the smart structure with freedom to reorganize the infrastructure for humor and joy. Undoubtedly, the concept of playful city will present its own challenges; however, as a continuous process, playful city will become a humorous part of city living with rich social interactions.

References

1. Sennett, R.: Classic Essays on the Culture of Cities. Prentice Hall, Upper Saddle River (1969)
2. Mumford, L.: What is a city. Architectural Rec. **82**(5), 59–62 (1937)
3. Jacobs, J.: The Death and Life of Great American Cities. Random House, New York (1961). Vintage
4. Lefebvre, H.: The Production of Space, vol. 142. Blackwell, Oxford (1991)
5. de Lange, M.: The playful city: using play and games to foster citizen participation. In: Skaržauskien, A. (ed.) Social Technologies and Collective Intelligence, pp. 426–434. Mykolas Romeris University (2015)
6. Townsend, A.M.: Smart Cities: Big Data, Civic Hackers, and the Quest for a New Utopia. WW Norton & Company, New York (2013)
7. Vestergaard, L.S., Fernandes, J., Presser, M.A.: Towards smart city democracy. Geoforum Perspektiv **14**(25) (2016)
8. Cheok, A.D., et al.: Human pacman: a wide area socio-physical interactive entertainment system in mixed reality. In: Extended Abstracts on Human Factors in Computing Systems, CHI 2004, Vienna, Austria, pp. 779–780. ACM
9. 2014 Shadowing Playable City. http://www.watershed.co.uk/playablecity/winner/2014. Accessed 1 Apr 2016
10. Nijholt, A.: Designing humor for playable cities. Procedia Manufacturing **3**, 2175–2182 (2015)
11. The works of 'My grandfather road' artist. http://multimedia.asiaone.com/static/multimedia/gallery/120605_stickerlady/. Accessed 18 Mar 2016
12. Smart. The Dancing Traffic Light Manikin. Smart Campaigns, For a Safe City. http://int.smart.com/en/en/index/smart-campaigns/whatareyoufor/for-a-safer-city.html. Accessed 1 Apr 2016

Play in the Algorithmic City

Troy Innocent[(⊠)]

Swinburne University of Technology, John Street, Hawthorn, Vic., Australia
tinnocent@swin.edu.au

Abstract. In this paper, the algorithmic city is introduced as a framework for understanding urban space in terms of its underlying code and systems. It is connected to urban codemaking, a playful approach to public art that asks players to engage with codes of urban space. To connect these two concepts in a framework for pervasive game design, players are framed as sensors and actuators within the algorithmic city to make it more playable.

Keywords: Urban codemaking · Playable city · Pervasive game design · Public art

1 Introduction

Over the past five years the practice of urban codemaking has explored the experience of the city as a set of codes and systems for players to discover and decode through a series of public art projects. The city is experienced as a giant board game or puzzle, with its spaces and structures recoded and repurposed for play. Can this approach be expanded by defining players as sensors and actuators, and articulate a form of pervasive game design based on the affordances of the algorithmic city?

First of all, what is an algorithmic city? During the 1970 s, the influential study 'limits of growth' [1] revealed the constraints and limitations of urban growth and the accompanying rise in human population intrinsically linked to increased consumption of resources, construction of infrastructure, and manufacturing of stuff. Will Wright, designer of SimCity [2], used these same algorithms to inform the design of the game abstracting them into a set of game rules [3].

Geoffrey West is the physicist who set out to 'solve the city' [4]. Based at the Sante Fe Institute researching cities, scaling and sustainability, he has developed mathematical formulae that apply to practically any city in the world, no matter where they are – the city is represented as a set of algorithms. Another set of researchers has identified four common patterns that based on a sample set of 131 cities, created a 'typology of street patterns' [5]. These perspectives bring into focus our understanding of cities as complex adaptive systems that arise from the interaction of a multitude of systems and processes.

Play has had an increasing role in urban life over the past century. The situationists [6] used play as a strategy to subvert the norms of city life, and combat urban alienation created by the homogenisation of cities. One of these, the dérive, developed the practice of psychogeography in which a player navigates city streets using their own personal landmarks, sensations, and experiences. There are parallels between this

© ICST Institute for Computer Sciences, Social Informatics and Telecommunications Engineering 2017
R. Poppe et al. (Eds.): INTETAIN 2016, LNICST 178, pp. 266–270, 2017.
DOI: 10.1007/978-3-319-49616-0_26

practice and location-based games [7], geocaching, GPS navigators, and local search and discovery mobile service apps. These experiences situate the player in relation to the city both as an individual, and as a node in the algorithmic city as a whole.

Players of SimCity may develop a different perspective on what a city is by reflecting on the processes and systems captured in the algorithms of the game. GPS navigational systems may also reinforce this systemic view in their positioning of the player as an entity in relation to data, such as the map of a city. More recently, the immediacy, ubiquity and pervasive nature of mobile devices have changed the relationship of the individual to the city. This is the second view of the city - data visualisation representing the algorithmic city in action.

We have two views here: the systemic view of the city as algorithm (macro), and the procedural view of the city as a process (micro) in which the individual is embedded. How do these viewpoints afford opportunities for pervasive game design in big cities? One way to approach the algorithmic city is to articulate players as sensors and actuators in the mixed realities of urban space.

2 Sensors and Actuators

Mixed realities are mediated experiences that situate layers of media and data in relation to the real world. Milgram's virtuality continuum [8] articulated mixed realities across a spectrum created by increasing degrees of mediality or virtuality, indicating that there is not one definition of mixed reality but rather a multiplicity of possibilities. These could be immersive, using Augmented Reality (AR) to situate digital media into urban space; contextual, providing relevant information about a place; or poetic, activating narrative potential of a location.

This paper presents a new approach to framing the player. This approach aims to use mixed realities to set up a new set of relations between players and the city. A player may be a sensor – reading codes, observing situations, being in spaces. The player may collect data for their own experience or to share with the collective, to provide input and feedback to the game. The player is also an actuator – making places, performing actions, leaving traces. In this way they may operate as a node in the system, triggering state changes and generating new data. The idea of player as sensor/actuator may be extended to relate to the micro and macro views of the city introduced earlier – they may sense data or trigger events either locally or globally.

How does this way experiencing the city make it more playable? First of all, the playing mind [9] sees the world in a different way. The usual form and function of urban space may be cast aside to imagine new possibilities. City blocks may become zones in a board game, security cameras become eyes of the city, landmarks and buildings become checkpoints, and so on.

In addition to reframing existing objects and spaces, digital layers augment the experience and add layers of narrative. These may be used to direct players to coordinates, set up communication between players, rename locations and introduce characters, keep score, and track the game. However, these experiences are typical of many urban games – the intention with this approach that defines players as sensors/actuators is to embody them within the city as a simulation, the city is not the backdrop for play but it becomes the site for play in a more literal sense.

This approach to pervasive game design aims to make the player feel embedded and integrated in the city through the potential for action – to create a city within the city that provides the space for play. This is perhaps the most important aspect in the algorithmic city – the player's realisation that they are part of the algorithm and have increased agency compared to non-players who don't perceive urban space in this way. The intention with this approach is to relate the player to the algorithmic cities in terms of its codes and operations, to make them part of the system.

How does this work in practice? In what ways does the view of player as sensor/actuator activate the existing infrastructure of the city for play?

3 Urban Codemaking in the Algorithmic City

This approach has emerged through observation of players and reflections on the design of a collection of street games have been staged in Melbourne, Ogaki, Istanbul, Sydney and Adelaide over the past five years. The primary mechanism for activating each city is the practice of urban codemaking [10], which is based on the placement of temporary markers in the city that operate as wayfinding markers, game tokens, and signifiers of mixed realities. Small and portable and immediately recognisable by their distinct style, urban codes (see Fig. 1) are deployed onto the streets en masse transforming the city into a game.

In the games *Urban Codemakers* [11], *Zydnei* [12] and *Xawthorn* [13] the urban codemakers are game designers surveying and tagging locations in the city to make it more playable. Each urban code tags a site as part of a survey city infrastructure – one week all of the sites that had a active security camera were tagged, another week unidentified doorways, and so on. As they collect and claim urban codes they are operating as sensors (mapping the space defined by the game) and actuators (activating the sites by visiting them) by generating stories in the game via their participation. Players choose one of three clans that frame their approach to urban space: revert the city to its past, renew the present, or remake the future. Urban planning is typically a lengthy bureaucratic process that aims to balance a network of systems and rules that

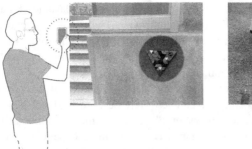

Fig. 1. Various types of urban codemaking in action. Codes may be scanned or collected.

are social, institutional, spatial, commercial and cultural. This game asks the question: what would happen if players recoded the city from within?

Another game, *noemaflux* [14] situates a mixed reality within a city to create abstract architecture. Thematically, it combines street art, geometric abstraction, synaesthesia and pictorial language. Each edition of the work is staged in a different city, and through strategies of urban codemaking aspects of the intersubjectivity and performativity of outdoor play are explored. It aims to create 'placemaking' encounters situated around large urban codes in cities such as Ogaki, Istanbul or Hong Kong. Activating a code using a mobile device displays abstract architecture that responding to the space of each site, accenting site lines and other structural aspects. Players are sensors (scanners of codes) and actuators (revealing the digital layer).

A more recent iteration of the project uses a similar strategy, but with a more deliberate emphasis on the player as sensor/actuator. In *navitag*, players find and scan codes using a mobile device as part of a multiplayer experience, and may sense the proximity of other players via Bluetooth. The codes simultaneously operate as a visual notation system, as wayfinding markers, signifiers of an alternate world, tokens in a game, and as material objects. In this game, the city becomes a site for spatialised musical notation and a competitive game of tag.

These examples foreground the possibilities of relatively simple interventions into urban space that activate its potential for play. Framing the player as a sensor/actuator in an algorithmic city opens up a different set of relations and affordances in the design process.

4 Conclusion

The algorithmic city opens up the possibilities for certain modes of play with the city. Unlocking urban codes and readymade sites for game design by providing the right contextual framework for play transforms infrastructure already existing in smart cities. Integrating players into the framework as sensors and actuators provides a way to explore pervasive game design in almost any urban environment – even if it does not meet the usual expectations of a smart city.

Activating players as sensors and actuators also sets them up in relation to one another both via immediate interaction or asynchronously through the traces and codes they may leave behind in the city. This way of thinking is presented as an approach to play that blends micro and macro views of the algorithmic city that frames the game design process in terms of simulation and systems, an approach common to digital game design but perhaps novel in the pervasive game design.

Urban codemaking demonstrates the initial potential in applying this framework to create playable cities, and articulates a particular approach to game design that focuses on the algorithmic city. Future work will explore these ideas further, working with both greater games literacies in players and an increased awareness in cities of the potential they afford for play.

Acknowledgments. Games cited in this paper were developed with the assistance of the ANZCA and City of Melbourne Laneway Commissions program.

References

1. Forrester, J.W.: Urban Dynamics. The MIT Press, Cambridge (1969)
2. Lauwaert, M.: Challenge everything?: construction play in will Wright's SIMCITY. Games Cult. **2**(3), 194–212 (2007)
3. Bogost, I.: Unit Operations: An Approach to Videogame Criticism. The MIT Press, Cambridge (2008)
4. Lehrer, J.: A physicity solves the city. NY Times Mag. (2010)
5. Louf, R., Barthelemy, M.: A typology of street patterns. J. R. Soc. Interface **11**(101) (2014)
6. Debord, G.: Society of the Spectacle. Zone Books, New York (1994)
7. Montola, M., Stenros, J., Waern, A.: Pervasive Games Theory and Design. Morgan Kaufmann, Burlington (2009)
8. Milgram, P., Takemura, H., Utsumi, A., Kishino, F.: Augmented reality: a class of displays on the reality-virtuality continuum. In: Proceedings of Telemanipulator and Telepresence Technologies, vol. 235, pp. 282–292 (1994)
9. Dekoven, B.: The Well-Played Game: A Player's Philosophy. The MIT Press, Cambridge (2013)
10. Innocent, T.: Code switching in mixed realities. In: Cleland, K., Fisher, L., Harley, R. (eds.) Proceedings of the 19th International Symposium of Electronic Art (ISEA2013), Sydney, 11–13 June 2013, pp. 1–5 (2013)
11. Innocent, T.: The lost art of urban codemaking. Commun. Res. Pract. **1**(2), 117–130 (2015). Terry Flew (ed.)
12. Innocent, T.: Urban Codemakers. Melbourne (2010). http://urbancodemakers.net/
13. Innocent, T.: Xawthorn. Hawthorn (2014). http://xawthorn.net
14. Innocent, T.: Zydnei. Sydney (2013). http://zydnei.net

Visual Abstraction for Games on Large Public Displays

David Gullick, Daniel Burnett, and Paul Coulton$^{(\boxtimes)}$

Imagination Lancaster, LICA, Lancaster University, LA1 4YW, Bailrigg, UK
{d.gullick,d.burnett,p.coulton}@lancaster.ac.uk

Abstract. From its earliest developments video game design has arguably been closely coupled to technological evolution particularly in relation to graphics. In very early games the limitations of technology led to highly abstracted graphics but as technology improved, abstraction has largely been left behind as developers strive towards ever-greater realism. Thus, games are generally drawing from conventions established in the mediums of film and television, and potentially limiting themselves from the possibilities abstraction may offer. In this research, we consider whether highly abstracted graphics are perceived as detrimental to gameplay and learnability by current gamers through the creation of a game using very low-resolution display that would accommodate a range of display options in a playable city. The results of trialing the game at a citywide light festival event where it was played by over 150 people indicated that abstraction made little difference to their sense of engagement with the game, however it did foster communication between players and suggests abstraction is a viable game design option for playable city displays.

Keywords: Game design · Graphics · Abstraction · Realism · Resolution

1 Introduction

While many game players will cite fun or gameplay as the most important attributes for a game, examining the marketing material produced by developers and publishers over many years might lead one to the conclusion it is primarily about graphics. This is because in its early days, games development were closely coupled to technological developments which were often intrinsically linked to notions such as Moore's Law [1]. The fidelity of the graphics was the simplest and quickest way that consumers could compare systems, and the complexity of graphic detail became the main area in which games would compete for customers. This concentration on graphics created a distinct change of style of the visual imagery, from abstraction to representation (often referred to as realism) [2, 3].

Early video games relied heavily on abstraction in that they simplified visual assets to a few essentials and basic forms due to the very limited graphical capabilities of early arcade machines and consoles. These early games could be considered abstract in both appearance and behavior, because at the time of their development game interaction conventions were in their infancy.

© ICST Institute for Computer Sciences, Social Informatics and Telecommunications Engineering 2017
R. Poppe et al. (Eds.): INTETAIN 2016, LNICST 178, pp. 271–275, 2017.
DOI: 10.1007/978-3-319-49616-0_27

272 D. Gullick et al.

With the development of the so-called third generation consoles we observed a shift to a concentration on representation, which seeks to create a resemblance and reproduce something; abstraction became more of an artistic choice than a technical default. This means there has been "a shift from perceptual abstraction to conceptual abstraction" [4].

Mark Wolf explains this shift in relation to art theorist Wilhelm Worringer, 1908 treatise, Abstraction and Empathy, within which he suggests that "there are two fundamental aesthetic impulses that are mutually exclusive, the desire for abstraction and the desire for empathy" [4]. This straightforward argument is that, as with Art, people will more readily engage with realism than abstraction, and this, in some way, explains the popularity of representational graphics within games.

Further it has been shown that a certain level of learnability can be beneficial in games [5], but how that level of learnability is achieved is different for every game. Modern games often rely on in-game tutorials to help increase the rate at which users can become familiar with a game, even though it is not always effective [6]. However, many older abstracted games such as Tetris allow users to learn through discovery whilst playing the game, which it has been argued gives the user a deeper understanding of the game as a whole [7].

In this research we consider whether rather than trying to avoid or sublimate abstraction, game design can usefully incorporate abstraction, resulting in new gaming experiences and game conventions which we believe would be relevant for creating a variety of flexible displays for a playable city of various resolutions.

2 Game Design

The game presented in this research is a two-player side scrolling game, similar in the style of early Atari favorites Defender and Chopper Command [8]. The player pilots the 'ship', only on the vertical axis, through a randomly generated tunnel avoiding obstacles and collecting power ups. The tunnel gets narrower and the number and complexity of obstacles increases the further down tunnel the player's progresses. Damage reduces the length of the ship whereas power ups increase its length, and the game is over when either of the players' ship's length reaches zero as shown in Fig. 1.

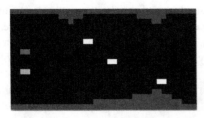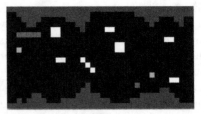

Fig. 1. (a) Game Graphics. Left are Player 1 (purple), Player 2 (green), the tunnel walls (blue, top and bottom) and 3 'bullet' type enemies. (b) In this graphical representation of the screen, we can see player 1 has more life than player 2, and we can also see the 'block', 'spinning' and 'bullet' type enemies, and 2 power ups (right). (Color figure online)

The game display exists as a large LED matrix of individually addressable RGB LEDs. Using a Teensy 3.1 each of the LEDs is addressable much like a pixel on a low resolution screen. From here, a small application running on a nearby computer duplicates a small area of a computer screen and forwards this to the teensy/LEDs. The screen itself has an extremely low resolution of 38 pixels wide by 20 high, and measures 122 cm wide by 70 cm high. The LEDS are covered by an acrylic diffuser, and the whole matrix is mounted on a stand that can be set as portrait or landscape (although we mainly used landscape). It is worth noting that this is a much lower resolution than would have been experienced in many of the early games. Additionally, the system is hooked up to a large speaker which plays background music in addition to audio for particular in game events (e.g. loose life, gain power up, hit wall, game over). In order for players to interact with the system, we provide two Leap Motions controllers (differentiated by the colored disks, shown in Fig. 2) that limit user control to the vertical axis. When a user places their hand over the sensor, the players game character mimics the movement of the user's hand. Additionally, the players also have a large press button that they can use to start the game as shown in Fig. 2(b). As the players progress through the game, the frequency of enemies, their speed and the height and frequency of spikes on the walls increase, which makes the game more difficult. There is no 'win condition' for this game, but rather the game mechanic is to not be the first player to loose, or in other words, to 'beat' your opponent.

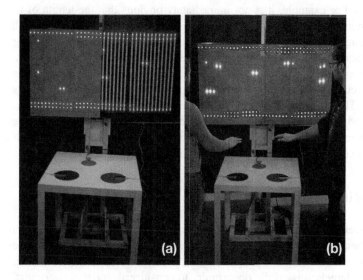

Fig. 2. Abstracted game

3   User Trials

Whilst we carried out small-scale play testing throughout the design process, the preliminary user trial was conducted at a local winter event called 'Light Up Lancaster'. Light Up Lancaster is a festival of lights held yearly in Lancaster City Center with numerous attractions and this game was one of these. In the space of 3.5 h, the game was played by well over 150 people, with a wide range of ages from small children to pensioners. When no one was playing the game, the screen invited people to 'Press Start', which initially attracted people to the stand. Subsequently the crowds waiting to play seemed the main encouragement for new players to join in.

Working with such a low resolution creates a difficulty in implementing a tutorial for game learnability, thus we offered players a number of 'practice plays' before playing the game. Furthermore, designing the game in this way promoted discovery and exploration by players. Whilst players often needed an explanation in how to control the ships with the Leap Motion controller, they were able to quickly understand the basic principles. Interestingly though, many younger players seemed to want to touch the controller and some players would start moving their hand back and forward rather than up and down after playing the game for a while. Similarly, some players had initial difficulties with the automatic range calibration of the Leap Motion controller. If they began the game with their hand too close to the sensor, they would be unable to move their hand closer to the sensor in order to move the ship down. As the playing time of the games was short (typically 2–3 min max) we did not have any incidents of fatigue in terms of holding hand in an elevated position which is a design concern that should be considered for gesture control in games [9].

What was noticeably different about this more abstract game was the way in which players communicated with each other in order to fully understand all of the game mechanics. For example, it is not immediately obvious that the length of the player's ship represents their remaining lives, as this is not labeled. This resulted in the players collaborating in exploring the game mechanics. More so, those playing the game often would explain the hidden mechanics to those watching and waiting to play in the crowd of spectators. With a more traditional less abstracted or high-resolution games, all of these aspects would probably have been explained by in game text or more expressive graphics. Thus, as perhaps might be expected, abstract games are harder to learn initially and require more trial and error discovery by players. It is hard to determine if this difficulty is due to the abstraction within the game, or the reliance on 'learnability though discovery' as these two elements are tightly coupled.

4 Conclusions

Game development has always been intrinsically linked to continuing technological enhancements with graphics being the main beneficiary since they are an easy way to make a distinction between products in the eyes of the consumer. This means games design has largely missed the opportunity to consider abstraction conceptually as well as perceptually. Therefore, this research considers how using abstraction as a deliberate design choice, rather than a forced design constraint, affects the experience of players.

The results from the preliminary event are very encouraging considering the high numbers of players that played the game. Despite the difficulty in observation and recording, the numerous positive comments and returning players, showed that this form of abstracted game is both engaging and welcomed across a wide demographic. In fact, the abstraction was often considered part of the game challenge. Whether this success is solely due to the abstracted nature of the designed game is hard to determine, however it does suggest that the role of abstraction in video games has been under-explored, and encourages further work in the area.

Acknowledgements. We thank all the early play testers at Lancaster Institute for the Contemporary Arts and players at Light Up Lancaster for their enthusiastic playing of the game. This work was supported by the RCUK Digital Economy project, Creating and Exploring Digital Empathy (Grant Reference EP/L003635/1).

References

1. Ernkvist, M.: Down many times, but still playing the game: creative destruction and industry crashes in the early video game industry 1971–1986. History of Insolvency and Bankruptcy 161 (2008)
2. Collins, S.: Game graphics during the 8-bit computer Era. ACM SIGGRAPH Comput. Graphics **32**(2), 47–51 (1998)
3. Masuch, M., Röber, N.: Game graphics beyond realism: then, now and tomorrow. In: Level UP: Digital Games Research Conference. DIGRA, Faculty of Arts, University of Utrecht (2004)
4. Wolf, M.J.: Abstraction in the video game. The Video Game Theo. Reader **1**, 47–65 (2003)
5. Jørgensen, A.H.: Marrying HCI/Usability and computer games: a preliminary look. In: Proceedings of the Third Nordic Conference on Human-Computer Interaction. ACM (2004)
6. Andersen, E., O'Rourke, E, Liu, Y.E., Snider, R., Lowdermilk, J., Truong, D., Cooper, S., Popovic, Z.: The impact of tutorials on games of varying complexity. In: Proceedings of the SIGCHI Conference on Human Factors in Computing Systems, pp. 59–68. ACM, 5 May 2012
7. Ryan, W., Siegel, M.A.: Evaluating interactive entertainment using breakdown: understanding embodied learning in video games. In: Proceedings of DiGRA (2009)
8. Kent, S.: The ultimate history of video games: from pong to pokemon and beyond... the story behind the craze that touched our lives and changed the world. Three Rivers Press (2010)
9. Kim, Y., Lee, G., Jo, D., Yang, U., Kim, G., Park, J.: Analysis on virtual interaction-induced fatigue and difficulty in manipulation for interactive 3D gaming console. In: Consumer Electronics (ICCE), pp. 269–270 (2011)

Workshop: Virtual Agents for Social Skills Training

project SENSE – Multimodal Simulation with Full-Body Real-Time Verbal and Nonverbal Interactions

Hossein Miri[1], Jan Kolkmeier[1(✉)], Paul J. Taylor[1,2], Ronald Poppe[3], and Dirk Heylen[1]

[1] University of Twente, Enschede, Netherlands
{h.miri,j.kolkmeier,d.k.j.heylen}@utwente.nl,
p.j.taylor@lancaster.ac.uk
[2] Lancaster University, Lancaster, UK
[3] Utrecht University, Utrecht, Netherlands
r.w.poppe@uu.nl

Abstract. This paper presents a multimodal simulation system, project-SENSE, that combines virtual reality and full-body motion capture technologies with real-time verbal and nonverbal communication. We introduce the technical setup and employed hardware and software of a first prototype. We discuss the capabilities of the system for the investigation of *cooperation paradoxes* and the effects of *direct nonverbal mimicry*. We argue that this prototype lays the technological basis for further research in interpersonal and social skills, as well as the social and emotional consequences of nonverbal mimicry in sustained interactions.

Keywords: Virtual reality · Motion capture · Interactive conversational agents · Mimicry · Social skills · Interpersonal sensemaking

1 Introduction

Interpersonal sensemaking is the cognitive process of understanding, predicting, and responding to the actions and inferred beliefs of others [1]. A critical, but under-explored, aspect of interpersonal sensemaking is *cooperation paradoxes*. A cooperation paradox occurs when the cooperative/competitive orientation implied by a person's *verbal* behavior does not correspond with the cooperative/competitive orientation of their *nonverbal* behavior [2]. This occurs, for example, when a person is verbally cooperative, but fails to *mimic* their partner's nonverbal behavior (i.e. they fail to imitate poses, gestures, and facial expressions) [3]. Understanding these paradoxes is important because they are often implicated as being at the heart of communication misunderstandings and conflicts in contexts such as law enforcement interviews [4]. To understand how people respond to paradoxes in *mimicry*, it is necessary to be able to measure or simulate the matching/mismatching of verbal and nonverbal behavior; henceforth orientation-matching between interactants. See Table 1.

© ICST Institute for Computer Sciences, Social Informatics and Telecommunications Engineering 2017
R. Poppe et al. (Eds.): INTETAIN 2016, LNICST 178, pp. 279–284, 2017.
DOI: 10.1007/978-3-319-49616-0_28

Table 1. Characterizing the Type of Behavior

		Verbal behavior	
		Cooperative	Competitive
Nonverbal behavior	Cooperative	*Cooperation*	*Paradox*
	Competitive	*Paradox*	*Conflict*

When examining communicative channels in *simulation* environments through virtual characters, orientation-matching requires a degree of realism of the characters with respect to their appearance, nonverbal movements and behaviors, and speech. Currently, there is limited technology available for virtual reality, motion capture, and avatar interfaces, capable of reproducing replicas that are animated by users' movements and include real-time verbal communication. We adopted several technologies and developed an interactive training simulation in which verbal and nonverbal modes can be manipulated. We developed a proof-of-concept prototype to facilitate *prolonged interactions* with a realistic-looking embodied conversational character in an immersive virtual environment, through the use of a state-of-the-art MoCap device. The virtual character is capable of real-time verbal and nonverbal behavior generation, as well as mirror-mimicking participants' full-body movements at an *adjustable delay*.

In a dyadic setting, a computer representation of an interviewee (e.g. a suspect) interacts with the user (e.g. a trainee officer) using mannerisms that are responsive to his/her actions, while also playing out a training scenario. By allowing the manipulation of, and capture of, verbal and nonverbal behaviors, the resulting interactive training environment simulates each of the cooperation paradoxes in a single platform and allows for the social skills training for law enforcement professionals.

2   Virtual Reality (VR) Technology

VR offers an appealing alternative for managing human-computer interactions. Part of the appeal is attributed to the fact that users can interact with virtual characters and artifacts in the environment using their *natural senses*. This increases the sensation of *immersion* or feeling of *embodiment* in the synthetic environment through the use of powerful graphics rendering engines, as well as interfaces with Head Mounted Display (HMD) devices. We selected the Oculus Rift [5] for project-SENSE as it is a high-powered light-weight high-resolution HMD for VR environments, designed to provide an immersive experience. With its wide field of view and low latency 360° head tracking, this HMD allows to virtually step inside any environment and interact with it.

3   Motion Capture (MoCap) Technology

MoCap technologies are being exploited to identify and study *nonverbal correlates of human interactions*, while also allowing users to view and review their own movements. When coupled with MoCap technology, interactive and immersive VR systems can provide remarkable realism and accuracy in simulating *human movements and behaviors*. A full-body MoCap system allows for a refined measurement of nonverbal behavior and enables the investigation of movement in all human limbs and joints. Marker-less and wireless MoCap technologies, in particular, have gained popularity due to their ease of use and precision. We selected the Xsens MVN Awinda system, along with the MVN Studio BIOMECH software application [6], for project-SENSE. It consists of wearable straps with 17 motion trackers, aligned with anatomical landmarks of the human body by means of a 5-second calibration procedure. It records the position, orientation, velocity, acceleration, angular velocity and angular acceleration of 23 segments of the body, as well as magnetic field and body's center of mass. The sensors are easily secured to various limbs without hindering natural movement. The system does not require external cameras, emitters, or markers, and can be used both outdoors and indoors. The use of the Xsens MVN Awinda system provides an efficient measure of nonverbal behavior, in particular mimicry, that is less susceptible to the subjectivity associated with observational coding of behavior [7].

4 Real-Time Interaction Technology

The Virtual Human Toolkit (VHTK) is a collection of modules, tools, and libraries, to allow for the creation of virtual conversational characters [8]. We fused the VHTK with Oculus Rift and Xsens MVN Awinda system, in order to augment the nonverbal method of examining behavior with real-time verbal capabilities. The power of this toolkit is in the combination of a wide range of integrated capabilities. Specifically, we took advantage of its NPCEditor and SmartBody. The NPCEditor [9] controls the spoken behavior of the characters, as well as the structure and logic of their interactions. It contains a list of questions that the user can ask, along with answers that the character can give, as well as the links between them. It uses a statistical text classifier to determine the best character responses to user input. The interaction is done through *text* (i.e. typing) or *speech* (i.e. microphone). SmartBody [10] is a character animation platform and library that provides synchronized locomotion, steering, object manipulation, lip syncing, eye gazing, and nonverbal behaviors in real-time. It is, in effect, a Behavioral Markup Language (BML) realization engine that transforms BML behavior descriptions into real-time animations. The use of VHTK serves to provide a unified framework for audio-visual sensing, nonverbal behavior understanding, speech recognition, natural language processing, dialogue management, nonverbal behavior generation and realization, and text-to-speech [11].

5 Development Platform

We used the Unity3D [12] as a common development platform for the hardware tools and software solutions. Unity3D is a modern visualization, rendering, and game engine with an accessible editor that also includes functionality to interface recent VR devices; e.g. the Oculus Rift. We also integrated into Unity3D the MVN Studio (application software for Xsens products) through a specialized plug-in for accessing live motion

Fig. 1. MVN Studio character (*left*) and VHTK avatar, Brad (*right*)

data from the Xsens MVN Awinda system. Finally, the VHTK was integrated into the project-SENSE prototype. See Fig. 1 for a schematic, showing the MVN Studio and VHTK avatars.

6 Prototype Operation

The application starts off with a menu that features selectable toggles for choosing one of the four training scenarios: *verbal cooperation with mimicry, verbal cooperation without mimicry, verbal competition with mimicry, and verbal competition without mimicry.* The experimenter makes the selection, thus determining the mode of communication prior to the commencement of the session. The application then proceeds to the training simulation. Participants are instructed to engage with the avatar that, in mimicry scenarios, replicates their behaviors similar to a VR mirror, with an adjustable delay. This mirror-mimicry is achieved through 'piling up' the animation/motion data into a queue and then streaming it into the character (Unity, SmartBody, etc.) after a certain delay. The avatar also utters scenario-specific dialogues, with associated natural-looking facial expressions and body gestures. In the other two scenarios, the avatar stands idly, ready to interact. Previously-designed scenario contents determine what responses by the VHTK digital character ensue, as well as what behaviors and facial expressions are generated.

7 Discussion

Nonverbal behavior carries significant social meaning in spoken communication [13] and its analysis contributes significantly to our understanding of how *human interaction* works [14]. A central construct to human interaction is behavior accommodation or *mimicry*, which we defined here as the degree to which two interactants align their verbal and nonverbal orientations. Previous research has shown that increased mimicry can lead to greater cooperation (e.g. [15, 16]), increased empathy for others (e.g. [17–19]), and greater social influence (e.g. [4, 20]). Mimicking agents have shown to be more persuasive and received more positive trait ratings than non-mimickers, despite participants' ability to detect direct mimicry after a while (e.g. [21]).

The precision of a full-body wireless MoCap device, the sensation of immersion in a VR world, and the realistic speech generation, facial expressions, eye gaze, and lip synchronization, all in real-time, have been combined in our first prototype. Our goal was to deliver a proof-of-concept system that combines behaviors in this way for law enforcement training. The objective of the system is to simulate each of the cooperation paradoxes in order to teach users (e.g. a trainee law enforcement officer) various effects and consequences of their verbal and nonverbal behaviors (as interpersonal stances and attitudes) on an interviewee (e.g. a suspect). This mixed-reality simulation environment enables the presentation of multimodal behaviors consistent with what occurs in real-life situations; e.g. *conflicts*. It can be used to model human reactions to *cooperative* and *competitive* behaviors, in conjunction with the presence and absence of *mimicry*. This modeling will utilize both verbal and nonverbal methods of examining behavior, as well as studying the dynamics of human cooperation in social interactions. It will, also, teach good conversational and social skills, and provide a valuable evidence base that informs better training and social coaching for law enforcement. It is thus particularly valuable to front-line professionals whose training needs are too complex (and therefore too costly) or too dangerous to simulate in real-life. We, therefore, propose this system for the investigation of human users' behaviors when interacting with a mimicking embodied conversational agent.

8 Future Work

Previous works have mainly focused on *single-action mimicry* and demonstrated its effects on mimickees. In project-SENSE we have set the groundwork for capturing the social and emotional effects of *direct behavioral mimicry* in *sustained and prolonged interactions* with individuals. This will be made possible by examining the MVN recordings of participants and measuring movements along various dimensions. A similar approach was taken by [7] to extract precise amounts of movements (e.g. fidgeting) from the Xsens MVN Awinda motion data. They recognized that in most studies, measuring behavioral mimicry is performed through manually coding events from video recordings (e.g. [22]) that raises issues such as *subjectivity* [23] and making comparisons merely between *isolated behaviors* such as face touching [7] although numerous *facial mimicry* research works also use EMG (e.g. [24]) and facial tracking systems (e.g. [25]). We also intend to integrate the Microsoft Kinect camera [26] into the project-SENSE prototype, as an *affordable* replacement for the Xsens MVN Awinda. Comparing the performance and precision of the *OptiTrack* as a professional MoCap system similar to the Xsens MVN Awinda is, furthermore, a future avenue we will be exploring.

References

1. Taylor, P.J.: The role of language in conflict and conflict resolution. In: Holtgraves, T. (ed.) The Oxford Handbook of Language and Social Psychology, pp. 459–470. Oxford University Press, New York (2014)
2. Taylor, P.J., Larner, S., Conchie, S.M., Van der Zee, S.: Cross-cultural deception detection. In: Granhag, P.A., Vrij, A., Verschuere, B. (eds.) Deception Detection: Current Challenges and Cognitive Approaches, pp. 175–202. Wiley-Blackwell, Chichester (2014)

3. Gottman, J., Markman, H., Notarius, C.: The topography of marital conflict: a sequential analysis of verbal and nonverbal behavior. J. Marriage Fam. **39**, 461–477 (1977)
4. Chartrand, T.L., Bargh, J.A.: The chameleon effect: the perception-behavior link and social interaction. J. Pers. Soc. Psychol. **76**, 893–910 (1999)
5. OculusVR, Copyright © (2016). https://www.oculus.com/
6. Xsens Technologies, Copyright © (2016). https://www.xsens.com
7. Poppe, R.W., Van Der Zee, S., Heylen, D.K.J., Taylor, P.J.: AMAB: automated measurement and analysis of body motion. Behav. Res. Methods **46**(3), 625–633 (2014)
8. Virtual Human Toolkit, Copyright © (2016). https://vhtoolkit.ict.usc.edu
9. Leuski, A., Traum, D.: NPCEditor: a tool for building question-answering characters. In: Paper presented at the 7th International Conference on Language Resources and Evaluation (LREC), Valetta, Malta, 19–21 May (2010)
10. SmartBody, Copyright © (2016). http://smartbody.ict.usc.edu
11. Hartholt, A., Traum, D., Marsella, S.C., Shapiro, A., Stratou, G., Leuski, A., Morency, L.-P., Gratch, J.: All together now: introducing the virtual human toolkit. In: Aylett, R., Krenn, B., Pelachaud, C., Shimodaira, H. (eds.) IVA 2013. LNCS (LNAI), vol. 8108, pp. 368–381. Springer, Heidelberg (2013). doi:10.1007/978-3-642-40415-3_33
12. Unity3D, Copyright © (2016). http://unity3d.com/unity
13. McNeill, D.: So you think gestures are nonverbal? Psychol. Rev. **92**, 350–371 (1985)
14. Kendon, A.: Movement coordination in social interaction: some examples described. Acta Psychol. **32**(2), 101–125 (1970)
15. Taylor, P.J., Thomas, S.: Linguistic style matching and negotiation outcome. Negot. Confl. Manage. Res. **1**, 263–281 (2008)
16. Chartrand, T.L., Lakin, J.L.: The antecedents and consequences of human behavioral mimicry. Annu. Rev. Psychol. **64**, 285–308 (2013)
17. Stel, M., Van Baaren, R.B., Vonk, R.: Effects of mimicking: Acting prosocially by being emotionally moved. Eur. J. Soc. Psychol. **38**, 965–976 (2008)
18. Hasler, B.S., Hirschberger, G., Shani-Sherman, T., Friedman, D.A.: Virtual peacemakers: mimicry increases empathy in simulated contact with virtual outgroup members. Cyber Psychol. Behav. Soc. Networking **17**(12), 766–771 (2014)
19. Stel, M., Vonk, R.: Empathizing via mimicry depends on whether emotional expressions are seen as real. Eur. Psychol. **14**, 342–350 (2009)
20. Richardson, B., Taylor, P.J., Snook, B., Conchie, S.M., Bennell, C.: Language style matching and confessions in police interrogations. Law Hum. Behav. **38**, 357–366 (2014)
21. Bailenson, J.N., Yee, N., Patel, K., Beall, A.C.: Detecting digital chameleons. Comput. Hum. Behav. **24**, 66–87 (2008)
22. Stel, M., van Dijk, E., Olivier, E.: You want to know the truth? then don't mimic! Psychol. Sci. **20**, 693–699 (2009)
23. Scherer, K.R., Ekman, P.: Methodological issues in studying nonverbal behavior. In: Scherer, K.R., Ekman, P. (eds.) Handbook of Methods in Nonverbal Behavior Research, pp. 45–135. Cambridge University Press, New York (1982)
24. Likowski, K.U., Mühlberger, A., Seibt, B., Pauli, P., Weyers, P.: Modulation of facial mimicry by attitudes. J. Exp. Soc. Psychol. **44**, 1065–1072 (2008)
25. Stel, M., Blascovich, J., McCall, C., Mastop, J., Van Baaren, R.B., Vonk, R.: Mimicking disliked others: effects of a priori liking on the mimicry-liking link. Eur. J. Soc. Psychol. **40**, 876–880 (2010)
26. Microsoft Kinect, Copyright © (2016). https://www.microsoft.com/en-us/kinectforwindows/

A Conversational Agent that Reacts to Vocal Signals

Daniel Formolo$^{(\boxtimes)}$ and Tibor Bosse

Department of Computer Science, VU University Amsterdam,
De Boelelaan 1081, 1081 HV Amsterdam, The Netherlands
{d.formolo, t.bosse}@vu.nl

Abstract. Conversational agents are increasingly being used for training of social skills. One of their most important benefits is their ability to provide natural interaction with humans. This work proposes to extend conversational agents' benefits for social skills training by analysing the emotion conveyed by the user's speech. For that, we developed a new system that captures emotions from human voice and, combined with the context of a particular situation, uses this to influence the internal state of the agent and change its behaviour. An example of the system's use is shown and its limitations and advantages are discussed, together with the internal workflow of the system.

Keywords: Virtual agents · Social skills training · Speech analysis · Vocal signals · Emotions

1 Introduction

Embodied Conversational Agents (ECAs) can be defined as computer-generated characters 'that demonstrate many of the same properties as humans in face-to-face conversation, including the ability to produce and respond to verbal and nonverbal communication' [1]. As research into ECAs is becoming more mature, conversations with ECAs are increasingly being perceived as natural, or at least 'believable'. As a result, there is a growing interest in the use of ECAs for training of communicative skills, such as negotiation, conflict management or leadership skills (e.g., [2–7]). The main motivation is that a training system based on conversational agents provides a cost-effective method to replace (or at least complement) human actors, as it can be used anytime, anywhere.

Despite this promising prospect, developing effective conversational agents for communication training is far from easy. An important requirement for effective ECAs is their ability to react to behaviour of the trainee in a similar manner as a human interlocutor would do. Otherwise, there is a risk that the system reinforces the wrong behaviour. For instance, a virtual agent that only listens to you if you address it with a submissive attitude is probably not very useful for leadership training. Hence, making an ECA show the appropriate response to the appropriate behaviour of the trainee is crucial. However, this introduces another challenge, namely to define what is 'appropriate behaviour' of the trainee. Obviously, one relevant aspect of behaviour involves the *content* of what the trainee says. And indeed, most ECA-based training systems

© ICST Institute for Computer Sciences, Social Informatics and Telecommunications Engineering 2017
R. Poppe et al. (Eds.): INTETAIN 2016, LNICST 178, pp. 285–291, 2017.
DOI: 10.1007/978-3-319-49616-0_29

have been designed in such a way that the ECA's responses depend on what the user says (e.g., by analysing the user's speech, or by generating appropriate responses based on selected options within a multiple choice menu).

However, although most ECAs respond to *what* the user says, they often do not respond to *how* the user says it. This is a serious limitation, as the style of a person's speech is very important during social interactions: as discussed in [8], humans heavily rely on vocal cues (such as volume, or speed of talking) to infer other people's emotions. For example, the phrase 'sorry sir, we cannot accept 100 Euro bills' can be perceived as very friendly when it is uttered calmly and gently, but it can be perceived as offensive when it is uttered with a quick and monotone voice. Especially for communication training it is important to take such differences into account, as it allows professionals to learn not only what to say during their job, but also how to say it. Hence, this paper proposes the use of ECAs for social skills training that adjust their behaviour based on vocal signals that are extracted from the user's speech[1]. The paper first presents global architecture to develop such feature in the agents, followed by a discussion on how the system can be used for specific types of communication training.

2   Emotions in Vocal Signals

Many factors influence the generation of emotion in humans. Emotions can remain stable for a long time or may come and go fast, and sometimes various emotions are mixed at same moment. In the literature, roughly three theoretical perspectives may be distinguished. First, *categorical theories* are based on the assumption that there is a limited set of basic emotions categories such as joy, sadness, fear, anger, and disgust [9]. Second, *dimensional theories* view emotions as states that can be represented as points within a continuous space defined by two (or three) dimensions, namely valence and arousal (and dominance) [10, 11]. Valence refers to the level of pleasure, while arousal refers to a general degree of intensity. Third, *componential theories* highlight the role of different components that play a role in the emotion generation process, such as the desirability and likelihood of the events that trigger the emotion, cf. appraisal theory [12]. In the current paper, we will mainly make use of the dimensional approach, using the dimensions of arousal and valence. Both valence and arousal are expressions of brain circuits involving amygdala, orbitofrontal cortex, the insula and various brain areas [13], and the emotions that arise from those areas have a direct reflection in the human voice.

To recognise such affective features in human speech, the presented approach builds upon a vast body of previous work. For instance, in [14] an approach was put forward to detect emotions in speech in terms of arousal and valence. Similarly, [15] has shown that more specific emotions (e.g., aggression) can be identified as well. Moreover, Rodriguez et al. analyse changes of vocal patterns in humans when they interact with ECAs [16].

---

[1] Obviously, vocal signals are not the only aspect of behaviour that is relevant for communication training. Other aspects include facial expression, gestures, and posture, among others. However, these aspects are beyond the scope of this paper.

Inspired by these developments, a number of recent systems use vocal cues to trigger the behaviour of virtual agents. For example, in [17] vocal cues are used to generate *backchannels* (i.e., non-intrusive signals provided during the speaker's turn). Acosta and Ward proposed a system that uses speech and prosody variation to build rapport between human and agent [18], and Cavazza et al. used vocal signals for character-based interactive storytelling [19]. Furthermore, the virtual human SimSensei Kiosk uses voice, speech and other features to analyse user emotions in the context of healthcare decision support [20]. As can be observed, these works are closely related to the proposed system, although they focus on different applications than social skills training. In contrast, one recent system that does focus on communication training (in the context of job interviews) is put forward in [21]. This paper presents an ECA that adapts its behaviour to vocal cues according to social constructs such as attitude and relationship. One way in which the current system extends this work is by considering the context of the conversation more explicitly.

3 The System

The proposed system is expected to be easily integrated within different serious games or other specialised systems. The final module is a library that is available in the Windows platform as a DLL and that may be extended to Linux-like operating systems. Figure 1 shows an overview of the system (i.e., the ECA). It contains various modules, including an interface to capture the user's speech, the off-the-shelf openEar tool to process this speech [22], and a module to generate a response to the user.

The openEar tool performs the task of identifying which emotion is currently experienced by user; however, it can also be replaced by any other tool, because the sub-components are completely independent. One only needs to adjust the connection between them. Some voice features used by openEar and consequently by the system to analyse emotions are Pitch, Formants and Bandwidth, and Temporal characteristics. The output of openEar is a set of emotions and their values. That information is processed by the Context Awareness Module, which deals with ambiguous outputs received by the previous module through a decision tree algorithm combined with

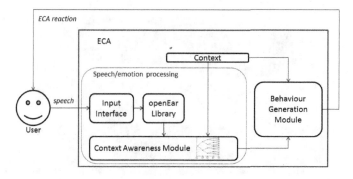

Fig. 1. Flow diagram of the proposed system.

context information provided by the ECA's beliefs. As mentioned before, it is difficult to distinguish between emotions with similar arousal, even if their valence levels are completely opposite (like anger and joy), [13, 23]. However, by using the context information, this module can minimise problems like that. The output is a set of emotions and their levels, varying from 0 to 100.

Next, this output is provided to the Behaviour Generation Module, which generates an appropriate response to the user. Obviously, this module can be very complex in itself (e.g., including modules for dialogue management and speech generation), but this is outside the scope of this paper. As a simple proof of concept, the Behaviour Generation Module currently just makes the ECA show a facial expression that is similar to the human emotion that is perceived. However, in other situations it might be more effective to respond in a different way to the perceived emotion (see the more extensive discussion below).

Currently, the system is still in development, and need improvements mainly in the Context Awareness and Behaviour Generation modules.

To illustrate its working, one prototype application composed of an ECA that responds to the inferred emotion captured from voice was developed. Figure 2 shows 4 different emotions expressed by the ECA, which reflect the voice of the user. However, the system could also be applied in many different situations in which the ECA not only mirrors the emotions of the user but also shows variations of those, like in negotiations, where a happy emotion from the user could produce an angry reaction from the ECA.

Another application that we are currently focusing on is aggression de-escalation training. In this domain, there is an interesting difference between so-called *emotional aggression* and *instrumental aggression*. The main difference is that emotional (hot-blooded) aggression is caused by an agent's goals being frustrated, whereas instrumental (cold-blooded) aggression is caused by an agent using intimidation as a means to achieve its goals [2]. This distinction is interesting for our system because an *emotionally aggressive agent* will calm down if the user approaches it empathically. Concretely, this means that the ECA first identifies the emotion conveyed in the user's

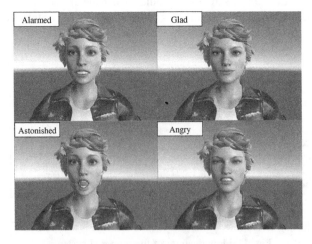

Fig. 2. Example of recognised emotions transferred to avatar.

voice, and if it recognises this as an empathic reaction it will become less aggressive. Similarly, if it interprets the user's utterance as non-cooperative, it will become more aggressive. Instead, for *instrumentally aggressive agents* this will be the other way around: if such an agent identifies the user's behaviour as empathic, it will become more aggressive, and if it interprets it as non-cooperative, it will calm down. Based on such an application, users could train to take the more suitable conversation style in the appropriate situation. This is very relevant, e.g., for employees in domains such as law enforcement and public transport [2].

Note that we presented here two possible applications of the system, where an ECA generates mirroring and opposite emotions, respectively. However, the application is not limited to these two situations. Generally, the system provides ECA developers the possibility to develop variance in emotional representation for a variety of aspects, for example, developing a sentiment of trust during a conversation. As another example, during an interaction, an supportive ECA could perceive irony in a user's voice and as a consequence become less empathic for the rest of the conversation. In principle, the possibilities cover the entire spectrum of human interactions; nevertheless, its success depends on the capacity of capturing the real emotion that the user is transmitting.

4 Discussion

This paper proposes the use of vocal signals that are extracted from the user's speech as one additional component to adjust ECAs' behaviour. To achieve this goal, we developed an adaptable system that processes human voice and returns a set of emotions and their intensity levels. The system can be easily plugged in into ECAs or other specialised systems that can enrich user experience. Especially for ECAs, the emotional information of a person's voice provides a new element to model their internal behaviour, which may make the interaction between ECAs and humans more natural and effective for training applications. A second innovation is the use of context information to extract emotions from human speech more accurately. Often, context conveys crucial information that is neglected by systems and serious games.

Nevertheless, there are circumstances that might limit the use of the proposed system; for example, when the user's environment is noisy or has more than one person speaking at the same time, the system cannot provide precise information. In other cases, the user might not interact much with the system, which could also limit the emotional information extracted by the system. Besides this, it is important to combine the emotional information provided by the user's voice with other sources like facial expressions, gestures and text. Despite these limitations, the system is an important addition to the state-of-the-art of the development of ECAs. For future work, it is necessary to refine the system, analyse its accuracy in different contexts, and test it in real world applications.

Acknowledgments. This research was supported by the Brazilian scholarship program Science without Borders - CNPq {scholarship reference: 233883/2014-2}.

References

1. Cassell, J., Sullivan, J., Prevost, S., Churchill, E.: Embodied Conversational Agents. MIT Press, Cambridge (2000)
2. Bosse, T., Provoost, S.: Towards aggression de-escalation training with virtual agents: a computational model. In: Zaphiris, P., Ioannou, A. (eds.) LCT 2014. LNCS, vol. 8524, pp. 375–387. Springer, Heidelberg (2014). doi:10.1007/978-3-319-07485-6_37
3. Bruijnes, M., Linssen, J.M., op den Akker, H.J.A., Theune, M., Wapperom, S., Broekema, C., Heylen, D.K.J.: Social behaviour in police interviews: relating data to theories. In: D'Errico, F., Poggi, I., Vinciarelli, A., Vincze, L. (eds.) Conflict and Multimodal Communication. Computational Social Sciences, pp. 317–347. Springer, Heidelberg (2015)
4. Hays, M., Campbell, J., Trimmer, M., Poore, J., Webb, A., Stark, C., King, T.: Can role-play with virtual humans teach interpersonal skills? In: Interservice/Industry Training, Simulation and Education Conference (I/ITSEC) (2012)
5. Jeuring, J., Grosfeld, F., Heeren, B., Hulsbergen, M., IJntema, R., Jonker, V., Mastenbroek, N., Smagt, M., Wijmans, F., Wolters, M., Zeijts, H.: Communicate! — a serious game for communication skills —. In: Conole, G., Klobučar, T., Rensing, C., Konert, J., Lavoué, É. (eds.) EC-TEL 2015. LNCS, vol. 9307, pp. 513–517. Springer, Heidelberg (2015). doi:10. 1007/978-3-319-24258-3_49
6. Kim, J., Hill, R.W., Durlach, P., Lane, H.C., Forbell, E., Core, C., Marsella, S., Pynadath, D., Hart, J.: BiLAT: a game-based environment for practicing negotiation in a cultural context. Int. J. Artif. Intell. Educ. **19**(3), 289–308 (2009)
7. Vaassen, F., Wauters, J.: deLearyous: Training interpersonal communication skills using unconstrained text input. In: Proceedings of ECGBL, pp. 505–513 (2012)
8. Juslin, P.N., Scherer, K.R.: Vocal expression of affect. In: Harrigan, J.A., et al. (eds.) The New Handbook of Methods in Nonverbal Behavior Research. Oxford Press, Oxford (2005)
9. Ekman, P.: An argument for basic emotions. Cogn. Emot. **6**(3–4), 169–200 (1992)
10. Russel, J.A.: A circumplex model of affect. J. Pers. Soc. Psychol. **39**, 1161–1178 (1980)
11. Yik, M., Russel, J., Steiger, J.: A 12-point circumplex structure of core affect. Emotion **11** (4), 705–731 (2011)
12. Scherer, K.R., Shorr, A., Johnstone, T.: Appraisal Processes in Emotion: Theory, Methods, Research. Oxford University Press, Canary (2001)
13. ElAyadi, M., Kamel, M.S., Karray, F.: Survey on speech emotion recognition: features, classification schemes, and databases. Pattern Recogn. **44**, 572–587 (2011)
14. Truong, K.P., van Leeuwen, D.A., de Jong, F.M.G.: Speech-based recognition of self-reported and observed emotion in a dimensional space. Speech Commun. **54**, 1049–1063 (2012)
15. Lefter, I., Rothkrantz, L.J.M., Burghouts, G.: Aggression detection in speech using sensor and semantic information. Text, Speech and Dialogue **7499**, 665–672 (2012)
16. Rodriguez, H., Beck, D., Lind, D., Lok, B.: Audio analysis of human/virtual-human interaction. In: Prendinger, H., Lester, J., Ishizuka, M. (eds.) IVA 2008. LNCS (LNAI), vol. 5208, pp. 154–161. Springer, Heidelberg (2008). doi:10.1007/978-3-540-85483-8_16
17. Bevacqua, E., Pammi, S., Hyniewska, S.J., Schröder, M., Pelachaud, C.: Multimodal backchannels for embodied conversational agents. In: Allbeck, J., Badler, N., Bickmore, T., Pelachaud, C., Safonova, A. (eds.) IVA 2010. LNCS (LNAI), vol. 6356, pp. 194–200. Springer, Heidelberg (2010). doi:10.1007/978-3-642-15892-6_21
18. Acosta, J.C., Ward, N.G.: Achieving rapport with turn-by-turn, user-responsive emotional coloring. Speech Commun. **53**, 1137–1148 (2011)

19. Cavazza, M., Pizzi, D., Charles, F., Vogt, T., Andre, E.: Emotional input for character-based interactive storytelling. In: Proceedings of the 8th International Conference on Autonomous Agents and multi-agent systems, AAMAS 2009, pp. 313–320 (2009)

20. DeVault, D., et al.: SimSensei kiosk: a virtual human interviewer for healthcare decision support. In: Proceedings of the 13th International Conference on Autonomous Agents and Multi-agent Systems, AAMAS 2014, pp. 1061–1068 (2014)

21. Ben Youssef, A., Chollet, M., Jones, H., Sabouret, N., Pelachaud, C., Ochs, M.: Towards a socially adaptive virtual agent. In: Brinkman, W.-P., Broekens, J., Heylen, D. (eds.) IVA 2015. LNCS (LNAI), vol. 9238, pp. 3–16. Springer, Heidelberg (2015). doi:10.1007/978-3-319-21996-7_1

22. Eyben, F., Wöllmer, M., Schuller, B.: openEAR - introducing the munich open-source emotion and affect recognition toolkit. In Proceedings of the 4th International HUMAINE Association Conference on Affective Computing and Intelligent Interaction 2009 (ACII 2009). IEEE, Amsterdam (2009)

23. Nwe, T., Foo, S., De Silva, L.: Speech emotion recognition using hidden Markov models. Speech Commun. **41**, 603–623 (2003)

Supporting Group Reflection in a Virtual Role-Playing Environment

Julia Othlinghaus$^{(\boxtimes)}$ and H. Ulrich Hoppe

Faculty of Engineering, Department of Computer Science and Applied Cognitive Science, University of Duisburg-Essen, Lotharstr. 63/65, 47048 Duisburg, Germany
{othlinghaus,hoppe}@collide.info

Abstract. This paper presents an approach to supporting group reflection in a virtual role-playing environment with intelligent support designed for the training customer complaint management in electronic shops. The single-player design involves a player and an AIML chat bot in a 2D web-based virtual environment. Building on this, a group reflection tool was designed, which is supposed be used in a training center environment. It features a dashboard design which includes different visualizations of player performance based on automated individual analyses of players' communicative behavior, as well as enriched replays of their conversations, and the ability to make annotations. The separation of the application into the actual role-playing game and the group reflection tool is assumed to support the learning process of responding to customer complaints by changing perspective, receiving feedback, and recognizing different ways of problem solving.

Keywords: Group reflection · Role-play · Intelligent support · Serious games · Multi-agent architecture · Chat bots

1 Introduction

Role-play allows participants to "play a role" in a situation: to act as themselves or otherwise in an environment without fearing irreversible consequence [1]. This makes it essential for a wide-range of education and training scenarios [2]. Authentic simulated environments provide learners with meaningful and near-real experiences: they "learn by doing" [3]. Customer complaint handling skills are often trained by role-playing with simulated customers. Correctly handling customer complaints has become an increasingly important social skill [4, 5]. However, traditional role-play in this context can be time-consuming, hard to administer, and lacking repeatability, while virtual role-plays can provide portable, safe and continuable environments.

This paper presents an attempt to train customer complaint handling skills by building on role-playing in a virtual simulation environment and providing a tool for after-action review. This takes the form of guided group reflection based on automated analysis of player performances.

© ICST Institute for Computer Sciences, Social Informatics and Telecommunications Engineering 2017
R. Poppe et al. (Eds.): INTETAIN 2016, LNICST 178, pp. 292–298, 2017.
DOI: 10.1007/978-3-319-49616-0_30

2 Background and Related Work

Serious Role-Playing Games. Serious games increase in being acknowledged as efficient and powerful tools for promoting learning and encouraging behavioral change [6], and thus have a great potential for professional training [7]. This article is in line with the work of Malzahn et al. [8], Emmerich et al. [9] and Ziebarth et al. [10]. It focuses on serious role-playing games in 2D and 3D environments for training specific social skills and follows a scenario-based approach. In scenario-based learning environments, conditions, characters, circumstances and parameters are drawn to simulate a real-life context for learning [11]. Table 1 provides a summary of the existing approaches, the training scenarios and their key aspects. The distinctive feature of the approach presented here is the explicit support for group reflection.

Table 1. Overview of existing approaches.

Year	Application domain	Constellation	Support/emphasis
2010	Job interviews	Single-user + chat bot	Scaffolding, Evaluation
2012	Conflict management	Multi-user + chat bot	Collaboration
2014	Patient-centered medical interviews	Single-user + chat bot	Gamification
2016	Customer complaint management	Single-user + chat bot	Explicit group reflection support

Customer Complaint Management. The successful handling of customer problems enhances customer satisfaction, trust and commitment [4], which are essential elements in establishing strong long-term customer-firm relationships [5, 12] and building sustainable market share [13]. While increasing investments in handling complaints can be recognized, firms are lacking effective strategies and programs [4]. Principal evaluative criteria of customer complaints are: (1) the resolution procedures, (2) the interpersonal communications and behavior, and (3) the outcome [4]. General guidelines for handling complaints are, amongst others, provided by the British *Institute of Customer Service* [14]. They include concrete recommendations on how to behave towards a complaining customer, such as thanking the customer for complaining, putting oneself in the place of the customer, always assuming that the customer has a valid point, getting all the facts, correcting the mistake, and responding at any time. Those guidelines have served as a compendium for the performance evaluation and rating.

Group Reflection. Reflection is an important activity in which people recapture, rethink and evaluate their experience in order to lead to new understandings and appreciations, which is very important for learning [15]. Learning processes cannot exclusively be reflected by oneself, but preferably in groups, which enables collective exchange and thus collaborative learning [16]. The term 'group reflection' describes a sort of meta-communication within a group about the learning process [17]. Furthermore, Kim et al. found out that effective instructor intervention is a crucial component leading to the better performance of a group in terms of learning [18].

3   *CuCoMaG*: **The Game**

The effects of a role-play, in particular the pedagogical outcome, usually depends on the post-role-play reflection, since without feedback the transfer to real-world situations cannot be secured [2]. After-action review is a method that helps learners to identify and share effective practices and strategies derived from the experience [19]. This requires a change of perspective. In our approach, this is facilitated by the differentiation of phases of immersion (role-play) and reflection (group session), which is considered to be conducive to learning as meta-cognitive activities are advanced [8].

Game Design. In the role-playing part, the player has the role of an employee who is responsible for customer service in a shoe-selling online shop. He finds himself in a conversation with a chat bot acting as a customer, who reports a certain problem. The player communicates with the customer through a simple chat environment (Fig. 1). Each chat message consists of a sentence opener which the player needs to select from a predefined set, and free text, which (a) gives the player the possibility to express himself more naturally and (b) allows a more detailed analysis of the communicative behavior. Based on the sentence openers, the chat bot can interpret the player's intentions and is able to detect and adequately react to e.g. aggressive or rude behavior by the player.

Fig. 1. Chat interface

Each scenario is kept simple and comprehensible to support understanding of the role and task, and to allow the player to focus on the problem-solving process. The main goal is to come to a resolution at the end of the conversation by showing appropriate behavior and choosing beneficial strategies of managing the complaint. A scoring system was implemented to evaluate the individual communicative behavior of each player and to make the performances of different players comparable. Relevant factors that influence the player's score in either a positive or a negative way are politeness, aggressiveness, rudeness, use of forbidden terms and phrases, message time, message length, moments of silence, answer quality (unhelpful/neutral/helpful), the total amount of answers and the quality of the final solution.

Implementation. The conversational behavior of the chat bot has been implemented using the *Artificial Intelligence Markup Language* (AIML), an XML-based solution for passive chat bots, which follows a simple pattern-matching mechanism [20]. The passive nature and the limited capabilities of AIML have required creative work-arounds in order to enable the bot to become active (by using external triggers) and to show appropriate reactions to the player's input (by preprocessing and using sentence openers) without having an extremely complex script.

In order to ensure platform independence and easy access, the logic and interface of the game client has been realized as a web-based application using common web technologies, such as HTML, CSS and JavaScript. The analysis of the player's performance has been designed as a multi-agent system which includes 11 agents (individual programs implemented in C#) in addition to the client. The multi-agent architecture has resulted in a loosely coupled system that can be easily extended and adapted. It is based on *SQLSpaces*, an implementation of the tuple space concept, which supports various programming languages and is built on a relational database [21]. Each of the agents is responsible for one certain aspect of either input analysis or game control. They mainly check the text input against predefined lists of words, expressions or phrases, or measure certain quantitative aspects, such as the time needed to send the message. The results of the agents' evaluation influence the player's score as well as the answering behavior of the chat bot.

4   Group Reflection Support

The reflection tool has been designed to be used in training centers and requires a trainer or expert to support the group reflection process. This involves a group of participants who have played the game before the start of the session. Since the tool has been realized as a detached application, the reflection phase does not necessarily take place right after the gaming sessions, so the trainer has time to inspect the material and to prepare the group discussion. The tool provides comprehensive preparation and visualization of the analyses' results to the trainer to support the group reflection process.

The design of the reflection tool has been kept simple and plain (Fig. 2). The application allows the trainer to load the game data of different participants; it provides a transcript of their chat conversations annotated with the analyses' results; it offers different chart-based visualizations of each user's score and certain aspects of the communicative behavior; it also facilitates the option to make notes with the help of a notepad. The transcripts give the trainer the possibility to replay the whole chat conversation of each participant or just certain passages from them. The transcripts are enriched with annotation tags showing the analysis agents' findings. In regards to the different chart-based visualizations, the trainer can select one or more players and one or more evaluative factors, such as politeness, aggression, rudeness, moments of silence, answer quality (unhelpful, neutral and helpful) and no-go answers, to display

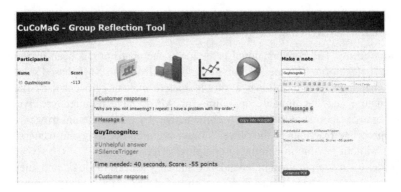

Fig. 2. Group reflection tool

them in the form of a bar chart or line chart. The bar chart shows how many times the selected factors occurred in the selected participants' performances, while the line chart presents the development of the participants' scores over time, with the option to highlight occurrences of the selected factors. The line chart is directly connected to the chat transcripts. This means that the trainer can switch from the chart to a certain point of the conversation by clicking on the graph. The notepad features the option to make notes for each participant. It is also possible to copy parts of the transcripts into the notepad and annotate them. The content of the notepad can be exported at the end of the reflection session to create a report for each participant.

The reflection tool has been designed as a web-based application and implemented using HTML, CSS, JavaScript, as well as JQuery[1] and Highcharts[2] libraries.

5   Conclusion and Future Work

We have presented a virtual role-playing environment for the training of customer complaint handling with group reflection support. The unique feature of this approach is the combination of an immersive role-playing scenario supported by an AI-controlled chat bot, with a separate group reflection phase reinforced by an evaluation tool based on automated performance analysis. Using a chat-based virtual role-play for training customer complaint handling in electronic shops is especially useful, since it provides a realistic training environment which simulates everyday work situations. The group reflection session is supposed to be guided by a trainer, who can use the tool to arrange the interactive after-action review process. With the help of the tool, the trainer can show important sequences from the participants' chat conversations, review specific actions and reasons for the outcome of the game, highlight certain aspects of the communicative behavior, give feedback, and initiate group

---

[1] http://www.jquery.com/.

[2] http://www.highcharts.com/.

discussions in order to enable reflection by the participants on their actions and to help them improve their performance in the future.

Due to the flexible multi-agent system architecture, the application can easily be adapted to other contexts and scenarios. Future tasks include usability and field studies, as well as the generation of additional scenarios featuring different customer and problem types to increase repeatability and diversity.

References

1. Ladousse, G.P.: Role Play. Oxford University Press, Oxford (1987)
2. Lim, M.Y., Aylett, R., Enz, S., Kriegel, M., Vannini, N., Hall, L., Jones, S.: Towards intelligent computer assisted educational role-play. In: Chang, M., Kuo, R., Kinshuk, Chen, G.-D., Hirose, M. (eds.) Edutainment 2009, LNCS, vol. 5670, pp. 208–219. Springer, Heidelberg (2009)
3. Slator, B.M., Chaput, H.C.: Learning by learning roles: a virtual role-playing environment for tutoring. In: Frasson, C., Gauthier, G., Lesgold, A. (eds.) ITS 1996. LNCS, vol. 1086, pp. 668–676. Springer, Heidelberg (1996). doi:10.1007/3-540-61327-7_167
4. Tax, S.S., Brown, S.W., Chandrashekaran, M.: Customer evaluations of service complaint experiences: implications for relationship marketing. J. Mark. **60**, 60–76 (1998)
5. Sirdeshmukh, D., Singh, J., Sabol, B.: Consumer Trust, Value, and Loyalty in Relational Exchanges. J. Mark. **66**(1), 15–37 (2002)
6. Cheong, Y.-G., Khaled, R., Grappiolo, C., Campos, J., Martinho, C., Ingram, G., Paiva, A., Yannakakis, G.N.: A computational approach towards conflict resolution for serious games. In: Proceedings of the Sixth International Conference on the Foundations of Digital Games. ACM, New York (2011)
7. Marr, A.C.: Serious Games für die Informations- und Wissensvermittlung: Bibliotheken auf neuen Wegen. Dinges & Frick, Wiesbaden (2010)
8. Malzahn, N., Buhmes H., Ziebarth S., Hoppe H.U.: Supporting reflection in an immersive 3D learning environment based on role-play. In: EC-TEL 2010, pp. 542–547. ACM, New York (2010)
9. Emmerich, K., Neuwald, K., Othlinghaus, J., Ziebarth, S., Hoppe, H.U.: Training conflict management in a collaborative virtual environment. In: Herskovic, V., Hoppe, H.U., Jansen, M., Ziegler, J. (eds.) CRIWG 2012. LNCS, vol. 7493, pp. 17–32. Springer, Heidelberg (2012). doi:10.1007/978-3-642-33284-5_2
10. Ziebarth, S., Kizina, A., Hoppe, H.U., Dini, L.: A serious game for training patient-centered medical interviews. In: IEEE 14th International Conference on Advanced Learning Technologies (ICALT), pp. 213–217. IEEE, New York (2014)
11. Herrington, J., Oliver, R., Reeves, T.C.: Patterns of engagement in authentic online learning environments. In: Proceedings of World Conference on E-Learning in Corporate, Government, Healthcare, and Higher Education 2001. AACE, Chesapeake (2002)
12. Orshinger, C., Valentini, S., de Angelis, M.: A meta-analysis of satisfaction with complaint handling in services. J. Acad. Mark. Sci. **38**(2), 169–186 (2010)
13. Urban, G.L., Sultan, F., Qualls, W.J.: Placing trust at the center of your internet strategy. Sloan Manag. Rev. **42**, 39–49 (2000)
14. The Institute of Customer Service. https://www.instituteofcustomerservice.com/research-insight/guidance-notes/article/handling-complaints

15. Boud, D., Keogh, R., Walker, D.: Promoting reflection in learning: a model. In: Boud, D., Keogh, R., Walker, D. (eds.) Reflection: Turning Experience into Learning, pp. 18–40. Kogan Page, London (1985)
16. Schuster, R.J.: Gruppenreflexion als Kommunikationsinstrument. In: Management und Wirtschaft. Schriftenreihe zur wirtschaftswissenschaftlichen Forschung, vol. 13, pp. 7–23. Fachhochschule des bfi Wien, Wien (2010)
17. Hilzensauer, W.: Theoretische Zugänge und Methoden zur Reflexion des Lernens. Ein Diskussionsbeitrag. In: Häcker, T.H., Hilzensauer, W., Reinmann, G. (eds.) Bildungsforschung, vol. 5(2) (2008)
18. Kim, P., Hong, J.-S., Bonk, C., Lim, G.: Effects on group reflection variations in project-based learning integrated in a Web 2.0 learning space. In: Interactive Learning Environments, vol. 19(4), pp. 333–349. Routledge, London (2011)
19. Morrison, J.E., Meliza, L.L.: Foundations of the after action review process. In: ARI Special Report, vol. 42. U.S. Army Research Institute for the Behavioral and Social Sciences, Arlington (1999)
20. Wallace, R.: The Elements of AIML Style. ALICE AI Foundation (2004)
21. Weinbrenner, S.: SQLSpaces – A Platform for Flexible, Language-Heterogeneous Multi-Agents Systems. University of Duisburg-Essen (2012)

Author Index

Printed in the United States
By Bookmasters